Nietzsche's New Darwinism

Nietzsche's New Darwinism

JOHN RICHARDSON

UNIVERSITY PRESS

2004

OXFORD
UNIVERSITY PRESS

Oxford New York
Auckland Bangkok Buenos Aires Cape Town Chennai
Dar es Salaam Delhi Hong Kong Istanbul Karachi Kolkata
Kuala Lumpur Madrid Melbourne Mexico City Mumbai Nairobi
São Paulo Shanghai Taipei Tokyo Toronto

Copyright © 2004 by Oxford University Press, Inc.

Published by Oxford University Press, Inc.
198 Madison Avenue, New York, New York 10016

www.oup.com

Oxford is a registered trademark of Oxford University Press

Library of Congress Cataloging-in-Publication Data
Richardson, John, 1951–
Nietzsche's new Darwinism / John Richardson.
p. cm.
Includes bibliographical references (p.) and index.
ISBN 0-19-517103-9
1. Nietzsche, Friedrich Wilhelm, 1844–1900.
2. Darwin, Charles, 1809–1882. I. Title

B3317.R458 2004
193—dc22   2003066224

9 8 7 6 5 4 3 2 1

Printed in the United States of America
on acid-free paper

To my daughter, Katie

Acknowledgments

All four chapters of this book began as presentations, and I am grateful to those who invited these talks, and for the criticisms offered by their audiences. These venues and inviters were: chapter 1: State University of New York at New Paltz (Eugene Heath); chapter 2: University of Santa Clara (Thomas M. Powers); chapter 3: University of Illinois at Urbana-Champaign (Richard Schacht); chapter 4: University of Texas at Austin (Brian Leiter). A version of chapter 1 appeared in *Philosophy and Phenomenological Research*, and I benefited from the comments of an anonymous reader for that journal. I discussed the ideas of the book in a graduate seminar at New York University and am grateful to the participants: Winston Chiong, Mathilde Cohen, David Enoch, John Fox, Todd Gitlin, Bruno Haas, Ian Jackson, Jim Jensen, Peter Kung, Angel Lozada, Jessica Moss, Ryan Preston, Daniel Shah, and Masahiro Yamada. I have also discussed these ideas with many people over the years, and would especially like to note the advice of Maudemarie Clark, Ken Gemes, and Brian Leiter. A number of people gave me very helpful written comments on one or another chapter: R. Kevin Hill, Clancy Martin, Graham Parkes, Peter Poellner, T. K. Seung, and Sharon Street. And finally, two people gave me written comments on the entire book, for which I am most grateful: David Enoch and Bernard Reginster.

Contents

Note on Citations

I cite Nietzsche's published works by their (English) acronyms, as follows:

A	*The Antichrist*
BGE	*Beyond Good and Evil*
BT	*The Birth of Tragedy*
CW	*The Case of Wagner*
D	*Daybreak*
EH	*Ecce Homo*
GM	*On the Genealogy of Morals*
GS	*The Gay Science*
HH	*Human, All-Too-Human*
NCW	*Nietzsche contra Wagner*
TI	*Twilight of the Idols*
UM	*Untimely Meditations*
Z	*Thus Spoke Zarathustra*

I cite passages in these works by the acronym, followed by a lowercase Roman numeral for a part or chapter with separately numbered sections (if any), followed by an Arabic numeral for the section. For example: TI.ix.36. In the bibliography, I list these works in their order of composition and with their years of composition. I also describe the various complications to my citations of them.

Nietzsche's *Nachlass* includes a number of early essays, which I cite by their titles, as well as voluminous notes. If a note is included in *The Will to Power* (a selection by later editors), I cite it by WP followed by its number there. If it is not included in WP, I cite it by the volume in the *Kritische Studienausgabe* (ed. G. Colli and M. Montinari; Berlin: de Gruyter, 1980), followed by the notebook number and—in brackets—the note number, e.g., 9.6 [145]. In order to flag that these are mere notes, I also give in brackets their year; this lets them be placed against the published works. If a note has been translated in Breazeale 1979, I add in parentheses P&T plus the page number there. Again, for further details see the bibliography.

I cite works by other authors in scientific format, with the exception of the following works by Darwin and Spencer, for which I use shortened titles:

Data: Spencer's *The Data of Ethics*
Descent: Darwin's *The Descent of Man*
Origin: Darwin's *On the Origin of Species*

Nietzsche's New Darwinism

Introduction

Most of what Nietzsche says about Darwin and Darwinism is hostile. Indeed the most striking things he says reach the pitch of denunciation and personal insult. He likes to call Darwin "mediocre," and attacks Darwinism on a host of theoretical and evaluative grounds.

But I think this pointed animosity is—here as often elsewhere in Nietzsche's campaigns—misleading. He is so eager to distinguish himself, because he knows how much he has taken over from Darwin—how big a part of his own view, this Darwinism looms.

I think Nietzsche profits when we notice and expose this shared ground. His position is stronger when we become aware—against his own efforts—of this Darwinian element in it. His views on a range of basic questions turn out to be more credible when we do justice to this element.

This Darwinian part or aspect may seem minor or peripheral to Nietzsche—an intrusion of something foreign. But I claim that we see better what's distinctively Nietzschean by setting all the rest of his views down on this Darwinian ground. The novelties in his positions lie with remarkable consistency in the ways he breaks from—and his view advances (in intent) beyond—Darwin.

This book's four chapters detail this Darwinism in four areas of Nietzsche's philosophy: his biology, metaethics, ethics-politics, and aesthetics. This may seem a disjoint and selective subset within his multifarious views.

But I think, in fact, they give us together the gist of his thinking. They include, in turn, his ontology for the things he's most interested in (humans as animals and organisms), his way of drawing values from his insight into these things, the particular values he derives in this way, and the aesthetic cast he gives to these values.

This book's main aim is to show that on all four topics, and so on that gist, it's of great use to recognize Nietzsche's relation to Darwin—both his important agreements, and his strong disagreements, his "similarities and differences." His differences depend, I'll try to show, on agreements: Nietzsche appropriates the central idea of Darwinism, and his attacks on Darwinists really express the ways he tries to extend or build beyond it. Getting a clear view of this relation to Darwinism shows his positions on all four topics to be stronger, more plausible than they would otherwise seem. It helps us to see how these positions hang together, and how (Nietzsche thinks) they're *grounded* or justified.

The similarities—the Darwinian parts—give his views the naturalistic grounding he hopes for them. They are the ways he appropriates explanation by natural selection. These give him, I will try to show, his crucial beginnings for his explanations of human beings and their values. He then uses these explanations in his *diagnoses* of our values—diagnoses that in turn support his own "revaluing." We need to see that Darwinian beginning in order to follow this broad argument.

The differences are the ways he builds differently than Darwinists do, on this ground. He sets something distinctively his own on top of (explanation by) natural selection. He proposes a second kind of selective mechanism—likewise nonindividual and largely noncognitive—that operates over human societies. This gives him a dual account of our values, as made by both natural and (what I'll call) social selection—a more complex account of what our values are *for* (i.e., were designed for). Nietzsche has insights and arguments in favor of the ways he here breaks with Darwinists.

Of these similarities and differences, the former are harder to remark, because Nietzsche harps so loudly on the latter: his disagreements are all he tells us about. But he is aware of what he has borrowed, and aware that he profits from it. He prides himself in his naturalism—in his study of contemporary science, and in his philosophy's incorporation of its truths. He claims to know what that science knows—and something else besides.

By analyzing these similarities and differences with Darwinism, we can answer some of the pressing interpretive problems that arise over Nietzsche. These problems concern certain obtrusively apparent *flaws* in his overall position—ways it *repels* us, whether as false or contradictory, as bad or silly. For each of those four topic areas, I'll stress a different such problem, and try to show that his neo-Darwinism gives Nietzsche a way to answer it. These problems will be, I hope, some of the objections or suspicions that most incline or dispose us against him. Let me quickly preview them, along with the main topics of the chapters.

Under his *biology*, I understand in particular Nietzsche's famous notion of "will to power," as well as his less-remarked but much more pervasive notion of "drives." The latter are, throughout his very rich diagnoses and analyses of us, his principal explanatory tokens. He attributes drives to all life, and analyzes organisms (and persons) as complexes of drives. However, I think this strikes many sober readers as to his discredit. It looks, at first blush, like a residual animism, a remnant of Schopenhauer's ontology of will. It seems to import an intentionality and a teleology at odds with that naturalism. How can we take his psychological explanations seriously, when they assign everything to these drives? However, when we set Nietzsche's notion of drives—as well as his famous notion of will to power—back on that Darwinian basis, as *products of selection*, we see how these notions can be de-animized, and naturalized in quite non-Schopenhauerian terms.

Under his *metaethics*, I understand the epistemic status Nietzsche claims for his own values, and more broadly the intent or force with which he says them to us. Familiarly enough, he announces that his values are "just his," i.e., express his perspective. Yet on the other hand he also thinks his values "higher" than ours, and higher thanks to some better wisdom or insight he has. The puzzle that strikes us here is how to reconcile his values' perspectivity with the priority he claims for them. Without seeing how these fit together, we won't ever correctly catch the "tone" or "force" with which he says his values. Again I think the answer lies in his neo-Darwinism. This gives him *diagnoses* of our values, and he thinks these diagnoses give him a basis for educing *new* values. Seeing how his values rest in these quasi-Darwinian diagnoses, we understand his claim that they're both wiser than ours but also "his perspective."

Under his *ethics-politics*, I treat the content of Nietzsche's values, or his values themselves. Here the challenge is the (apparent) moral odiousness of these values, at the level of both ethics and politics. We abhor his ethics of selfishness, conflict, and looking down on others, as well as his politics of hierarchy-inequality, and the weeding out of the weak and sick. Here the problem seems to be precisely that Nietzsche *is* a particular kind of Darwinist, a "Social Darwinist" who takes many of their typical positions, espousing for example the necessity for competition and selection in society. Here the continuities with (these) Darwinists looks to be precisely the problem. My argument is again that there *are* agreements, but that here Nietzsche's differences—especially those recognized already in his biology and metaethics—point his ethics-politics a different way, which makes them (at least somewhat) less egregious to us.

Under his *aesthetics*, I treat the way in which Nietzsche means his values "aesthetically." Here the problem is not just the subjective and perspectival character this gives them (treated under his metaethics). It's that Nietzsche is attributing his values to the exercise of a faculty that seems inappropriate or unreliable for this serious task. To choose values aesthetically is to entrust them to a relatively primitive faculty, which judges by sensory and superficial properties. Indeed, Nietzsche himself says that art and beauty—what the aesthetic power appreciates—are *lies*. So when he proclaims the aesthetic standing not just of his values, but of his philosophy as a whole, shouldn't this count *against* them? But once again his Darwinism helps him, I'll try to show: it gives him a plausible justification for so weighting this aesthetic choice. But it shows how this aesthetic value is pursued in tandem with a commitment to truth, which keeps Nietzsche in the company of philosophers.

Let me comment on some further features of the overall argument. The crux of Darwinism is of course the theory of evolution by natural selection. I'll examine how fully Nietzsche accepts this crux in chapter 1. I'll argue that he, at the least, uses natural selection as a major explainer of *drives*. The further question is the explanatory relation between natural selection and *will to power*: is the latter an independent (and indeed a prior) *co*-explainer of drives, or does natural selection explain (not just drives but) will to power too? I'll argue that although the former is Nietzsche's *dominant* view—the view I developed in *Nietzsche's System*, of will to power as basic ontology—he does *sometimes* think the second, more fully Darwinian point: that living things are selected to will power. And when he does, he grasps the way he *really can* naturalize "from the ground up" his explanations of us by our drives and wills. He can naturalize, in particular, what I'll call the "teleology" in these explanations—the ways they make outcomes explanatory.

So Nietzsche's degree of success in naturalizing his biology (and psychology, as likewise insisting on our willing power) depends on how far he can see this will to power as a selected product, not an ultimate principle or life force. However it's important to bear in mind that even when he does think of will to power as a prior such force, he still thinks of selection as *shaping* it. He still explains much or most of the character of organisms' and persons' drives by ways that selection has culled that ur-force into behaviors that can survive and continue. So I claim that chapter 1 shows the real naturalistic basis for Nietzsche's biology/psychology of drives— even if he does sometimes add a metaphysical basis we likely reject. He has naturalistic senses for the ways drives "value" and are "toward ends," to precisely the extent that he explains them by selection.

Because even the partial use of natural selection can give *some* naturalistic support for Nietzsche's drives—and more than they would otherwise have—it is basis enough for the further claims about human values that I go on to treat. So my chapters after the first do not depend on the more thorough Darwinism sketched there as Nietzsche's "minority view." I hope they will be of interest even to readers who don't accept that stronger link—and even to those who don't care whether Nietzsche got his biology right or not. Clearly his interest for us lies not in what he says about the evolution of biological drives, but in his social and psychological diagnoses, which seem a quite separate thing. But I will try to show that Nietzsche borrows from Darwinism here too, by modeling a new kind of selection on natural selection.

In chapter 2 I introduce this further selective mechanism that Nietzsche discovers at work in human societies, which is dominant over natural selection in shaping our moral values. These values have been made by a *social* selective process superimposed on natural selection, which Darwinists have altogether missed. This "social selection" shares broad structural features with natural selection, yet works in favor of quite different overall outcomes. I will try to show that we can specify somewhat the special *logic* that Nietzsche attributes to this second selective process. And it is chiefly his diagnosis of this social selection that leads to his "revaluation" of values, the topic of chapters 3 and 4.

Nietzsche uses *both* selective processes—natural and social—to explain human values. These selective mechanisms constitute our values, I will try to show, by giving us certain *goals* or *ends*. I will operate with a rough definition of an end, as an *outcome that explains*. It's only because selection lets drives' outcomes explain, that we can value by or in (having) these drives. This suggests how "teleology"—explanation by ends—will play a large role in my reading. And this may seem perverse or misguided, given Nietzsche's many attacks on teleology. Instead of treating Darwinism as naturalizing teleology, doesn't he rather see it as compelling a nonteleological position? But I will show that he doesn't really give up explaining by ends. His key notions of wills, drives, and values all involve directedness or aiming. His attacks on teleology are really attacks on a certain cognitive or psychic model for this directedness—as indeed are also, I think, the doubts many of his readers share against teleology. The key point Nietzsche takes from Darwin is a *different model* for teleology, which he extends and applies.

It's this core Darwinian insight that lets him naturalize his wills and drives: goals can be set into organisms—they can be designed for certain outcomes—by processes that don't at all "represent" or "foresee" those outcomes. Long-term, stochastic processes such as natural selection can set into us aims and values of which we're quite unaware—and can give the values of which we *are* aware further meanings and functions that we don't at all suspect. So Nietzsche sets up a "thin" sense for the teleology and intentionality of drives and will to power. I try to specify the logic of these naturalized ends in chapter 1, adapting certain recent analyses of function in philosophy of biology; this logic is shared by the ends generated in social selection, added in chapter 2.

Nietzsche's naturalized teleology is, unusually, a teleology of suspicion: it finds these ends not to validate them, but to estrange us from them. We get our goals and values from these overall selective processes, which lie "behind" us in our society and species. We don't really know why we think and feel and act as we do, since all of these have been designed into us for outcomes set by those selective logics. We need *genealogy* to uncover these real meanings and ends, by exposing that selective history. And it's this way that we are usually unaware of our real purposes that points Nietzsche to his own principal end or ideal: *freedom as self selection.* I will argue that this ideal issues reasonably from that genealogy. By seeing how, we fit together two main aspects of Nietzsche usually held apart: his biologism (with its insistence on "fate") and his value of freedom.

Throughout, I try to state a position with a kind of argumentative coherence and specificity, which it may seem implausible to say are Nietzsche's. Often, it will be clear, I connect his ideas to one another with arguments he himself rarely or never states quite so—and which he surely never organizes so systematically. So should I say that the position is *not* Nietzsche's, but one constructed from the pieces of his views (or the pieces of his works)? I would at least like to claim that it is made from large and important such pieces, that it connects these pieces in ways he often *did* "have in mind," and that it connects them in ways that *enhance* his views— i.e., gives them their best chance of being near to the truth.

Nietzsche's well-known multiplicity makes this the strongest kind of claim any single reading can plausibly make for itself: to pick out *one* voice or aspect in Nietzsche's writings, and show how to see that voice as somehow dominant, somehow trumping or subordinating the many other incompatible voices also there. I don't deny that Nietzsche often saw things in different and in fact explicitly contrary ways to how I will read him; I will make a point of recognizing such countervailing evidences throughout. But I think every interpretation faces such explicit contradictions. What I claim for *this* voice, again, is that with it Nietzsche may have come closest to the naturalistic truth that he wants too.

1
Biology

Nietzsche's relation to Darwin deserves a different kind of attention than I think it has received.[1] Looking closely at its logic brings us quickly to the middle of his thought, where it opens up a better reading of his famous notion of "will to power," together with such allied and far more pervasive notions as "drive" and "instinct." It gives us a prospect or chance to *naturalize* these notions, and, since they are Nietzsche's key explainers, thereby to set all the rest of his ideas on a firmer footing than they have been realized to have.

In this chapter I try to lay that firmer foundation by giving a precise account of Nietzsche's *biology*, i.e., his explanation of organisms by those drives and wills.[2] The following chapters will then show how this analysis both clarifies and supports his further, and much more interesting, ideas about our (humans') values. I claim that we can't understand his views

1. Some recent accounts: Stack (1983, 156–94); Stegmaier 1987; Poellner (1995, 138–73 *passim*); Ansell Pearson (1997, 85–122); Morrison (1997, 73–87). The discussion in Dennett (1995, 181–86 and 461–67) is of special interest. More recently (and too recently to affect my discussion as much as it otherwise would) is the excellent treatment in Moore 2002; whereas Moore's task is to "historis[e] Nietzsche's biologism" (15), mine is rather to philosophize it—i.e., to develop and weigh its argumentative coherence.

2. This runs against the advice of Heidegger, who warns against reading Nietzsche's thinking as "biologism" (1961/1979–1982, III/41; also /122).

on our values without seeing first and precisely how he thinks we are animals with drives. And we should only take those views about values seriously, if we have reason to think these foundations might let them be true.

The better sense of drives and will to power emerges through our recognizing Nietzsche's close affinity with Darwin. His biology profits, naturally enough, from the ways he agrees with Darwin—whereas as our attention shifts in the following chapters to human values his disagreements will have increasing credit. So this first chapter will play the possibly tedious role of stressing Nietzsche's *agreements* with our evolutionary theory—but as a necessary step toward clarifying and defending his disagreements, as built on what he shares. I'll ask whether he shares enough to entitle him to Darwinian ways of explaining organisms.

Still, to do justice to that notion of will to power we also need to recognize how Nietzsche explicitly asserts it *against* Darwin—and how this makes his drives different from Darwin's, too. Indeed, I think we best understand both that affinity, and its limits, by focusing on those attacks, and examining how Nietzsche proposes will to power in pointed contrast with a Darwinian "struggle for survival." Our task is to map, conceptually, how far down that opposition extends.

There are, I will argue, two ways to read this opposition—or rather two ways Nietzsche does indeed (at different times, even in the same breath) mean it. Most often, he conceives will to power "metaphysically," as a universal force more basic than Darwinian selection. In this role, will to power is Nietzsche's *basic* explanatory principle. I've elaborated elsewhere[3] this "power ontology," and shown how it pulls together the greatest share of his other main ideas; I remain convinced that this is his dominant view. Yet this metaphysics has small plausibility for most of us.

However, we can also identify a second, *minority* way Nietzsche intends will to power: as a kind of internal revision of Darwinism itself. While this recessive sense, by paring the notion down to a "power biology," prevents it from doing quite so much work in his system, it gives it a far better chance to be true. In this chapter my primary project is to analyze and assess this recessive but promising view. But I will also show how even when Nietzsche thinks of will to power ontologically, he still relies on selection in ways that help to naturalize his claims.

---

3. Richardson 1996, especially chapter 1. The view is "metaphysical" *not* in treating that force as transcendent, or as knowable a priori, but as primitive—uncaused and unexplainable.

It should be stressed that these findings bear not only on will to power, which some Nietzsche readers may think too isolated (or too *Nachlass-bound*) a notion to be worth worrying over. But drives are everywhere in Nietzsche: they are his main explanatory devices, throughout his psychology and sociology. His *diagnoses* of our values and practices, which attract so much of our interest in him, all work by attributing them to drives or instincts. The question of whether Nietzsche has a viable notion of drives—one that can bear the weight of these diagnoses—should be harder to dismiss. At issue, in particular, will be how Nietzsche can attribute the *end-directed* character he clearly does to these drives and wills, without illicitly anthropomorphizing an implausible mentality into them.

The same issue arises for Nietzsche's conception of "values," since he treats all living things as valuing. Valuing, he often insists, is something that happens already in our bodies, and indeed in the bodies of all organisms. It happens precisely in that end-directedness of bodily drives, in the way they are "toward" and "for" certain outcomes. Nietzsche insists that this is not a conscious or mental directedness, so that valuing isn't, in most cases, a mental activity either. To naturalize this valuing, and render it something that his science (genealogy) can study, he needs to naturalize drives' directedness. It is only once we have this concrete sense for valuing and values that we'll be able to understand his penetrating diagnoses of our moral values—the ideas that most interest us in him.

The task of naturalizing these drives and values is the task of naturalizing *ends*—since a drive's values are precisely the goals it drives toward. Throughout, I will operate with a root or background definition of an end: it is an *outcome that explains*, i.e., explains the process, behavior, disposition, and so on that has this outcome, and explains more particularly the specific things this disposition does. The famous problem with teleology is *how* an outcome, which (it seems) comes later, can explain the process that issues in it.[4] The obvious way is by a *representation* of the outcome occurring before or during the process, and steering it.[5] But Nietzsche denies that drives have goals in this cognitive way. So the challenge will be to supply some other analysis for the directedness of drives and wills. My claim is

4. By "teleology" I mean a claim or theory that purports to *explain by ends*; since ends are by (my) definition already explanatory, merely to assert ends is already to purport to explain by them.

5. On this cognitive model it is not strictly an "outcome" that explains, but the representation of an outcome. This reflects a certain flexibility in applying the notion of an "outcome that explains." It will be stretched in a different direction by the Darwinian teleology I'll sketch—to cover the way that *functions* explain in selection theory.

that Nietzsche's key borrowing from Darwin is a general answer to this challenge—a way to decognitivize and naturalize life's directedness.

As mentioned I will proceed by examining Nietzsche's sharp attacks on Darwin. But first we should take a quick orienting look at their context—the broad background of agreement these attacks presuppose, no matter which sense they have. Although Nietzsche mentions Darwin only sporadically, and then usually to rebuke him, his thinking is deeply and pervasively Darwinian. He writes after and in the light of Darwin, in persisting awareness of the evolutionary scenario.[6] Here, as often elsewhere, his seemingly dismissive remarks express his own sense of closeness: he sees it as his nature to repel where he most feels an affinity.[7] I'll eventually argue that his affinity with Darwin extends much further than we expect, but here let's start with some general and programmatic links. These also suggest the *valuative* aspect to his relation to Darwin, an aspect I'll mostly avoid in this chapter, the better to focus on his ontology-biology.

Nietzsche associates with Darwin certain "critical"—skeptical and nihilistic—lessons. He thinks he sees and feels the full troubling force of these lessons better than Darwin or his followers, but also a way to build a more positive view from and upon them.[8] He takes Darwin to have these critical consequences by his decisive step in *naturalizing* life—i.e., in explaining it by processes that are nondivine and indeed noncognitive. To be sure, this broad lesson is that of (modern) biology generally; it's not peculiarly Darwinian. Nietzsche associates it also with the older material-

6. Indeed, he passes through a period (the mid- to late 1870s) in which his views on Darwin and Spencer are quite favorable—reflected in (and influenced by) his friendship with the Darwinist Paul Rée. In 1879 he urges his publisher to obtain the rights for a translation of Spencer's *Data of Ethics* (see his letter to Schmeitzner in November 1879). Simmel (1907/1991, 6): "Nietzsche in his later period probably misjudges the influence of Darwin on him."

7. HH.ii.252: "Not in how a soul draws near another, but in how it distances itself from it, do I recognize its kinship and commonality with the other." WP655 [1885]: "The weaker presses itself to the stronger, from a nourishment-need; it wills to slip under it, if possible to become *one* with it. The stronger, on the contrary, fends off from itself." See also GM.iii.18, TI.v.2, EH.i.7. For my procedures in citing and translating Nietzsche, see the bibliography and vocabulary.

8. So, familiarly, Kaufmann says (1950/1974, xiii) that Nietzsche was "aroused from his dogmatic slumber by Darwin." UM.ii.9: "[T]he doctrines of sovereign becoming, of the fluidity of all concepts, types and kinds, of the lack of any cardinal distinction between human and animal — [are] doctrines that I hold to be true but deadly"; also 7.19[132] [1872–1873] (P&T43). WP69 [1885–1886] classifies Darwinism under nihilism. UM.i.7–9 attacks David Strauss as too cowardly for Darwin's radical implications; Nietzsche will make a similar criticism of Darwin himself.

ism in German biology, which he learns especially from Lange.[9] He is especially interested, of course, in applying this general naturalizing move to humans. We are organisms continuous with the rest, and our special capacities, above all our "reason," are to be explained by the same natural and ultimately physical processes.[10] The existential force of this lies in a way that it is *deflating* (or insulting) to the human.

Darwin can stand for that broad lesson, because he discovers evolution by selection, which is the most important of these noncognitive processes, the one operating over the longest time-scale, and producing not just individual organisms, but even their *types*. Part of Darwin's insight is just evolution itself: species "become," are created and destroyed, including the human species.[11] But more important is his account of what drives that evolution: a struggle or competition in which all organisms—ourselves included—are engaged. Darwin shows that organisms, in their types, are shaped by and for such struggle, and so pursue a basic selfishness. And the application of *this* point to humans deflates or insults us a further way, that is more peculiarly Darwinian.[12] This is why Nietzsche counts Darwin so decisive a factor in modern nihilism (although Darwin himself fails to face, Nietzsche thinks, how fully deflating his own insight is). Our species, and our special capacities, are the products of a long history of such selfish struggles, and are designed precisely and merely to struggle so into the future.[13] This diagnosis bears an obvious, broad resemblance to Nietzsche's own explanations of the human by will to power. How does he set himself apart?

9. See Leiter 1998a on Lange's influence on Nietzsche, and Leiter 1998b on Nietzsche's naturalism. Also Stack 1983. Lenoir 1982/1989 very usefully reviews the varieties of teleology developed in nineteenth-century German biology.

10. A14: "[W]e have placed [the human being] back among the animals"; "what is generally understood today about the human, goes just as far as it is understood mechanistically [*machinal*]." GS109: "When will we be able to begin to *naturalize* [*vernatürlichen*] humanity with the pure, newly discovered, newly redeemed nature!" Also BGE230; and see the opening of "Homer's Contest". Nietzsche recounts his vocational switch from philology to "physiology, medicine, and natural sciences" at EH.HH.3; also EH.ii.2.

11. D49, Z.i.P.3. HH.i.2 says that we take humans' current instincts as eternal because they evolved prior to the 4,000 years we know about. In recognizing becoming, Darwin expresses a main modern advance. GS357 says that Hegel made this idea of "evolution" [*Entwicklung*] possible for Darwin; also 11.34[73] [1885].

12. Compare Dennett's account of Darwin's idea as "universal acid: it eats through just about every traditional concept" (1995, 63).

13. UM.i.7: "[A]ccording to Darwin, [the human] is quite thoroughly a natural being [*Naturwesen*] and . . . has evolved to the height of the human . . . by feeling himself the stronger and gradually bringing about the destruction of the other, weaker examples of his kind."

1. Nietzsche's Arguments against Darwin

These programmatic agreements with Darwin help to explain the vigor of Nietzsche's rejection of him—his eagerness to distinguish himself, his indignation at being called a Darwinist.[14] Darwin and his followers are among his recurring targets; he titles sections "Anti-Darwin" and "Against Darwinism,"[15] and attacks them often elsewhere not by name but by their phrases (for example, "struggle for existence," "adaptation").[16] He attacks them from the Left, i.e., from a position claiming to radicalize, to carry still further, their own critical lessons.

However, it must be said at the outset that the movement presents to him a broad target; he marks few distinctions among individual proponents. Tellingly, he seems not to have required of himself a direct acquaintance with Darwin's own writings before addressing his attacks.[17] He knows the movement primarily by way of the English and German Social Darwinists. So, in particular, he refers more often to Spencer than to Darwin; he has Spencer but not Darwin in his library.[18] He also relies on several critics of Darwinism, in particular Wilhelm Roux and William Rolph.[19] This introduces several angles of misconception into his attacks.

So, as we turn to his criticisms of Darwin, we find that many of these are ill informed: Nietzsche attacks him for positions Darwin doesn't hold.[20]

14. EH.iii.1 says that "scholarly oxen" have suspected him of Darwinism because of what he says about the overman. In this chapter I set aside attacks bearing more against the *values* Nietzsche thinks Darwinists have smuggled into their science, for example, their faith (as he thinks) in *progress*. I return to these in chapters 2–4.

15. "Anti-Darwin": TI.ix.14; WP685 [1888], WP684 [1888]. "Against Darwinism": WP647 [1886–1887].

16. "Struggle for existence" [*Kampf um's Dasein; Kampf um Existenz*]: HH.i.224; 11.34[208] [1885], WP588 [1886–1887]. "Adaptation" [*Anpassung*]: GM.ii.12; WP645 [1885], WP681 [1886–1887].

17. The one exception: his letter to Rée in August 1877 suggests that he has read Darwin's "A Biographical Sketch of an Infant" in a recent issue of *Mind*.

18. Also tellingly, even Spencer he has only in translation; Nietzsche's lack of appreciation for things English is surely effect as well as cause of his disuse of the language. See *Nietzsche's Bibliothek*, which classes the works in biology and Darwinism partly under "*Neuere Philosophie. Psychologie*" and partly under "*Naturwissenschaften. Mathematik.*" Note that the books listed under "*Englische und amerikanische Literatur*" are virtually all in translation.

19. See nn. 26 and 89 below.

20. Dennett (1995, 182): "[H]is acquaintance with Darwin's ideas was beset with common misrepresentations and misunderstandings. . . . On the few points of specific

Often, Nietzsche's "corrections" bring him to points Darwin already holds: (1) he misreads Darwinian "struggle" as physical combat, and "fitness" as muscular strength. So he takes the latter to exclude all the indirect devices he labels "cunning" (*List*).[21] But of course Darwin makes clear that organisms "struggle" in many different ways; see, e.g., his account of the cuckoo's instinct to lay its eggs in other birds' nests (1859/1961, 216ff.; hereafter I cite this as *Origin*). Nietzsche's uncharitably literal reading of the Darwinian term ironically foreshadows the similar misreading his own term "power" has often received. (2) Nietzsche also misconceives the speed of the evolutionary change Darwinists claim—for example, when he replies that we can *see* that animals don't adapt to new environments.[22] He seems not to have absorbed the extreme slowness and gradualness of evolution, as Darwin conceives it (*Origin* 108–9, 312–14).

Other of Nietzsche's criticisms and amendments are wrong not about Darwin, but about the facts, as we now know them; on these points Darwin has been confirmed, and Nietzsche's doubts carry no weight: (1) he argues, against the efficacy of selection, that since mating is random, extreme traits are not preserved but returned to the average. WP684 [1888]: "The most disparate individuals unite with one another, the extremes are mixed into the mass." This is a version of the common criticism by Darwin's contemporaries, that variations will be blended back into the average; it is answered by Mendelian inheritance. (2) He carries much further a Lamarckism that Darwin also accepts, but uses much less.[23] Here Nietzsche follows Darwin's followers more than he does Darwin: Spencer and Haeckel, for example,

criticism he ventures, he gets Darwin utterly wrong." But the example he goes on to give gets Nietzsche wrong; see n. 104 below.

21. WP684 [1888]: "We have convinced ourselves, conversely, that in the struggle for existence . . . cunning often prevails over strength." TI.ix.14: "Darwin forgot the spirit (—that is English!), *the weak have more spirit* . . . by 'spirit' I mean care, patience, cunning, simulation, great self-control, and everything that is mimicry." Also WP685 [1888]. And see how Darwinism is characterized as a "philosophy for butcher-boys" in 8.12[22] [1875].

22. WP684 [1888]: "When [creatures with exterior markings to protect them] live in places where their dress ceases to hide them, they do not by any means approach [*nähern an*] the new milieu." (Ironically, Kettlewell's study of melanism in moths is now the best-known case in which natural selection has been purportedly observed.)

23. GS143 describes animal species as having completely translated their "customs" [*Sittlichkeit der Sitten*] into "flesh and blood." See BGE213 on how the philosopher must receive in his "blood" virtues worked up by his ancestors. WP995 [1884] also speaks clearly of transmission of acquired traits.

both stress the inheritability of acquired traits.[24] Nietzsche tends to blur or ignore the difference between genetic and cultural inheritance.[25] He tends to focus on the latter, and to extrapolate from there—from the human case—to the rest of life. This distorts his theory in some predictable ways; we'll often see its influence below. So we find a jumble of mistakes about Darwin and mistakes about biology.

However, the disagreements so far are secondary ones. We can peel them away from Nietzsche's primary criticism of Darwin, because they neither rest on the latter, nor support it. (They are, as it were, charges that Nietzsche "tries out"—or collects from others—to support his main attack. He has little allegiance to some of them.) That main disagreement is with Darwinism's stress (Nietzsche thinks) on **survival** or preservation, instead of on **power** or growth. He offers this as his key amendment to Darwin's account of organisms' ends or aims. WP688 [1888]: "It can be shown most clearly for every living thing, that it does everything, *not* in order to preserve itself, but to become *more*."[26]

I'll give a fuller account of "power" (*Macht*) later on, but from the start we should hear it with the two main senses Nietzsche gives it: broadly, he uses it for any kind of growth or increase; more strictly, he limits it to growth in control over other processes. In both senses, he contrasts it with "preservation" (*Erhaltung*). Here Darwin attracts fire from a much broader campaign: Nietzsche frequently advances his idea of will to power by attacking opponents he interprets as offering something like a will to the status quo. He particularly links such a theory—of a "will to existence" or "will to life"—not only with Darwin, but with Spinoza.[27] We need to judge whether, in this main disagreement, Nietzsche is once again at odds

24. Lange (1866/1950, III/46–47) argues for Lamarck; he attributes (/60) the view to Darwin too. On Lange's influence on Nietzsche's conception of Darwin, see Müller-Lauter (1971/1999, 232). On Lamarck, see Bowler 1992.

25. Consider his famous account in GM.ii of how a "memory" was "burned into" precivilized humans: this memory is fixed not by selection of those who can remember, but by the acquisition of pain associations that are inheritable.

26. These passages make this criticism of Darwin or Darwinism: GS349, TI.ix.14. These make the point without (explicit) reference to Darwinism: BGE13; 11.34[208] [1885], 12.2[68] [1885–1886], WP650 [1885–1886], WP774 [1886–1887], WP488 [1887], WP651 [1887–1888], WP634 [1888], WP689 [1888], WP688 [1888], WP692 [1888]. Many of these are quoted from, below. The point is touched on by Kaufmann (1950/1974, 246); he recounts (179) Nietzsche's sister's tale about a wartime source for the contrast. See also Moore (2002, 46–55), who shows the important influence on Nietzsche here of William Rolph's *Biologische Probleme*.

27. BGE13, GS349; 9.11[193] [1881], 11.26[313] [1884], WP688 [1888].

with the facts about Darwin and/or about organisms themselves. His errors above don't encourage confidence in him here.

Let's set some passages before us. First, from *Thus Spoke Zarathustra* (ii.12), here is Zarathustra purporting to quote life telling him a secret:

> Indeed, the truth was not hit by him who shot at it with the word of the "will to existence [*Willen zum Dasein*]": this will — does not exist [*giebt es nicht*]! / For, what does not exist [*was nicht ist*] cannot will; but what is in existence [*im Dasein ist*], how could that still will to existence [*zum Dasein wollen*]! / Only where life is, is there also will: not will to life but—thus I teach you — will to power!

Then, in the 1886 addition to *The Gay Science* (349), and with specific reference to Darwinism:

> To will to preserve oneself [*Sich selbst erhalten wollen*] is the expression of distress, of a limitation of the genuinely basic drive of life [*Lebens-Grundtriebes*] which aims at *the expansion of power* [*der auf Machterweiterung hinausgeht*] and in this willing frequently risks and even sacrifices self-preservation. . . . The struggle for existence [*Kampf um's Dasein*] is only an *exception*, a temporary restriction of the life-will [*Lebenswillens*]; the great and small struggle always turns upon superiority, upon growth and expansion, upon power, in accordance with the will to power, which is just the will of life [*Wille des Lebens*].

Finally, in *Twilight of the Idols* (ix.14):

> *Anti-Darwin*. As for the famous "struggle for *life* [*Kampf um's Leben*]," so far it seems to me to be asserted rather than proved. It occurs, but as an exception; the total-aspect of life is *not* distress, not hunger, but rather riches, profusion, even absurd squandering, — where there is struggle, one struggles for *power*. . . . One should not mistake Malthus for nature.

Our main interpretive challenge is to say precisely *where*—in what role—Nietzsche thinks this substitution of "power" for "survival" occurs.[28] Apparently, from such passages, he conceives these two to be competing answers to the question of the **end** or goal of life: he takes Darwin to

---

28. This substitution also has a valuative aspect which I will, as I've said, largely defer to chapter 2.

claim that organisms are "toward" survival, and he argues that they're toward power. More specifically, he supposes that *both* of these are meant as goals of a "will" or "basic drive" of life, which is *zu* or *auf* or *um* them. Nietzsche's main point is that this life will (*Lebenswille*) is *not* a will *to* life (*Wille zum Leben*), but to power.[29] What is the force of this "to"? What type of goal does it imply? In what sense, if any, does Nietzsche intend a *teleology*? Here hangs the viability of his own view, and of his critique of Darwin.

2. Problems in the Main Attack

There are problems, however, in taking this to be Nietzsche's basic dis-agreement with Darwin—his claim that power, not survival, is living things' end or goal. We have reasons for both *thinking* and *hoping* that he here misstates his own position.

First, and despite such seemingly direct statements as the above, it's problematic how Nietzsche can consistently hold this view, given his other strong positions. For he frequently *attacks* "teleology," and denies any "purpose" (*Zweck*) or "goal" (*Ziel*).[30] Such rejections indeed seem part of that radical lesson we've seen that he draws from Darwin's naturalism.[31]

29. Also GM.ii.11: "[T]he genuine life-will, that is out for power [*auf Macht aus*]"; BGE259: "[T]he will to power . . . is the will of life." But Nietzsche isn't always faithful to this contrast; in places he posits a "will to life." TI.x.4: "For it is only . . . in the psychology of the Dionysian state that the *basic fact* of the Hellenic instinct expresses itself — its 'will to life'." See the rest of that section, and the next. Also germane are the many passages criticizing the "self-preservation drive" (*Selbsterhaltungstrieb*), e.g., BGE13; 9.11[108] [1881], 11.26[277] [1884].
30. GS109: "no purposes . . . no accidents." TI.vi.8: "We have invented the concept 'purpose': in reality purpose *is absent*." 11.25[96] [1884]: "My presuppositions: 1) no end-'causes.' Even in human actions the intention [*Absicht*] of the doing explains *not at all*." 11.26[432] [1884]: "When I think on my philosophical genealogy, I feel myself connected with the anti-teleologists, i.e., the Spinozistic movement of our time, but with the differ-ence, that I also hold 'the purpose' and 'the will' *in us* to be a delusion." Also WP666 [1886–1887] ("an action *is never caused by a purpose*").
31. D122: "*Purposes in nature.* — Whoever, as impartial investigator, pursues the history of the eye and its forms among the lowest creatures, and shows the whole step-by-step becoming of the eye, must come to the great conclusion: that seeing was *not* the intention in the arising of the eye, but rather appeared, as *chance* put the apparatus together. A single such example: and 'purposes' fall away like scales from our eyes!" Consider BGE14 on "the Darwinists and anti-teleologists." See n. 10 above.

Yet these rejections seem at odds with his insistence on a will "to" power.[32] What can that towardness be, if *not* an end-directedness?

This is hardly the only case in which Nietzsche seems on the one hand to attack and dismiss an idea, yet on the other to employ it in one of his principal positive thoughts.[33] Here on the issue of teleology, as often elsewhere, there are so many passages on both sides of the issue—both positing and rejecting ends (we'll look at samples of both below)—that we can't dismiss either large set as "not Nietzsche's real view." Charity requires, I think, that we attempt to read his positive ideas in ways consistent with his refutations. So we must work to reconcile his critique of teleology with his own continued reliance on it.[34] We must do so by distinguishing senses: the one in which ends are denied and the other, novel sense in which life has power as its end. A main challenge in the following will be to analyze the latter sense.

There's a second kind of problem with reading Nietzsche's main objection so: it makes him seem amateurishly wrong about Darwin, who surely says nothing about any "will to life." This would add, to all those local and sporadic mistakes I cataloged above, a more fundamental error about the logic of Darwin's view. It's worth examining what kind of mistake this would be—what it misses in Darwin's core point about natural selection. Nietzsche seems guilty of a twofold confusion: about what the "end" of selection is, and how it's an end.

First, he misidentifies the selective criterion in Darwinism, the standard by which natural selection selects: this is reproduction, not survival, and emphatically not the organism's own coming-into-existence, as in the *Zarathustra* passage.[35] Darwin warns against this misreading of his terms: "I should premise that I use the term Struggle for Existence in a large and metaphorical sense, including dependence of one being on another, and

---

32. Often rejection and insistence coincide, e.g., WP552 [1887]: "That the apparent *'purposiveness'* . . . is merely the result of that *will to power* playing out in all events." Nietzsche treats will to power as occupying a middle ground between teleology and mechanism, which he also rejects.

33. Other important examples are "will" and "true."

34. By contrast Moore suggests (2002, 32) that Nietzsche was simply unaware of the problem: "(Strangely, he does not seem to be aware that to redescribe perfection in terms of a will *to* power does not make evolution any less teleological.)"

35. See also WP651 [1887–1888]. Nietzsche is misled, perhaps, by Darwin's own chosen terms; the rest of the title of *On the Origin of Species* is *by Means of Natural Selection, or the Preservation of Favoured Races in the Struggle for Life*; one of the book's key chapters is entitled "Struggle for Existence."

including (which is more important) not only the life of the individual, but success in leaving progeny" (*Origin* 62). Nietzsche seems to hear that tag-phrase much too literally.

In current neo-Darwinism, survival through maturity is only one factor in an organism's *reproductive success*—which indeed includes not just the number of its offspring, but their viability, and even their fertility, and so reaches well beyond the organism itself. Natural selection occurs when the "fitter"—those with a greater "propensity" for such success—do in fact out-reproduce their competitors. The possibility that this propensity might fail, and chance factors (e.g., random drift) favor the less fit, shows the nontautologous status of "the fittest reproduce best."[36] The selective criterion, then, is this "reproductive fitness," not survival or existence.

I think this first point is answerable. Often enough, Nietzsche uses "survival" in the same extended way Darwin does: for survival not of the individual, but of the lineage, the reproducing line—which he often understands broadly as the species. Often, indeed, he seems to concur with Darwin, so understood. So GS1 says that "to do what is good for the preservation of the human species . . . this instinct is *the essence* of our kind and herd."[37] When he elsewhere presses power as his alternative to survival, it is as often the survival of the lineage or species he has in mind, as of the individual. Let's use "survival" in this larger sense below.

But a second problem is more serious. Nietzsche seems to misread Darwinian survival as an "end" in too literal a sense: as the aim of a will or drive or instinct, analogous to that suspect will to power with which he replaces it. So BGE13: "Physiologists should consider before positing the self-preservation drive [*Selbsterhaltungstrieb*] as the cardinal drive of an organic being. Something living wills above all to *discharge* [*auslassen*] its force — life itself is will to power—: self-preservation is only one of the indirect and most frequent *results*." Nietzsche's terms "will" and "drive" suggest an intentional end-directedness—that either power or survival is an *intended goal*. And this in turn suggests that there is some kind of *representation* of the goal, which picks it out in advance and steers behavior toward it.

---

36. The standardly cited statement of this point is Mills and Beatty 1979. See also Brandon 1978/1996 (which calls this propensity "adaptedness" rather than "fitness").

37. Also GS4 (entitled *"The kind-preserving"*), TI.x.4. I return to Nietzsche's views about (what we would call) the "unit of selection" in section 4 below; see n. 92 below.

But Darwin's core point about natural selection posits no such "self-preservation drive," nothing that "aims" or "steers" organisms at reproduction. It rather describes a long-term *structural* property of evolution: traits that improve fitness tend to persist and accumulate; this mechanism, operating over long periods, explains organisms' most striking features. Those features have been designed for certain functions, by which they improved the organism's fitness (capacity to reproduce itself). The organism need no more "will" or "intend" those functions, or reproduction, than brooms will to sweep. Those functions, and reproduction, are not represented goals, but the outcomes for which those biological features were selected. So it appears that Nietzsche offers power to replace survival (reproduction) in a role the latter was never meant to play.

This seems to me the doubt against Nietzsche's critique of Darwinism that reaches deepest into his thought, and most threatens to uproot it. It reinforces our strongest reservation against his notorious will to power. For I think we immediately hear this notion to mean that will "aims" at power in a quasi-human way: "intending" it by somehow "representing" it. And this worry extends to his notions of "drive" and "instinct," which are so extremely widespread in his diagnoses. Here too Nietzsche appears to anthropomorphize life, by attributing a certain intentional and representational content to it, and using this content to explain what organisms do. Indeed, he readily attributes "perspectives" to all of these drives. So despite his attacks on our mental model, it is hard not to suspect that he falls back on it in thinking of wills and drives.

Sometimes it seems that he has simply displaced this mental model "beneath consciousness"—making wills and drives intentional in an unconscious way that still mirrors all the structure of consciousness. So drives would still operate with beliefs and desires, about their means and goals especially, even though these beliefs and desires never "rise to consciousness." And drives would still represent their goals, and steer unconsciously by these previews of them. This is already implausible, given how widely (among animals and even plants) Nietzsche wants to ascribe these wills and drives. But sometimes he goes even further, and insists that this intentional structure *is* conscious.[38] And this not only spreads consciousness

38. 11.25[401] [1884]: "There must be an *amount of consciousness* and will in every complex organic being. . . . The smallest organic creature must have consciousness and will." Poellner 1995, e.g., 276, 281, reads him so. Also supportive are passages saying that it's the *"feeling* of power" that is the end, e.g., WP649 [1886–1887]; see n. 122 below.

out to all organisms, but also carries it into each distinct will or drive—both very implausible. Moreover, he insists that this mental directedness goes beyond (is not reducible to) the physical or material processes that science discovers. So wills and drives are not susceptible to a mechanistic explanation, and Nietzsche seems to offer a version of vitalism. Thus GM.ii.12 opposes "the ruling instinct and current taste . . . which would rather endure the absolute fortuitousness [*Zufälligkeit*], even the mechanistic sense-lessness of all events, than the theory of a *power-willing* playing itself out in all events." Quoting this, Dennett seems right to judge such will to power "one of the stranger incarnations of skyhook hunger, and, fortunately, few find it attractive today" (1995, 466).

These points suggest a diagnosis of Nietzsche's error: he slips back to that mental model because he misses the unconventional form of Darwin's teleology—the precise sense in which organisms "struggle for existence."[39] He misunderstands the logic of natural selection, and how it makes survival an end. And then he models his "correction" of survival to power on this mistake. In this case he would fall, ultimately, into Leibniz's implausibility—his wills merely another kind of monads—and would fail ignominiously in his effort to out-radicalize Darwin.[40] In sum: if his main criticism is indeed this claim "power, not survival," this apparently gives him not just a weak attack, but one that threatens to unravel basic ideas of his own.

However, this criticism also shows us, in negative, how Nietzsche might save drives and will to power from mentalism and vitalism, by cleaving closer to Darwin than we've supposed. What if his criticisms of Darwin are more local or secondary than we've supposed? What if he gets right, after all, the sense of Darwinian selection—how it is and isn't teleology—and builds his own will to power and drives in parallel? By rooting these in selection, he would free them from the need to be conscious or representational; he would have a way for power to be life's "end," without illicitly anthropomorphizing. We should consider whether Nietzsche might grasp that sense after all, and then adapt it to make his own

---

39. Consider WP646 [1885] on evolution: "There are analogies, e.g., to our memory another memory, which makes itself noticeable in heredity and evolution in forms. To our inventing and experimenting, an inventing in the application of tools to new purposes, etc." Taken one way, Nietzsche here anthropomorphizes evolution itself (though taken another, he doesn't mean "memory" and "inventing" literally, as mental).

40. Moore (2002, 43): "Nietzsche appears to be genuinely oblivious to the fact . . . that his anthropomorphic vision of a world permeated by spirit and will is also strikingly reminiscent of the pan-animism of Leibniz." See too Poellner (1995, 277).

point about power.[41] If he does, then his criticism "power, not survival" would play the role of an internal amendment to Darwinism itself; he could make it while still claiming that he's accepting and radicalizing Darwin's nihilistic thrust. I'll argue that Nietzsche *sometimes* takes this view.

We have more reasons than wishful thinking for exploring such a reading of will to power: while some passages suggest a mental will, I think there are many more that reject it. Nietzsche attacks not only the "anthropomorphizing" extension of this mental model to the rest of life, but even its use in explaining the paradigm, the human case. He frequently raises doubts against the causality not just of consciousness, but of motives and purposes, and often states these as attacks on "will." So TI.vi.3: "The will no longer moves anything, hence does not explain anything either — it merely accompanies events, it can also be absent. The so-called 'motive' [*Motiv*]: another error."[42] Nietzsche introduces his drives and will to power not as versions of that mental model, but as alternatives to it; his point is that we are more like animals than we thought, not that they are more like us.

For these reasons I think we must not treat will to power as something mental or representational, that can plausibly apply only to humans.[43] We must search for a different analysis of both drives and will to power,

41. Nietzsche can be presumed familiar with the option of reading Darwin as grounding rather than demolishing teleology, since Lange sees it; cf. 1866/1950, III/33–34, /36, /66 ("a teleology which is not only compatible with Darwinism, but is almost identical with it"), /68. Dennett too says (1995, 65, 126) that we can read Darwin either as (in Marx's words) dealing a deathblow to teleology, or as finally giving it adequate grounding. Lennox 1992 argues that Darwin himself considered natural selection and teleology compatible.

42. WP526 [1888]: "Where there is a certain unity in the grouping, one has always posited *spirit* as cause of this coordination: for which there is no ground whatever. Why should the idea of a complex fact be one of the conditions of this fact? or why must the representation of a complex fact precede it?" WP666 [1886–1887]: "[I]s it not an illusion to name as cause that which rises to consciousness as an act of will?" See also GS360, TI.iii.5, A14; WP676 [1883–1884], WP478 [1888]; also n. 30 above. Elsewhere he argues that will occurs only in a few organisms: GS127. Note too how he explicitly renounces his earlier view that our practices originated from *motives* that were later forgotten: 9.6[366] [1880].

43. Leiter argues (2002, 252) that Nietzsche's "paramount" doctrine of will to power treats it "as a psychological hypothesis about the best explanation for human action in most, if not all, cases." So too Kaufmann (1950/1974, 204, 420). But I think one of Nietzsche's main ambitions with the notion is to explain humans *in the same way* as he does animals; he treats this as a crucial "naturalization," for which see n. 10 above.

consistent with Nietzsche's attacks on that mental model.[44] But this analysis must, at the same time, show why he so often attributes to drives and wills the teleology and intentionality he elsewhere denies them; it must explain his dividedness here. I will offer an account of drives' and wills' end-directedness, and argue that it legitimates attributing to them a "thin intentionality" not dependent on mentality; it legitimates Nietzsche's assigning to them "perspectives." When we see how drives are "toward goals," we see how they can also "intend" and "mean" things without representing them.

3. Kinds of Teleology

But in what sense can Nietzsche think wills are "toward" power (or drives toward their respective goals), if *not* in this purposeful, quasi-human way? The challenge is to catch the precise force of his attribution of ends, to give him neither *too much* teleology—this is what a mentalist reading of will to power (and drives) does—nor yet *too little*.

I think it will be helpful to step a bit back from Nietzsche, to distinguish the main options for a *naturalized teleology*, as they are presented in a well-known recent literature analyzing functions.[45] This excursion will help us to sharpen our unfocused sense of teleology. What makes it the case that the heart—to take this literature's favorite example—is "for" pumping blood? What makes this its function? The main answers in that literature offer us potential ways to naturalize Nietzsche's claim that wills are "toward" power. We can clarify the logic of his will to power by locating it among these options.

---

44. Nietzsche shows his interest in finding some nonmental account of purpose in WP526 [1888]: "We will guard ourselves against explaining purposiveness through spirit: there is no ground at all for ascribing to spirit the properties of organizing and systematizing. / . . . [Consciousness] plays no role in the total process of adaptation [*Adaptation*] and systematization." WP676 [1883–1884]: "[A] *purposiveness* rules in the smallest events, which our best knowing is not up to, a precaution [*Vorsorglichkeit*], a selection, a bringing-together, making-good-again etc."; "In short: supposing that purposiveness in the working of nature could be explained without the assumption of an ego positing purposes: could perhaps also *our* positing of purposes, our willing, etc., be only a *sign-language* for something altogether different, namely not-willing and unconscious?" WP660 [1885–1886]: "The 'purpose'. One should start from the 'sagacity' of plants." Note the subtitle of a book by Wilhelm Roux that much influenced Nietzsche: *A Contribution to the Completion of the Doctrine of Mechanistic Purposiveness*; see n. 89 below.

45. A recent selection from this literature is Allen et al. (eds.) 1998.

A first, most austere possibility is this: pumping blood is a function of the heart, just because this is something the heart (usually) *does*:

(1a) A part's functions are the results it tends to produce.

In parallel, we might take Nietzsche to think of wills as "to" power, merely in the sense that this is a (or the) result they tend to cause:

(1b) Will to power is the disposition to cause a certain result, i.e., power.

Then his wills or drives would be mere causal *dispositions* or tendencies, and power just their tended *result*.[46] This would be a quick and (relatively) unproblematic way to naturalize will to power's directedness. On this reading, Nietzsche makes the empirical claim that all or most organisms tend toward this same (type of) result: their own *growth*, and especially their growth by incorporating or *controlling* other organisms. Living things are toward power, insofar as their behaviors tend to produce it. So even an amoeba "wills to power," just by its causal tendencies to grow and to eat.

However, in this bare form the definition is clearly too weak to capture our notion of functions or ends. Familiarly, the heart has many other tended results, such as its thumping sound, that we would not consider functions. We don't count just *any* dispositional state as "toward" its results as ends—not the raindrop's tendency to fall, or the sun's to heat, for example. Nor (I think) would Nietzsche treat these mere tendencies as wills or drives. To be sure, in some moods he attributes wills even to nonliving things.[47] But in doing so he imagines them as "toward" their outcomes in a richer sense than just by tending to produce them. He has

46. Evidence here is 8.23[9] [1876–1877]: "In general the word drive is only a convenience and will be used everywhere that regular effects [*regelmässige Wirkungen*] in organisms are still not reducible to their chemical and mechanical laws." Schacht (1983) interprets will to power as a "disposition," "simply the basic tendency of all forces . . . to extend their influence and dominate others" (220). Anderson (1994) argues that Nietzsche's will-to-power biology denies the purposiveness of Darwin's struggle for existence, since "it appeals to a simple instinctual drive to expend force in the environment," which "operates without any particular end in mind, i.e., without any particular idea of how the environment ought to be transformed" (738); he holds that Nietzsche allows teleology only where there are "intentions."

47. Consider in this regard GS310's elaborate image of will as a wave—which then claims there's something really in common: "Thus live waves, — thus live we, the willers! — more I shall not say." And (to the wave): "You and I, we are indeed from one species [*Geschlecht*]! —You and I, we have indeed one secret!"

in mind a fuller kind of directedness, in his ideas of both will to power and drive.

It's natural to seek sufficiency by *adding* conditions to (1), e.g., by specifying some *kind* of disposition, as that whose tended results count as goals. Many different such added conditions are of course feasible here— and many have been offered as analyses of function. We can treat the whole family of these analyses as **dispositional**; they build on a common stem, (the supposition of) a causal tendency to some result. I think we can distinguish in the literature two main versions of this dispositional approach. The first adds conditions by specifying the disposition, the latter by specifying the result.

The first requires that the disposition be "plastic" in its tendency to bring about its result: if one route is blocked, it shifts to another.[48] The disposition bifurcates (trifurcates, and so on) but then reconverges: it is a tendency to respond differently in different contexts, in such a way that the same result ensues. Such plasticity might plausibly be denied the raindrop and the sun, but seems pervasive among organisms and their parts: they adjust their output in response to circumstances, in such a way that they consistently reach certain outcomes. So the heart's rate adjusts in order to maintain an adequate supply of blood to other parts of the body:

(2a) A part's functions are the results it tends to produce plastically.

And what makes eating the amoeba's goal is not just that it tends to that result, but *how* it does: it responds to stimuli from prey with behaviors appropriate for that outcome. (Among other things, perhaps, it changes direction in response to the prey's movements.)

Might Nietzsche mean by "will" or "drive" something like such a *plastic disposition*? Then:

(2b) Will to power is a *plastic* disposition to cause a certain result, i.e., power.

I think it's clear that Nietzsche thinks of wills or drives as plastic in this way; this is obvious, for example, wherever he treats their responses to

48. See, e.g., Braithwaite 1953 and Nagel 1977. Bennett (1976/1990, 38–42) gives a clear statement of the criterion; Woodfield (1976, 45ff.) diagrams the convergence it requires.

obstacles, or the adjustments they make in reaching "balances of power" with other drives.[49] This plasticity importantly contributes to the teleological sense in which wills are toward power, or drives toward their goals. Yet Nietzsche insists that such "adaptation"—i.e., this responsiveness and self-adjustment to environmental conditions—is a secondary and derivative feature of drives, a "mere reactivity."[50] We need to look elsewhere for what their directedness chiefly involves.

The other main version of the dispositional approach to functions adds a different criterion, and adds it in a different place—to qualify not the disposition itself, but its result. What makes a result a function is not the way the process tends to it, but an independent feature of that result— something about the result in its own right, apart from how the process is toward it. It's not (just) how the heart accomplishes pumping, but something about that outcome that makes it an end. In the literature analyzing functions, we find several candidates for this feature that makes a result an end; for our purposes two are most relevant.

At the root of this strategy is the intuition that it's the *goodness* of certain results that constitutes them as functions or ends—their goodness, that is, *for the organism* (or for whatever *has* the disposition).[51] So, among the various results the heart tends to produce, it's those that are good or beneficial that are picked out as its functions, what it's "for":

(3a) A part's functions are the good results it tends to produce.

Similarly, among the outcomes the amoeba tends toward, it's only the good or advantageous ones that are its ends—and not, for example, the one result that *every* organism might tend toward, its own death.

If Nietzsche thinks that wills are toward power in this way, then:

(3b) Will to power is a disposition to cause a certain *good* result, i.e., power.

---

49. E.g., WP636 [1888]: "[E]very specific body strives to become master over all space and to expand its force (— its will to power:) and to push back everything that strives against its expansion. But it pushes constantly against other bodies similarly striving and ends by arranging ('unifying') with those sufficiently related to it."

50. GM.ii.12 complains against the prevailing (Darwinist) tendency to place "'adaptation' in the foreground, that is, an activity of the second rank, a mere reactivity." See n. 125 below.

51. See especially Bedau's argument (1991, 1992) that teleology requires that the outcome be good.

Again I think it's clear that this is part of his conception of will to power. Power *is* a "good result," inasmuch as willing power involves *valuing* power, which is thereby "good for" what wills it. Similarly, Nietzsche stresses that drives value their distinguishing outcomes—which are thus their "goods."[52]

This order of dependence is important: what's basic is will's end-directedness, and Nietzsche will define/explain both "valuing" and "goods" in terms of it. To value is precisely to be so end-directed, and a good is always just an end in such a directedness. I'll develop these relations in chapter 2. For now they show us that adding "good" to our analysis of teleology can't help: since goodness follows teleology, it can't be a criterion to define it. Nietzsche denies that any results are *independently* good, (logically) prior to their being valued or to their being aimed at by wills or drives.[53] It's not a result's goodness that makes it an end, but vice versa. So we still need an account of what kind of disposition it is that makes drives tend toward their results—in such a way as to "value" them, and render them "good for" the drives.

We should be glad that Nietzsche doesn't rely on goodness as a criterion here, since if he did the directedness of wills and drives would be nonnatural: science couldn't identify and study an independent good. But if Nietzsche can give nonnormative criteria for end-directedness, science could study this, and by doing so study the "values" and "goods" he defines in terms of it. One way to find such criteria might be by finding nonnormative analogues for the goodness that teleology will construct. There are two versions of this strategy in the literature analyzing function.

One such naturalized analogue of goodness—offered in analysis of functions—is "contributing to some *system*'s working."[54] We pick out the heart's function, from among its many tended results, by identifying its role in the system to which it belongs. But once again we can see that this is not Nietzsche's point. He does indeed recognize such functionality of drives—how they can serve encompassing systems. But he denies that this is the crux of their directedness: such functionality is *imposed upon*

52. 11.25[433] [1884]: "In all willing is *valuing* — and will is there in the organic." 11.26[72] [1884]: "Every 'drive' is the drive to 'something good,' seen from some standpoint."

53. Z.i.15: "First through valuing is there value." Again, I treat issues about values in chapter 2.

54. Cummins 1975 is the best-known statement of this. Cummins leaves it to our interest to determine *which* system the result will be considered as functional for; hence he denies that functions are explanatory, or teleological.

drives that are already "toward" goals of their own.[55] Wills and drives have their primary ends prior to such self-subordinating service.

Another approach in the function literature is more germane: a result might be rendered a function by virtue of its being "fit"—i.e., by its enhancing the organism's reproductive capacity or "propensity."[56] On this view the heart's blood-pumping counts as its function because this result (but not, presumably, its thumping) increases fitness:

(4a) A part's functions are the ways it tends to improve the organism's fitness.

This analysis has obvious ties to Darwinism (whereas (2a) is rooted rather in behaviorism and cybernetics). It identifies fitness as the end-constituting feature of (some) results, because fitness seems a kind of "Darwinian good," or a naturalized substitute for "good." The very logic of natural selection seems to assign organisms the overall end of surviving-to-reproduce, making it natural to single out results promoting this, as functions.

Might Nietzsche think of will as a disposition to results that tend to reproduce the disposition? And of power as an end, by being such a result?

(4b) Will to power is a disposition to cause a certain *fitness-enhancing* result, i.e., power.

In this case something would be toward power not just by tending to cause it, nor even by doing so plastically. Also needed to make power its end is a feature of power itself—that it helps the thing to sustain or reproduce itself. Similarly, drives would be "to" those results that serve this reproductive end. Again I think this is often part of Nietzsche's conception of wills and drives, but let me defer the evidence for now.[57]

For I think we can see the inadequacy of all our options so far—(1b), (2b), (3b), and (4b), whether singly or in combination—by noting some-

55. GM.ii.12: "[A]ll purposes, all utilities are only *signs* that a will to power has become master over something less powerful and has imprinted upon it the sense of a function."

56. See especially Bigelow and Pargetter 1987; also Canfield 1964, Ayala 1970. Often this view is presented as an addition to the previous: it specifies *which* system is relevant (the organism), and what proper working of this system (its fitness) the result must be functional for.

57. See n. 76 below. I defer it because this evidence is entangled with evidence for the option (5b) below. At issue will be whether wills' and drives' ends are constituted by what *does*, or by what *has* enhanced fitness, and the evidence is often ambiguous between these.

thing basic they all leave out. Each gives an element in Nietzsche's (and our) sense of end-directedness, but none supplies the crucial ingredient. So they don't really make his view teleological, after all. For I take it to be crucial to teleology that its ends are *explanatory*,[58] and (I think) Nietzsche thinks this of drives: for each, its goal explains what the drive does.[59] It is not merely a brute fact that we have the disposition to eat and that it takes the steps it does; these happen because of what eating is.

But none of the above analyses captures this explanatory role of the end. They cannot, so long as they refer only to present features of the disposition (its plasticity) and/or to future features of its result (its goodness, its fitness). For this omits reference to a certain past cause of the disposition, which is needed for teleology. Why is there this drive, aimed at eating? What is it about eating that has brought about this disposition toward it? These analyses refer only to how the disposition *is* (or to what it will do), not to how it came about—and came about "for the sake of" that outcome/end.

To be sure, the disposition—at least as embodied in a certain material state—can itself explain *some* things: the process ensuing, and its result. Indeed, the disposition can explain more tellingly if it is either plastic (when it explains the shifting outputs) or fitness-enhancing (when it explains future Darwinian success). Both criteria are explanatory—but not of the right explananda. In both, the tended result is what's explained, not what explains; so the result can't yet be an *end*. (If it is mentioned in the explanation, this is only as a shorthand way of specifying the tendency, which is the real explainer.) And in neither case is the disposition itself explained; so it can't be end-directed.

I think Nietzsche wants to rescue, despite all his attacks on teleology, this central explanatory claim.[60] And it's this renewed insistence that power must *explain* as an end that so tempts him back to mental models of will to power. For mentalism—attributing representations of ends—is the most obvious way to convert ends into explaining causes. It gives the result a kind of causal presence in advance, in an anticipating representation of it. A "preview" of the result steers behavior, and this is what constitutes the

58. As Aristotle makes the "for the sake of which" (*hou heneka*) his chief (kind of) cause or explainer (*aitia*).

59. Poellner (1995, 165) argues that will to power is teleological, in a sense similar to mine.

60. WP675 [1887–1888]: "that one takes the doing-*something*, the 'goal,' the 'intention,' the 'purpose' back again into the doing, after one has artificially removed it and thereby emptied the doing."

result as an end, and lets it explain the behavior. But since Nietzsche is otherwise convinced that this mental model is misguided, he needs another option here—some kind of nonmental teleology.

Darwinism supplies another kind of "presence in advance" for the result. The organ's function/result explains the organ, inasmuch as "ancestral" results caused by the organ's ancestors explain its presence and structure now (in this organism). By the logic of natural selection, *some* of the organ's tended results are singled out as of special causal relevance: it was by pumping blood that this heart's lineage survived; it was by (increasingly) *better* pumping blood that its main features evolved, were "designed." "The heart"—thinking of it now as a type or *lineage*—was incrementally built and then preserved, because having this "result"—treating it too as a lineage—rendered the heart (or its organism) more reproductively fit. Here, by contrast with (4a), it is *past* fitness that's at issue, not present; only past fitness can be genuinely explanatory (of something present).[61]

This point is captured by another main approach in recent analyses of functions and goals—the **etiological** or "historical."[62] This approach denies that the present dispositional state (even if it's plastic, even if it's fit) is sufficient to constitute it as toward its results—it also needs to have had a certain past, a certain causal history. So, it's not an organ's "fitness for the future" that constitutes its (present) functions, but its "fitness from the past"—or not the way this organ is *fit*, but the way it's an *adaptation*.[63] What makes it the heart's function to pump blood is the way its parts and processes have been selected for this result:

(5a) A part's functions are the results it was selected to produce.

By contrast with the dispositional analysis, I think this catches a genuinely teleological sense, by making the result properly explanatory.[64]

This etiological analysis not only allows results to explain in the manner of ends, it also shows how *all* organisms can, in a sense, have the *same*

61. See the account of the logic of natural selection in Brandon 1981/1996.

62. The chief statements of the view are by Wright (e.g., 1973) and Millikan (e.g., 1989).

63. See West-Eberhard (1992, 13): "In contemporary evolutionary biology an 'adaptation' is a characteristic of an organism whose form is the result of selection in a particular functional context."

64. So Brandon (1978/1996, 41) on this teleology: "Put cryptically, trait *A*'s existence is explained in terms of what *A* does. More fully, *A*'s existence is explained in terms of effects of past instances of *A*; but not just any effects: we cite only those effects relevant to the adaptedness of possessors of *A*."

end. For each biological item and its specific function, the latter explains the former in the same general way: that result has enhanced the reproductive fitness of the item. In each case we can distinguish between the general and structural end of survival/reproduction, and the specific result(s) this item has recurrently had, by which it has furthered that "highest end." Organisms have many different functions, but all of them are subjoined to the same structural end; by this subjunction, Darwinism justifies attributing to organisms a common end.

Now if Nietzsche means by a will's or drive's "towardness" no more than this kind of teleology sanctioned in Darwinism, then his scatter-gun attributions of these to organisms won't necessarily sink him. He can avoid mentalism for wills by some such analysis as this:

(5b) Will to power is a disposition to cause a certain result, i.e., power, and past such results caused (produced) this disposition.[65]

This would give him a thin sense of "will" consistent with his many attacks on the notion. Moreover, this thin sense for will's directedness can be extended into thin senses for the intentional terms Nietzsche so often uses in talking about wills (and drives).[66] It lets us read will's "intentions" and "perspectives" with a quite different logic than on our usual mental model—and lets us reconcile it with Nietzsche's attacks on that model.

Indeed, I suggest that *it's only* if Nietzsche means this that his claims about will to power can be nonmentalist. And the same applies to his much more common claims about drives—each identified by what it is "to." Without selection to make each end explanatory—to give it presence in the past, to let it have caused the tendency toward it—he can't avoid slipping mentality back into these wills and drives, by implicitly positing an aim or desire or some other *representation* of the end, as an alternative past cause of the tendency. Nietzsche means to explain wills and drives by citing what they are toward, but he can only do so consistently with his critiques of mind and consciousness, if he grounds that "toward" in natural selection. But does he do so?

---

65. I.e., the past results (selection for them) caused *this occurrence* of the disposition, in this organism now. It is an important and difficult task to specify *how* this causing works—to determine more precisely the logic of "selection"; I forgo a closer look here.

66. Poellner (1995) stresses that when he speaks of "the actual mode of operation and agency of these drives, which he in fact seems to conceive of as the ultimate agents, Nietzsche invariably uses intentional-mentalistic terms" (215).

As I will gradually try to show (not just in this chapter but also in the next), this etiological analysis squares with something very deep and pervasive in Nietzsche: his continual effort to find out why we have our drives and practices, by means of a diagnosis or *genealogy* that uncovers how they have evolved. The *meanings* of our drives and practices, what they are truly after ("for"), lie in this evolutionary history. Since the latter is mostly quite unknown and opaque to us, we don't really know why we think and act as we do. The reasons lie not in our (conscious or unconscious) motives and decisions, as our mental model for teleology has always had it. Our own ends and goals, which explain what we do, have been settled before us in that past. We need genealogy to dig them out.

4. Drives as Selected

I think the evidence is much clearer that Nietzsche treats *drives* as selected than that he treats will to power so. The eventual harder question will be whether will to power is a separate principle from selection that has an *independent* role in explaining drives. This will be so if, as often seems, Nietzsche thinks of will to power as the source of the ever-new "variation," over which selection then operates in generating drives. I'll defer these further questions about will to power until section 5. I begin with the clearer point about drives—with how selection explains them. This order is the more appropriate, because it will turn out that drives are the primary "units" of will to power.

These drives or instincts are, as I've said, themselves the principal proximate explainers in Nietzsche's rich and influential psychological and social diagnoses.[67] Leaving aside (as for now we generally are) the *evaluative* aspect of these diagnoses, it's clear that they are crucially *explanatory*: they

---

67. The term *Trieb* is extremely common in Nietzsche's books and notebooks. It occurs in the first section of his first book, *The Birth of Tragedy*, applied decisively to the Apollonian and Dionysian "art-drives" (rendered by Kaufmann as "art impulses"). And it is still just as common in his last books, and in the same explanatory role; see its use in *Twilight of the Idols*, ix.39, for example. It is used together with a host of related expressions, including *Antrieb*, *Getriebe*, *Betrieb*, and the verb *treiben* (commonly built up as *übertreiben*, *zutreiben*, and so on). Most of these occurrences are not evident in the available English translations. By contrast, *Instinkt* is less common in Nietzsche's early works, but becomes remarkably pervasive later on; this term tends to survive English translation.

explain our practices, feelings, and attitudes as expressions of particular drives. Citing the drives, Nietzsche claims, shows the sense or significance of those practices or attitudes.

But as we've often seen, this explanatory scheme is rendered suspect by the dubious character of these drives. They have the same mysterious teleology as will to power. Each drive is identified in terms of a certain outcome it is "to" (*zu*), so that Nietzsche speaks of drives "to" life, knowledge, and so on.[68] And—I submit—he means something stronger by this "to" than just that these drives *tend to cause* (or bring about) life, knowledge, and so on. Nor is it enough to add that this causal tendency is "plastic" (or responsive) toward those results—though I think this too is part of his conception of drives.

Drives are more than just plastic dispositions, because their outcomes are more than just tended results. When Nietzsche names a drive by citing the outcome it is "to," he means that outcome to explain what the drive concretely does. It's because of what eating is that the drive to eat performs the specific behaviors it does (e.g., hunting and killing). By contrast a mere disposition's outcomes don't explain it: a stream has a disposition to erode its bed, but this eroding doesn't explain why the stream does it. Indeed—I claim further—Nietzsche *identifies* what the drive is "to," not with all the outcomes it has, but with precisely those that explain it in this way. It's not just because they all result in eating that we collect those behaviors together under a "drive to eat," but because eating is *why* those behaviors occur.

This makes it sound as if the drive has *foresight* of that outcome (e.g., eating), which threatens to turn it into something mental—a preview or precognition of that goal. Yet it's key in Nietzsche's story that we are *not*, generally, conscious of or in these drives or instincts.[69] They are nonmental dispositions, which we share with animals and even plants. They are not transparent to us, but must be dug up with craft and labor. Nor is it merely consciousness that Nietzsche denies to drives—we're not to think of them as "previewing" or "preconceiving" their outcomes unconsciously either,

68. By contrast, *Instinkt* is said to be *für* something—likewise teleologically, I think.
69. D115 says that we have language and consciousness only for the extreme degrees of our drives, whereas "the milder, middle degrees, and especially the lower degrees which are constantly playing, elude us, and yet it is they that weave the web of our character and our destiny." Also D119. See too n. 42 above; on the other side, see n. 38.

as if the whole mental structure were simply displaced "beneath consciousness." No such advance representation of the outcome is needed, conscious or not. But then, how else might he think that the drive's outcome explains? What else might he mean by that "to"? He means, I claim, that the drive was *selected for* that outcome.

I think there's overwhelming evidence that Nietzsche does think of drives as (at least in large part) products of selection. However, this evidence does not include many explicit statements of these points (though it does include some).[70] This is partly due, I think, to how thoroughly Nietzsche has absorbed this Darwinian way of explaining things: he uses its logic, without thinking of himself as explaining "by Darwinian selection."[71]

The point is also obscured by the way he presents his *differences* from Darwin. I claim that he (often at least) takes over Darwin's central point, about the logic of selection and how it explains drives by functions. But he associates Darwin not with this structural point, but with a further claim about the *kind* of drive this selection most favors. Nietzsche thinks Darwin assumes that what reproduce best are "instincts for survival," i.e., drives plastic or sensitive toward the organism's continued existence. And Nietzsche rejoins that it's drives of a quite different sort that succeed: drives that press single-mindedly at their specific and "selfish" goals— goals different from the organism's survival, yet (in aggregate) functional for it. Drawing his difference from Darwin here, he underrepresents his true continuity with him.[72]

70. Consider the following notes, spread through his philosophical years. 7.19[132] [1872–1873] (P&T43): "The horrible consequence of Darwinism, which by the way I hold to be true. . . . [I]nstincts are already the product of an endlessly long continued process." 9.6[366] [1880], speaking of drives: "The purpose is achieved, but not willed. *The* kinds of pleasurable movements which serve the purpose of preservation, are preserved through selection [*Selektion*]." 11.26[69] [1884]: "The thought, that only the life-capable is *left remaining*, is a conception *of the first rank*." And WP315 [1887]: "*[A]ffects* and *basic drives* in every race and in every class express something of their existence-conditions (— at least the conditions under which they have succeeded for the longest time)."

71. This evidence of his use is also less evident to us, because *we* take such explanations for granted.

72. Another motive I mentioned above: Nietzsche's "agonal" inclination to stress differences even or especially where he sees similarities; see n. 7 above. See n. 124 below for an especially clear case of Nietzsche arguing against a "preservation-drive" with an argument that is in fact Darwinian.

An important hint to Nietzsche's recognition of selection is his fascination with "breeding" (*Züchtung*).[73] His attention shows that he sees how
differential reproductive success (a generic "selection") can cause and explain biological characters. "Breeding" in the strict sense—selection *by*
humans, whether *of* humans or not—redirects a formative process already
at work in nature. To be sure, Nietzsche often applies the term to that
process as well, speaking as if nature "herself" breeds.[74] We might worry
that he thinks of nature's selection as likewise foresighted—and has misread Darwin after all. But elsewhere he shows himself alert against any
such anthropomorphizing, which I think is clearly at odds with his skeptical
and debunking heart; we'll see many examples below. Those personifica-
tions of nature must be as metaphorical as Aristotle's.[75] Nietzsche recognizes a formative natural selection that is not at all mental.

The drives that Nietzsche is most concerned to explain are not such
"animal" instincts as hunger or sex. Instead they are our dispositions for
complex social and cognitive practices. Nietzsche diagnoses these practices,
showing what they are "to" or "for," by showing what selective advantages
they have conferred. Our logic, our concepts, our beliefs, our virtues and
values are all as they are because they enabled our ancestors to survive
and reproduce.[76] They are, as Nietzsche says repeatedly, our "existence-

73. E.g., BGE62, BGE262, TI.vii.2–5. Note that Nietzsche conceives of his thought
of eternal return as a "means of breeding and selection" (WP462 [1887]; also WP1058
[1883–1884], WP1053 [1884]). 12.2[100] [1885–1886]: "The hammer: a teaching, which
by *unchaining* of death-seeking pessimism works a *selection* [*Auslese*] of the *fittest* [*Lebens-
fähigsten*]." Conversely, one of Nietzsche's complaints against Christianity is that it
interferes with (natural) selection, and "breeds" mediocrity: again BGE62, BGE262; also
A7, EH.iv.8; 13.14[5] [1888], WP246 [1888]. I return to Nietzsche's conception of breeding
in chapter 3.

74. The beginning of GM.ii.1: "To breed up [*heranzüchten*] an animal that *may
promise* [*versprechen darf*] — is this not indeed that paradoxical task which nature has
set itself with regard to the human?" Later in the section he speaks of the human species
"breeding itself." (Here some of "nature's" work might be done by deliberate social
selection, so the mental model could in this case have a special point.) See UM.iii.6
(nature "presses towards humans") and iii.7.

75. The metaphorical character seems clear in UM.iii.6: "And just this attitude
should be planted and grown in a young person, that he understand himself as so to
speak [*gleichsam*] a failed work of nature, but likewise as a witness to the grandest and
most wonderful intentions of this artist; it turned out badly for her, he should say to
himself, but I will honor her grand intention by serving her so that one day it turns out
better."

76. 9.6[184] [1880]: "Our thoughts are to be viewed as *behaviors*, corresponding to
our drives, like all behaviors. Darwin's theory is to be applied." Some notes conveniently

conditions."[77] And I think he clearly means that we have these practices because they *have been* such conditions. What those social and cognitive practices are really after, their identity or meaning, lies in what they have done, as such conditions. And this entitles Nietzsche to an etiological analysis of the ends he ascribes to the drives.

I claim: a Nietzschean drive is a disposition that was selected for a certain result; this result is its individuating goal, which explains its presence and its character. In most cases the drive will also be plastic toward this result.[78] And of course this result will also, usually, *continue* to enhance fitness (though not if, e.g., the drive's environment changes, e.g., by the arrival of new competitors). Hence the drive's relation to its result will usually also satisfy criteria (1a), (2a), and (4a) above. A drive is a plastic disposition to a result enhancing fitness. But it's (5a)—the etiological criterion—that says how the drive's result is its end, since this is what lets the end explain. That the disposition is plastic, and that its result raises fitness, are *signs* of a drive and its end, but what counts is that source in selection,

grouped in *The Will to Power*: WP497 [1884], WP496 [1884], WP498 [1884], WP493 [1885], WP494 [1885], WP520 [1885], WP505 [1886] ("we have senses for only a selection [*Auswahl*] of perceptions — those with which we have to concern ourselves in order to preserve ourselves"), WP507 [1887] ("all our *knowledge-organs and -senses* are evolved only with regard to preservation- and growth-conditions"), WP515 [1888]. Also WP480 [1888]: "*The usefulness of preservation* . . . stands as motive behind the evolution of the knowledge-organs." Already in "On Truth and Lie in an Extramoral Sense": "[I]ntellect . . . was certainly allotted to the most unfortunate, delicate, and ephemeral beings merely as a device for keeping them a minute in existence." The point is common in his books, too. GS1: "Whether I view humans with a good or evil eye, I find them always at one task, all of them and each one in particular: to do what helps the preservation of the human species. Not indeed from a feeling of love for this species, but simply because nothing in them is older, stronger, more inexorable and unconquerable than this instinct, — because this instinct is even *the essence* of our kind and herd." See Poellner's discussion (1995, 138ff.) of "Nietzsche and Evolutionary Epistemology."
77. "Existence-conditions": GS1, GM.i.10, EH.iv.4; WP507 [1887], WP515 [1888]. "Life-conditions": BGE4, BGE62, BGE188, BGE276, A25. "Preservation-conditions": EH.BT.2. I think Nietzsche clearly means this conditionality in a Darwinian rather than Kantian fashion: they're not logical conditions for being, e.g., human, but the conditions that have enabled the kind to survive and increase. Nietzsche's use is a bit different from Darwin's own, however: Darwin (*Origin* 206) identifies "conditions of existence" with the environmental conditions to which selection adapts the organism; Nietzsche—a typical difference—thinks rather of the fit-making powers of the organism itself.
78. For a time Nietzsche thinks that selection makes drives that are plastic or sensitive toward certain *pleasures*, that have been made to coincide with what "preserves." See especially 9.6[366] [1880]. I return to this in section 5b.i below, and again in discussing the "selfishness" of drives in chapter 3, section 2.

since only this gives the result a past causal role. In this sense, Nietzsche can plausibly attribute drives not just to persons, but to all organisms and their parts.

Contrary to the tendency of most "evolutionary epistemologists" since, Nietzsche's main thrust is that it's *errors* (as well as *lies*)[79] that have been thus functional. Our cognitive practices are crucially built out of dispositions designed to get things wrong—i.e., out of drives to simplify and otherwise distort reality. Nietzsche interprets Kant's categories as precisely such requisite mistakes: we all instinctively structure our experiences into substances and causes, because these fictions helped our ancestors to cope quickly and roughly with their surroundings. WP515 [1888]: "The categories are 'truths' only in the sense, that they are life-conditioning for us: as Euclidean space is a so-conditioned 'truth'."[80]

The most basic such instinctive error is that involved in our general terms; already in grouping individuals into types, we misidentify them as "the same." So GS111: "Those . . . who subsumed too slowly, who were too cautious in subsumption, had lesser probabilities of surviving [*Fortleben*], than those who, for all similar things, guessed immediately at equality."[81] This instinct "functions" to assimilate unequals, not just by tending to do so, but by having evolved for this role; it "aims" at this end not by intending or wanting it, but by having been selected for it. Our thinking is the upshot of a struggle among many such adapted instincts.[82]

79. "On Truth and Lie in an Extramoral Sense": "The intellect, as a means to preservation of the individual, unfolds its main forces in dissimulation." I'll treat the aesthetic (and sexual) cases of these lies in chapter 4, section 2b.

80. Also WP497 [1884], WP507 [1887], WP514 [1888], WP584 [1888]. Contrast Quine 1969, 126: "Creatures inveterately wrong in their inductions have a pathetic but praiseworthy tendency to die before reproducing their kind." Nietzsche can agree that this is so for "empirical" truths, but claims that these depend on "transcendental" lies.

81. HH.i.18 expects it to be shown how this tendency began to evolve in the lower organisms. GS110: "[A] few of these [errors] proved to be useful and kind-preserving: those who hit upon these, or inherited them, fought their fight [*Kampf*] for themselves and their progeny with better luck." Also HH.i.16. 9.11[286] [1881] says that without this "faith" neither human nor animal would be "fit" (*lebensfähig*). WP515 [1886–1887] denies that this tendency was adopted intentionally: "No preexisting 'ideal' has worked here: but the usefulness, that only when we see things made coarse and equal do they become calculable and handy to us." I return in chapter 4 to examine this claim that it's *errors* (not truths) that are selected for.

82. GS111: "The course of logical thoughts and inferences in our brain today corresponds to a process and struggle of drives that are individually all very illogical and unjust; we ordinarily experience only the result of the struggle: so quickly and so secretly does this primeval mechanism now play itself out in us."

In explaining these social-cognitive practices Nietzsche often uses a second kind of selection, besides the (strict) Darwinian selection among inheritable traits. For these practices are replicated not only by inheritance ("in the blood"), but by training/learning ("in habits").[83] Hence they are selected not only by the comparative fitness (for surviving/reproducing) these habits confer on the persons who possess them, but also by these habits' comparative propensity to diffuse through society by persons learning or imitating them. The latter is a kind of "fitness" these practices have in their own right, to copy themselves independently of the genetic route. I'll develop this second kind of selection in much more detail in chapter 2; I'll call it "social selection." For now I'll just note that this second selective mechanism likewise explains drives in a way that gives them "etiological ends," as analyzed above.

In evolving our deepest and most settled habits, this social selection has worked by the same unconscious and stochastic logic as natural selection. Practices became widespread and fixed not because social planners imposed them deliberately, but because of selective advantages these practices had over competing ones. Such advantage can lie in many things, but Nietzsche pays special attention to a few. One is the extent to which the practice can serve, and thereby be favored by, other practices already widespread and settled: practices, like drives, typically begin as means or devices for existing practices (drives). Another key selective advantage explains practices but *not* drives: practices are generally designed to *unify* the society, in particular by rendering its members *alike* or homogeneous. It's because of this special logic in social as opposed to natural selection that Nietzsche thinks a "herd instinct" has been bred into us.[84]

Now Nietzsche often speaks of practices as imposed deliberately, with foresight, by individuals; for example he treats the priests as inventors and inducers of slave morality.[85] This suggests, once again, a mental model for the teleology of these practices: their ends and meanings would lie in the intentions of their founders, and not in the implicit selection I'm developing. But first, I think this "social planning" is relatively recent and

83. In his Lamarckism, Nietzsche blurs the boundary between these: he thinks that *habits become blood*—that they become inheritable if practiced for long enough. I return to this in chapter 2, section 3.

84. BGE199: "[O]bedience has been practiced and bred best and longest among humans." Consider how explicit or implicit this breeding is conceived to be, in BGE62. Again, I return to these topics in chapter 2.

85. WP513 [1886–1887] says that categories such as substance were created by "the greatest abstraction-artists." See, e.g., GM.i.7 on the priest as creating slave values.

exceptional in our species' history, according to Nietzsche. And second, he stresses the ways even these planners "don't know what they're doing"—i.e., ways they are merely tools employed by larger and impersonal selective logics. Their views succeed, and their kind rises to power, because of ways their values are *needed* by the social body, i.e., ways they really do help this body persist. So, e.g., society uses the priest to medicate itself in the ways it needs, to cope with the pains of social life. The ultimate point of slave morality lies not in the priest's intentions, but in this broad function it has played.[86] And so for practices generally.[87]

Because both drives and practices are designed over "deep" time, they are subjected to a succession of quite different "breeding" pressures, by different external drives and practices. They survive and increase by serving a succession of prevailing forces (or complexes of forces). So a drive or practice is bred for a series of different functions, being successively readapted for each. Each period of service alters the practice, the better to serve its new function, and these changes accumulate through time. So a practice today displays design features dating to various periods of formation, and various functions. Nietzsche puts these points in his important discussion of the practice of punishment in GM.ii.13:

> [Today] the concept "punishment" no longer represents one sense [*Sinn*], but a whole synthesis of "senses": the previous history of punishment in general, the history of its exploitation [*Ausnützung*] for the most various purposes, finally crystallizes into a kind of unity that is hard to dissolve, hard to analyze and, what one must emphasize, quite completely *undefinable*. (Today it is impossible to say definitely *why* one punishes: all concepts in which an entire process is semiotically combined elude definition; only that which has no history is definable.)

The meanings of our practices stretch back through their design history; they're not given by the present consciousness in which we engage in them.

86. GM.iii.13 presents the priest as crafting the ascetic ideal, yet its point "is the opposite of what those who revere this ideal suppose, — : . . . the ascetic ideal is an artifice in the *preservation* of life"; see also iii.28. I return to this point in chapter 3, section 6a.

87. 11.40[54] [1885]: "The *intentionality* [*Absichtlichkeit*] of actions is not decisive in morality (belongs to the short-sighted *individualistic* tendency). 'Purpose' and 'means' are in relation to the whole kind, from which they grow, only symptomatic, in themselves many-meaninged and nearly ungraspable. The animal and plant show their moral charac-

It's because drives' and practices' identities are etiological—lie in what they're selected to be—that Nietzsche requires a *genealogical* method to discover them. He looks to the past, because this is where their ends are assigned or constituted. This is why genealogy tells us not only what, e.g., slave morality *was*, but what it *is*: what it *is for* is what it was selected for, which genealogy bares. Nietzsche insists on the persistence of even deep past functions, as contributing to present identity—they persist in minority or occasional expressions, even when some new and conflicting function is laid over them. So the "meaning" of a drive today is a layering of the functions it was serially selected for, in becoming what it is.[88] All of these go into explaining why the drive is here now.

Such is Nietzsche's quasi-Darwinian scenario. It shows, in some aspects, a certain sophistication and prescience: he anticipates ideas recently promoted in neo-Darwinism. While most are traceable in Darwin himself, they're little acknowledged by his early followers (through whom Nietzsche mainly knew Darwin). Let me quickly list a few:

Sub-individual competition: Nietzsche insists that the basic competition occurs at the level of the drives and that the whole organism is merely the upshot of their intramural struggles. WP647 [1886–87]: "The individual itself a struggle of parts (for food, space, etc.): its evolution [is] tied to a *victory* or *predominance* of individual parts, to an *atrophy* or 'becoming an organ' of other parts."[89] In recent terms: the "unit of selection"—the unit upon which natural selection primarily works—is the drive. More pre-

ter, by the life-conditions in which they arose. Behind 'intentionality' lies the decisive." Also BGE32.

88. The remnant signs of prehistoric functions are a theme in the early sections of HH.i; for example i.12–13 says that we reenact primitive thinking in our dreams, and i.43 gives earlier stages physical presence in "grooves and convolutions" in our brain, "no longer the bed in which the stream of our experience runs." WP659 [1885]: "The human body, in which the most distant and nearest past of all organic becoming again becomes living and corporeal." Also HH.ii.223 ("the past flows on within us in a hundred waves") and GM.ii.3 (on how the terrible mnemotechnic has an after-effect in our seriousness).

89. Here Nietzsche was influenced by the anatomist Wilhelm Roux and his book *The Struggle of Parts in the Organism*; see Müller-Lauter (1971/1999, 163ff.) and Moore (2002, 37–38). While reading Roux's book Nietzsche writes: "As cell stands beside cell physiologically, so drive beside drive. The most general picture of our being is *an association of drives*, with ongoing rivalries and alliances with one another" (10.7[94] [1883]). See also 11.27[27] [1884]. The famous statement of "gene selectionism" is Dawkins 1976/1989; its antecedent is Williams 1966/1996. This view is *not* in Darwin, who makes the individual the unit of selection—and in one case (in explaining human morality) the group.

cisely, drives are the basic "replicators," the units transmitted between generations. Nietzsche conceives of these drives as interacting both within the organism (combining to produce its behavior) and between organisms (by their interacting behaviors). Drives are selected for their effects on the individual's behavior—i.e., for the success of the behavior, as so affected.[90]

"Population thinking": Nietzsche rejects the "essentialist" view of species as constituted by some abstract form by which individual members are explained.[91] WP682 [1887]: "[T]he species is a mere abstraction from the multiplicity of these chains [of members] and their partial similarity." Nietzsche takes seriously this ontological point. The primary biological entities are neither individual organisms, nor kinds or types, but these "chains" of individuals—what I have called "lineages."[92] (Or, combining this point with the previous one, the basic units are such chains of drives.)

Exaptation: As we've seen, Nietzsche stresses that functional roles can change. Usually, an organ or drive is not built "from the ground up" by and for the same function—the same way of enhancing survivability. In GM.ii.12: "[T]he entire history of a 'thing,' an organ, a practice can . . . be a continuous sign-chain of ever new interpretations and adaptations [*Zurechtmachungen*]." A drive, as a selected tendency to cause some result R, can be appropriated into different functional contexts, so that doing R enhances survivability in different ways. Another drive appears, for example, that can use it in some new way, can give it a different way to improve fitness, so letting selection work on it in a new direction; usually R and the process to R will then be gradually redesigned for that new role.[93]

90. So whereas drives are Nietzsche's replicators, organisms or behaviors are his chief "interactors"—to employ a distinction in recent discussions of the problem of the "unit of selection." The distinction owes especially to Dawkins 1976/1989 and Hull 1980.

91. Here he takes over Lange's attack on the "absolute idea of species" (1866/1950, III/27, n. 54).

92. See also 9.11[178] [1881] and WP521 [1887] on species; compare Sober's defense (1980) of "population thinking." Nietzsche's claims for the chain or lineage resemble recent arguments for the "species as individual"; cf. Hull 1978. They express Nietzsche's view that what's real are not beings but becomings. He depicts the whole lineage as somehow present in each individual organism, not as merely its cause; see WP678 [1887], WP687 [1887], WP785 [1887], WP379 [1887], WP373 [1888]. 9.11[7] [1881]: "We are buds on one tree."

93. On exaptation, see the definition by Gould and Vrba (1982/1998, 55): "[C]haracters . . . evolved for other uses (or for no function at all), and later 'coopted' for their current role." Dennett (1995, 465) calls this "Nietzsche's most important contribution to sociobiology." He and others have denied Gould's claim to novelty here; cf. Dennett (1995, 281), Kitcher (1993/1998, 266). Nietzsche's fullest treatment of the topic is in GM.ii.12–13; here he sees functions as superimposed on preexisting functions. 10.7[172]

Now the way Nietzsche sometimes describes exaptation might seem to undermine my claim that he intends an *etiological* sense for terms like "purpose" and "function." GM.ii.12 again: "[T]he cause of the arising of a thing and its eventual utility, its actual employment and place in a system of purposes, lie *toto coelo* apart." In distinguishing origins from purposes, isn't he denying that a drive's ends are determined by its "design history"? I don't think he is. This is his hyperbolic way of alerting us to how drives are successively revised by being selected for new criteria. But as he soon makes clear, in GM.ii.13, these revisions are never complete: they leave much of the current behavior reflecting earlier selective criteria—signs or traces of much older functions. (Indeed, selective forces that once were formative may continue to operate in a secondary, merely sustaining way.) So older functions are not left in the past, but laid into the complex meaning the drive has now; the new role is only the most obvious meaning, layered on top.

All of this entails a very different conception of the "meanings" of our drives and practices than we naturally expect. These drives aren't "to" and "for" their goals by virtue of intending them, whether consciously or not. So their meanings and goals are far less transparent and available to us than we think. The individual who has a drive is not the only or even the primary determiner of its meaning; the latter lies "behind" it, in the forces that made it. But although this teleology is surprising, and presents new challenges for discovery, it is also a teleology by which Nietzsche can genuinely naturalize his life-wide drives, as he cannot on the mental model.

5. Is Will to Power Selected?

However, all of this ignores the role of will to power itself. We can't be satisfied with this account of drives until we settle that role, since it so often seems that Nietzsche thinks will to power *also* explains drives—and does so independently of selection. All of those drives with their diverse goals are also wills to power—are somehow "toward power," as well: "every drive seeks mastery [*ist herrschsüchtig*]" (BGE6). The question is what the role of will to power is in drives, and whether it indeed introduces

---

[1883] is another clear statement of this point. Elsewhere he suggests that functions can accrue to things that arise quite without functions (i.e., arise not by selection); see D122, GS11. (Sometimes, however, he is thinking that the source of such things is not random mutation, but again that ur-tendency to power; see WP647 [1887].)

a nonselective factor. Granting that Nietzsche gives Darwinian explanations of those various drives and instincts, does he give one for will to power itself—explaining it too by selection?

So what *is* the relation between will to power and natural selection, for Nietzsche? There are two options here, both I think represented in his texts: (a) he offers will to power as a life will that is, explanatorily, fully basic and prior in particular to natural selection; or (b) he offers will to power as a product of natural selection and uses selection to explain (why or how there are) these wills. On the first line of thought, Nietzsche treats will to power as a primordial ur-tendency in nature and Darwinian selection as merely its consequence or by-product; on the latter, he recognizes selection as basic, but argues against Darwinism that it fashions wills to power, not to survival.

There are also two ways of applying these options to Nietzsche, and here too we must decide: they can be read either (1) as competing hypotheses about his one real position; or (2) as coexisting aspects or moments of his position, as layers or levels within it. I prefer the latter. Each of (a) and (b) is a view Nietzsche *sometimes* thinks and states; the challenge is to see whether either is somehow dominant. We should judge this partly by the frequency and directness with which he expresses these views, but also by their comparative fit with the rest of his positions. And we should also consider the separate question: which of these views gives Nietzsche his *strongest* position—the one that looks closest to being true?

a. The Dominant View: Will to Power as Basic Explainer

Let's begin with the evidence that Nietzsche thinks that *will to power precedes selection*—that it's a preexisting life force, not itself the product of selective processes.[94]

In his metaphysical moods, Nietzsche thinks that although drives may well be shaped by selection, this selection works on a raw material supplied to it by and as will to power itself. Here he modifies a response to Darwinian

---

94. Moore (2002, 28–29) reads Nietzsche so. So too Schacht (1983, 247): "'[W]ill to power' for Nietzsche is a disposition that is both conceptually and actually distinct from the promotion of the kind of utility associated either with natural selection or with the emergence of successively 'higher' forms of life." I develop this "power ontology" viewpoint in detail in Richardson 1996.

selection made by others before him: selection is a secondary operation that shapes and prunes tendencies generated by an independent "force" in life. These theories replace what we treat as a "chance" factor—random mutation—with a directed tendency that adds an independent vector to evolutionary change. So new drives are generated by and as wills to power, and selection then tests these new wills against those already current.

On this line will to power is a precondition for selection—or at least for effective selection. Without will to power's supply of ever-new variations, selection could never have the cumulative and constructive effects we observe—could never evolve an eye, for example. Moreover, will to power initiates selection in this further way: it already makes drives that aim to control one another, and so sets up an immediate conflict among them. Natural selection then merely modifies or directs this conflict, designing drives to control one another *as a means to* reproducing themselves.

The passage most explicit on will to power's priority to selection may be WP690 [1887–1888]: "One cannot discover the cause *that* there is any evolution [*Entwicklung*] at all by way of research on evolution; one should not will to understand it as 'becoming,' even less as having become . . . the 'will to power' cannot have become."[95] But there's a great variety of other evidence that suggests this priority (of will to power over selection) less directly.

Generally, Nietzsche's frequent insistence on will to power as *primary* seems to count against its having been due to natural selection.[96] Moreover, the great number of times he explains by citing will to power—and *doesn't* go on to say how this will in turn results from selection—all weigh indirectly against his explaining it so. If he has this explanation in view, why doesn't he mention it more?

Another piece of evidence may seem decisive: he attributes will to power even to the nonliving. WP692 [1888]: "It is even less a matter of a 'will *to life*': for life is merely a *special case* of will to power, — it is quite arbitrary to maintain that everything strives to enter into this form of will to power."[97] Nietzsche thinks he can do not just biology with his concept,

95. See too WP636 [1888] on physicists' omission of the "perspectivism" of forces: "They suppose this is 'evolved,' arrived at — / But even the chemist needs it."

96. Z.ii.12: "the will to power — the unexhausted procreative life-will [*der unerschöpfte zeugende Lebens-Wille*]." A6: "Life itself I count as instinct for growth, for duration, for accumulation of forces, for *power*: where the will to power is lacking, there is decline."

97. WP655 [1885]: "The drive to approach — and the drive to push back, are the bond in the inorganic as in the organic world. The entire distinction is a prejudice."

but chemistry and physics too. He attributes it not just to drives, but to all "forces" (WP619 [1885]) and "dynamic quanta" (WP635 [1888]). If even atoms have will to power, how could selection be what sets that end?

To be sure, Nietzsche stresses that this application to the inorganic is a hypothesis, a tentative extrapolation from the primary case, that of life.[98] And he more often attributes will to power to *life*, than to *everything*. Still, how could he even hazard the extension as a guess, if he thought that will to power is formed by natural selection? The hypothesis alone suggests that he doesn't have this basis (for will to power) in mind—hence that the "to" can't have its teleology grounded in selection by the etiological analysis.

Moreover, Nietzsche wants to use this inorganic will to power to explain the basic organic functions. He states a kind of "preformationism." So BGE36 hypothesizes matter "as a more primitive form of the world of affects, in which everything still lies closed in a powerful unity, which then branches off and develops in the organic process . . . , as a kind of drive-life, in which all organic functions, including self-regulation, assimilation, nourishment, elimination, and metabolism, are synthetically bound, — as a *pre-form* of life?" Elsewhere he specifies how the inorganic "ramifies" into these organic functions.[99] For example, the nutritive drive, or hunger, "is a specialized and later form of the drive, an expression of a division of labor, in the service of a higher drive that rules over it" (WP651 [1887–1888]).[100] So this nutritive drive initially arises as a form of will to power;

WP688 [1888]: "[A]ll driving force is will to power, . . . there is no other physical, dynamic or psychic force than this." See also WP619 [1885], WP1067 [1885], WP634 [1888], WP692 [1888].

98. WP689 [1888]: "The will to accumulation of force as specific for the phenomena of life, for nourishment, procreation, inheritance, /for society, state, custom, authority /should we not be permitted to assume this will as a motive cause in chemistry also? /and in the cosmic order?" See also BGE36.

99. 12.6[26] [1886–1887]: "The *organic functions*, [to be] regarded as development [*Ausgestaltung*] of the will to power." WP688 [1888]: "That the will to power is the primitive affect-form, that . . . all other affects are only its developments." Also relevant are Nietzsche's accounts of will to power as a kind of indeterminate "energy" that demands expression in some way or other: WP995 [1884].

100. WP702 [1888]: "[T]he protoplasm stretches out its pseudopodia in order to seek something that resists it — not from hunger, but from will to power. Then it makes the attempt to overcome, appropriate, incorporate that thing: — what one calls 'nourishment' is merely a result-appearance, an employment of that original willing, to become *stronger*." Also WP658 [1885], WP660 [1886], WP657 [1886–1887], WP656 [1887], WP652 [1888].

selection just culls the versions of this drive into those that are fit (reproducible).

But most relevant for our Darwinian comparison is Nietzsche's similar account of reproduction, and of organisms' interest in it. This too he tries to explain as a spin-off from the primary project of power—whereas for Darwinism the organism's reproductive success is precisely what selection is ultimately for. Notice WP680 [1886–1887]:

> Against the theory that the single individual has in view [*im Auge hat*] the advantage of the *species*, of his posterity, at the cost of his own advantage: that is only *appearance*[.] / [T]he tremendous importance with which the individual takes the *sexual instinct* is not a *consequence* of its importance for the species: but procreation is the genuine *achievement* [*Leistung*] of the individual and consequently his highest interest, *his highest expression of power* (naturally not judged from consciousness, but from the center of the whole individuation)[.][101]

Even before Nietzsche thinks in terms of will to power, he argues that procreation results from drives that are ultimately *selfish*.[102] And he also offers several different accounts of how will to power results in procreation—including a theory that procreation is merely a matter of "casting off excess" which a will to power is unable to hold together in/as itself.[103] He surely sees himself directly opposing Darwinists here—denying that reproduction is the ultimate standard and replacing it with another.

It's clear this is a thick strand in Nietzsche's view: he often thinks of will to power as a sort of cosmic force, prior to selection—as a positive and creative principle that must already be there, before selection can begin to work negatively upon it. He does most to elaborate this view in his notebooks, but it's strongly present in his published works too. In this "power ontology," he denies that selection—"unconscious selection," he

101. 11.26[274] [1884]: "Reduction [*Zurückführung*] of generation to the will to power (! it must therefore also be present in the appropriated *inorganic matter*!)."
102. He argues that the sex drive aims at its own satisfaction, not at procreation: 9.6[55], [141], [145], [155] [1880]. He argues for the selfishness of this drive against those who treat procreation as an altruistic tendency built into all living things.
103. WP660 [1886]: "Procreation, [is] the crumbling that ensues through the powerlessness of the ruling cells to organize what has been appropriated." Also WP658 [1885], WP654 [1886], WP653 [1887].

calls it in WP684 [1888][104]—plays a genuinely constructive role in evolution, after all. This was of course a common response to Darwin; we find it in Lange, who posits (e.g., 1866/1950, III/51–58) a "law of development" as a purposeful force that supplies possible forms, from which natural selection chooses the actual forms. On this view, selection works merely to prune a variety generated by a more fundamental will—whose teleology, we should note, must be differently based.

This ontic priority of will to power goes together with an epistemic priority: will to power *explains* things, as science without it cannot do. Nietzsche attacks mechanism and argues that "matter in motion" is merely a way of describing events "for the senses"; it fails to explain them.[105] To really explain things, we need to think a will to power into them. So the familiar WP619 [1885]: "The victorious concept 'force,' with which our physicists have created God and the world, still needs a completion: an inner world must come to be ascribed to it, which I designate as 'will to power'."[106] Nietzsche doesn't limit this claim to biological things, i.e., organisms. Mechanism is inadequate even for physical forces, which likewise need to be explained by will to power.[107] And this means explaining them, we've seen, by the outcome of power—i.e., teleologically.

Nietzsche uses this independent source to explain some features of evolution that (in this mood) he thinks aren't adequately explained by the mechanism of natural selection. Most obviously, the source in will to power explains the aggressive and combative character of drives and organisms:

104. Dennett (1995, 182) misreads this as claiming that Darwin denies unconscious selection; instead Nietzsche attacks him for asserting it. (Kaufmann's edition misleads by inserting a paragraph break.) See n. 20 above.

105. WP634 [1888], WP635 [1888], WP625 [1888].

106. WP636 [1888] says that physicists have left out "this necessary perspectivism, by virtue of which every force-center — and not only the human — construes from itself outwards all the rest of the world, i.e., measures, touches, shapes according to [*an*] its force."

107. WP618 [1885] says that mechanists give up on explaining (*Erklären*) and content themselves with describing (*Beschreiben*); Nietzsche opposes a "dynamic" account to theirs. Also WP660 [1885–1886]. He often argues that explanations by cause and effect should be replaced by explanations by struggling wills: BGE21; WP631 [1885–1886], WP634 [1888], WP633 [1888]. BGE36 defends the hypothesis that "all mechanistic happening, insofar as a force is active in it, is indeed will-force, will-working," though the point may be that due to our limitations "we can't help but" suppose so—so that the passage may support the second option in my text below; so too WP689 [1888]. WP634 [1888]: "['Will to power'] expresses the characteristic that cannot *come to be* thought out of the mechanistic order, without thinking this [order] itself away." GS373: "[A]n essentially mechanistic world would be an essentially *meaningless* world!" Also GM.ii.12.

it sets these against one another "in advance" of the process of selection for fitness. They compete for power "before" they compete to survive and reproduce. Moreover, this source explains the way the lineage or species is likewise always striving to grow and strengthen itself, through the advances of its members.

And yet, as we've often noted, such a "cosmic" teleology is deeply at odds with other positions Nietzsche takes. By undercutting selection, it leaves him no other way to ground his will-to-power teleology than mentally. If not by selection, ends can have causal presence in advance of the explanandum only by being represented, in quasi-cognitions of them. In his metaphysical, Schopenhauerian mood, Nietzsche tolerates and even embraces this result, but elsewhere he sees good reasons to reject it.[108]

Nietzsche's doctrine of will to power seems somehow to forget or ignore these attacks elsewhere on wills, teleology, and so on. This makes it sit oddly with much of the rest of what he says. He seems to suspend, in this doctrine, the critical and skeptical faculty he so aggressively applies to doctrines of others.[109] How shall we read this situation? How can we reconcile these positive and negative moments?

One option is that the contradictions are really there, and Nietzsche simply misses or overlooks them. He really does mean will to power as fundamental and just fails to see that this reintroduces a mental principle into things. Some interpreters have defended this judgment.[110] I agree with it to this extent: Nietzsche *often* thinks of will to power in this way that contradicts his attacks. But I deny that he always understands it this way. It's implausible, I think, that such a central and glaring contradiction could have escaped him throughout.

A second option is that Nietzsche suspends his critical doubts purposely and overtly, because he offers will to power as a "useful fiction"— i.e., on pragmatic (or other nonepistemic) grounds. In this case will to

108. GS127 says that the expectation that every event is due to a will dates to a primitive period in which there was no thought of mechanism; it concludes: "[O]nly among intellectual creatures is there pleasure, displeasure, and will; the vast majority of organisms have nothing of it." TI.vi.3 rejects will and motive (*Motiv*), and says: "There are no spiritual causes at all!" See also n. 42 above for attacks on will, spirit, and so on, and n. 30 above for attacks on ends and so on.

109. Dennett's charge of "skyhook hunger" (1995, 466) may be apt for this side of Nietzsche's view.

110. E.g., Moore 2002; see n. 34 above. See Poellner (1995, 213–29) on the difficulty of construing Nietzsche's talk about drives and wills as involving an unconscious intentionality.

power would not really be a "doctrine," meant as true, but a kind of metaphor or image. This view too has able defenders.[111] And Nietzsche sometimes suggests he offers the thought in just such a way—as an ennobling or uplifting perspective, though no truer than others. Other times he suggests it is merely a concession to the framework we (by our own limited nature) need in order to feel that we understand or can explain.[112]

I'll defend a third option: that Nietzsche thinks he sees a way to avoid that contradiction, by understanding will to power in a sense that escapes the criticisms he makes against "will," and allied notions. So he can mean that claim seriously—as true—after all, but in a naturalistic fashion consistent with all those critical attacks. I'll defend this option by presenting a reading of will to power that abandons that ontic and epistemic priority, the better to find such a naturalistic ground. It does so, of course, by explaining will to power itself by selection.

b. The Recessive View: Will to Power Explained by Selection

Let's turn to the evidence that Nietzsche (also, sometimes) subordinates will to power to natural selection—treats it as the product of selection. Consider first this more general remark: "that we do not place our end forms of evolution (e.g., spirit) back as an 'in itself' *behind* evolution" (WP709 [1887]). Given this warning, and given how commonly Nietzsche uses the logic of natural selection to explain drives, it is unsurprising that he sometimes treats will to power this way as well. I claim that he *sometimes* thinks of will to power so, and that this is his *best* view—the one that best fits both the facts and the other positions important to him. In particular, it gives him a plausible account of how all or most drives, besides being toward their distinctive goals, are also toward power. I'll try to show that, as we reread important passages accordingly, this quasi-Darwinian line renders them more plausible than they had seemed before.

I think Nietzsche accepts that organisms are "designed for" reproductive fitness, but he argues that the design feature that most pervasively and effectively maximizes this is (some kind of) drive toward "power."

111. E.g., Clark (1990, chapter 7); she argues that Nietzsche's "cosmological doctrine of will to power" is really a metaphorical expression for his values, in particular the value of a psychological desire for power.
112. WP627 [1885–1886]: "The will to take power over a thing or to defend oneself against its power and push it back — *that* 'we understand': that would be an interpretation that we could use."

As we saw above, he uses this term both broadly, for any kind of growth, and narrowly, for growth in control over (other) processes. He claims that selection favors and develops certain dispositions to effect power, either growth or control. This tendency is "designed into" the organic, by the long operation of selection for it.[113]

Selection is, in a certain way, *for power*; but in what way? There are two options here: power is either (i) a function or goal shared by some or many selected drives, or (ii) a (higher-level) structural end of selection itself, which somehow squeezes in alongside or under Darwinian survival. For power to be a universal end, it seems it might need to play the latter, structural role. But perhaps it need not be universal to merit the priority Nietzsche claims for it. I begin by arguing for (i), then explore his options for (ii).

i. POWER AS THE FITTEST STRATEGY

Let's begin with the drive-selective context, within which Nietzsche argues design for power. We've seen that in his better moments he treats drives as designed by selection. They are so designed simply qua drives, in that organisms are crucially rendered fit by being equipped with *plastic dispositions* (drives): physical set-ups with causal tendencies that are plastic toward certain *results* (Rs). And drives are also so designed for those specific results that each of them is plastically toward. These results are selected for fitness, i.e., their contribution to replicative success, but are (usually) *different* from that success, highly specialized subsidiary means to it; photosynthesis is one such R. Just as the utilitarian might maximize utility by adopting or imposing nonutilitarian rules, so selection mainly maximizes reproductive fitness by crafting drives aiming at quite different

---

113. This reading *can* (in reply to the argument above) account for Nietzsche's occasional attributions of will to power even to the inorganic. We need not conclude from these that he can't be thinking of selection, and must mean a mentalist point. For even nonliving things and forces can be subject to a kind of selection—what has been called the "survival of the stable." Brandon (1981/1996, 34) calls this "physical evolution," of which "biological or genetic evolution is a special case"; he cites Dawkins 1976/1989 for the phrase "survival of the stable." Nietzsche's claim about power will be that it's not really stability that renders most fit (able to persist and replicate), after all. Even inorganic forces have—by selection—been "designed for" persisting by overcoming other forces. WP552 [1887]: "All events, all motion, all becoming, [is] . . . a fixing of degrees and relations of force, . . . a *struggle*."

goals than reproduction itself. This is involved in all organic "division of labor": specific tasks, means to that overall end, are assumed by parts whose horizons are confined to the tasks; only a few of these parts are responsible for replication (of the whole organism) itself.

As products of selection, these R(esult)s are teleological: they explain, by their (past) contribution to fitness, the drives that are toward them. This makes these Rs to be *goals* (Gs) for the drives. Drives "aim" at these goals in a sense that is dependent upon, but different from, the sense in which they aim at reproductive success. As plastic toward these Gs, the drives must somehow "sight" their relation to them and "respond" to this relation in their output. But they need not—and rarely or never do— similarly sight that structural *end* (E), reproducing. These drives are not, individually at least, plastic toward reproductive success; this end lies over their horizons, even though they're "designed for" it.[114] Those Gs, and that E, lie as it were at different levels in the organism's teleology.

Now although these G(oal)s are enormously diverse and specialized, there are also some widespread common features. In the first place, drives' Gs are generally *pleasant*: drives commonly pursue their Gs *as* pleasant, i.e., for the pleasure achieved in reaching the result. In his "positivist" phase Nietzsche treats pleasure as organisms' principal aim: he stresses that we pursue pleasure and not what's useful. Nevertheless, he still thinks that this pleasure in the result has been selected for its usefulness. So 9.11[5] [1881]: "Our instinct of drive grasps in every case at the nearest agreeable [thing]: but *not* at the useful. Of course in countless cases (namely on account of selection [*Zuchtwahl*]) the agreeable to the drive is also precisely the useful!"[115] So Nietzsche's picture is that drives are designed to be more devoted to their outcomes by being made to feel pleasure in those outcomes, and to pursue them as such.

But gradually Nietzsche decides that a different such common feature of goals is more important. Pleasure is itself just the "feeling of power."[116]

114. The Gs are internal, the E external, we might say. Compare Gibbard (1990, 28): "A person's evolutionary *telos* [reproducing his genes] explains his having the propensities in virtue of which he develops the goals he does, but his own goals are distinct from this surrogate purpose."
115. 11.25[427] [1884] says that the "principle of the *preservation of the individual*" lies at the basis of all feelings of pleasure and displeasure. 11.43[1] [1885]: "It is their life-condition, that they have pleasure in it for itself (the human has joy in the means to his preservation . . .)."
116. See n. 122 below.

So behind it, *power* is the really crucial property of most drives' goals; it is what they have mostly been designed to pursue. The first reading of "power"—(i)—takes it in this role. It reads power as a common property of many Gs (whereas the second will place it at the level of E). And it reads will to power as one kind of drive among others (whereas the second will make it universal).[117] This renders Nietzsche's claim about will to power at its least metaphysical, as simply this: the drives that have best served reproductive success and that dominate the drive economy of most organisms are drives whose goals involve some kind of *control*, either over other organisms, or over other drives in the same organism. It's not really the pleasure of the outcome, but the power or control it takes, that shows us what selection really favors in drives.

Now by contrast with this power or control, the "competition" involved in selection itself is less direct: fitness is the propensity to *outperform* competitors for given environmental niches. (There needn't even be direct interaction with them.) Such competition has the character of a *race*. I take Nietzsche to argue that within this Darwinian competition, selection most favors drives toward a sharper kind of struggle, a *fight*. He insists on the special effectiveness, in that competition, of drives to control or *incorporate* others—to divert others' projects to serve their own.

Nietzsche here makes an *empirical* claim: he invites us to *see* how widespread such dispositions are.[118] They include, of course, all the aggressive drives that set up the struggles for social rank, which have been found in so many species. So GM.ii.11 speaks of "another group of affects . . . of an even much higher biological value, than those reactive ones, [which] therefore deserve all the more to be *scientifically* evaluated and esteemed: namely the genuinely *active* affects, such as lust to rule [*Herrschsucht*], avarice [*Habsucht*] and the like."[119]

117. Compare two ways a *utilitarian* might defend the goal of power: (i) as (when widely adopted) mostly promoting utility, or (ii) as somehow part of (or necessary for) utility itself.

118. This satisfies Clark's requirement (1990, 210–11) that an empiricist reading of will to power defines it so that "the contrast between power and other possible motives is preserved."

119. 11.26[369] [1884]: "[A]ll the physiological-historical researchers of morality judge: *because* the moral instincts say *so* and *so*, therefore these judgments are *true*, i.e., *useful* in relation to the *preservation of the species*: because they have been left remaining! In the same way I say, that the *immoral* instincts must be true: only something else expresses itself than the will to preservation, namely the will forwards, to more, to — For is preservation the only thing, that a being wills?" See BGE230, BGE259; WP769

This competitive strategy—plasticity toward power over some other—is so effective that it becomes a pervading design feature of organisms. The many varieties of power drives are not descendants of some single ur-will, but strategies separately, repeatedly evolved—as, familiarly, is the eye. Nietzsche claims about this diverse lot that they are extremely widespread among organisms, and especially influential for their evolution.[120] This—I suggest—is at least *sometimes* the gist of Nietzsche's notion of will to power.

In the clearest, perhaps primary form, subjection is by killing and eating, but organisms evolve many subtler ways to turn others toward their ends. Nietzsche's main interest is of course in the human case, in what he calls the "spiritual" forms of these drives; these too evolve by and for success. And in us, these aggressive drives are also selected at the level of societies or groups—for how they help in those competitions. Nietzsche thinks such drives are especially bred when groups pass through periods of adversity and deadly struggle.[121]

It's important for Nietzsche that these drives are *plastic* toward power, i.e., toward the kind of control that is their G(oal). As conditions change, they adjust their behavior so that power still tends to result. By contrast, reproductive success generally lies beyond drives' horizons, as a structural end, part of the logic of the selective process; they need not be plastic

[1883], WP656 [1887] on incorporation. Nietzsche stresses the risks in this, if the system is unable to assimilate what's taken in; his own digestive problems gave him a ready case.

120. See GM.ii.12 on "the fundamental priority . . . that the spontaneous, aggressive, expansive, . . . and formative forces have." GM.iii.18 describes will to power as "the strongest, most life-affirming drive." In (the very early) "Homer's Contest": "Those human capacities that are terrifying and are counted as inhuman, are perhaps even the fertile soil out of which alone all humanity can grow in impulses, deeds, and works." See n. 13 above. When BGE13 counsels us to "beware of *superfluous* teleological principles! — such as the self-preservation drive," this is because these *other* drives explain what that one was supposed to: how we persist and prosper.

121. BGE262 can be read as a detailed account of how a group acquires both unity and its own will to power by selection; it begins: "A *kind* arises, a type becomes fixed and strong, through the long struggle with essentially constant *unfavorable* conditions." It goes on to say that the experience of breeders shows that a relaxing of selective pressures produces *variation* within the kind. This is a recognizably *frequent* view by Nietzsche, that adversity breeds strength (while reducing variation); his great cultural worry is that egalitarian comforts will cease to breed wills to power. See also his references to the "discipline [*Zucht*] of suffering," e.g., BGE225. I return to this topic (Nietzsche's seeming Social Darwinism) in chapter 3. Here what matters is how this story shows him thinking of will to power as a *product* of selection.

toward *it*. So these drives, by their plasticity toward power, "aim" at it in a way they do *not* aim at that Darwinian success; in this same sense they "prefer" power to that success.

Nietzsche often says that drives are "sensitive" toward power in a stronger, mental, and even conscious way. As we've seen, they recognize its achievement in a "feeling of power," which he sometimes identifies with pleasure.[122] Here it's hard not to hear him as implausibly attributing consciousness to all living things—as all capable of that feeling of power. But (I think) we read him more charitably if we interpret this universal "feeling" in the same thin sense we've found for drives' "aiming": every drive "feels pleasure" at achieving its G(oal), merely by its capacity to recognize it in such a way as to take steps to prolong it, to *stay* in that G.[123] Only *some* drives have evolved to "feel" that achievement in conscious experience—as only some predators have evolved to delight in catching their prey.

Nietzsche treats Darwin as an opponent here. He interprets him as making competing claims for "instincts for survival"—as claiming that *these* are the plastic tendencies most pervasively selected for. Uncharitably, he associates Darwin with this claim about Gs, and not with the structural point about E, where his revolutionary insight in fact lies.[124] So he thinks that Darwin presumes an isomorphism between selection's structural end and drives' concrete goals: selection favors not just drives that enhance Darwinian survival, but drives that plastically "aim" at it. Against this, Nietzsche presses the competitive strengths of power drives over survival drives; the former are fitter than the latter—better at surviving/reproducing. He depicts survival drives as passive or reactive tendencies, and argues that actively aggressive ones are more important.[125] It's important to credit

122. GS13, A2, and WP649 [1887] stress the feeling of power. WP693 [1888], WP689 [1888], WP688 [1888] analyze pleasure as this feeling; compare WP661 [1887].

123. Similarly, drives "interpret" others just by their plastic tendencies to incorporate them; I think we can read "interpret" in this thin sense in, e.g., WP643 [1886].

124. 8.23[9] [1876–77]: "Why accept a *preservation-drive* at all? Among countless non-purposive forms there occurred fit [*lebensfähige*], durable [*fortlebensfähige*] ones; million-year-long adaptations of individual human organs were necessary, until finally the current body can regularly arise and those facts regularly appear, which one commonly ascribes to the preservation-drive."

125. Nietzsche thinks that Darwinists' presumption that selection favors a passive kind of instinct also shows up in their portrayal of organisms as "adapting" to their environments; see GM.ii.12; WP681 [1887], WP647 [1887]. (On the other hand, he elsewhere credits adaptation; 9.11[274] [1881]: "Animal species, like the plants, have mostly *achieved* an adaptation to a particular continent, and now have something fixed and

how this frequent theme shows Nietzsche thinking of will to power as *something selected.*

But is there any reason to think that Darwin or Darwinists would care to enter this debate and argue for the prevalence of "drives to survive" or "drives to reproduce"? It might be natural to expect such isomorphism between G(oal)s and E(nd)—that organisms would be built out of processes aiming at survival, persistence, stability. And indeed in a general sense they clearly are, and have been viewed so; biologists often stress homeostatic and replicative powers, down to the level of cells. The organism and all its parts need to be maintained in largely constant conditions in order to function, and there are intricate mechanisms to detect and correct divergence.

When we turn to Darwin, however, we find no such stress on "survival drives."[126] His closest analogues to drives are "instincts"; his chapter on these (in *Origin of Species*) is revealing. He treats them as a diverse group of behaviors, not specifically aiming "to survive," though all ultimately selected "for survival." Nor of course does he treat them as aiming "to power." But two of the three examples he chooses for extended discussion ("the instinct which leads the cuckoo to lay her eggs in other birds' nests; the slave-making instinct of certain ants; and the comb-making power of the hive-bee" [*Origin* 216]) may invite that conception. And sometimes he puts the point more directly and generally: "[E]ach species tries to take advantage of the instincts of others, as each takes advantage of the weaker bodily structure of others" (*Origin* 211).

Some neo-Darwinists put still more weight on the role of "fight" in winning the Darwinian "race"; Dawkins is a prominent case.[127] They bring this struggle into the very places where identity of interest had seemed clearest: into the relation between a mother and her fetus, into the relation between different parts of a cell (between its nuclear and mitochondrial genes). We can also get a sense of the prevalence of this view from Keller's

restraining in their character.") Godfrey-Smith (1994b/1996, 315f.) discusses this view in Spencer; he presents (328f.) a critique by Dewey that resembles Nietzsche's. James (1878/1992) gives a similar argument against Spencer's too-passive view of the mind. And see the recent criticism of "the metaphor of adaptation" by Lewontin (1996, 8f.).

126. Except, that is, for some loose or heuristic remarks, e.g.: "[E]very single organic being around us may be said to be striving to the utmost to increase in numbers" (*Origin* 66).

127. Dawkins (1982, 56) (in a chapter entitled "Arms Races and Manipulation"): "This kind of unsentimental, dog eat dog, language would not have come easily to biologists a few years ago, but nowadays I am glad to say it dominates the textbooks."

attack on it: she argues (1992) that biologists' usual stress on "competition" expresses and encourages a misunderstanding of natural selection; with that term, biologists too unthinkingly slide along a range of meanings, from a minimum of "difference in viability and reproductivity" (in which it gets equated with selection itself), through the richer "joint reliance on a scarce resource" (the current technical sense), to "direct struggle with others." Keller thinks the last is too often used as a metaphor for the other senses, in a way that tends to obscure them.

Nietzsche takes the opposite view: (his) Darwinists tend to *under*estimate the role of such direct struggle. By their preoccupation with survival and adaptation, they conceive of the organism as self-focused and defensive, rather than aggressively outgoing.[128] They don't properly see the common character of so many organic processes—how they are "sensitive" toward control and use of other processes, how they press plastically to *improve* control. However, we've just seen that some Darwinists now do. Dennett complains (1995, 465) against Nietzsche's "characteristic huffing and puffing about some power subduing and becoming master," but I think we can now read it as a systematic rendering of a strong strain in neo-Darwinism itself. Nietzsche's will-to-power idea is, on this reading, a naturalistic thesis about a class of drives—tendencies toward power as control. These drives have control as their explaining goal, insofar as they've been selected for producing it; such drives are widespread, because control is *strongly* selected for. But it is allowed that other kinds of drives are often selected, too.

ii. POWER AS A STRUCTURAL END IN SELECTION ITSELF

I think this first reading of "power," as the internal goal of the drives most important in selection, fits most of Nietzsche's uses of it in particular cases. However, it does not do justice to the *universality* he so often ascribes to will to power. This reading makes power drives only a subset of drives, though a large and potent one. If power is to be an end for *all* wills or drives, as Nietzsche so often maintains,[129] we must find a way for it to be not just the selected goal of some drives, but intrinsic to the logic of them all. We must find a way in which even drives that are *not* toward power

128. I pursue Nietzsche's psychological diagnosis of these errors—which turns sharply ad hominem—in chapters 2–3.
129. See nn. 97 and 98 above.

in that sense (aren't selected as plastic dispositions to some kind of control) can still be "for power." I think there are two ways that Nietzsche might mean such a point. In the first, power is universal by being part of "what it is to be a drive"; in the second, it is universal by belonging to the process (selection) that makes all drives.

First, he might suppose that power is the goal of all drives, simply inasmuch as every drive aims to "achieve" its goal. Power might be, in its root and abstract sense, little more than "achievement"—reaching whatever result the drive is plastically toward. Or it might be just the drive's "power to achieve" its goal, which any drive wills in willing its goal.[130] In this achieving, the drive makes the rest of the world "obey" it, to the extent of making room in that world for its goal to be real or actual. It *imposes* its goal on the world. So perhaps WP689 [1888]: "[S]triving is nothing other than striving after power." Nietzsche's point is then cousin to Aristotle's about actuality—any power (*dunamis*) holding itself in its end (*entelecheia*).

I think this is indeed an element in Nietzsche's notion of power. He's sometimes driven to this point by his effort to universalize that end: this persuades him to read it as something intrinsic and essential to will, in general.[131] But I also think he doesn't *sustain* this view of power; he doesn't carry it into his actual *uses* of the notion (the ways he explains by power). In its abstractness, this sense carries too little of the force "over another" that he mainly hears in the term. Moreover, it expresses an a priori and speculative approach to power that he has strong reasons to disavow. However, he also has another, more promising option: he can try to ground even the universality of power *in selection*, in a way that preserves both power's aspect of control and the doctrine's empirical status.

To make power a universal end, Nietzsche must give it the same kind of *structural* role—as part of the "logic" of evolution by natural selection—that Darwinian survival has. He must make it an E(nd) contrasting with manifold G(oal)s, an E somehow designed into drives by the structure of selection itself, as is survival. Power must be not just one contingent strategy for selective success, but a necessary means to it, or even somehow an aspect of it. Then organisms would be "for" power,

130. Compare Clark 1990, interpreting will to power as a (Frankfurtian) second-order drive for "effectiveness" at first-order drives (211).

131. WP668 [1887–1888]: "that *something is commanded*, belongs to willing." In WP692 [1888] Nietzsche poses the question plainly: "[I]s 'will to power' a kind of 'will' or identical with the concept 'will'? does it mean as much as desiring? or commanding?"

even when they're not plastically aimed toward it—just as we've taken them to be for Darwinian survival.

Indeed, Nietzsche's commonest way to give power this structural role is to make it a *correction* to "survival," as what selection is ultimately for. He thinks Darwinists are constantly overstating the role of constancy and sameness in evolution, even or especially here at the crux. Biological entities are *not* selected for their capacity to "reproduce" themselves—in the strict sense of making copies. Rather, they're selected for their capacity to develop or improve themselves, in their "copies." Nietzsche aims to "dynamize" the ultimate selective criterion. But I think we best hear his point as *amending* (restating) the Darwinian criterion, not *replacing* it.

The basic application of this point is to the *lineages* that are Nietzsche's real beings (i.e., "becomings") here. A lineage lasts, over deep evolutionary time, not just by surviving or reproducing, but by successively overcoming stages of itself—by, indeed, *evolving*. Darwin's terms imply an identity or fixity through time in the members of the lineage, a repeated production of structurally identical Xs; Nietzsche claims that this isn't how selection works.

Not only does the lineage change even in its members' (Xs')[132] central features and functions, but it *must* do so in order to continue. For it competes with other lineages not just in the moment, but over stretches of evolutionary time, in which each is challenged to improve faster than the others.[133] A lineage can continue only by repeatedly revising itself. WP552 [1887]: "'*Preservation* of the species' is only a consequence of *growth* of the species, i.e., the *overcoming of the species* on the road to a stronger type."[134] My suggestion is that Nietzsche thinks lineages are *designed* for such growth, designed not for maximally replicating or duplicating, but

132. What counts these as members is their descendance relations, not—as the stress on survival suggests—their sharing a defining structure or features. Not only are members of a lineage L not determined by similarity relations, but L's success requires that they diverge. See nn. 91 and 92 above.

133. Compare Dawkins (1982, 61) on an "arms race" between lineages, e.g., a predator and its prey, each progressively improving its adaptations in response to the other.

134. GM.iii.27: "All great things bring about their own destruction [*gehen durch sich selbst zu Grunde*] through an act of self-sublimation [*Selbstaufhebung*]: thus the law of life wills it, the law of the *necessary* 'self-overcoming' in the essence of life." In Z.ii.12, life ascribes this necessity to itself. Z.ii.7: "[Life] wills to build itself into the heights. . . . / And because it needs height, it needs steps and a contradiction of steps and climbers! Life wills to climb and to overcome itself climbing." WP674 [1887–1888]: "The task, to spin forward the whole chain of life, *so that the thread becomes always stronger* — that is the task." Also GS33 on this evolutionary self-overcoming.

for evolving. As such lineage growth, power is natural selection's ultimate E(nd), for which *all* drives are designed.

Nietzsche's favorite term for such power is "self-overcoming" (*Selbstüberwindung*). This makes power somewhat different once again: in (i), power was control over others; previously in (ii), power was just achieving G(oal)s; here it is a kind of control over self. Again this control is a teleological "incorporation"—of something as a subordinate means or stage, into a fuller project or ability. So power over other organisms lies in turning them to use. And power over self, self-overcoming, is overcoming one's limitations—and thereby incorporating one's old self, as corrected past, into a fuller, more potent self.

Selection's ultimate E is this self-overcoming by lineages. They compete, across evolutionary time, in their capacity to evolve. All the organisms and traits that make up these lineages must ultimately serve this E—must collectively enable their lineage to overcome itself. This gives Nietzsche a way to naturalize his claim that all living things will power: each is designed for lineage growth.

Could anything like this be biologically viable today? The best candidate to be a design device for species change is presumably the *mutatability* of the genetic code. Could this itself be an adaptation? Could the cellular copying mechanisms for that code have been selected in competition with *more accurate* mechanisms that precluded the degree of variability needed? Here it suffices that we see what kind of selection *could* give Nietzsche's claim a ground. But he himself of course knows nothing of this.

Nietzsche envisions a much greater proliferation of designs for self-overcoming. Here his Lamarckism plays a major role. Whereas Darwinism attributes improving revisions (which selection then favors) to random mutation in the production of germ-cells—i.e., to the step *between* successive Xs in a lineage—Nietzsche thinks advances made within an X's own life can be heritable. Hence organisms can be designed to change themselves, as a means to changing their lineage. Individuals are bred for self-overcoming, as a means to the line's self-overcoming. So Zarathustra challenges his audience to work at overcoming the human (Z.i.P.3): "All beings so far have created something beyond themselves: do you will to be the ebb of this great flood and rather even go back to the animal, than overcome the human?"[135] In preaching the overman, Nietzsche sees himself appealing to aims deeply bred into us.

135. See how WP686 [1884] describes something that "flows on *under* the individual," shaping a future.

So far we've viewed lineages as descendant lines of *organisms*. But Nietzsche makes his point about lineages of other kinds too. The Xs that copy/revise themselves from generation to generation can also be *parts* of organisms, e.g., drives, or *groups* of organisms, e.g., communities. Nietzsche attributes competition at these other "levels" (than the organism) much more readily than Darwin.[136] And he thinks their lineages are also selected to be self-revising—and that this is also achieved by the heritable progress of the units themselves. Drives and groups are likewise "designed" to revise themselves, the better to revise their lineages.

Nietzsche's most important application of this point—design for self-overcoming—is to explain the prevalence of sickness and weakness. It poses a prima facie puzzle to him, why the sick and weak should be (as he thinks) so common—especially perhaps in certain periods, such as now. Why doesn't selection eliminate them?[137] Nietzsche proposes that it's the sick or weak that serve the lineage's self-overcoming most of all—and that they are selected precisely for this role. HH.i.224: "The strongest natures *hold* the type *firm*, the weaker help it to *develop further [fortbilden]*."[138] The picture seems roughly to be: the sick or weak, uncomfortable with the prevailing practice of their kind, work changes in it—introduce variation, over which selection operates. This variation in response to discomfort helps the lineage to change.

Nietzsche develops this account of sickness/weakness in elaborate and fascinating ways. I'll return to parts of it in chapter 2. But I think this gives us enough to draw some conclusions about this whole strategy for securing the *universality* of power as an end.

The strategy promised a naturalistic, empirical way for Nietzsche to attribute will to power to all organisms. But if it can successfully deliver anything at this biological level by its argument from lineage selection, it's at best an extremely attenuated kind of will to power—just "mutatability." All the richer ways Nietzsche thinks organisms are structured "for self-overcoming" collapse when we remove his Lamarckian support. With-

136. See n. 89 above.

137. WP864 [1888]: "It is senseless to assume that this whole *victory of values* [of the weak] is antibiological: one must try to explain it from an interest of *life* /the *preservation* of the type 'human' even by this method of dominance [*Überherrschaft*] of the weak and disadvantaged — ." Also GM.iii.13; WP401 [1888].

138. 8.12[22] [1875], a draft for this section, is entitled "On Darwinism." Elsewhere he suggests different roles the weak and sick may be "for"; see, e.g., WP685 [1888]. In chapter 2 I develop yet another reason: it's because humans are subject to a "social selection" that favors and spreads a "herd instinct" that humans are pervasively "sick."

out it, organisms *can't* be designed to overcome themselves ("in their lives"), as a way to improve the species. The only place design for evolution occurs is in the copying process.

Nietzsche's richer claims about self-overcoming collapse—as biology, that is. We can still try to rescue them by converting them into points about "cultural evolution"—about a hidden selective logic in that. And Nietzsche himself sometimes sees that his points about self-overcoming belong not to biology but to anthropology. For he sometimes treats self-overcoming as a distinctively human way of willing power. It's our capacity for this that has carried us so beyond the other animals—though at the cost of great self-inflicted pain. In chapter 2 I elaborate the different way selection works in this cultural process.

It is the argument in (i) that gives Nietzsche his best ground—most consistent with his other main claims—for attributing will to power to organisms generally. Power, as control over others, is a goal all organisms must pursue, in many ways at many levels, since without such a pervasive design they could not compete with those that do have these aims.

Summary

In *Nietzsche's System* I interpreted "will to power" as a hypothesis about the basic character of all reality—a hypothesis not claimed proven by a priori argument, but offered as a candidate to fit and explain our overall experience. I continue to believe that this is how Nietzsche most commonly means it, and that it's in this role that the notion ties together the greatest share of his thoughts. However, this "power ontology" is incredible for most of us. The claim that *everything* is toward power leaves Nietzsche with no alternative to a mental vitalism, reading mind into all things, despite his explicit disavowals. For how else can he find a directedness, a teleology there?

Recoiling from this apparent absurdity, it can be tempting, as a way to rescue will to power for viability, to scale back the claim into a "power psychology": a proposal about an underlying "motive" in *human* intending and purpose. Perhaps we can save enough of Nietzsche's point by restricting it to cases in which a mental account of the teleology is available.[139] But besides being dubiously plausible in its own right, this psychological will to power casts off too much of what Nietzsche wants to say with his

139. This approach is defended by Leiter 2002; see n. 43 above.

notion. (It loses, in particular, his naturalist insistence on the deep continuity of the human with the rest of life.) I think we do better on both counts by pursuing instead a "power biology."

I've tried to show how this biological reading of will to power gives Nietzsche's idea its strongest form. By treating that will as a product or element of natural selection, we find a nonmental sense for directedness toward power—and a sense that can explain why Nietzsche is surest about calling only all *life* will to power. This quasi-Darwinian reading saves Nietzsche from a mentalism he has his own good reasons to avoid; it converts a weakness at the center of his thought into a strength there. To be sure, this account of will to power is not, to my knowledge, ever directly articulated by Nietzsche. But it is an easy and natural application of his pervasive use of selection to explain drives and instincts. While less to the front of his mind than that ontological claim, it's still there in the background. And it's this power biology that sets most of his thoughts on a firmer ground. We'll go on to see how it supports his views about values, in particular.

2

Metaethics

Nietzsche's connections to Darwin can help us understand other parts of his thinking better too—in particular his values. I'll pursue in more detail this valuative side through the rest of this book.

First, in this chapter, I'll examine the interface between Nietzsche's values generally and the claims of fact sketched in chapter 1. How does he relate his values to his facts? I ask in particular whether and how he means to *ground* or *justify* his values by his psychological and social explanations in terms of drives and will to power. I'll argue that, just as his explanations are variants on Darwinian ones, so is his way of making his *transition* from explanations to values.

In order to study this interface between his facts and values, we need to add to our account of his facts—we need to build that account right out to the interface. We need to examine the facts that most affect his own values, and these are *facts about valuing*. In chapter 1 we looked at the general logic of drives and will to power, which we saw are his principal explanatory devices. Now we go on to see how he uses those devices to explain ("our") valuing and values, for it's *these* explanations that most motivate his own valuing. To explain our values requires more than the Darwinian mechanism of natural selection, however. It requires, I'll try to show he thinks, a *second kind of selection*—social selection—which Darwinists have missed. Here we pass from chapter 1's biological story to an anthropological one. Treating values as products of not just natural but social selection sets them in quite different light than Darwinists had done.

Once we've determined how Nietzsche explains values, we'll be ready to address his *metaethics*—in particular this question about the ontic and epistemic relations between his facts and his values. Nietzsche not only *studies* (tries to find out the naturalistic truth about) valuing, he also *engages* in valuing. And he uses what he learns in that study to orient his own valuing. Specifically, I'll try to show, he uses his quasi-Darwinian facts about the sources of our values to raise himself (as he thinks) into a superior valuative stance, from which he carries out his "revaluation of values." This stance gives credit or support to the "new values" that result from this revaluation. So these new values are partly based on his (purportedly factual) "genealogy" of human values.

In claiming such support for his values from his evolutionary facts, Nietzsche shares some of the program of Darwin and (especially) his "Social Darwinist" followers. His attacks on the way Darwinists try to ground their values really serve to point us toward his own revision of their strategy. To be sure, his genealogy recognizes more kinds of selective factors than Darwinian natural selection. And the revaluation will turn out to be "based" on this genealogy in an unfamiliar way. So Nietzsche has good claims to novelty and difference from Darwinism; his attacks are, in this respect, not inflated. Still, I'll argue that his metaethical approach is a recognizable descendant of the Darwinian one he criticizes.

By uncovering these Darwinian roots, we can address what I think is the main interpretive puzzle about Nietzsche's metaethics: how to reconcile his emphatic "perspectivizing" of all values, including his own, with his equally vehement "ranking" of values—a ranking that so clearly purports to some privileged status. So, on the one hand, he stresses the perspectivity of all values, and rejects any effort at objectivity: his own values are "merely his," and have no worth for, or bearing on, persons different from him.[1] Yet these relativizing moves seem to clash with Nietzsche's own great assurance in valuing—reflected especially in his highly confident rankings. It seems obvious that he thinks his values are *better* than Christian values— and if not for all persons, at least for the *best* persons.[2] It's hard to hear this "better" and "best" as relativized to (and valid only for) his own single

---

1. Zarathustra says: "'This — is now *my* way — where is yours?' so I answered those who asked me 'as to the way.' For *the* way — that doesn't exist!" (Z.iii.11.2).
2. See nn. 105 and 107 below, for example.

viewpoint and as claiming no extrinsic priority over different rankings. When he values, he does so with a vehemence that seems to renounce the perspectivism he affirms in *studying* values.

Nietzsche's insistence that values are perspectival belongs to his naturalizing move: values are precisely the goals of an organism's drives or wills. But when he passes from explaining values to valuing, on his own behalf, he seems to do so in a way that forgets that naturalistic lesson. As we might crudely put it, he seems to forget that his values are "just his perspective"—that they express the "existence conditions" of the very specific organism (and spirit) he happens to be. He claims a priority or privilege for his values that jars with their status as perspectives.

I'll argue that we can reconcile Nietzsche's naturalizing perspectivism with these claims to higher status for his own values, by going back to his Darwinian beginning. Nietzsche thinks that he completes a naturalizing movement begun by Darwin, by which he can at last *explain* our human values. He thinks his new grasp of this explanation permits a privileged ranking of these values, and also points the way to certain new values that will rank higher still. He thinks the privilege and priority of his own values lie in the way they issue out of his genealogy of values. Still, this priority doesn't keep them from being "perspectives"—not objective nor absolute.

My strategy will be to show how what's at issue is "selection" of values—and how Nietzsche thinks in terms of several kinds or "levels" of selection. He begins with a Darwinian story about a *natural selection* of values: values are "designed," by the differential survival and reproduction of their bearers, to enhance success in surviving and reproducing. But Nietzsche thinks this Darwinian point is not enough to explain our own values. He builds on top of natural selection a second kind of selection, a *social selection*, which he thinks has a different logic, not recognized by the Darwinists. And he then goes on to construct still a third kind of selection upon the other two—the kind of individual or *self selection* he advocates to us. Our best way to the whole logic of his view about values is through these levels of selection.

Now in the previous chapter I introduced two separate readings of whether/how the will to power is a product of natural selection. I argued that Nietzsche's dominant view is that it is not, but a prior life force that generates the variation on which selection then works. But this more metaphysical claim clashes with other of his ideas, in particular his conviction that will to power explains in a quite different way than our usual mental model of purposes.

Sometimes, however, Nietzsche treats will to power too as "designed" by selection, and I argued that this gives him the novel way of explaining us—and of explaining us *as organisms*—that he is generally convinced he has.[3] It gives him the "thin" versions of teleology and intentionality, which clarify his ambivalence on these topics. Drives and wills have "ends" and "intentions" in a very different way than we expect—a way that even Nietzsche himself struggles to keep in view.

It's this second conception of will to power that I'll use in the following. Still, I think most of my account will hold true even within the first, more metaphysical conception. For even that gives selection a crucial role in "designing" drives spun up by will to power. So the ends and intentions generated by selection still hold; it's just that there are *also* ends and intentions of a mysterious sort contained in drives' character as will to power.

I'll begin, in sections 1–4, by describing what Nietzsche thinks values are, and how they're constituted by those three kinds of selection. Then in section 5 I'll turn to the question of Nietzsche's own values, to show how they issue out of that study.

1. What Values Are

My eventual question will be: how far does Nietzsche think his "naturalization" of values brings him toward his business of ranking or evaluating them? But first I'll need to show how I think that naturalization goes.[4] Before looking at his *ranking* of values, we have to see what he thinks values *are*. He prides himself, sometimes, even on *discovering* this problem—the task of studying values in a truly scientific way. GM.P.7: "It's a matter of traversing, with quite new questions and as if with new eyes,

---

3. Or rather, it gives him that different way *complete*, since he has a part of it even when he makes will to power ultimate: he still thinks natural selection works upon the variation introduced by will to power. Although one key aspect of drives—their willing power—is independent, the ways they will power are products of selection.

4. WP462 [1887]: "In place of *moral values*, purely *naturalistic* values. Naturalization [*Vernatürlichung*] of morality." WP299 [1887]: "I might designate the tendency of these reflections as *moralistic naturalism*: my task is to translate apparently emancipated and *denatured* moral values back into their nature — i.e., into their natural 'immorality'." On Nietzsche's broader naturalism, see Leiter 1998b; also BGE230 ("To translate man back into nature") and GS109.

the enormous, distant, and so hidden land of morality — the morality there really [*wirklich*] has been, that has really been lived: and doesn't this mean nearly to *discover* this land for the first time?"[5]

More plausibly, Nietzsche claims merely to address this question (what values are) in a new way, on the basis of certain fresh insights. He offers these insights as *improvements* on the Darwinian ways of naturalizing values. He tries to vault to status, over them, by carrying their project further than they could themselves. Here his main point will be (I claim), that Darwinian natural selection is only a *first stage* in the formation of values, and a first factor in explaining them. There are *other* selective mechanisms besides this one, that also operate in forming values, and must be added in explaining them.

Before turning to this story of how values are explained by selection, we must do a bit of background work: we should say a few things to settle the logic or meaning of this notion of "value." First, we need to mark an important duality in Nietzsche's conception. We must distinguish a value (1) as a *taking-for-good* (a viewing-good) versus (2) as a *taken-for-good* (a viewed-as-good): on the one hand the act or activity of **valuing** some content—positing it as good—and on the other the **valued,** the content so posited. So "Christian values" could refer either to such goods as relief from suffering, or to the attitudes valuing such goods.

Nietzsche observes this difference in his terminology. For the most part, he refers to values-as-valuings using a family of terms built upon *schätzen* (*Schätzung, Abschätzung, Geringschätzung*, and so on). (He also uses *Werthung*, however.) I'll generally translate these as "valuing" or "valuation." We should hear these to refer to a certain activity, or a certain (thinly) intentional stance.

On the other hand, Nietzsche usually refers to values-as-valueds using **Werthe**, which I'll translate with "valued" or (just plain) "value." This refers to the content that is posited as good, by some valuing act or attitude.

---

5. GM.P.6: "[T]here is needed a knowledge of the conditions and circumstances in which [moral values] grew, under which they evolved and changed . . . a knowledge of a kind that has never yet existed or even been desired. One has taken the *value* of these 'values' as given, as factual, as beyond all question." In the "Remark" appended to GM.i, Nietzsche enlists the academic faculties of history and linguistics, as well as physiologists and doctors; the philosopher is to mediate among these. See GS345's call to explore "the history of the origins of these feelings and valuations" in morality. Compare Darwall et al. (1992, 188): "[M]ore careful and empirically informed work on the nature or history or function of morality is needed."

It refers to the thing that is valued, but *as* valued, e.g., not to what relief of suffering is "in itself," but to a relation or aspect it bears, as good for (Christian) valuing.

This relation of valued to valuing becomes explicit in such terms as *Werthschätzung* and *Werthurteile*, which show *Werthe* as a content for a valuing attitude. Nietzsche takes seriously this status of values. A first important way in which he "naturalizes values" is precisely by insisting on their dependence, as contents, on those activities of valuing—so putting them back into their natural setting.[6] A value is always "for" a valuing; it is an intentional object of that valuing and ontologically dependent on it. There can only be goods, as posited by a valuing viewpoint. GS301: "Whatever has *value* in the current world, has it not in itself, from nature — nature is always valueless — but one has once given it a value, as a gift, and *we* were these givers and gifters!" Z.i.15: "First through valuing is there value."[7]

As these passages make clear, the dependence of values on valuings does not imply that there *are no* values; rather, it tells us what they are. There *are* values in the world—he is ready enough to say—precisely because valuers have put them there, by their aims and intents.[8] As I will put this point, he thinks that values are *real* (i.e., there *are* values in the world, which science must study) but not *objective* (i.e., values always exist for a "subject"—construed very broadly to include the drive or will he finds in all organisms).[9] Nietzsche's "perspectivism" includes this refusal

6. I suggest that we think of a value not as "within" the valuing organism, but as the thing or event that is valued—this thing in a certain relation to the valuing. It is the mouse, for example, in its aspect as prey for the cat. Since Nietzsche denies (on my reading) that the cat-drive "represents" the mouse, there's no obvious candidate within the cat to play this role.

7. Also in Z.i.15 ("On the Thousand and One Goals"): "The human first laid values into things, to preserve himself, — he first created a sense for things, a human-sense! Therefore he named himself 'human,' that is: the valuer." See too WP260 [1883–1884].

8. Here I disagree with Hussain (unpublished), who argues against attributing to Nietzsche a "subjective realism" about values. I address his antirealism in section 5c below.

9. Here my reading is similar but my terms differ from Clark's, when she argues (1998, 67–68) that in *The Gay Science* Nietzsche remains a "value anti-realist," though he abandons his earlier "error theory" about values: "Value is not already in the world, waiting for us to discover it. But there is no necessary error involved in none the less discovering value in the world, finding it there. The only error is at the metalevel: the error of failing to recognize that value can be discovered in the world only because 'we' put it there."

to allow any values or goods that are *not* the intentional objects of some valuing; there's only a value if there's a valuing of it. But although values are not objective, there can still be objective facts *about* values—i.e., objective facts about those perspectival stances, about what valuing attitudes there are, and what they value. This point is an obvious and constant one in his metaethics—and will play an ongoing role for us.

Now these two senses of value, as valuing and as valued, leave aside another, which Nietzsche might need too. Those two senses may well be sufficient when he *studies* values, in his genealogies and diagnoses of us. But how about when he himself *engages* in valuing—when he values, e.g., strength or honesty? It seems he here might need to "posit values" in a different way than when he studies them. So, perhaps, in and for his own valuing, strength is "a value" in a way that relief from suffering is not, inasmuch as (he thinks) strength is "of value" or "valuable," and relief from suffering is not (despite the fact that Christians so value it).

I'll return in section 5 to the questions of how Nietzsche values, and whether this involves his "positing values" in a way that goes beyond the two senses above. Our earlier questions of whether values are "real" or "objective" will need to be readdressed with respect to such a positing within valuing. But as we examine Nietzsche's genealogies of values in sections 2–4, we treat the values that he posits only within his naturalistic study of valuing and its aims. We must refrain from reading into his genealogical references to "values" that he thinks they're of value or values them. As scientist or genealogist, he posits only the values internal to the valuing he studies.

We should bear in mind that this valuing need not—and principally does not—occur in a conscious act. Nietzsche attributes valuing very widely, to animals and indeed living things generally. "Valuations [*Werth-schätzungen*] lie in all functions of the organic being" (11.26[72] [1884]).[10] The continuity with other life is important to him. He thinks we commonly suppose that goods and values are confined to an autonomous human and psychological domain—that we alone have values by virtue of our singular mentality.[11] We suppose that "our values" are those we put into *language* and *consciousness*—so that they are and must be precisely what

10. 11.25[433] [1884]: "'Higher' and 'lower,' the selecting of the more important, more useful, more pressing arises already in the lowest organisms. 'Alive': that means already *valuing* [*schätzen*]: — /In all willing is *valuing* — and will is there in the organic."
11. Admittedly, Nietzsche sometimes seems himself to limit valuing to humans; see Z.i.15 in n. 7 above.

we believe they are.[12] But according to Nietzsche, not only do we share values with other creatures, but even in us the really effective or influential values are not those conscious ones, but values we have, as it were, through the plant or animal in us. Values are built into our bodies, and their conscious and linguistic expression is something quite secondary.[13]

This denial that values depend on conscious acts is a second way Nietzsche means to "naturalize" them. He needs some other account or analysis for this "valuing," that doesn't require consciousness. His main candidate for this role is his pervasive notion of a **drive** (*Trieb*), which we looked at carefully in chapter 1. He takes the role of valuing (and thereby making values) away from a central ego-will-mind, and disperses it among a multitude of drives, with a quite different kind of teleology and intentionality. Each drive is a valuing. So 11.26[72] [1884]: "Every 'drive' is the drive to 'something good,' seen from some standpoint." HH.i.32: "[A] drive without a kind of knowing valuation [*erkennender Abschätzung*] of the worth of the goal, does not exist among humans." A person's overall valuing is the synthetic product of these valuings by drives. And a person's explicit or conscious values are an indirect expression of those valuings in drives.[14]

What are these "drives"? Let me quickly recall my analysis in chapter 1—the parts that bear on our inquiry about values. I suggest that we think of Nietzschean drives as—to begin with—**dispositions** to *behavior*, i.e., as an organism's causal tendencies to act in certain ways. In most cases, this behavior itself tends to issue in some usual *outcome*—so we can say that the drive is also a disposition to this result. Moreover, a drive is a **plastic**

12. As elsewhere, Nietzsche sometimes uses "valuing" and "value" to refer to what we commonly think they are (our valuative beliefs), and sometimes to what he thinks is really going on (our valuative drives and their objects). For the former: WP676 [1883–1884] asks "whether all conscious *willing*, all *conscious purposes*, all *evaluations* are not perhaps only **means**, with which something essentially *different is being achieved*, than appears within consciousness." For the latter: see n. 13 below.

13. WP314 [1887–1888]: "N[.]B[.] Our most sacred convictions, what's unchanging in regard to [our] highest values, are *judgments of our muscles*." BGE3: "[B]ehind all logic and its seeming self-mastery of movement there stand valuations, put more clearly, physiological demands for the preservation of a certain kind of life."

14. D119: "[O]ur moral judgments and valuations are only images and fantasies upon a physiological process unknown to us." BGE187: "[M]oralities are also only a *sign-language of the affects*." BGE268: "Which group of sensations is awakened, takes words, and gives commands in a soul most quickly, is decisive for the whole rank-order of its values and ultimately determines its table of goods." Also WP258 [1885–1886].

disposition to this outcome, inasmuch as it tends to produce different behaviors in different circumstances, in such a way that the same outcome is reached, by different routes, in all of them. So the hunger drive is an organism's disposition to certain behaviors (e.g., hunting and chasing) which tend plastically toward certain outcomes (catching and eating the prey).

Such plasticity depends on a capacity to "respond" to circumstances, which requires being able to "sense" them, in some minimal way. But this way can be minimal indeed. On this pared-down notion of drives, even a plant's phototropism can count as one: it shows a plastic responsiveness to a light source, even though this consists in nothing more than the tendency of the leader to grow more quickly on the shaded side. It's in terms of such minimal units as these plastic dispositions that Nietzsche means to build his naturalism of drives.[15] It lets him find drives—and thereby values—very widely, in all life, yet without anthropomorphizing them as psychic states.

Given this much, a drive's value is simply the outcome it tends plastically (and responsively) toward. But this isn't yet enough. It leaves out the twofold *explanatory* interest Nietzsche has in values. He wants on the one hand to count the value as explaining behavior—explaining it as aimed at the outcome. And on the other hand he wants to explain the value—why the organism has a drive that aims at just this.[16] As I argued in chapter 1, section 4, Nietzsche has one main way of explaining drives: as **selected**. And this allows him to set values in both explanatory roles: they explain behavior, by being the outcomes that it was "selected for."

Put most abstractly, all such selection is for (replicative) "fitness": what explains the drive's outcome is the way this outcome improves the drive's own capacity to survive and reproduce.[17] Drives are selected for their fitness; their outcomes are designed to maximize this fitness. So we have a drive to eat, because eating is an outcome that makes a drive fit. This way of explaining the outcome allows it in turn to explain—seemingly

15. WP704 [1887–1888]: "In order to understand what life is, what kind of striving and stretching life is, the formula must apply as well to tree and plant as to animal."

16. WP257 [1888]: "Formerly one said of every morality: 'by their fruits shall you know them'; I say of every morality: 'it is a fruit, by which I know the *soil* from which it grew.'"

17. I put aside the possibility that Nietzsche means to modify the very criterion of selection—reproductive fitness—by recasting it as evolutionary "self-overcoming"; see chapter 1, section 5b.i.

against the directions of causation and time—the behavior that brings it about: it's the fitness benefit of eating that explains why the organism hunts. So:

(1) Behavior *is selected for* outcome *is selected for* fitness.

Hunting is for eating is for fitness. And:

(2) Fitness *explains* outcome *explains* behavior.

Fitness explains eating explains hunting.

Consider by contrast a merely physical process, such as water freezing; its result (water frozen) is explained only by the process toward it and in no way explains the process. But an organic process ("behavior") can have outcomes that explain why the process occurs. When water *does not* freeze in a cell, this can be the "function" of certain parts of the cell, which have been selected for that effect. So the "behavior" of those parts is explained by that outcome—and more particularly by the way this outcome improves fitness. Here the outcome explains the chemical processes by which the freezing is avoided. Here we have, in other words, "teleology," an *explanation by ends*.[18]

It's only when an outcome explains in this way that it counts as a "goal"—and a "value." Water doesn't value freezing, but the cellular process or ability *does* value not freezing, Nietzsche thinks. It values it, by having been designed to pursue it plastically, responsively. So here we can give these definitions of "value" and "valuing":

(3) Valuing = being disposed to responsive behavior for a selected goal.
(4) Value = the selected goal of a responsive behavior (and its disposition).

The definition of "value" is equally a definition of "good": a drive's goods are precisely its goals—the outcomes it was selected to bring about.

So not only are values explained by selection, but qua values, they logically depend on it: it's having-been-selected that makes an outcome a valued goal. A behavior—and even a single instance of a behavior—has many different causal effects; it's only the disposition's selective history

18. As noted in chapter 1, section 3, I here appropriate the etiological analysis developed by Wright (e.g., 1973) and Millikan (e.g., 1989) for "functions." This gives, I claim, a sense of "teleology" that survives Nietzsche's many attacks on the notion; it gives the sense in which will to power itself is something teleological.

that determines which among these effects is the behavior's goal and value—it tells *what* is really being valued here. So, to uncover the meaning of our values we need to study their past. *Meaning is settled by genealogy.*

This supplies a further reason why our values are not immediately or inevitably available to us. It's not just that they lie mainly in our drives, rather than in our conscious purposes. It's also that these values are "in" our drives not just by virtue of how those drives are *now*, but by their past. My values are settled by selection that worked largely before me—in the history of my species and society. And even there, this selection worked quite above or behind my ancestors' conscious sense of what they valued and why. The mechanisms selecting values are opaque to us, despite our ordinary confidence that we understand and choose our own values. We don't really know what we want. To find out, we need genealogy.[19]

How, concretely, has this selective mechanism designed the values we see or hold? Nietzsche believes, I'll argue, that selection has worked in several ways, each with a somewhat different "logic." Let me quickly preview these kinds of selection, before treating them separately in the following sections.

Darwin gives the start of this story: values are selected for how they help the organism to survive and reproduce. As I'll try to show in detail, Nietzsche has two strong reactions to Darwin's account. On the one hand he is deeply impressed with what natural selection explains about humans—with how our behaviors are indeed directed by this mechanism at basically selfish aims, contrary to our pretensions and self-conceptions. But on the other hand he is also convinced that this Darwinian model needs to be supplemented in this application to humans: there's a somewhat different form of selection that is, with us, superimposed on the natural selection that more completely explains plants and animals.

Most crucially, this new mechanism is social selection. By it we acquire our distinctively human features, such as self-consciousness and language. But this social selection, which makes us human, has a negative aspect as well: it renders us "sick." This overall diagnosis is one of the major themes through all Nietzsche's works—we are "human, all-too-human," the "sick

---

19. Nietzsche often states this determination of meaning outside the individual, by identifying the individual with the evolutionary "line" (*Linie*) to which it belongs. WP379 [1887]: "[T]he individual has not been grasped by science: it is *the whole previous life in one line* and **not** the *result* of this." WP373 [1888]: "Every individual is the entire line of evolution besides (and not only, as morality [conceives] him, something that begins with birth)." Also WP678 [1886–1887], WP687 [1887], WP785 [1887], WP682 [1887]. I return to this idea in chapter 3, sections 6–7.

animal," this infection showing especially in our religions and moralities, and in the "nihilism" they express and tend toward.[20] I will argue that this sickness is ultimately due to a certain logic of *selecting values*, which characterizes our social life.

Similarly, it's by changing again this mode of value selection that Nietzsche aspires—as he does through all his works—to escape or rise above this sickness, into what he eventually calls a "great health." He conceives this step as redeeming from the sickness characterizing the human, so that it deserves to be called "superhuman" (*übermenschlich*). I will try to show that this too is crucially another *mode of selection of values*, different from both the natural and the social.

So I think we can distinguish, in Nietzsche's account of values, a certain overall dialectic of stages, different *levels of selection*. Of course he doesn't consistently and explicitly think in terms of such discrete levels, but I think we find that the bulk of his remarks coalesce on them. There are these different ways our behaviors have been selected: first the Darwinian, explaining the *animal* in us, then the social which explains our more peculiarly *human* behaviors, and finally a certain *superhuman* possibility we're pointed toward. This overall dialectic will eventually show us how Nietzsche means to "ground" his own values in his explanations of our values so far.[21]

2. Animal Values, by Natural Selection

Let's see first how Nietzsche appropriates the basic Darwinian mechanism—natural selection—to explain our values.[22] This mechanism sets into us, he thinks, the basic and most settled of our values. The other selective mechanisms that can produce values set theirs upon and against these values long sedimented into us by "nature." Nietzsche associates these basic values with the "animal" in us, and with our "body." Indeed, some of these values express conditions for life generally; they were selected in

20. See n. 37 below.

21. The dialectic animal-human-superhuman is important in *Zarathustra*'s preface, e.g., Z.i.P.4: "The human is a rope, tied between animal and superhuman."

22. Again, I'm here assuming and operating within Nietzsche's "strong selection" view, in which he treats not just drives but will to power itself as arising by selection; I sketch this view in chapter 1, section 5b. But remember that much of this account remains true within his "metaphysical" view of will to power as ultimate: selection still designs, though it designs things with a certain prior unselected aim.

a distant evolutionary past.[23] (Bear in mind that we still confine ourselves to his *study* of these values, and defer the question of how/whether he himself values them.)

Values and drives selected in this first way are those carried in the "blood" of organisms (e.g., BGE208, 261, 264), and transmitted in that blood to genetic descendants. Insofar as a drive replicates (is copied in another organism) *only* through blood transmission—in genetic descendants of the organism that bears it—the drive will be selected *only* for how it favors that transmission, i.e., raises the organism's reproductive fitness. If this is how selection "gets a grip" on a drive, it will shape it to serve biological fitness. And along with the drive, it will so shape its value. WP507 [1887]: "[I]n valuings *preservation-* and *growth-conditions* express themselves."[24] Nietzsche also expresses the point that values are designed this way by saying that they reflect our "life" or "existence conditions."[25]

We should recall (from chapter 1, section 5b.i) the distinction between two levels of "goods" in these drives' valuing. The drive is a disposition for behavior plastic toward a *goal* (G), and the G is itself selected as a means to the overall *end* (E) of reproductive fitness or success. We could speak of the drive as valuing either G or E or both. The drive stands in a different relation to each. It—or its behavior—is plastic toward the G: it adjusts to changing conditions in such a way as to stay "on track" toward G, as the predator stays on track toward its prey. But the drive and behavior are probably *not* plastic or responsive toward that ultimate E (reproductive success), which lies (as it were) over its horizons. Although all drives are "designed" for that outcome, none need "track" it or "sense" it.

This lack of plasticity toward the E—the ultimate selective end—means that in special cases in which the drive's G(oal) is *not* a means to E, the drive still pursues G: even when eating lowers fitness, the hunger drive

---

23. 11.40[69] [1885]: "But our valuations betray something of what our *life-conditions* are (in smallest part the conditions of the person, more broadly the [conditions] of the species 'human,' in greatest and broadest [part] the conditions under which *life* is possible)."

24. WP715 [1887–1888]: "[T]he viewpoint of 'value' is the viewpoint of *preservation-enhancement-conditions* with respect to complex forms of relative duration of life within becoming. . . . 'Value' is essentially the viewpoint for the increase or decrease of these dominating centers." WP567 [1888]: " . . . according to values, i.e., in this case according to the viewpoint of utility in regard to the preservation and power-enhancement of a particular species of animal."

25. BGE268: "The valuations of a human betray something of the *structure* of his soul and where it sees its life-conditions, its genuine need." Also WP260 [1883–1884]. See n. 77 in chapter 1.

still wants it. So, although the drive was designed for E, its horizons reach only to G, which has in this respect a better claim to be what the drive values. Nietzsche sometimes reflects this by treating the drive's G as its value and the E as the "meaning" of its value.[26] There remains a sense in which the drive "misfires" in those special cases: unbeknown to itself, it's deeply for that E. By such divergences between G and E, an "internal value criticism" is possible even within the scope of a single drive; this will be important when we turn from explaining to assessing values.

When values arise by natural selection, their ultimate E is "reproductive success," which Nietzsche interprets as the success of the *reproducing line* or lineage of the organism—this can be the family or tribe or species, conceived as stretching through time. And by this reproducing line's success, he means its preservation and—more particularly—its development or *growth*.[27] So our animal values are ultimately designed to serve our lineage's preservation and growth. For this basic level of our valuing:

(5) Animal value = the goal of a responsive behavior, naturally selected to preserve/increase the lineage.

If an organism (an animal or plant) is made only by such selection, then all of its drives and structures are for this end, not only individually but as a package: "Every drive has been bred as a temporary *existence-condition*. . . . A determinate degree of the drive in relation to other drives will, as able to preserve, always be transmitted further, an opposed one vanishes" (11.26[72] [1884]). What most prevents an individual drive from pursuing its G to the detriment of the E for which it (with all the other drives) was designed is that it occurs in just that degree of strength that lets it be appropriately reined in and limited by the other drives. Hence there is an "organic unity" in the animal's manifold behaviors, as in its physical structure. No drive stands out and presses its project to a degree that hinders the organism's preservation and growth. This functioning together of the drives, in coordinated service of the single reproductive end, is the simple "health" of animal life—with which Nietzsche will contrast our human case.[28]

26. This distinction plays a role in Nietzsche's argument for drives' (and organisms' and persons') selfishness: what they really value is satisfying themselves at their goals— even if their goals have been selected as means to the lineage's or species' success. I discuss this in chapter 3, section 2.

27. On lineage and growth, see chapter 1, section 5b.ii.

28. Bear in mind that we continue to defer the question of whether/how Nietzsche himself values fitness, health, and so on; we remain within his naturalistic explanations of these values.

In his analysis of drives as due to natural selection, we've seen that Nietzsche has one main disagreement with Darwinists: he thinks they miss how crucial to reproductive success are the *aggressive* drives, the drives for "power over" other organisms or processes. Achieving power in one form or another is the fittest strategy. Darwinists miss how pervasive drives aiming at this general outcome/goal are—the extent to which organisms can only survive and reproduce by being largely steered by active, aggressive, and hostile tendencies. Because natural selection favors such drives, it builds into our bodies values more cruel than we've supposed. So 11.40[61] [1885]: "Our intellect, our will, even our experiences are dependent on our *value-judgments*: these answer to our drives and their existence-conditions. Our drives are reducible to the *will to power*."

I developed this disagreement with Darwinism at length in chapter 1. Here instead I turn to a disagreement not about how natural selection itself operates, but about a second kind of selection, which Nietzsche claims is superimposed upon it.

3. *Human Values, by Social Selection*

Darwin goes wrong this further way in our human case. In us, the very mechanism of natural selection has been modified—or rather, there has been imposed upon it a second kind of selection with a somewhat different logic. This selection not only works in a different way, but also toward a different overall end: it "designs" our drives and values for different ultimate ends than the organism's reproductive success. Darwin gets part of the story: he sees that behavioral tendencies can be replicated (transmitted) not just genetically, but socially.[29] But he fails to see just how selection works on this new kind of replication—what its logic and direction are.

For Nietzsche the key innovation lies in *custom (Sitte)*, as a new mechanism for propagating or replicating behavioral dispositions. As we'll see, this depends on the development of memory—the capacity to sustain habits distinct from wired-in drives. An organism's causal tendency to behave in certain ways—the "program" that determines its activity in given conditions—is now acquired not by genetic inheritance, but by copying

---

29. Darwin's account of the rise of the moral virtues, in *Descent*, chapter III, finds their root in certain "social instincts" evolved by natural selection even in lower animals, but then enhanced and built up into our "moral sense" by such social factors as "habit, instruction, and example" (I/102), abetted by praise and blame.

and remembering the practice of (other members of) the social group. Dispositions to behaviors that propagate widely through a group in this way will be called not "drives" or "instincts," but "customs" or "practices" (*Bräuche*) or "habits" (*Gewohnheiten*).

Now of course the capacity and propensity to form such customs arise and evolve by natural selection—and hence for the sake of reproductive goals. The genetic basis for these customs continues to be judged by its reproductive fitness: Darwinian selection by no means ceases to work. However, this capacity sets up a new replicative mechanism, in which habits get copied and thereby multiply in a nongenetic way. And a new selective logic will work on these new replicators: they will be selected for success at copying and dispersing themselves as social customs. How well a habit enhances genetic fitness may be one factor affecting how well it spreads, but there can be many others.[30]

So a new kind of selection— **social selection**—works on this new replicative process. Nietzsche's analysis of it is an ancestor to Dawkins's well-known account of selection over "memes."[31] Some dispositions are more "fit" for social dispersion than others: they will tend to be "selected for" their fit-making features, i.e., those that make them more likely to be copied by others, more likely to become customs or habits.[32] Here too this selection can gradually and incrementally fix and enhance those features that help behavioral dispositions to disperse. So these customs can evolve plastically toward certain "fitness peaks," at which those features are maximized.

Now of course some of the logic of this new selection remains the same—it's what entitles it to be called selection. The process still works by

30. A practice can spread even if it damages genetic fitness, even indeed if it destroys it (as, e.g., with the practice of celibacy)—though in the latter case there will of course be limits to how widely it can spread, for how long.

31. 7.19[87] [1872–1873] (P&T26): "Darwinism has title [*Recht*] also in picture-thinking: the stronger picture consumes the lesser." WP508 [1883–1884]: "[In the] original chaos of representations / the representations that got along with one another remained, the greatest number perished — and are perishing." And WP588 [1886–1887]: "Not a struggle for existence will be fought among representations and perceptions, but for mastery." Compare Dawkins (1976/1989, chapter 11). Dennett (1995, chapter 12), develops Dawkins's point, and later treats Nietzsche in these terms, an account that my own develops and modifies.

32. Like Dawkins, Nietzsche compares the spread of ideas to that of a disease. TI.ix.35 speaks so of altruistic, nihilistic values: "Such a judgment always remains a great danger, it works contagiously [*ansteckend*], — on all the morbid soil of the society it soon proliferates up to a tropical vegetation of concepts."

the differential reproduction of the elements, the behavioral dispositions. Moreover, Nietzsche conceives it as still, for the most part, an *incremental* and *aggregate* process. It is incremental, in requiring long periods of gradual approach to those fitness peaks, at which customs are best "designed" for continuing themselves. And the process is an aggregate one, in that it depends on the effectiveness of statistical differences in the relative fitness of two types, each represented by a "population" of instances. So this social selection is *not* carried out by any steering intelligence. Like natural selection, it is "stochastic," not intentional, and not the work of any deliberate selectors.[33] And it is not immediately perspicuous to individual participants—those who share in the practices.

The individual who has his/her behaviors from customs is unlikely to know what they mean. This is so partly because the individual is unlikely to be aware of why he/she adopts a certain habit or practice—*that* it is being copied from others, *why* he/she is copying it, *what* specific features in the behavior make it attractive now. But even if the individual had this very rare *self*-clarity, this would still not exhaust the meaning of this practice. For the practice gets its meanings and goals from its selective history, not just from the reasons the individual participant enters into it. It's that history that tells what the custom has been "designed for," and why it is present now.[34] Of course this history is even less available than those personal incentives.

By this superimposition of social on natural selection, a new set of behavioral dispositions arises and evolves, a web of practices that is both a rewriting and an overwriting of the dispositions shaped by natural selection. As I've said, Nietzsche sometimes calls these new dispositions "habits," reserving "drives" for those more ingrained "animal" instincts we inherit rather than learn. But he doesn't consistently observe this distinc-

33. I must acknowledge, however, that here as so often, Nietzsche also thinks along a second line. Sometimes he conceives of customs as the products of a deliberate invention and imposition by aristocratic "masters." So GM.ii.17 attributes the first "state" to "a pack of blond beasts of prey," whose "work is an instinctive form-creating, form-imposing." But I believe he thinks this is subsequent to a more primeval phase during which developed such basic human powers as memory and language, a phase steered by social selection; see in GM.ii.19 that the noble tribes occur in an *"intermediate age."*

34. In chapter 1, section 4, we looked at GM.ii.13 on the complexly evolved practice of punishment: "[Today] the concept 'punishment' no longer represents one sense [*Sinn*], but a whole synthesis of 'senses': the previous history of punishment in general, the history of its exploitation for the most various purposes, finally crystallizes into a kind of unity that is hard to dissolve, hard to analyze and, what one must emphasize, quite completely *undefinable.*"

tion, often calling learned tendencies "drives" as well. The boundary is a permeable one for him, because he accepts a Lamarckian "inheritance of acquired traits."[35] So he often suggests that these learned practices can acquire a genetic footing ("in the blood") and be inherited. Still, he treats them as less securely or solidly or deeply settled in this way than our animal inheritance; they can go as quickly as they came.

Nietzsche thinks that Darwinists have failed to notice the special character of this social selection. His account of it highlights its differences from natural selection. And indeed it works, to an extent, *against* natural selection. It works to modify behaviors designed for the organism's survival and reproduction, and to re-aim them toward goals serving a different overall end. So taught behaviors oppose or counter inherited behaviors. And because the design by natural selection persists "in the blood," this conflict is not a passing phase, in which the one set of dispositions—designed for genetic reproduction—are erased and replaced by ones replicating socially. Nietzsche thinks that much of our "animal nature," fashioned by natural selection, is impervious to redesign through social selection.[36] So customs must constantly work to oppose and suppress inherited drives—which Nietzsche refers to as humans' "taming" (*Zähmung*) and "domestication" (*Domestikation*) (I return to these in chapter 3).

This persisting conflict is Nietzsche's first reason, I think, for describing humans as "the sick animal."[37] Our habits conflict with our drives, as is not the case with other animals. This division, our dispositional commitment to two incompatible sets of behaviors, with incompatible goals and values, causes a new kind of *suffering*, which is distinctively human. GM.ii.16: "But thus began the greatest and uncanniest illness, from which humanity still today has not recovered, the suffering of the human *over the human, over himself*: as the result of a forcible sundering from his animal past."

What kinds of behaviors *are* favored by this social selection? Not exclusively, and not primarily, those advancing the reproductive success of the organism that bears the disposition. To be sure, *one* way a habit can

35. As does Darwin, e.g.: "It is not improbable that virtuous tendencies may through long practice be inherited" (*Descent* II/394).
36. WP684 [1888]: "[E]verything that escapes the human hand and breeding, turns almost immediately back again into its natural condition. The type remains constant: one cannot *'dénaturer la nature'*."
37. See A14 on the human as "the most ill-formed [*missrathenste*] animal, the sickest, that has strayed most dangerously from its instincts"; GM.iii.13 on how sickness is "normal" among humans. Nietzsche attributes humans' sickness to their taming: GM.iii.13, 21, TI.vii.2.

replicate itself is by helping the individual to have offspring it can train into that habit. But since habits don't depend on this transmission to offspring, they will not be designed simply and solely for genetic success, as inherited drives must be. A much more effective way for a habit to replicate itself is by social transmission—not to descendants, but "laterally." So habits will be designed for their "habit-forming powers," for their "capacity to become custom," in a given social environment. They will be selected for traits that allow them to persist and spread, in that environment.

a. Structure of Social Selection: Herd Instinct

I think much of Nietzsche's pessimism about humanity stems from his analysis of the "logic" of this social selection, and the kinds of customs/ values it tends to favor and establish. His diagnosis of the defects of this mechanism, and the values and practices that have evolved by it, is extremely complex. I can only try to organize some of the main points.

To begin with, social selection designs drives and practices that serve the survival or expansion of the social group (and not the individual or species). That is, the practices that replicate best are those that preserve and expand the "medium" within which they propagate—the social group. So each individual human acquires behaviors that have been "designed," by this selection, not principally to serve the lineage's preservation and growth, but the group's. So:

(6) Human value = the goal of a responsive behavior, socially selected to serve the group.

So GS116: "These valuings and rank-orders [of a morality] are always the expression of needs of a community and herd: that which benefits *it* first — and second and third —, that is also the highest measure for the values of all individuals. With morality, the individual is trained to be a function of the herd, and to ascribe value to itself only as function."[38] Thus far

38. HH.i.96: "[Tradition] is above all directed at the preservation of a *community* [*Gemeinde*], a people." 11.25[398] [1884]: "Preservation of the *community* (the people) is my correction for 'preservation of the species'." Also 11.26[369] [1884]. HH.ii.89 "The origin of custom goes back to two thoughts: 'the community is worth more than the individual' and 'an enduring advantage is preferable to a fleeting one'; from which the conclusion follows, that the enduring advantage of the community is to take unconditional precedence to the advantage of the individual." GS21: "Upbringing [*Erziehung*]

Nietzsche's position accords with Darwin's account of selection of social groups.[39]

But Nietzsche also has a subtler point in mind. Social selection favors habits that not only preserve this social medium in which they replicate, but that also shape or adapt this medium to suit their own replication. That is, it favors habits that produce a kind of society, and a kind of person, in which habits generally can most readily spread by copying—can best become widespread and stable customs. So, most basically, this social selection, by its very logic, favors a drive *to copy*, i.e., a disposition to imitate others, to want to do the same as they do. This is the "meta-habit" of learning habits by copying others; it is so basic and long-standing a product of social selection that it has become a stable drive itself.

Nietzsche's name for this metahabit is "herd-instinct" (*Heerden-Instinkt*). It's a strength of our Darwinian approach that it lets us naturalize this important idea of his: we can tell a scientific story of how it arises, which doesn't leave it dangling unexplained. So BGE199: "Inasmuch as at all times, as long as there have been humans, there have also been human herds (clans, communities, tribes, peoples, states, churches) and always a great many obeyers, compared with the small number of commanders, — considering, then, obedience has been practiced [*geübt*] and bred [*gezüchtet*] best and longest among humans, one may fairly assume that on average the need for it is innate in everyone, as a kind of *formal conscience*"; and later: "the herd instinct of obedience . . . is inherited best."[40]

always proceeds so: it tries to determine the individual through a series of attractions and advantages into a way of thinking and acting that, once it has become habit, drive, and passion, rules in him and over him *against his ultimate advantage*, but 'to the general good'." See how BGE201 associates "the utility of the herd" and "the preservation of the community." Also HH.iii.44; WP789 [1885–1886].

39. Darwin uses a group-selection argument to help explain the development of social virtues such as fidelity, courage, and obedience: "[A]lthough a high standard of morality gives but a slight or no advantage to each individual man and his children over the other men of the same tribe, yet . . . an advancement in the standard of morality . . . will certainly give an immense advantage to one tribe over another" (*Descent* I/166). So the social virtues and instincts have been selected to favor "the general good or welfare of the community," which Darwin offers as "the test of morality." (Darwin's argument is here genetic, not memetic as I read Nietzsche's to be.)

40. BGE268: "The humans who are more similar, more ordinary, have had, and always have, an advantage"; hence there has been "a natural, all too natural *progressus in simile*, the continual development of humans toward the similar, ordinary, average, herd-like — *common*!" GS76: "[T]he greatest labor of humanity so far was to agree [*übereinstimmen*] with one another about very many things and to impose on itself a *law of agreement* — regardless of whether these things are true or false." Also WP509 [1886–1887].

Sometimes, to be sure, Nietzsche treats this herd instinct as a more local and derivative phenomenon—an event in human history, not its constant theme. He depicts the rise of the herd instinct as a later development, preceded by an aristocratic society with the "instinct of commanding"; he depicts it as arising under the compulsion of those "masters'" rule, as a secondary reaction against that rule. In GM.i.2, for example, the herd instinct, instead of being endemic to all societies, is a degeneration in some of them. And BGE202 says, "Morality in Europe today is herd animal morality."[41]

But elsewhere he treats this herd instinct as more fundamental to our becoming human at all. It's this line I'll develop. I suggest that we hear the herd instinct as a kind of "structural" (second-order) social drive, one that plays the crucial background role of maintaining the social medium so that practices can replicate within it. This structural drive will be reinforced and abetted by all the practices that benefit from this conducive medium. (Any habit that enhances social copying will thereby enhance its own prospects for being copied and replicated. The metahabit of copying habits acts as a kind of "booster" to the fitness of other habits.) And this structural drive is also selected, because the social cohesion it promotes makes the society more successful and survivable.[42]

This herd instinct contains many subhabits that cultivate copying—beginning with the habit of being pleased to be in agreement with others.[43] It also involves the habit of blaming and suppressing other people who refuse to copy, who desist from common practices. And it opposes and disvalues one's own impulses to new behaviors and discourages "individuality." Z.i.15: "Pleasure in the herd is older than pleasure in the I: and so long as good conscience means the herd, only the bad conscience says: I." And GS117 describes "herd remorse" as the bad conscience humans were

41. See BGE62 on how the European of today has been bred as a herd animal; also D132 on a recent European movement "*to adapt* the individual to general requirements" by spreading a "[social] body- and member-building drive." GM.ii.17 attributes the formation of a social order to a "conqueror and master race," "born organizers" who impose form.

42. By contrast, natural selection—which works ultimately for survival and growth of the lineage or species, according to Nietzsche—may have little or no tendency to promote this through any "cohesion" in that lineage or species.

43. HH.i.371: "Why are inclination and aversion so contagious, that one can scarcely live in the proximity of a person of strong feelings, without being filled like a barrel with his For and Against? . . . [W]e gradually accustom ourselves to the way of feeling of our environment, and because sympathetic agreement and accommodation is so pleasant we soon bear all the marks and party colors of this environment."

trained to feel over their own freedom or individuality: "[T]hroughout the longest time of humanity nothing was more terrible than to feel oneself individual [*einzeln*]"; "[T]he more unfreely one acted, the more the herd-instinct rather than any personal sense spoke in the action, the more moral one esteemed oneself."[44]

So long as social selection prevails, there *are no* "individuals," in Nietzsche's stricter sense.[45] On the other hand social selection can only work if certain "mental" powers are present in the population. These powers are then developed and enhanced by the selection they permit; together, these powers constitute what Nietzsche often calls "spirit" (*Geist*). Eventually this development will bring these powers to a point at which a new kind of selection becomes possible, by full-fledged individuals. But before this a very long and complex development must proceed. Nietzsche often divides this development into two phases, the "ethic of custom" (*Sittlichkeit der Sitte*) and "morality" (*Moral*). They are distinguished as different ways that values can be made by social selection. I'll sketch them now, focusing on their role in designing those important mental or epistemic powers.

I'll focus on three such powers: memory, consciousness, and language. Together I think they give us the gist of Nietzsche's account of "cognition" or "thinking"—the activity that other philosophers had found so distinctive and honoring to us. He argues that these mental powers are all designed to serve that socializing function—to make humans better able to form habits in that social way. But they do so differently under the ethic of custom and under morality.

b. First Phase of Social Selection: The Ethic of Custom

The ethic of custom is the long early phase of social selection, whose "tremendous eras . . . precede 'world history' as the *actual and decisive eras*

44. Cf. BGE201 on how the herd instinct is opposed to individuals and brands them evil. Also D107, GS328. WP685 [1888]: "[T]he strongest and most fortunate are weak when they have against them organized herd instincts, the timidity of the weak, the majority."

45. 9.11[185] [1881]: "Egoism is something late and always still rare: the herd-feelings are stronger and older!" 9.11[182] [1881]: "[The human] has begun as a part of a *whole*, which has *its* organic properties and makes the individual into its organ — so that through unutterably long habituation humans **immediately** feel the *affects of society* against other societies and individuals and all the living and dead, and *not* as individual[s]!" See also 9.11[193] [1881].

of history which determined the character of mankind" (D18). Its most important work is to inculcate the habit of (following) custom.[46] It does so by training and breeding into people the first of those epistemic powers, what Nietzsche calls "memory" (*Gedächtniss*).[47] It does so, most notably, by the public warning and enforcement of horrific punishments for forgetting—by "blood, torture, and sacrifices," which Nietzsche details with some relish in GM.ii.3. These punishments give persons a highly striking point to "bear in mind"—and so help to create and strengthen their ability to bear things in mind.[48]

Broadly understood, memory is another "meta-habit," which makes humans able to form other habits, of the kind society needs. For this memory is simply the ability to "remember" social rules or practices, to be bound by them, in opposition to the "animal drives" ingrained by natural selection. It is a stronger form of the capacity that sets up social (memetic) selection in the first place: the ability to keep oneself within the social practice, even at those moments when one's drives or appetites are most urgently against it. One remembers not to steal this tempting food, even when very hungry. And correlative with this ability to remember is the ability to bind oneself into the future, to "promise."[49] Only someone able to remember commitments can properly make them.

By this social design, humans become capable of a new kind of behavioral disposition—a long-ranging will, the power to commit oneself in the future to behave a certain way, and then to behave so. Here see especially

46. D16: *"First proposition of civilization.* Among raw peoples there is a species of customs whose intention appears to be custom in general: painstaking and basically superfluous stipulations . . . which however keep custom constantly close, keep the uninterrupted compulsion to practice customs constantly in consciousness: to strengthen the great proposition, with which civilization begins: any custom is better, than no custom." See HH.i.96, 99.

47. Cf. UM.ii.1 on how the human emerges from the animal by the power of remembering, of learning from the past. Compare Darwin's different map of some of this same ground: it's not that social instincts are *stronger* than those to "self-preservation, hunger, lust, vengeance, &c.," but that they are "ever present and persistent," so that after one of the other instincts has been gratified and abated, the "ever-enduring" social instincts will work as "conscience [which] looks backwards and judges past actions, inducing that kind of dissatisfaction, which if weak we call regret, and if severe remorse" (*Descent* I/89–91; also II/392).

48. GM.i.15: "[W]e must seek the actual *effect* of punishment above all in a sharpening of prudence [*Klugheit*], in a lengthening of memory"; it produces "mastery of the desires: thus punishment *tames* humans, but does not make them 'better'."

49. GM.ii.2: "[W]ith the help of the ethic of custom and the social straitjacket, the human was actually *made* calculable," a precondition for being able to promise.

GM.ii.1–3: "[T]he severity of the penal code gives a striking measure [of] how much effort was taken to defeat forgetfulness and to keep a few primitive demands of social coexistence *present* to these slaves to the moment, of affects and desires" (ii.3). Nietzsche stresses how, in order to be able to promise, to be "responsible" (*verantwortlich*), humans must be made "necessary, uniform, like among like, regular and therefore calculable" (ii.2).[50]

The other two epistemic powers developed by social selection, which are crucial in making individuals possible, are *consciousness* and *language*. Nietzsche thinks that these arise in close connection with one another. Again, he rejects the natural assumption that humans have always been conscious, and have always chosen their practices with conscious intention, as if what I've called "social selection" were the mere upshot of all those individual choices.[51] Instead (he claims) we can explain (self-)consciousness itself as an artifact of that social process. It is again a matter of that habit selection "designing" a better medium in which to operate.

Nietzsche's key text here is GS354, half-ironically titled "On the 'genius of the species'." He begins by arguing for the secondary and dispensable status of consciousness: even thinking, feeling, and willing can take place without it, and in fact most of our own does. Consciousness is designed for *communication* (*Mittheilung*)—and hence reaches its greatest "fineness and strength" in social contexts in which there is the greatest need for communication. He envisions a period, that is, in which there was strong selection—compelled by circumstances—for communication. And in order

50. Note that Nietzsche speaks in these sections as if this development were supervised by a "breeder": first it's nature that breeds an animal that may promise, later it's this animal that breeds itself. But I think we can see, from the larger context of his works, that these expressions are metaphorical, and meant to be heard so. I suggest he really means the different kind of selection I've been analyzing. I return to the topic of breeding in chapter 3, section 6a.

51. So, to the challenge that individual (self) selection must precede social selection, because the group can only select through or in the individual choices of its members, Nietzsche replies that no such "individual choices" were possible until fairly late in society's development. 9.11[193] [1881]: "*Before* egoism, the herd drive is older than the 'will to self-preservation.' The human first *evolved* as *function*." 10.3[1].255 [1882]: "Originally [there was] herd and herd-instinct; the self experienced as exception, nonsense, madness by the herd." WP773 [1887–1888]: "[See] how far the *feelings of sympathy and community* are the lowest, the preparatory stages, at a time when personal self-esteem [*Personal-Selbstgefühl*], initiative in the individual for setting values are not yet possible."

to communicate needs to some other, a human must be able to "know" what he/she feels or wants.

Self-awareness arises to facilitate this sharing. Hence "only as a social animal did the human learn to become conscious of himself—he does it still, he does it more and more" (again, GS354). "Consciousness is genuinely only a connection-net [*Verbindungsnetz*] between human and human, — only as such did it have to evolve [*entwickeln*]." So consciousness belongs to our "communal- [*Gemeinschafts-*] and herd-nature," and it has "finely evolved" only in relation to "social- and herd-utilities." We become self-aware, that is, not because it's in our own interest, but because it enables us to be fuller members of the herd: we look inward, the better to align ourselves with others. And this inhibits us, Nietzsche thinks, from understanding ourselves individually, since we become conscious only of our "average" (*Durchschnittliches*). Our thoughts are controlled by this "genius of the species" that controls consciousness, and are "as it were *majoritized* [*majorisirt*] and translated back into the herd-perspective."

It's by this same story that Nietzsche explains the development and function of language: "[T]he evolution of language and the evolution of consciousness (*not* reason, but only the becoming-conscious of reason) go hand in hand" (again, GS354). Language too depends on the herd instinct's prior work to homogenize persons.[52] And language is itself a device for rendering them still more like one another—for further tightening the social bonds, and making the social medium more susceptible to the dispersion of customs within it.[53]

These factors—memory, consciousness, and language—transform the character of "values."[54] They allow a behavioral disposition to "aim" at its goals in new ways: foresightedly, self-consciously, and linguistically. Now

52. Like language's general terms, logic depends on "equal cases," and so on the herd instinct. WP509 [1886–1887]: "The earthly realm of desires, out of which *logic* grew: herd-instinct in the background, the assumption of equal cases presupposes 'equal souls.' *For the purpose of intelligibility and mastery.*"

53. See again BGE268 on how language allows ever-quicker understanding of others based on shared experience, so that "one associates ever more closely." See too Z.i.5 on how the act of naming a virtue turns it into something you share with others. HH.iii.55: "*Danger of language for spiritual freedom.* — Every word is a prejudice." (Here too, however, Nietzsche sometimes tells a different kind of story: that language is a more deliberate achievement, by "masters"; see GM.i.2.)

54. They make possible what we commonly call "values," but which Nietzsche treats as a secondary overlay.

the behavior makes the goal explicit to itself, sighting it in advance consciously, and naming it. It's only here that we arrive at values, as moral philosophers have known them—as goods we name, are aware of, and remember to live by. Still, there is something deceptive in this new foresight: the individual *doesn't* really choose the values he/she pursues in this way; these values are still dictated by social selection, working on behalf of the herd.

c. Second Phase of Social Selection: Morality

The ethic of custom makes these epistemic powers, and once made they institute a second phase of human history, which Nietzsche calls "morality." Now social selection takes a new form, since the habits copied are the habits of conscious speakers "with a memory." In this phase of morality, social habits are designed to bind these members still more firmly into the herd. They do so by shifting the "target" of evaluation from an action's consequences to its intentions; see BGE32. By this shift, social values are redesigned in ways that render them still "sicker"—still more hostile to the body and its drives.[55]

Again I can only sketch this phase, which Nietzsche so richly diagnoses. GM.ii in particular tells a famously intricate story about the multiple, interacting strands in the development of morality. But we should note some examples of our overall point: how social selection, dominated by the herd instinct, finds further ways to *use* those new powers so as to cultivate the spread and uniformity of social practices. Members are driven into tighter cohesion by selection's manipulation of their powers of memory, consciousness, and language. Let's quickly see how each of the three new powers gets used this way within "morality."

Take, first, *memory*. As we've seen, this capacity is selected in the first place as a memory *of the practices*: what we're trained to remember, above

---

55. See GS116: "These valuations and rank-orders are always expressions of the needs of a community and herd. . . . The conditions for the preservation of different communities were very different; hence there were very different moralities. . . . Morality is herd instinct in the individual." EH.iv.7 speaks of the "de-selfing morality" (*Entselbstungs-Moral*); also A54. This is "morality in the pejorative sense," in Leiter's phrase (1995). When values get posited in consciousness and language, the gap becomes clearer or wider between the real purpose of these values (what they are selected for) and the criteria by which these values aim (what the behavior thinks it is doing, or is aiming at).

all, is "what's done," the prevailing practice relevant to our situation. We guide our forward-aiming behavior "in the light of" this memory; we bind it back to this memory. So memory is a retrospective drag on our activity that aligns it with the current of what's generally done. Memory already functions this way in the earlier "ethic of custom."

But in morality, where a developed memory, consciousness, and language are all available, a more sophisticated use of memory by the herd instinct becomes feasible. Now society makes a collective kind of memory, in a story it tells itself about *ancestors* who created it by making these practices. It cultivates a sense of indebtedness to these ancestors, to strengthen the grip of these practices. So GM.ii.19: "[A]ll practices [*Bräuche*], as works of the ancestors [*Vorfahren*], are also their statutes and commands —: can one ever give them enough [obedience]?" The status of these ancestors is progressively inflated through generations, to tighten that grip. Eventually the ancestors are gods, and finally the absolute God of (for example) Christianity, which makes the indebtedness also absolute. So religion too is a design product of social selection and its ruling herd instinct: ultimately, we have gods to tie us to what's done.[56]

Similarly, the new power of (self-)*consciousness* gets put to further work in morality, by that same herd instinct. Initially self-awareness was selected as an aid to communication and sharing: it helps us liken ourselves to one another. Under morality self-awareness gets "moralized": members are trained to introspect themselves in a certain negative light—to take a certain critical angle of view "inside." They are trained to feel a "bad conscience" toward everything in them that resists that sharing—in particular toward their "animal drives." Within morality we're self-aware for the sake of self-blame. Bad conscience plays a double role: it contributes to control (suppression) of these drives and it counteracts the consequent pain.[57] It holds people steady to the practices in the face of this pain, by

56. See further in GM.ii.19–20, e.g.: "[I]n the end the forefather [*Ahnherr*] must necessarily be transfigured into a *god*"; "[T]he rise of the Christian God, as the maximal-god attained so far, has therefore brought to appearance on earth the maximum feeling of debt [*Schuldgefühls*]." Also HH.i.96: "To be moral, customary [*sittlich*], ethical [*ethisch*] means to hold obedience towards an old-established law or tradition [*Herkommen*]." "Every tradition now continually becomes more venerable, the farther away its origin lies and the more it is forgotten; the respect paid to it increases from generation to generation, the tradition at last becomes holy."

57. GM.ii.16 says that this suffering is due to the difficulty of suddenly guiding behavior by *something else* than the "regulating, unconscious, safely-guiding drives"; "I believe there has never been such a feeling of misery on earth, such a leaden discomfort

inducing them to blame themselves for the pain, by blaming their drives.[58]
This is also the first function of the "ascetic ideal": it supports socialization
by opposing the selfish drives.

Finally, in (the phase of) morality *language* is also developed to serve
herding. It originated as a device for aligning feelings and projects among
members of a group—at first by the simplest of signals. Eventually, in
morality, language plays this same function in the form of a supporting
ideology, which explicitly justifies the practices. The core of this ideology
is the branding of animal drives as evil, and promotion of the shared
practices as good. An elaborate story evolves to strengthen these values'
hold on us; it uses such notions as free will, responsibility, the afterlife,
and God.[59] This ideology intensifies the memory and self-awareness by
which persons are bound to social values. So, for example, GM.ii.22 describes
how bad conscience is made all the keener by being fused with that religious
indebtedness: people are trained to blame themselves before God.[60]

These adaptations of memory, consciousness, and language to serve
herd ends generally work by *concealing* those ends from the moral agent
they constitute. They bring values to consciousness and language, but most
often *not* the real meanings or purposes of those values—not why we
really have them. They are designed for the most part to conceal how
members really do sacrifice themselves in these values, i.e., weaken, sicken,
and homogenize themselves for the sake of herd. The moral agent is bred
to serve herd ends, but bred to serve in ignorance of this service.[61]

— and at the same time the old instincts had not all at once ceased to make their demands!
Only it was hard and rarely possible to humor them."

58. Indeed, for this purpose the herd instinct uses these drives themselves: it turns
them against themselves. The only outlet it allows for their aggressive energies is in
self-attack. GM.ii.16: "Those fearful bulwarks with which the political organization protected itself against the old instincts of freedom — punishments belong above all to the
bulwarks — brought about that all those instincts of the wild, free, prowling human
turned backward *against the human himself.* . . . [T]hat is the origin of 'bad conscience'."
GM.iii.16 says that the priest preaches sinfulness "to *exploit* the bad instincts of all
sufferers for the purpose of self-discipline, self-surveillance, self-overcoming."

59. WP7 [1887–1888]: "[O]ne has built these *social values* over humans for the
purpose of *strengthening* their voice, as if they were the command of God, as 'reality,'
as 'true' world, as hope and *future* world."

60. TI.v.4: "When [antinatural morality] says 'God looks at the heart,' it says No
to the lowest and highest desires of life, and takes God as *enemy of life.*" GM.ii.22: "He
grasps in 'God' the ultimate opposites of his own real and irredeemable animal instincts,
he reinterprets these animal instincts themselves as guilt before God."

61. WP492 [1885]: "Directly questioning the subject about the subject, and all self-
reflection of spirit has its danger in this, that it could be useful and important for its

4. *Superhuman Values, by Self Selection (Freedom)*

But these new epistemic powers can also be turned a different way: they make a new kind of value selection possible, which I'll call **self selection**, and which Nietzsche most often calls "freedom."[62] He insists that we stand before the possibility of a new way of making values, feasible now as never before. (Here his biological and anthropological story becomes historical.) This new possibility is the key to his overall assessment of "the modern age"—it's what he mainly hopes or aims for. Here I'll look at Nietzsche's *description* of this freedom, deferring to section 5 the questions of why/how he values it. So we complete our account of Nietzsche's science about values before turning to his promotion, as philosopher, of values himself.

Memory, consciousness, and language are necessary for this freedom, though of course not sufficient. They're initially selected in forms that preclude it, and they require a long period of modifications before they can be used for a new kind of selection. Z.i.15: "First peoples were creators, and only later individuals; indeed, the individual himself is the youngest creation." Why do these modifications take place? Why does this new possibility arise? Sometimes Nietzsche speaks as if the overall process "aims" at these self selecting individuals.[63] Elsewhere it seems they are fortuitous side effects of processes aiming elsewhere. The choice between these will be important in seeing how he values freedom, and I'll return to this question of its origins then.[64] Here we focus on what freedom is.

The self-creation or freedom that Nietzsche means lies in bringing the selective process into oneself. It lies in taking over, oneself, the selective role, so that one "creates" or "gives oneself" values. It involves a "will to self-determination [*Selbstbestimmung*], to self-value-setting [*Selbst-Werth-setzung*], this will to a *free* will" (HH.i.P.3). By this, one "becomes who one is," in Nietzsche's well-known phrase. So in GS335 (an important section

activity to interpret itself falsely. Therefore we question the body and reject the testimony of the sharpened senses."

62. EH.i.2 says that the "well-formed" (*wohlgerathner*) person "is a selecting principle [*auswählendes Princip*]; he discards much." But for the most part Nietzsche doesn't use Darwinian terms for this freedom.

63. In GM.ii.2–3 the individual is described as the "fruit" the ethic of custom has been ripening; GS149 says that the break from "crude herd-instincts and the ethic of custom" shows "that the egg is becoming ripe." See also HH.i.107 on how "*everything is streaming*: towards one goal." See n. 77 in chapter 3.

64. See section 5b below, and the discussion of "progress" in chapter 3, section 4.

on this topic): "We, however, *will to become those we are* [*wollen Die werden, die wir sind*] — human beings who are new, unique, incomparable, who give themselves laws, who create themselves."[65]

The key to becoming myself is to select my values, i.e., the goals of the dispositions that—in making my behavior—specify "who I am." It is to make myself the cause of these decisive bodily aims. Initially and as a matter of course, these aims are set by selection in the species' or society's past: how my body aims was selected—"became"—before I was born, within the natural and social processes that formed my drives and habits. To become myself is to make my values *during* my life, as well as by and for that life. I revise these drives and habits, selecting them to serve my individual will.

Nietzsche thinks such self selection of values is far more difficult to perform, and far rarer than we presume; he places it mainly off in our future.[66] Indeed, it appears as a "receding" ideal, which shows itself to be harder and harder with each step we take toward it. Nietzsche pushes the standard so high that he's often inclined to call it "superhuman"—as involving an evolution beyond the human.[67] So we can label it:

(7) Superhuman value = the goal of a responsive behavior, self se-
    lected to serve oneself.

Freedom makes an evolutionary step, not just within the old selective scheme, but by instituting a new kind or logic of value selection. Freedom requires a structural change, and by it a new kind of value comes on the scene, embodied in a new kind of disposition, neither drive nor practice. This radical change is exceedingly difficult and rare, Nietzsche thinks.

65. Also EH.ii.9 on "how one becomes what one is." See GS347 ("a pleasure and strength of self-determination, a *freedom* of will"); HH.ii.325 ("only he that wears them makes the clothes"). HH.i.P.6 says that the "great liberation [*Loslösung*]" begins to be unveiled when the "free, ever freer spirit" thinks, "You shall become master over yourself, master also over your virtues." TI.ix.38: "For what is freedom! That one has the will to self-responsibility."

66. WP886 [1887]: "Nothing is rarer than a *personal* action. A class, a rank, a race [*Volks-Rasse*], an environment, an accident — everything expresses itself sooner in a work or deed, than a 'person'." By contrast, GM.ii.2 may suggest that freedom is something already long attained—when it speaks of the "sovereign individual, like only to himself" that society's ethic of custom brought about. I think Nietzsche here treats this condition as already achieved in the masters. But elsewhere he sets higher standards on freedom: it requires that one "make one's values" in a way the masters (and even everyone so far) haven't and can't.

67. GM.ii.16: "[A]s if with him something were announcing and preparing itself, as if the human were not a goal but only a way, an in-between, a bridge, a great promise."

Our own self-conception, of course, is otherwise: we suppose that our conscious choice selects our values. Nietzsche is constantly reminding us of the ways this isn't so. Our real values lie in our inherited drives and inculcated practices, shaped in our species' and society's past.[68] Conscious "choice" is a tool of these, a tool in important part designed *not* to come to grips with them or question them. Indeed, the illusion that we self select is another part of the deceptive ideology of morality: agents are indoctrinated to believe that they (genuinely) *choose* to be moral. So in some respects Nietzschean freedom will involve really or truly being what we think we've been all along.

But what, concretely, does Nietzsche think we need to do, in order to wrest the power of selecting our values away from those natural and social selectings? I suggest he has in mind two main tasks. The first is to achieve *insight* into the ways our values have been made already. The second is to *incorporate* this insight, i.e., to build it into one's body—into the system of drives and habits that make behavior. By doing both, one enables this system (our body, our life) to make values of its own—to become what it is.

a. Insight

Let's begin with the requirement of insight into how our values *have* been selected so far.[69] This insight is the completion, in detail, of the explanations outlined above in sections 2–3—and their completion *as applied to oneself*, in a self-diagnosis of one's values. This insight is, I claim, a precondition for Nietzschean freedom. Consider GS335:

> To that end [being self-creators] we must become the best learn-
> ers and discoverers of everything that is lawful and necessary in the
> world: we must become *physicists* in order to be able to be *creators*
> in this sense — while hitherto all valuations and ideals have been
> based on *ignorance* of physics or were constructed so as to *contradict*

68. D104: "[W]e are mostly lifelong fools of judgments accustomed in childhood." Also HH.i.226.

69. GS335: "Your judgment 'this is right' has a pre-history in your instincts, likes, dislikes, experiences, and lack of experiences. '*How* did it originate there?' you must ask, and then also: 'What is it that impels me to listen to it?'" 9.5[48] [1880]: "The most frequent thing that happens is lying to oneself. The intellectual conscience is weak, and the *other conscience* stronger."

it. Therefore: long live physics! And even more so that which *compels* us to turn to physics — our honesty![70]

Let's approach Nietzsche's idea of this insight by way of this "virtue" he thinks it depends on. This "honesty" (*Redlichkeit*), which is Nietzsche's favorite virtue, is needed precisely for inquiry into the sources of our values—which is what it's both hardest and most important to be honest about.[71] It opposes our ancient and sedimented instinct not to question our values—especially values shared widely by our group and kind. The great stress and pain involved in exposing the sources of these values demands as ally the subsidiary virtue of courage (*Muth*)—which matters to Nietzsche only in this context, for the sake of that honesty.[72]

Consider how these virtues can be *absent*, and insight missed, taking the germane case of Darwin and Darwinists. It's their failure in honesty and courage in this inquiry that Nietzsche holds mainly against them. They name the key task or challenge—a naturalized understanding of values—but are too fully in the grip of their own (Christian, moral) values to carry it out.[73] In place of sober empirical study, they leap to hypotheses

70. EH.iv.1: "I know myself to stand in opposition to the mendacity of millennia. . . . I was the first to *discover* the truth by being the first to experience — *smell* — lies as lies. . . . My genius is in my nostrils." And EH.iv.5: "[Zarathustra] says that it was precisely his knowledge of the [morally] good, the 'best,' that has made him shudder at humanity in general; from *this* aversion he grew wings, 'to soar off into distant futures'."

71. EH.iv.3: "[Zarathustra's] doctrine and his alone has truthfulness as highest virtue." BGE295 speaks of Dionysus's "investigator- and discoverer-courage, . . . his daring honesty, truthfulness, and love of wisdom." Also BGE227.

72. EH.P.3: "Error (— faith in the ideal —) is not blindness, error is *cowardice*. . . . Every achievement, every step forward in knowledge *follows* from courage, from hardness against oneself, from cleanliness against oneself." The relevant pain is in exposing social practices; it is analogous to the pain in social selection itself, with its tense opposition to the naturally selected instincts. We feel a different range of discomforts in breaking from social norms than from inherited instincts—above all, we feel "the bite of bad conscience," to which the herd instinct trains us. D18: "Every smallest step on the field of free thought and the individually formed life has always been fought for with spiritual and physical torments." Z.i.17 ("On the Way of the Creator"): "'All loneliness is guilt' — thus speaks the herd. And you have long belonged to the herd. The voice of the herd will still be audible in you. And when you will say, 'I no longer have a common conscience with you,' it will be a lament and an agony." See n. 44 above.

73. WP253 [1885–1886] says that in Darwinism "even the basic conditions of life are falsely interpreted for the benefit of morality." WP685 [1888]: "The error of Darwin's school became a problem for me: how can one be so blind as to see falsely just *here*?" Also WP243 [1887]. UM.i.7 harps on Strauss's lack of courage for the valuative implications of natural selection.

that "valorize" their values—that confirm or justify them. These hypotheses are betrayals of their own naturalistic project.

First, taking over the prevailing self-advertisement in these values, Darwinists imagine them produced by—or at least justified by—the free rationality they suppose themselves, as persons, to wield. This claim to rationality is the common ideology of these herd-instinct values—an ideology developed under selection for the way it helps them to disperse and "universalize" themselves.[74] Yet this claim to a "grounding of morality" is "merely a scholarly form of the good *faith* in the ruling morality" (BGE186).

Second, offering then their own innovative further support for this ideology, Darwinists argue that not just reason but evolution itself converges on these same values: morality is the point to which selection will tend to progress.[75] It's to turn evolution to this justificatory work that they must misconstrue it as *progressive*.

So rather than attending to the evidence available—in languages, histories, literatures—about the factors really at work in this long process, Darwinists invent a retrospective story to justify the values they find themselves with.[76] They convert an insight that should be a step toward freedom into new dogma on behalf of the very customs that freedom should be from. They use natural selection to justify the values they have—to bind themselves more securely into them—instead of using it to lever themselves to the freedom of self selection. And this reinforced ideology bars them from seeing a whole raft of facts about our values' genealogy.

Nietzsche claims for himself the honesty and courage missing in Darwinists. He claims to pursue that inquiry into values' sources in a more genuinely scientific spirit than they do, by virtue of standing back critically

74. Nietzsche often states his scorn for this self-flattery of Christian values. Cf. BGE295.

75. *Descent* I/72: "The following proposition seems to me in a high degree probable—namely, that any animal whatever, endowed with well-marked social instincts, would inevitably acquire a moral sense or conscience, as soon as its intellectual powers had become as well developed, or nearly as well developed, as in man." Richards (1988/1998, 607) argues, against what he thinks to be a common recent misconception of Darwin, that he, like Spencer after all, thought that evolution progresses toward morality: "Both believed that evolutionary progress was to be expected, and it would be progress generally in the complexity of organization, and finally in the moral and intellectual faculties characterized by the higher races."

76. GS345: "These historians of morality (especially Englishmen) do not amount to much: usually they themselves stand unsuspectingly under the command of a particular morality, and serve, without knowing it, as its shield-bearers and followers." See n. 99 below.

from the values he studies. By this honesty, he brings to light sources and meanings of our values that had been missed by evolutionary explanations before. In particular he recognizes, as Darwinists could not, the logic of *social* selection, which has, in the ways we've seen, a less healthy face than does natural selection.

Nietzsche means to infect us with his honesty—i.e., to propagate this meme of his. He tries to shift us, very broadly, from intending our explanations of our values to *justify* these values, to intending them to *detach* or alienate us from our values. Each of his diagnoses is at once both a sample of a method of inquiry he invites us to emulate and a small tug *away* from our values, toward that position of detachment from which he wants us to proceed (on our own). He tries to pull us to a distance from custom and morality, by forcing our attention to the sick logic of social selection.[77]

Nietzsche thinks that this distancing belongs to the very project of truth. This is why he associates truth with asceticism, at the climax of the third essay in *On the Genealogy of Morals*. The effort at truth is an aggressive effort to "expose" or "violate." When it is directed at oneself and one's values, it works to undermine and disengage.[78] It does so particularly by exposing *lies* these values had told about themselves, as well as *contradictions* between these values' overt content, and what they were selected for.[79] "*All* science . . . is today [aimed] at dissuading the human from his former respect for himself" (GM.iii.25).[80] By this critical eye on our values, science begins to pry us loose from them.

Is this distancing sufficient for freedom? Does genuine scientific insight into the sources of our values suffice to let one select values oneself? Sometimes it seems Nietzsche thinks so—that all the important work is already done by this insight. GS335: "Your understanding *of the manner*

---

77. GM.ii.2 speaks of "the autonomous, super-ethical [*übersittliche*] individual (for 'autonomous' and 'ethical' exclude one another)." A54 speaks of the need to dislodge one's convictions: "[T]o be allowed to have a say about value and disvalue, one must see five hundred convictions *beneath* oneself, — *behind* oneself."

78. WP602 [1884]: "The deeper one looks, the more our valuations disappear — *meaninglessness approaches!*"

79. GS21: "[T]he *motives* [*Motive*] of this morality stand opposed to its *principle*." Genealogy also undermines values by undercutting certain beliefs on which they depend; so HH.i.133 says that "with the insight into that origin [of the belief in God] that belief falls away."

80. Also 9.7[19] [1880]: "We seek to kill [the passion] through analysis, through deriving its origin."

in which moral judgments have originated would spoil these grand words [duty and conscience] for you."[81]

On the whole, however, I think Nietzsche *denies* that this insight is enough to make one "free"—even when it's applied to the details of one's own values. Although these truths about values do detach from the values, they do so *only in theory*, i.e., only in *consciousness* and *language*. As we've seen, Nietzsche takes this to be a superficial and secondary kind of valuing. What we need to do, to be free, is to bring this insight down into our drives and habits, to give it substance there. It's only by its presence there that this insight gives rise to new dispositions, with new goals and values.

b. Incorporating Insight

Nietzsche's more characteristic view is that there's an important gap between knowledge and freedom.[82] He thinks of values as creatures not of consciousness but of our drives and habits, which are more obviously difficult to "select" than our opinions. If we realize that some habitual practice is the product of the herd instinct, this may do very little to release its grip on us—even if we expose a contradiction or lie in the practice, as Nietzsche so often does. It seems likely, even, that many of our drives and social habits could *never* be lastingly stilled—that the selective forces behind them will inexorably work in us, and we'll continue to value and *care* about things in the ways they've designed that we do. And I think this is Nietzsche's view.[83]

If we can't quell or quiet the values carried in our drives and social habits, we must find some way to oppose them where they work—to

81. EH.iv.8: "Whoever uncovers morality has also uncovered the disvalue of all values in which one believes or has believed." And see Z.i.1 ("On the Three Metamorphoses") about the lion's struggle against the dragon of values: "As his holiest he once loved the 'thou shalt': now he must find illusion and arbitrariness even in the holiest, so that from his love he may steal himself freedom."

82. WP254 [1885–1886]: "The question about the ancestry of our valuations and tables of goods does not at all coincide with their critique, as is so often believed: though certainly the insight into some *pudenda origo* brings with it a feeling of diminished value of the thing so arising, and prepares for a critical mood and bearing against it."

83. Already in HH.i.16: "Rigorous science is capable of releasing us from this world of representation only to a limited extent — and more is indeed not to be desired — , inasmuch as it is incapable of breaking essentially the power of age-old habits of perception: but it can gradually and by stages light up the history of origin of that world as representation — and lift us out of the entire proceeding, at least for moments."

oppose them not with mere beliefs, but with contrary dispositions and habits that work against the tendencies ingrained in us. Only so can we preempt the latter's claim to explain our thoughts and behaviors. We must work to give our distancing insight a causal presence in us, to *embody* it in our behavioral dispositions. And this too is Nietzsche's view.

What we try to build into ourselves are not counterdispositions to all of our drives and habits, just as such. Rather, we form dispositions that oppose drives and habits *where and insofar as* they express sources we choose against. We instantiate those diagnoses into a *felt distaste* for those aspects of our habits that reflect those rejected meanings. So GM.ii.24 advocates the attempt "to wed the *unnatural* inclinations, all those aspirations to the beyond . . . with the bad conscience."[84]

Nietzsche speaks of this challenge, to turn knowledge into real impulses, as its "incorporation." GS11: [T]he *"task*, [is] *to incorporate knowledge* and make it instinctive, — a task which will only be seen by those who have grasped that so far only our *errors* were incorporated and that all our consciousness relates to errors!" GS110: "To what extent can truth endure incorporation? — that is the question, that is the experiment."[85]

This incorporation requires that we push each diagnosing insight down into the details of our lives—to wherever the diagnosed value operates. We need to activate its critical eye in concrete cases, to the level of detail Nietzsche himself practices in his "miniatures," his so-called aphorisms. We need the long-term habit of diagnosing our everyday thoughts and habits, seeing why they express the values they do. We need, that is, to *embody honesty* in the details of our lives. This process of incorporating diagnostic critiques of our values involves "living through nihilism," and is highly unsettling.

Nietzschean freedom, I suggest, lies in incorporating insight in just this way. This freedom is clearly something quite different from the Kantian "uncaused cause"—something consistent with Nietzsche's many attacks on the latter, as false and indeed incoherent.[86]

84. CW.P describes Nietzsche's need for this "self-discipline . . . : to take sides *against* everything sick in me, including Wagner, including Schopenhauer, including all of modern 'humaneness'."

85. On incorporating knowledge, see also 9.11[141] [1881]. 9.11[164] [1881]: "I speak of *instinct*, when some *judgment* (*taste* in its lowest stage) is incorporated, so that it now moves itself and no longer needs to wait on a stimulus."

86. E.g., HH.i.106, BGE21. These attacks tend to obscure Nietzsche's deeper agreement with Kant, in making freedom the ultimate ideal (as I'll argue in section 5). Nietzsche

Nietzsche thinks we're wrong not just in thinking we *are* free, but also as to what freedom is. We imagine it the wrong way—as occurring in special moments of decision from a viewpoint poised on the moment, a "first cause" undetermined from the past. We need to see that self selection is a lot like natural and social selection: it operates in an aggregate way that need not be supervised by an overarching consciousness.[87] It possesses the same stochastic and statistical character of those other selective modes. It consists in an overall tendency or pattern of behaviors—a sustained series of uncoverings and diagnosings of many different practices and values in oneself. It lies in an overall pattern of suspicion or skepticism, practiced against one's instincts over a long period. In repeatedly tracing out the many ways that one's values have been made by natural and social selection, and acting in the light of it, one stands free (in the way we can be) of those other forces, and values for oneself.

So a behavior is self-selected and free, not by what happens in the moment of choice by itself—in that microsituation—but in the macrohistory by which the dispositions producing this behavior were designed. This is why Nietzsche stresses the long logic in his life, visible only in retrospect, not transparent in the moment (e.g., GM.P.2, EH.ii.9). By his past diagnostic work on his own values, he has won the right to his judgments now; these judgments have their meaning from that selective work long carried out in himself—and not by some transparency they possess "in the moment."

It belongs to Nietzsche's naturalization of freedom that he conceives it as not absolute—there are certain *limits* to the freedom we can have. This is because of the way some things are *settled* in us: there are values we can't disengage. Some of these are personal idiosyncrasies, as Nietzsche describes his own views about women: these belong to his "spiritual *fatum*, to what is quite *unteachable* 'down there'" (BGE231). Other unshakable attitudes belong to all of us, as human, as animal, even merely as alive. Such values constitute blind spots we can't manage to overcome, even if we can diagnose them. Self selection, in other words, can never be complete.

tries to show that true freedom is the self selection we're analyzing, and not what Kant imagines.

87. EH.ii.9: "That one becomes what one is, presupposes that one does not suspect in the least *what* one is." Nietzsche sometimes speaks as if this nonconscious direction lies in some emerging "idea"; e.g., again EH.ii.9: "[T]he organizing 'idea' appointed to mastery grows and grows in the depths, — it begins to command, . . . it develops the series of *serving* capacities, before it allows any hint of the dominating task, of 'goal,' 'purpose,' 'meaning'."

5. *Revaluing Values*

I want now to say what I think are the implications of this story, for Nietzsche's own values. How does he make the transition from *studying* values, to *valuing*, himself and on his own behalf? This step involves his "positing values" in a quite different way than that naturalistic study does. And it makes, in Nietzsche's terms, the transition from science into philosophy.

Back in section 1 we saw that Nietzsche understands a "value" as the "valued by a valuing": by his naturalism, values occur only as contents of valuing attitudes or behaviors. But when he passes from studying values to actually valuing, in his own right, it seems he must have a further sense for "value"—that he takes the things he values to be valuable in some *stronger* sense than the values he merely studies. When he calls *his* values "values," this means more than just that they're valued by a valuing.

It's tempting to put this as his holding that his values (by contrast with others' values) "really are" values—tempting but I think misleading, because even or especially in studying values he treats them as real. His ambitious genealogy of Christian values, for example, is a scientific description and explanation of quite real things, these valueds, as the teleological—and hence thinly intentional—objects of certain historical human processes.

So we can think of *both* (a) studying values and (b) valuing as different ways of "positing" (taking there really to be) values. But they have as their objects values of different kinds. I'll begin with a simple or minimal statement of these different senses, which I think will let us keep them clearly apart, the better to examine them. This examination will then help us to a fuller account of the difference, and especially of the sense in which Nietzsche "posits" his own values.

On the one hand, as scientist/genealogist, Nietzsche discovers values as contents to the valuing attitudes he studies. In particular, they are the goals for which responsive behaviors (drives or habits) were selected. Taking there to be a value of this sort—a "value to study," a **value/s**—does not involve valuing it:

(8) A value/s is a goal (teleological object) of some valuing that one studies.

In his genealogies Nietzsche counts, e.g., the Christian values of pity and altruism as "real," precisely as such selected goals. They are indeed all too real, playing crucial roles in explaining behaviors, thoughts, and feelings.[88]

But of course in another sense Nietzsche *does not* take these values to be real: he doesn't think they're "really of value," because he doesn't value these things himself. He doesn't take any of them as a "value to value"—a **value/v**:

(9) A value/v is a goal (teleological object) of one's own valuing.

Because Nietzsche does not (qua studier) value the values/s that he studies, he counts them "values" in a different sense than do the valuers—and than he does the values/v that he values himself.[89]

We need especially to analyze the sense in which Nietzsche values his values/v. We must specify whether and how he means these values to be "really valuable" in some sense the studied values are not. Here we need to place him between two extremes. One extreme is for the valuer to renounce any such claim: his values/v are valuable in just the same way as any values/s, simply *as* the "perspectival contents"[90] of a valuer; his values/v are simply the subset of values/s that *this* viewpoint values. The other extreme is for the valuer to insist on the special status of his values, by taking them to be "objective," i.e., to exist independently of any perspective, including his own—to take them as *not* essentially the "perspectival content" of a valuing. I think Nietzsche finds a way between these extreme options: he privileges his values, ontologically and epistemically, without however rendering them objective.

Now in examining (in sections 1–4) Nietzsche's facts about values/s, and reserving how he values (his values/v), it may have seemed that his facts come first, and his values after. But of course this is not at all the character of his writing: his genealogies are dense mixtures of values/s and values/v, of descriptive and evaluative stances. His studies of values are studded with appraisals and critiques of them, which express values of his own—his own criteria in the appraisals. But where, we naturally ask, does Nietzsche get these criteria for judging the values he studies?

---

88. Cats chase mice because this drive was selected to help them survive; people pray because this practice was selected to help them conform and cohere. In each case the goal explains why the behavior occurs.

89. Note that a value/s can be converted into a value/v, and vice versa, by shifting the stance one takes toward it: Nietzsche will diagnose his own values/v, and will also choose to value some values/s.

90. I use this rather than "subjective contents" because as we've seen Nietzsche denies that it is, in most cases, a "subject" that values.

What status does he think his own valuings have, what claim to our attention?

Nietzsche's genealogies have a claim to our attention if they're true (or even if they *might* be true, or *near* the truth). But what such claim can his valuings have? They appear to mix a personal element into his diagnoses, which inhibits and undermines their scientific status—and makes them less useful to readers interested in truth. They seem to expose his explanations of values to the same diagnosing critique he so witheringly applies to others. For the common drift of all his diagnoses is to reveal the limited, "perspectival" status of these values/s, and the way they distort any theoretical studies they affect—a lesson it seems that should extend to his own values.[91] Indeed, we'll see that he thinks these diagnoses expose a kind of "lie" or illusion in all valuing, in the very way it posits its values/v. Then Nietzsche, in valuing, would be subject to this illusion even while he diagnoses it in others. At the least, his values/v would be relativized to his own perspective, in a way that takes away any right or power to persuade our own. We must see whether Nietzsche can answer these doubts that his own insights work against his values/v.

It is already obvious *what* I think Nietzsche values: his principal value/v is precisely the freedom or self selection described in section 4. This is, we've seen, a way of selecting or choosing one's own values—so that the principal value is a way of valuing. The other things he values are either means to freedom, or products of it.[92] Our main questions will be *why* (section 5b) and *how* (section 5c) he values this freedom. We're interested especially in whether he values it *because* of the facts from his study of values. Does he think that his facts "justify" this value to his audience—i.e., give them a reason to value freedom themselves? Does he think that his genealogy shows this value to be somehow more real or true than what this audience might have valued instead (privileging it ontologically or epistemically)?

These questions about the interface between his facts (about values) and his values are the part of Nietzsche's metaethics I'll most consider. This will extend into the next chapter, where I'll treat this fact-value relation with respect to the (relative) particulars of Nietzsche's values: in his positive

91. He states the general lesson, e.g., in WP259 [1884]: "[W]ith all evaluation it is a question of a definite perspective," and "there is only a perspectival valuing." Also HH.i.P.6.

92. In this respect freedom plays a similar role for Nietzsche as it does for Kant. I'll develop the comparison between Nietzsche's and Kant's conceptions of freedom and their uses of it in their values.

ethics and politics, *as* rooted in his diagnoses of our ethical and political values so far. Here in this chapter I'll treat this interface more abstractly. I'll examine how Nietzsche understands, generally, the *difference* and *relation* between these two attitudes he takes: diagnosing values and valuing. And I'll show how his basic valuing of freedom depends on that diagnosis.

I'll argue that Nietzsche relates his studying and valuing in this strong way: the diagnosis decisively *guides* his valuing. Indeed, his conception of freedom is most distinguished by the way it presupposes diagnosis; I think it's this that most marks it as "Nietzschean" rather than Kantian.[93] Valuing freely, as self selecting one's values, is precisely to value in the light of an understanding of why one values. It is to "incorporate" insight into the selective processes—Darwinian and cultural—that made the values of one's body and spirit. Moreover, that prior diagnosis isn't just a formal requirement on valuing: it also helps to specify the content that gets valued. It "guides" the choices of specific values/v.

First and above all, diagnosis guides the free spirit to choose freedom itself, i.e., to enhance his/her ability to self select values. Nietzsche, we'll see, has arguments why genealogy—the overall story in sections 2–3— should lead the genealogist to this basic value/v. This story convinces Nietzsche of freedom's preeminence, and he expects it to convince us. However these arguments have a more complex and contingent character than most philosophical arguments leading from facts to values. Nietzsche doesn't claim to "deduce" his values from his facts.

Eventually indeed I'll distinguish *two* ways Nietzsche tries to justify his value/v of freedom by his genealogies of human values/s. A first strategy is to find that value already present in all those values/s—such that it turns out that we (his audience) all really or deeply value freedom already. I'll call this Nietzsche's "intrinsic" justification of his values. His second strategy is to insist that his value/v really is something new, a value he "creates," yet to argue that his genealogy of human values supports or justifies this creation. I'll call this second kind of justification "constructive." Nietzsche is tempted by both ways of defending his ultimate value/v.

The value of freedom is only the beginning of the "revaluing" the self selector will carry out. From the standpoint of freedom he/she will diagnose and revise the particular values formerly taken for granted. This will lead to many further new values/v—for example, new rules for comport-

93. Kant thinks of freedom as "freedom from" desires—as not having one's choice determined by "impulse or inclination." But he thinks of these desires as far simpler and more evident than the motives Nietzsche finds behind our values.

ment toward others, i.e., a new "ethics." These more specific values will likewise depend on genealogical facts about the values they replace. But more than the basic value of freedom, they will also depend on personal facts about the self selector—for example, about his/her specific system of drives. So Nietzsche will insist on the great variance among the values that different self selectors will choose. Again the facts guide values, but by even more complex inferences than those for the value of freedom itself.

a. From Facts to Values?

Before turning to these positive arguments, I must recognize some reasons—they will already have struck many readers—for *denying* that Nietzsche tries to ground his values/v in facts in any such way. I'll pause to treat two such reasons; both can be given considerable textual support. They are two ways of "deflating" the claim Nietzsche makes in his values, of *denying* that he thinks these values are privileged by being in some way *grounded in the facts*. Since I want to read Nietzsche in just this way, I must rebut these two deflationary readings, which I think will seem recognizably "Nietzschean."

A first way of denying that he so supports his values is to deny that he thinks there's anything firm—any facts—to provide such support. It may seem that he *doesn't* think his genealogy grasps "facts" distinct enough from values to be *able* to ground them. How *could* he claim to find such facts, when he so completely infuses his genealogies with his own sharp evaluations and assessments? Rather than his values being "based" on his facts, values and facts are woven together throughout his diagnoses. His analysis and history of value selection—the famous distinction between master and slave moralities in GM.i, for example—is not soberly neutral, but tinged and even saturated with his personal preferences and ratings.[94]

Such frequent and thorough intermixings of his values into his theory may make us suspect that the two are not just mixed but *fused*, in such a way that no purely "factual" analysis or history is even intended by Nietzsche. Perhaps he offers us his "facts and values" as a package, and not in such

---

94. In GM.i.12 he describes a hardship in his genealogical inquiries: "What is really completely unbearable for me? That I cannot be done with, that makes me choke and faint? Bad air! Bad air! That something mismade comes near me; that I must smell the entrails of some mismade soul!"

a way that the former are separable grounds for accepting the latter.[95] We might find this fusion of factual and valuative sense in his common terms "healthy" and "sick," for example. These quasi-scientific "medical" terms seem chosen precisely to bear this dual meaning—to be values that simultaneously count as (a kind of) facts. And so indeed, in his important "Remark" appended to the end of GM.i, Nietzsche calls on physiologists and doctors to address the question of the *value* of different values—by studying how those values bear on the physiological health of their adherents. So science is already engaged in valuing, it seems, and can't offer the sort of "neutral" or objective base for Nietzsche's values that I was suggesting it might.

There's a second reason for doubting that Nietzsche uses his genealogy this way: it comes from the side of his values (rather than his view about "facts"). He often announces that his values(/v) are "created," not "discovered," and seems to deny that they are any "truer" or more adequate to reality than other values are.[96] We've already seen (in section 1) that he denies that *any* values inhere in reality independently of valuings: he denies any "objective" values. There are values only by and in our valuing them; values are always "for" a valuing perspective. And Nietzsche apparently embraces this conclusion's application to his own values/v: they too are inescapably perspectival, existing in the world only as intentional (perspectival) contents for himself, as he values.

It therefore seems that Nietzsche only offers his values *as his own*, and not as specially justified or privileged over other values (including ours). And this is why, this response may conclude, he insists that the philosopher's act is to "create" values, not to find them, through any fuller vision than the scientist's, in the facts themselves (in any stronger sense than

95. Still another possibility is that his argument works in just the opposite direction to mine, and he means his values to justify (persuade us to) his facts. This may indeed be his rhetorical effect on most of his audience: they (we?) are persuaded first by his scathing assessments—by, as it were, the way he "looks down" on things, rather than how he simply "looks at" or describes them. His stories often have their main appeal, not in their independent claim to be true (his evidence is after all very thin), but in the striking verdicts they issue in. Then Nietzsche's descriptions would be (meant as) "facts" only in some odd sense consistent with this different way of being supported or justified—as cohering with certain values. In this case it would be especially misguided to read Nietzsche's genealogy as a naturalistic, objective, scientific theory that grounds his values. This position is antipodal to my own.

96. WP979 [1885]: "Basic thought: the new values must first be created. . . . The philosopher must be like a law-giver."

others' values are there).[97] His values' "createdness" proves the *absence* of any epistemic grounding in facts—even if there were such facts. Once again it seems that Nietzsche's histories and psychologies of values can't (be meant to) justify his own values.

As I try to show how genealogy can still play that role, I'll try to handle these two objections. They present alternatives that my position must find a space between. On the one hand, I must preserve a distinction between facts and values, and prevent these from diffusing into one another—in such a way that there are no discrete facts to support his values. On the other hand, I must prevent his values from floating altogether free from the facts, as products of a creating that pays no attention to them. Since Nietzsche gives evidence of holding both of those alternative views, I'll need not just to find that space between, but to show that Nietzsche moves into it from both of those sides.

Let's begin with the objection that Nietzsche treats science—and genealogy—as already infused with values, and not as uncovering objective facts, in which his own values might then be grounded. Nietzsche does indeed think that values enter science, but it's important to distinguish the two ways he thinks so—and to see that neither threatens my point.

A first way is what the objection has in mind: Nietzsche diagnoses scientists as failing to achieve the objectivity they claim. They're still in the grip of values—their own values/v—that bias their inquiries and findings.[98] They engage in valuing, but without noticing that they do, and so without being on guard against how these valuings might distort their studies. So one of Nietzsche's favorite occupations is detecting such biases in scientists, baring various concrete ways in which science too, despite its own self-advertisement, still expresses values.

However, it's important to see that in this sense Nietzsche is *critical* of values' presence in science—and not just of scientists' self-ignorance about them. He thinks that scientists should struggle to overcome these valuative elements, which subvert their efforts. So we saw above (in section 4) how he diagnoses Darwinists as misled by their Christian values into misreading the evolution of morality; those values make them get it *wrong*. Nietzsche aims to overcome this bias and to give a more clear-sighted

---

97. BGE211 says that the philosopher's task "demands that he *create values*. . . . *Genuine philosophers . . . are commanders and legislators*: they say, '*thus* it *shall* be!'" GS320: "I want more, I am no seeker. I want to create for myself a sun of my own."

98. BGE23: "A genuine physio-psychology has to struggle with unconscious resistances in the heart of the researcher."

account of morality. So his genealogy aspires to do better at getting to the facts about values' history, precisely by overcoming subjective biases to which Darwinists were prone.[99]

But there's a second way values can enter into science: as its subject matter, as the values of the entities it studies, i.e., as values/s. Nietzsche approves of and even insists on "values in science" in this sense. Biological science at least will need to study values, since these are involved in all organisms' drives: drives are for goals, and are explained by their goals, because they were selected for these goals. Values are built into all organisms, as the goals explaining their drives and behavior. Biology cites values, in explaining by Darwinian functions and goals.

Indeed, biology is even licensed to *apply* these values *to* the organism: it conveys crucial information about it to say *how it stands* with respect to the outcomes it was selected for. So biology will include, within its description of the organism, judgments of it by the ends for which it was designed. In particular, biology will judge it by the ultimate end given by natural selection—fitness for surviving and reproducing.[100] Here biology describes and applies (what I call) "intrinsic" values, intrinsic that is to the organisms it studies.

It's in this sense, I think, that Nietzsche uses the terms "healthy" and "sick," which are so common in his genealogies. These are simply applications to the organism of values it has by its own selective history— the goods that explain why it's here (with the physiology and behavior it has). Nietzsche principally uses these terms to rate organisms in their fitness—in the physiological well-functioning of the many bodily systems. Health is simply the way of functioning whose past fitness explains the organism's existence and structure. To rate an individual organism by this criterion economically conveys this important information about its

99. An important extended passage, admittedly early, is UM.i.7. It attacks David Strauss for failing to follow up his avowed Darwinism into the ethic it implies; he takes his values from what "we" value, conventionally, rather than being led to them by a "love of truth." GM.P.7 invites Rée to look for "an actual *history of morality*" by paying attention to "what is documented, what can actually be established and has actually happened." GS345 complains that prior historians of morality show little "scientific curiosity." See BGE207 on the "objective human" as a "mirror," to be used by the philosopher.

100. Leiter (2002, 147) claims that Nietzsche thinks there's an "objective fact of the matter" as to "welfare or prudential goodness—what is good or bad for particular sorts of person[s]." I take it these facts are determined, in each case, by the goals of a person's drives and habits.

relation to its history. It's by such intrinsic standards that doctors and biologists can legitimately "evaluate."[101] They judge the organism by how well it (or some part) does what it was naturally designed to do.[102]

But when science "values" in this way, it hasn't really posited any values/v. It applies only the standards it finds in the things it studies; it rates them only by ends they set themselves—or rather, ends that have been set for them by the selective process that produced them. The doctor simply *describes* the patient as sick, rating him/her by the ends the body was "designed"—selected—for. So scientists need not—and should not—introduce any values of their own: when they evaluate, it's not in their own voice, but that of what they study. This lets Nietzsche's notion of science remain "naturalistic": the valuations he allows to science, and includes in his own elaborate analysis and history of value selection, do not prevent them from being, by intent, an account of "the facts" (I'll so refer to them).

But Nietzsche stresses that the philosopher's way of valuing is different from the scientist's. In the memorable ending to the "Remark" at the end of GM.i: "*All* sciences have now to do advance-work for the future task of the philosopher: this task [is to be] understood as, . . . to solve the *problem of value*, to determine the *rank-order of values*."[103] So science's "intrinsic" assessments of organisms as healthy and so on fall short of—although they are useful for—some *different* way of evaluating values, the philosopher's. The philosopher makes use of those naturalistic studies of value, but goes beyond them to posit new values of his own.

When he sees himself as *creating* values this way, Nietzsche does not try to justify his values/v as ones we already implicitly share—his ends aren't already in reality's design. Yet he still does, I think, try to justify them to us, and indeed by facts about that design. He still uses those facts to single out his own values, even though his values aren't "in" the facts. But how can this be?

101. See section 2 above. Nietzsche extends the notions of health and sickness into the psychic and social spheres, by analogy with bodily well-functioning. The psyche and the society are analogues to the body: wholes selected/designed with parts "for the sake of" functions. Here too instances can be judged as healthy or sick by their aptitude for so functioning. So psychologists and sociologists can likewise deploy "intrinsic" values.

102. This is consistent, I think, with Nietzsche's insistence that each individual has his/her own peculiar conditions of health, such that there is no "normal health" (GS120).

103. EH.GM describes GM as "[t]hree decisive preliminary studies of a psychologist for a revaluation of all values."

We can zero in on Nietzsche's way of justifying his values by returning now to the second objection, which denies just this. It claims that his values/v float free and independent from his historical and psychological facts about values/s. It points out how he stresses that he "creates" his values, rather than discovering them in reality. And it cites his perspectivism, which seems to renounce any claim to priority or status for his values— any pretense that they're better than other values.

Taking first the point about "creating" (*Schaffen*), I agree we must do justice to Nietzsche's insistent self-description. He prides himself that nobody before him has had quite *his* values. Since these values could only be by being for a valuer, the lack of any predecessors implies that these values have never been before. So his values are not "intrinsic" to the processes his genealogy describes: they're not built into the world, nor into us. This means that he can't persuade us to his values/v by showing them to be especially pervasive or basic values/s.

Still, we should notice two features of this value creating: (a) it is not *ex nihilo* (it remakes existing values); and (b) it is not uninformed (it remakes values from lessons it learns about them). Nietzsche thinks he makes his new values on the basis of insight into values so far. Although his values/v aren't uncovered among values/s, study of the latter is still what justifies valuing the former. The values he creates have their distinction, and their claim on us, by their proceeding from the genealogy. So though not perhaps *compelled* by the facts, his values are crucially *informed* by them.[104]

But what, second, about Nietzsche's perspectivism? Doesn't this show that all values are on a par, none more "justifiable" than others? I agree that (for Nietzsche) every value is for—exists as the goal of—some valuing perspective. So there can be no "objective values," existing independently of any valuing. And this means that perspectival values can't be ranked by their fidelity to such objective values. They are, in this respect, all "equally perspectival."

Nevertheless, Nietzsche's perspectivism is *not* the relativism with which it is so often conflated. We must always remember that it coexists with his breathtaking confidence that his own values are "better" or "higher" than other values—better above all than the prevailing Christian morality. He expresses this confidence when he speaks of "rank" or "rank-

104. GM.ii.24: "[T]he creative spirit [is one] whose compelling strength [*Kraft*] always pushes away [*wegtreibt*] from every Away and Beyond, whose loneliness . . . is only his absorption, immersion, penetration *into* reality."

order," and when he claims to be able to recognize cases of "ascent" and "decline."[105] He shows none of the modesty in valuing we expect from a relativist, whose metaethic puts different values on a par. Instead, Nietzsche's ratings and critiques show a certain knowing superiority that is not, I think, tempered as true or good only for his own self and perspective.[106]

Moreover, this height is, fundamentally, an *epistemic* matter. Nietzsche thinks he looks down on other perspectives, by virtue of understanding more and better than they do. He claims to have "seen through" the viewpoints lower on the *ladder* (*Leiter*) (a favorite image) of perspectives—to have once seen things their ways, but now better. HH.i.P.7 (on what "free spirits" can say): "Here a long ladder upon whose rungs we ourselves have sat and climbed, — which we ourselves at some time have *been*! Here a higher, a deeper, a beneath-us, a tremendous long ordering, a rank-ordering, which we *see*."[107] His own confidence in his values and judgments, and also whatever credit we might grant him, are due to the plausibility (the chance to be *true*) of his factual, psychosocial story. If we're persuaded to his assessments, it's because he seems so preternaturally keen in his insight into psychological and social phenomena.[108] But we need to see how that insight can help his values.

---

105. EH.i.1: "I have a finer nose for the signs of ascent and decline than any human has had, I am the teacher *par excellence* for this, — I know both, I am both."

106. Leiter (2002, 154) argues against inferring from Nietzsche's emphatic way of stating his values that he must be a realist about them: "*[T]he rhetoric is forceful, but the language of truth and falsity is conspicuously absent.*" But I think Nietzsche binds his values up with his facts all the time; he commonly couches his evaluations in terms with strong diagnostic and factual aspects, such as "sick" or "decadent." Although he doesn't think his values themselves are "truer" than others', he does think they're better supported by truths. See A9 for one case where he so uses the "language of truth and falsity" in attacking Christian values.

107. EH.iv.6: "Nobody yet has felt the *Christian* morality as *beneath* him: that involves a height, a far view, a formerly quite unheard of psychological depth and abyssal-ness." As we see here, this epistemic height involves bearing a psychological depth, which is accomplished precisely by bearing the whole ladder along within you. HH.i.292 speaks of this internal ladder of viewpoints: "[Y]ou have in yourself a ladder with a hundred rungs, upon which you can climb to knowledge." In EH.i.1 Nietzsche claims for himself "dual descent, as it were, both from the highest and the lowest rung on the ladder of life"; his innovation lies in his ability to occupy this whole range of viewpoints. See also Z.iii.12.19, EH.Z.6.

108. EH.iii.5: "That from my writings a *psychologist* speaks, who does not have his equal, is perhaps the first insight reached by a good reader." So I reject the view expressed in n. 95 above.

b. *Justifying Values*

So just how, finally, *do* these diagnostic insights into values/s (the values he studies) support Nietzsche's values/v (the values he values)? What reason do they give us—if we accept those insights as true—to concur in valuing his values/v ourselves? I come at last to my positive sketch of his position. (The full answer—the account of Nietzsche's value lesson—will extend into the following chapters.)

We must start by distinguishing two levels in Nietzsche's values/v. First there's the ur-value of freedom as self selection (of values); second there are all the particular values that arise by this selection (that get selected freely). Nietzsche makes different claims about these levels of his values. He most wants (I think) to proclaim and persuade us to the first—to valuing our own self selecting.[109] He allows that *some* of the second sector of his values—what he selects from that freed stance—is idiosyncratically his, with little or no claim to be selected and valued by us too.[110]

So to an extent, what matters most is not the content of Nietzsche's values—his particular ethics and politics—but how he makes them. Many of these values are *not* "justified" in a way binding on us. They're not inferred from certain facts, such that we are obliged to infer the same values from these facts. Rather, these values have their status ("higher") from his making them in knowledge of the facts, since this is making them freely. And if we make *different* values in that same knowledge, they will have that status too. If, for example, we value pity or democracy—as Nietzsche certainly does not—what matters most is whether *we* have selected these values, i.e., hold them after having "incorporated" the truth about their source in the herd instinct. What mainly gives values status is how they're made, not which values they are.

Nietzsche principally offers us not his values—though he claims them higher than our own—but his method for making values. He offers us himself as an example—perhaps the first ever[111]—of how one may make one's values in knowledge of how values *have* been made (and so what

109. GM.ii.2: "The 'free' human, the owner of a long, unbroken will, has in this possession also his *value-measure*."

110. By contrast Kant thinks freedom chooses the same in every individual case, because freedom is detaching from all individuating desires.

111. EH.iv.1: "*Revaluation of all values*: that is my formula for an act of the highest self-reflection by humanity, that has become flesh and genius in me. My fate wills, that I must be the first *decent [anständige]* human."

they've really been for). Only now that we can understand the logics by which natural and social selection shaped our values do we have a chance at the kind of freedom that is really most germane to us. Nietzsche invites us to make values for ourselves, from this same stance. This gives a further point to his "perspectivism": what matters about values is precisely that they be our own, not that they match some end built into reality.

Nevertheless, all of this requires that there is one of his own values that Nietzsche *does* mean us to adopt: the value of that method for making one's values. His other values are accredited by their source in his own self selecting, his freedom. With many of them he makes no claim on our own—hence his frequent reminders that he wants no "disciples."[112] But the value of self selection itself has a different status: he *does* mean for (the best of) us to follow him in this (in not being followers). So it's here that the question of justification really arises. What support do his genealogical facts give for this crucial (meta)value? How can they justify it to us?

First a preliminary point. For a start, the facts "support" that value in this unexpected way: to be taking account of these facts, in the right way, *is already to have* this value. To value self selecting is precisely to have taken on the task and habit of "incorporating" that genealogical insight—of pushing it down into the details of one's everyday valuing, as described in section 4b. By this incorporated insight, one "controls" (aspects of) those other selective forces. And "freedom" simply lies in exercising this control, as one values. So in *studying* values/s in Nietzsche's way, one is already *valuing* his basic value/v of freedom. There is less of a step from studying to freedom than might have seemed.

To an extent, then, Nietzsche *induces* this value (freedom) in us, simply by drawing us into his diagnostic practice. He brings the value in by the back door, all the while he's conveying his insights of fact.[113] As we read, he involves us in judging whether our values *do* have the genealogy and meaning he attributes to them: he engages our power of assessing his claims about the facts. Still more, he engages our power of assessing our own values, in the light of these facts about their origins. So the genealogy "supports" the revaluing of values, inasmuch as carrying out the genealogy

---

112. Z.iii.11.2: "'This — is now *my* way, — where is yours?' so I answered those who asked me 'as to the way.' For *the* way — that doesn't exist!" Compare GS.JCR.7, GS255. In chapter 3 I'll show that Nietzsche thinks self selection dictates *some* further ethical and political values—which Nietzsche thinks other free spirits will or should share.

113. EH.BGE.1 describes his books as "fish-hooks."

involves us in (is itself part of) practicing and valuing that very self selection, which the revaluation promotes.

Nietzsche here absorbs us in an activity that we, his willing readers, already incline toward. He draws us further into this project, shows us how it can be refined and perfected—how rich and subtle are the sources and meanings of our values, and how hard it is to bring this knowledge into a *choice* about or among them. His books are meant as trainings in this practice—are meant to be "habit forming," to form the habit of diagnosing all of our other habits. And of course they're only so meant for those already prepared for this practice, who have certain tributary drives or values. He often stresses that he writes for a narrow audience.

In this strategy of inducing his values in us, Nietzsche relies on certain values preexisting in us. His aim is to shift our values not "from the bottom up," but by appealing to values we already bring to our reading—for example, the values of self-understanding and self-determination. By his genealogical facts, he shows us that these are *far harder* to achieve than we had supposed. Our valuing and values had seemed transparent and obvious, as carried in our own free choice. Nietzsche's light on the logic of socially selected values shows that they are really quite opaque—that such selection has cultivated our self-ignorance (has designed us for it). We thought we were already *honest* in our values, but now see we must work much harder to become so. Such virtues, which we had presumed for ourselves, need more work: it's only in the self selection he describes that they can really be what we want them to be. In such ways, Nietzsche tries to show his (narrow) audience that his values are *improvements* on theirs—better values to which their own can be led, by being shown certain facts. He gives arguments or insights that are meant to bridge from their values to his.

To the extent that Nietzsche relies on appeal to preexisting and "local" values like self-understanding, his justification of his value/v (freedom) is only hypothetical, not categorical. *If* we want to be honest, we'll be led to his ideal. Our existing values give *some* of us reason for adopting his ideal. But the justification has no grip on individuals who either lack those preexisting values, or little value them. Often, Nietzsche is happy to leave it at that. But I think he also takes himself to have, in reserve, grounds for a priority of self selecting that transcends such merely local and hypothetical support.

Here we come to the crux—to Nietzsche's reasons for his extraordinary confidence in his values, a confidence apparently at odds with his perspectivism. He is convinced, I think, that "freedom is best": it's the best or highest a human can be—*any* human, and not just those who are suited and predisposed for it by their individual tastes and abilities. How could his genealogies of human values support this conviction? We can distinguish two kinds of arguments, "intrinsic" and "constructive."[114]

Nietzsche wavers between two ways of relating his value (freedom) to his genealogical facts—and to the values genealogy uncovers already in us. Sometimes he treats freedom as implicit in—or directly implied by—a single basic value, power, built into us all. He makes (what he treats as) a direct and simple inference from that basic value to the value of freedom, as power's fullest form. So he purports to reveal that freedom is what we've really wanted all along. Elsewhere, however, he treats freedom as a value he "creates," in response to a certain problem or dilemma he claims we face, as a culture or indeed a species. This problem lies in a conflict between a *pair* of basic values. Nietzsche offers freedom as resolving this conflict—as an effective way of synthesizing those basic values. This second way of justifying freedom still relies on those (claimed) preexisting values, but treats freedom not as implicit or intrinsic in them, but as something new constructed out of them.

On the one hand Nietzsche justifies his value/v by claiming it is already covertly present in all of us—in all humans, and even in all organisms. This argument runs through his notion of will to power. He claims to identify a deep, pervasive aiming already in all living things—missed by scientists so far, yet within their proper scope and domain.[115] He argues that drives (organisms' behavioral dispositions) are principally selected to pursue power—so that power is a basic and pervasive value/s, built into the viewpoint of life itself.[116] And his first way of justifying his value of freedom is to argue that self selection is the greatest or fullest power we can have.[117]

114. Sharon Street has persuaded me not to call these "internal" and "external," since in Bernard Williams's well-known sense for these terms *both* of my Nietzschean positions count as internal—i.e., both argue from values that it's claimed the audience already has. The difference lies in how direct or immediate the argument from these values is.

115. Z.ii.12: "Only where life is, is there also will: not will to life but — thus I teach you — will to power!" Also BGE259, GS349, GM.ii.11, TI.ix.14. We saw the details of this "power biology" in chapter 1, section 5.

116. Nietzsche sometimes (e.g., WP674 [1887–1888]) describes this argument as revealing "objective values"—but I think he rather means "universal perspectival" ones.

117. See especially EH.P.3: "How much truth does a spirit *bear*, how much truth does it *dare*? [T]hat became for me ever more the genuine [*eigentliche*] measure of value." BGE39 hypothesizes that "the strength of a spirit would be measured by how much of

By this first argument Nietzsche claims to "discover" that freedom is something we already value, in valuing power. The value of freedom is "intrinsic" to us:

> (10) Intrinsic justification: we already basically value freedom (because we basically value power).

Nietzsche does, to be sure, need to draw an inference from power to freedom—he needs to give reasons that freedom is the best form of power. He argues that by self selecting his/her drives and habits, the free human achieves a power over him/herself that transcends the power achievable simply by those drives and habits. The human's independence is marked by the way he/she *controls* and *employs* the drives and habits: freedom has not just the power *in* them, but a power *over* them. This argument is direct and, in a way, a priori—it justifies freedom as picked out by the mere concept of power. I developed a non-Darwinian version of this reading in *Nietzsche's System*,[118] which could readily be restated in the selective terms of this book. But here I want to pursue a somewhat different argument that I think he also makes.

For more commonly Nietzsche offers his values not as the ultimate built-in goods—which his audience already implicitly shares—but as "constructive," as values he creates and gives his audience, not discovers within them. This belongs to Nietzsche's strong conception of himself as a philosopher not a scientist: as a philosopher his main role is to make new values, whereas the scientist can only study those already on the scene.[119] As a philosopher he achieves a kind of independence from those prevailing values; he steps somewhat "apart" from them, and so can "revalue" them, as the scientist never does.[120] To revalue our values he needs to step out of these values somehow—these values can't revalue themselves. So he prides himself in *not* discovering his values already built into us.

However, I think it's crucial to see that this value creation still depends on his facts about what values *are* built into us—and still appeals to those values in us. Nietzsche justifies his new values as created in the light of

the 'truth' it could endure." In both cases, I suggest, the "truth" Nietzsche mainly means is truth about one's values. Also GS347, A50, A54, EH.iv.3, 5; WP327 [1887], WP1041 [1888].

118. See Richardson 1996, chapter 3, especially section 1.

119. See n. 97 above. On "creating values" also see Z.i.1. GM.iii.25 says that science never creates values.

120. CW.P: "What does a philosopher demand of himself first and last? To overcome his time in himself, to become 'timeless'."

a lesson he learns from his study of our values so far. He tries to lead us to his values by that lesson about our own. That lesson makes an appeal to our values, though without ceding ultimate authority to them. It tries to teach us something about these values, which will change them into his new values. So although his values are distinct from our own, they are justified by a lesson to and about our own:

> (11) Constructive justification: our basic values justify creating the new value of freedom.

I'll argue that this is Nietzsche's primary way of propounding his values/ v. It licenses his claims that they are "new" and "his" (perspective)—but also his claim that they're better than our own. It lets his new values appeal to our own, but also claim superiority to our own, yet still without claiming to be objectively real.

Nietzsche's main strategy here, I suggest, is to uncover a basic *conflict* in our human values: we all aim at two contrary sets of ends, designed into us by two selective regimes. CW.Epilogue: "The modern human represents, biologically, a *contradiction of values*, he sits between two stools, he says in one breath Yes and No." Nietzsche claims to discover and describe these regimes empirically. They are of course the systems of dispositions designed by natural and social selection—our competing systems of drives and social habits.

On the one hand our bodies and drives have been adapted for an animal, physical health—for fitness to further the reproducing line. This involves a deep egoism. But our "spirit"—our habits of memory, consciousness, and language—has been adapted by selection over a different field of replicators, for a different and in fact conflicting end. Habits are selected to bind us into society, and the most effective means, under both the ethic of custom and morality, are habits that attack and undermine our drives and their natural "healthy selfishness." Hence we find ourselves—and this is the sum of Nietzsche's dual diagnosis—"the sick animal," "human, all-too-human": our two deep projects frustrate and interfere with one another, and subject us to a pervasive suffering. Nietzsche lays such stress on this diagnosis, I claim, because it is his main support for his own values.

Nietzsche diagnoses this conflict of values, and he proposes a certain solution to it. This solution, freedom, is a strategy for redesigning ourselves toward a new basic project that assumes priority over the other two. It synthesizes our natural and social values into a new value not predelineated in either. This new project uses the other two, and it also satisfies them better than they currently can be—it overcomes their mutual frustration. The project of freedom can both *advance spirit* and *reclaim health*, though it does so only by making something else more important than either spirit or health. So Nietzsche tries to use those built-in values to motivate and justify a new value different from both.

HH.iii.350 gives an early version of this argument:

> Many chains have been laid upon the human so that he should unlearn behaving like an animal. . . . But now he still suffers from wearing his chains for so long, for lacking clean air and free movement for so long: — these chains are . . . those heavy and significant errors of moral, religious, metaphysical representation. Only when this *sickness from chains* is also overcome will the first great goal be fully achieved: the separation of the human from the animal.

(Nietzsche goes on to say that this overcoming is through "freedom of spirit.")

By devising a value/v that coordinates the basic values/s of our human and animal aspects, Nietzsche thinks he solves the problem of our dual design. So he thinks this value/v has a claim on everyone who shares that design. Sometimes Nietzsche suggests that this value was somehow prefigured and preordained in that design, but for the most part he denies this.[121] That sequence of natural and then social selection wasn't aimed at making self selection possible. Darwinists (he thinks) depict their morality as preordained that way, in the tendency of natural selection itself. But when we see the complexity and multivalence of the processes that have made us, we see that there's no single aim or end to evolution—including as it does those conflicting selective regimes. There's nothing ineluctable in evolution by selection, leading to self selection or freedom. Evolution doesn't make this value—Nietzsche makes it by his insight into evolution.

So the main parts of his argument are these: he promotes his ideal of freedom as a way of living (or aiming) that (a) uses the powers of both body and spirit, and (b) satisfies the values of body and spirit, but also (c) does both by raising a new value above them.

Take first the project of spirit, i.e., that whole vector of social values evolving by social selection and culminating in morality and the ascetic ideal. Despite Nietzsche's obvious aversion to this whole family of values, he still means to channel and assimilate it into his new value. Part of what credits his new value is the way it advances the key aims and powers of

---

121. I return to these topics in my account of Nietzsche's views about "progress" in chapter 3, section 4; see n. 77 there.

spirit. We saw in section 4 how self selection depends on spirit's powers of memory, consciousness, and language; these originated in order to herd us, but can be redirected into genealogy, to uncover how herding has worked and to help us to overcome it. Moreover this new use lets those powers play a role they have long been assumed to play but really have not: freedom makes good on how spirit (cognition) has always advertised itself—as enabling each person to choose his/her thoughts and values.

So freedom both uses spirit's powers, and satisfies its values—and does these better than was possible before. Above all freedom takes up the value of truth. Near the end of *On the Genealogy of Morals* Nietzsche famously argues that the will to truth is the "kernel" of the ascetic ideal. This diagnosis of the value of truth is of course meant first of all to call it into question. But I think it also has a second role. Nietzsche insists that truth is the *crux* to the ascetic ideal because he intends to synthesize the value of truth into his new ideal—and wants thereby to take up the whole family of values evolved by social selection. He wants the will to truth to be a kind of epitome or essence of morality, so that his use of it within his ideal of freedom can coopt that whole system of values—can do a kind of justice to it, by preserving that epitome. He "redeems" that whole system by redirecting this kernel into his new project.

But on the other side Nietzsche also takes up the project and values he associates with the body and drives. Rather than blocking and vilifying our ingrained drives, his new project of freedom tries to use and to satisfy them—while redirecting them. He insists that we pay close attention to the conditions—climatic, nutritional, behavioral—of our health as organisms. So EH.ii gives an account, down to banal details, of his discovery of the nutrition, place and climate, and recreation that are healthiest for him. (See EH.ii.10 on the importance of these "small things.") Subtle mistakes about what's best for our bodies can have calamitous consequences for our "spiritual" health; they can cut a person off, in particular, from freedom: "[T]he animal vigor has never become great enough in him, for him to reach the most spiritual, overflowing freedom" (EH.ii.2).[122] We need to see to the health of our bodies, understood as systems of drives. Science needs to learn and teach better here. But more important is for each individual to use its general findings to doctor him/herself, *as* a quite specific, distinctive system of drives.

---

122. Also in EH.ii.2: "The tempo of the metabolism stands in a precise relation to the mobility or lameness of the *feet* of the spirit; the 'spirit' itself is indeed only a kind [*Art*] of this metabolism."

Freedom doesn't just presuppose the general health of the drives, it also uses the drives more directly. The kind of insight that freedom presupposes—insight into our values—requires a sensitivity to the nuances of our drives, a sensitivity that depends on learning to step into their viewpoints.[123] More than this, Nietzsche wants us to use the "taste" of our bodily drives to judge the social values laid over them.[124] We evaluate the health of a social practice or viewpoint by reviving an ability bred into our bodies, to "smell" sickness and decline. So Nietzsche insists that our cognitive powers not be divorced from our drives and feelings, that we not try to isolate them in a neutral and objective space. Our values must be rerooted in the healthy instincts bred (not trained) into us.[125] As we'll see in the following chapter, this restores a "selfishness" natural to these drives.

With these arguments on both sides, Nietzsche tries to take up into his new ideal both of these conflicting value systems, which all of us have as "human animals." Freedom uses and satisfies both sets of powers—in our body, in our spirit. It synthesizes these powers by adjusting each to fit with the other into a new project. It adjusts each with the help of the other: it uses the healthy taste in the drives to heal spirit, and it uses spirit's truths to redirect drives. So it finds a form of each power in which it no longer opposes and interferes with the other—a form in which both values can be satisfied together. Inasmuch as we all share these basic values, we all have reason to value this synthesis.

By appealing to these basic values in us, and also to our cognitive grasp of his story about their conflict, Nietzsche means both to motivate and to justify our adoption of his new basic value of freedom. Once we adopt it, it has a value of its own, and not simply that of those natural and social values. Similarly, although the overall project of self selection draws on the projects of health and truth, it is more than just the sum of them—it is a single project that deploys both others. Nietzsche stresses the new unity he thinks he brings. Z.ii.20: "I live among humans as fragments of the future: . . . I compose [*dichte*] and carry together into one, what is fragment and riddle and horrible accident."

---

123. I develop this "phenomenological" use of the drives in chapter 4, section 4, of Richardson 1996.

124. Z.i.3: "Listen . . . to the voice of the healthy body: this is a more honest and purer voice." I'll pursue the "aesthetic" character of this taste in chapter 4.

125. TI.v.4: "Every naturalism in morality, that means every *healthy* morality, is ruled by an instinct of life. . . . *Anti-natural* morality, that means almost every morality that has so far been taught, revered, and preached, turns, conversely, *against* the instincts of life, — it is a . . . *condemnation* of these instincts."

The argument is, in a way, dialectical and Hegelian. The conflict between these opposing principles (natural and social selection, with their distinct values) is resolved in a new synthesis. But of course Nietzsche has many differences from Hegel. In particular, he insists that the development is not inevitable. To be sure, it sometimes seems that *part* of it is: our culture's moral values are ineluctably undermining themselves, at the hands of the will to truth, their "kernel."[126] But it's *not* inevitable that this undermining self-critique will give us the new ideal of self selection. It may instead leave us in an inert, long-lasting "nihilism" or valuelessness: once we see through all our values, nothing might matter to us. Nietzsche's well-known worry that human culture could get stuck in nihilism shows the contingency of the step to his new ideal.[127]

Nietzsche interprets Darwinists as in thrall to the Hegelian claim of inevitability: they imagine that natural selection leads ineluctably to human morality. I'll return to this disagreement over "progress" in chapter 3. But in another way Nietzsche's developmental theory is *more* Hegelian, because it's more dialectical: it works, as we've seen, by positing a deep conflict between values, and finding its resolution in a kind of "synthesis" of the opposing values. Nietzsche claims novelty in creating this resolution. Darwinists, by contrast, offer an "intrinsic" argument: a tendency already present in natural selection leads to (and justifies) morality; science claims to discover this single end built into reality (organisms as selected).

Nietzsche's view, as I here read him, has some affinity to (what have been called) "practical reasoning theories" in recent metaethics.[128] These argue that (a kind of) objectivity in ethics is indeed feasible, but depends not on theory's matching independently real goods, but on the proper exercise of practical reason. There are certain "universal demands" imposed by reasoning over reasons for acting. These demands arise either in Hobbesian fashion (as rational pursuit of the agent's interests), or in Kantian (as conformity with categorical reasons). And now Nietzsche, as I've read him, offers a third version: practical reason properly requires a certain kind of *insight into* one's own values. Hobbes and Kant presume

126. WP.Preface [1887–1888]: "For why is the arrival of nihilism now *necessary*? Because our values so far are drawing their ultimate conclusion [*Folgerung*]; because nihilism is the logic of our great values and ideals, thought to the end." Also GM.iii.27.

127. On this contingency see, e.g., BGE203.

128. See the survey in Darwall et al. (1992, 131ff.); they mention Baier and Gauthier as giving Hobbesian versions of the view, and Nagel, Korsgaard, Donagan, Darwall, and Gewirth as giving Kantian versions.

to have all the insight needed into their values as they act, but they miss the genealogies of their own values, hence their real aim or point. Nietzsche describes, and enacts, a new discipline of practical reasoning. It rests heavily on empirical insights: science's facts about our species' and culture's evolutionary paths, extended in each case into an individual's insight into his/her personal makeup. Nietzsche's ultimate value is this new discipline.

In sum, Nietzsche uses his genealogy to promote his new value/v (freedom) in two ways. First, simply by engaging his readers in that genealogy, exposing how their values have been selected outside them, he induces and even forces them to hold their values in a new awareness. Here he appeals to readers' contingent values, such as curiosity and honesty, to lead them into his diagnostic practice. But Nietzsche also thinks this practice *would* be better even for persons who lack such "gateway" values as honesty. He claims it solves a structural problem in humans generally, due to our dual design for clashing ends. Even humans without those contingent virtues encouraging to freedom can still be judged by the standard of freedom, since they too suffer that structural problem, and without becoming free, they will never be more than "all too human."

c. Valuing's How

So much for Nietzsche's argument in favor of his ultimate value. Now let's return to the question of how he values it. We began this section with the difference between studying and valuing values—treated as different ways to "posit" values. A value as studied—as the genealogist studies it—is a teleological explainer: it's the (tended) outcome that explains some (probably human) behavior, as toward and for it. But in valuing, it seems, we posit the value as a quite different kind of reason—not the reason we are, but the reason we *should* be doing this. So what, finally, does Nietzsche think is the force of this "should"? Given that freedom is what he basically values, and given his reasons for himself and others to value it, what can we say about that "how" (to value it)? And in particular, in valuing it does he posit it as "real" (or really valuable) in any way that he does *not* so posit the values he studies?

Here we need to distinguish (i) the attitude that Nietzsche thinks valuing usually but misguidedly takes from (ii) the attitude he thinks he adopts himself, in valuing, e.g., freedom. And we must also consider (iii) what these have in common—and in particular what it is, generally, to value, or in what way *both* he and the moralists "posit values" in valuing.

Some of the differences between Nietzsche's and others' (the usual) ways of valuing have emerged already. I'll recall two.[129]

Nietzsche doesn't "value his values" by positing them as objective, i.e., as existing "in the world" independently of valuings—as he thinks our prevailing valuing posits them. He attacks the implication in morality that a thing has value "in itself" (*an sich*), and intends to withdraw this implication from his own valuing.[130] He holds on, as he values, to his own role in making these be values, by his valuing. They have their value in relation and in proportion to the way he values them.

Second, Nietzsche also doesn't "value his values" in the sense of thinking that they're the values *everyone* should hold: he refrains from positing them as "universal" in this way.[131] He insists on the need for values to be tailored to each individual's constitution. And he repeatedly stresses that we should not all assume that his values are addressed to us. Again I think we should read this restriction into the "tone" with which he (not just speaks but) values his values.[132]

So these are mistakes built into our usual valuing, which Nietzsche thinks he can avoid. He's eager to prevent us from misunderstanding the force of his values, and so he pares away these (and other) errors in how we commonly value. He intends, ambitiously, to initiate a new valuative practice in which those faulty implications are absent. These changes— renouncing objectivity and universality—are key ways he wants to carry us out of morality, "beyond good and evil." Morality is characterized not just by a certain content, but by this force or tone, which Nietzsche wants to remove.

We can see that valuing *can* renounce those claims (objectivity and universality)—that they're not part of "what it is to value"—by recalling (from section 1) that Nietzsche thinks that valuing extends all the way down

129. Another implication he hears and rejects in our moral valuing is that agents (those we evaluate, and ourselves *as* we evaluate) are free to choose differently.

130. We've already seen from GS301: "Whatever has *value* in the current world, has it not in itself, from nature — nature is always valueless — but one has once given it a value, as a gift." WP12 [1887–1888] says that our values have been "falsely *projected* into the essence of things." Also GS299; WP260 [1883–1884].

131. GS382: "Another ideal runs on ahead of us, a strange, tempting, dangerous ideal to which we do not wish to persuade anybody, because we do not easily concede *the right to it* to anybody." Also BGE43.

132. Nietzsche stresses the importance and difficulty of hearing correctly Zarathustra's "tone," in EH.P.4.

to the level of drives, the inherited behavioral powers of all organisms. The designed-in goals of these bodily capacities are already values, yet these capacities make no such posits of objectivity or universality. Even the simplest organism—e.g., an amoeba—has such drives and values.[133] But the amoeba doesn't take, e.g., eating to be valuable "in itself," nor to be valuable for "all" amoebas (or all life). These posits arise, rather, in the context of human spirit (memory, consciousness, language) and its social values. They arise as part of the practice-justifying *doctrine* (dogma) that evolves in the "ethic of custom" and still more in "morality," a doctrine selected for its power to herd us into common practices. The assumptions that values are built into the world, and that they're universally binding, belong to a *kind* of valuing—a kind Nietzsche aspires to overcome. In overcoming it he tries to reinstitute some of the "innocence" with which our drives have valued all along.

Here it will help to contrast my account with Hussain's persuasive reading (unpublished). He argues that Nietzsche thinks every valuing counts its value as "valuable in itself," and that Nietzsche therefore (as a free spirit who "conceives reality as it is") refrains from valuing, himself. Hussain applies Walton's analysis of art as make-believe to argue that Nietzsche engages in a "fictionalist simulacrum of valuing": he "makes believe" that he values. He merely pretends to regard some X as valuable in itself, hence he merely pretends to value it. In this way, Hussain thinks, Nietzsche offers his values as "honest illusions."

Now I agree that Nietzsche raises a doubt or criticism against all valuing—a doubt sometimes expressed as the charge that it always "lies." But I deny that this essential criticism is that valuing always (essentially) claims objectivity.[134] I also deny that Nietzsche takes the doubt he does raise as reason to refrain from valuing, himself. I think he considers himself really and genuinely to value—not to engage in a simulacrum of it. If the latter were his view of himself, we would need to hear scare quotes in all

133. Nietzsche mentions the amoeba to bring out the continuity of life in WP501 [1886–1887], WP653 [1887]. He similarly speaks of "protoplasm" in WP656 [1887], WP651 [1887–1888], WP702 [1888].

134. I think the evidence that Hussain (unpublished) cites to show that Nietzsche attributes this error to all valuing can be read as (sometimes hyperbolic) attacks on the way people *usually* value, or *have* valued *so far*. I think Nietzsche shows his satisfaction with the perspectivity of values—his refusal to hold against them that they're not objective—in WP1059 [1884]: "[N]o longer [use] the humble phrase 'everything is *merely* subjective,['] but 'it is also *our* work!' let us be proud of it!"

expressions like these: Nietzsche "values" freedom, freedom is one of Nietzsche's "values,"[135] But I don't think we should. He means to modify his/our valuative practice, not to break away from it altogether.

The doubt Nietzsche does raise is against a different kind of "posit" that all valuing makes. Now it might have seemed, when we reminded ourselves that valuing extends down to the drives, that this would show that valuing doesn't essentially make *any* posit, not just that it doesn't posit objectivity or universality. It seems implausible that the amoeba seeking food "posits" eating it as good or valuable. However we must remember that Nietzsche insists on treating such cases—and indeed all life processes—as (thinly) intentional, as involving "wills" and "perspectives." And this insistence showed us his minimal conditions for perspectivity: a perspective is constituted *merely by virtue* of a responsive or "plastic" system having been selected to bring about some outcome. The amoeba's adapted pursuit itself amounts to a "viewpoint" on the world. And we must think of the "posit" in valuing in a similarly minimal sense: the amoeba "posits" the value of feeding, in and by the way its perceptive and motive systems have been selected to bring about feeding. By extension, humans posit values by having had their drives and habits designed for natural and social functions.[136]

On this story, valuing's posit is initiated in the selective history that designed the organism's systems. Our conscious "values," the rules or principles we consciously advert to, and cite to ourselves and others as what we're for and after, are superimposed on that basic valuing.[137] To a large extent, these "announced values" are superficial, Nietzsche thinks, and either turn no wheels, or are merely tools of the basic projects—i.e., are used to help us to propagate, or to herd.[138] To the extent that these conscious values *do* effectively oppose the project in our drives, it is merely in support of our social habits. So the meaning even of the values we posit

135. There's an analogue to this for Nietzsche's (seeming) factual claims: it might be argued that he doesn't, strictly speaking, "believe" any of his historical or psychological claims, since here too the posit of objectivity is part of "what it is to believe"; so he would engage in only a simulacrum of belief as well. (Perhaps favoring this is WP15 [1887].) I rebut such a reading of Nietzsche in Richardson 1996, especially chapter 4.

136. As we saw in chapter 1, it's not the bird's pursuit systems *as they are now* that makes them "for" that goal; rather, it's the selective history by which those pursuit systems were "designed" for that outcome. It's that evolutionary process that dictates the goal and point of the bird's pursuit—it's really this that "posits" that value.

137. See Schacht (1983, 403ff.) on the contrast between these kinds of value.

138. WP392 [1888]: "Moral values are *apparent values* [*Scheinwerthe*], compared with physiological [values]."

consciously depends on our culture's history: they explain what we do only via that history.

Now it may be hard to see how this designedness could really amount to a "posit" of the end as valuable. It does so in an unexpected sense, which is Nietzsche's key to the force of valuing. Whereas in studying a value we posit it as explainer, in valuing it we posit it by our *being explained* by it as an end. It's the outcome that explains our behavior; it's what our behavior is designed for. We posit it practically, precisely in acting for it: it *is* our end. So to value is simply to be telic, i.e., to be explained (explainable) teleologically. Nietzsche thinks of valuing as the essential posit of *will*: it posits in being aimed at an outcome, i.e., in having an outcome that explains what it does.

We can formulate the contrasting ways values are posited, in studying them and in valuing them:

(12) X posits Y as a value/s = X explains by Y as an end.
(13) X posits Y as a value/v = X is explained by Y as an end.

These formulations show how the study of values studies them as they really are, despite the difference between studying and valuing. It studies them *as explainers*, which is precisely the role they essentially play for the valuers. So a valuing's own values/v are properly treated as values/s by a genealogist. Nietzsche admits nothing nonnatural in his explication of valuing. Valuing per se—by contrast with its development as morality—posits nothing supernatural, nothing beyond genealogy's scope.

Nevertheless, as I've mentioned, Nietzsche still finds a kind of "lie" in all valuing. We need, finally, to understand this in relation to the practical kind of posit that valuing involves. The epistemic fault lies not in a mismatch with objective reality—not in a failure at correspondence[139]—but in a "methodological" inadequacy in how the practical posit gets made. The lie consists, I suggest, in these two things: first, the narrowness or "partiality" in being toward *this* end rather than others; and second, the arbitrariness or "blindness" of the selecting process that created/set the end. Each of these is a way that valuing's "posit" is always, though to varying degrees, limited or flawed.

An aiming is always (to some extent) "partial," in that it pursues its end by ignoring and excluding other ends.[140] It is one perspective on things'

139. I.e., to the *absence* of any values "in things themselves."
140. Here Nietzsche means something similar to Anaximander's metaphysical "injustice" in all particularity.

value, but there are many others. Values are put in the world by *all* the wills (or aiming organisms) there are. So the adequacy of our own values gets judged not by whether they match the values in things themselves (there are none), but by how they stand toward that field of competing values. Things have, besides the values I give them, all those other values as well. My values will be *less* partial to the extent that I somehow recognize or encompass or supersede some of those others.[141]

An aiming is always (to some extent) "blind," in that it fails to understand itself; it "doesn't know what it's doing." This is the case, first of all, because values are almost always simply inherited—received as bodily drives or social customs. Even value creators are for the most part instruments of larger selective forces: they make the values the historical situation needs.[142] And the selective forces that design drives and habits work mechanically; they are merely stochastic logics in large populations, favoring fitness and conformity, respectively. To be sure, Nietzsche is largely positive toward the mechanism of natural selection: he admires how resourcefully life finds a way to continue and further itself. But he also stresses how this mechanism is both partial and blind: it ignores other values (such as the production of higher individuals), and in no way "chooses" its structural end against alternatives.

It's important that on this account the "lie" in valuing is a matter of degree. The error or injustice will be less to the extent that the valuing perspective includes or recognizes other and different values, and knowingly chooses its own against them. It's not, as the antirealist reading of Nietzsche's metaethics holds, that all valuing posits entities that don't exist—in which case all would be equally guilty of the same mistake. Nietzsche denies that true and false are "opposites," by which he means exclusive and exhaustive alternatives.[143] By his notion of truth as "perspectival," he means that it is cumulative: a perspective is "truer" depending on how many other perspectives it encompasses.[144] So consider this long extract from HH.i.P.6:

141. Here I defend a kind of perspectivism attacked by Clark (1998, 76), though she is focused on perspectives about facts not values.
142. See n. 86 in chapter 1.
143. BGE34: "[W]hat forces us in general to the supposition, that there is an essential opposition of 'true' and 'false'? Is it not enough to assume grades of apparentness and, as it were, brighter and darker shadows and shades of appearance . . . ?"
144. I analyze this notion of perspectival truth in Richardson 1996, chapter 4, section 5.

You should get control over your For and Against and learn
how to disengage and again engage them, according to your higher
goals. You should learn to grasp the perspectival in every valuation
— the displacement, distortion and seeming teleology of horizons
and everything belonging to the perspectival; also the piece of stu-
pidity in relation to opposed values and the whole intellectual loss
which every For, every Against costs. You should learn to grasp the
necessary injustice in every For and Against, injustice as inseparable
from life, life itself as *conditioned* by the perspectival and its injustice. You should above all see with your own eyes, where the injustice is always greatest: there where life has evolved at its smallest,
narrowest, neediest, most incipient, and yet cannot avoid taking *itself* as the goal and measure of things. . . . — you should see with
your own eyes the problem of *rank-order* and how power and right
and comprehensiveness [*Unfänglichkeit*] of perspective grow into the
heights with one another.[145]

Nietzsche concedes, I think, that his values too will be partial and
therefore "lies" and "unjust." But partiality is a matter of degree, and he
claims that his values are *less* so than others. They are so by his enhancement
of the value-selecting stance. By genealogizing his received values, he takes
a selective stance that takes account of the aims of those other selective
forces, but also "sees more" than they do—it selects from a wider set of
goods. By taking up into his new value of self selection both our natural
and social values, he assimilates their practical perspectives into his own.
So his values are less partial and less blind than prior values—they better
recognize the whole *sum* of values there are, by the valuings of humans
and other organisms.[146]

I'll return to this question of the "tone" of Nietzsche's valuing in
chapter 4, when I pursue the "aesthetic" character of his thought. Nietzsche
compares the "lie" in valuing to that in art—and means to embrace this
affinity in the way he values. For now what's important is that this lie is

145. On exercising this control of opposite perspectives see also BGE284, GM.iii.12,
and EH.i.1. EH.Z.6 says that Zarathustra is highest because he is most comprehensive
(quoting Z.iii.12.19).
146. I think Nietzsche means this comprehensive view in EH.BT.2: "This ultimate,
most joyous, most abundantly playful Yes to life is not only the highest insight, it is
also the *deepest*, the most strictly confirmed and supported by truth and science." He
calls this comprehensive stance "Dionysian"; see WP1041 [1888].

not the egregious one of "speaking of what is not," a lie that would rule out his values being still "truer" than others'. Nietzsche admits a kind of lie and injustice in even his own valuing, but a kind of lie that is overshadowed by the way his values are generated by a superior method for valuing, and (in *that* sense) are "truer" than other values. This shows us the middle ground between the extremes, of either renouncing all claims to truth in valuing, or claiming one's valuing to be true by matching values "in themselves."

3

Ethics-Politics

In the last chapter I argued that Nietzsche's primary value is freedom or self selection. This is a way for a person to be "toward him/herself." Nietzsche insists, generally, on the proper priority of this concern for oneself. But we may ask next: what consequences does this self-concerned aim at freedom have for the person's relations to other people? In this chapter I turn to Nietzsche's values(/v)[1] "toward others"—to the goals by which he governs relations to other people. Once again I think these values are clearer when we see them under his Darwinian aspect.

I will broadly sort Nietzsche's other-regarding values into (what I'll call) his "ethics" and his "politics." These will be the values governing, respectively, (a) how he means to feel and act toward (particular) other people, and (b) what he wants society to be like (how he wants it to be structured or organized). Nietzsche emphatically expresses values of both sorts. And in each case he clearly wants his readers—some of his readers at least, the ones he writes for—to take over his values for themselves. These values are—I think for many readers today—among the *least appealing* of his strong views.

1. Remember that I'm calling a studied value (a value-as-studied) a "value/s," and a valued value (a value as valued) a "value/v." When Nietzsche speaks *about* values in his genealogy, he means values/s; when he *expresses* values, he means values/v.

To focus my treatment of his ethics and politics, I'll examine a couple of particular values within each—or rather, a couple of particular *revaluings*, since in each case Nietzsche means to revise or replace a value he had taken for granted, and that he thinks his readers still do. In each case we therefore have a pair: the prevailing value and Nietzsche's revision of it, a revision he encourages us to emulate.

Within his ethics, I'll treat two personal traits he counts as virtues to govern his (and his readers') relations to others: **hardness** (*Härte*) and **selfishness** (*Selbstsucht*). These are, as it were, his basic policies or stances toward others. He means them to replace what seem to be opposite traits, which our prevailing values count as virtues instead: **pity** (*Mitleid*) and **altruism** (*Altruismus*). Nietzsche's attacks on these are quite pervasive. I think our ethical dissatisfactions with him are well represented by these attacks and revisions.[2]

Within his politics, I'll treat two societal traits he esteems as virtues for societies: **rank order** (*Rangordnung*) and **breeding** (*Züchten*). These are the basic policies or projects he wants the whole society to adopt. Again they replace their seeming opposites in our current values, the virtues for societies of **equality** (*Gleichheit*) and **civilizing** (*Civilisiren*) (which Nietzsche relabels "taming" [*Zähmung*]). His apparent preference for a society that "breeds inequalities" likewise catches the gist of our aversion to his politics.

In examining these particular values we'll test how well chapter 2's schematic account of freedom-by-genealogy applies to cases. Can we see how his genealogy of pity frees him to self select it—and why this self selection revalues it just as it does? In examining these specific revaluings, we can also address further metaethical questions. Does the genealogical insight (into, e.g., pity) somehow determine or require that revaluing—such that *every* self selector would or should choose hardness too? Does the basic value of freedom specify and settle the values that guide comportment toward others?

Now Nietzsche's set of ethical and political values reminds us very strongly of Social Darwinism. Indeed, I think we tend to interpret how he means these values in the light of that movement, and what we know of

When he calls something a value in the former sense, he means "someone values it"; when he calls it a value in the second, he means "I value it." (See chapter 2, section 5.)

   2. Schacht (1983, 359–62) singles out pity and selflessness as moral values that Nietzsche revalues. Nussbaum 1994 gives an extended analysis and critique of Nietzsche's attacks on pity.

its positions, policies, and social effects. We tend to hear his pronouncements in their spirit: we hold against him some of what we understand about them. To clarify Nietzsche's revaluings, it will be helpful, I think, to examine how close his positions really are to theirs.

In section 1, I'll take a first look at this relationship, surveying in particular those four revaluings and how they seem to link Nietzsche with these Darwinists, to his discredit. Then in the rest of the chapter I'll try to sort out more carefully both the affinities and differences, building on what we've already seen of his biology and metaethics. I will argue that the differences—and above all his novel ideal of self selection—manage to set his new values of hardness and selfishness, breeding and rank order in a more favorable light.

Nietzsche's ideal of self selection (or freedom through genealogy) affects his revaluings in two basic ways: (a) insofar as those revaluings need to be carried out in/by self selection; and (b) insofar as that revaluing first of all "chooses itself," i.e., chooses the values that preserve and improve this very freedom. Both points alter the force or sense of Nietzsche's ethical and political revaluings.

First, given chapter 2's account of his aspiration to freedom, we can see that Nietzsche wants to "self select" his ethical and political values, i.e., to choose them "in the light of" his genealogical insight into how such values *have been* made. Moreover, what he wants for his favored readers is that *they* self select their ethical and political values as well. So he does not, after all, want those readers simply to take those values over from him. If he does still hope they'll arrive at these values, it will be by choosing them on the basis of genealogical insights they achieve themselves.

This first role of self selection shows that Nietzsche's revaluings of pity and so on have a different intent than we thought. His principal purpose is not to transmit those values of hardness and so on, but to teach the method of freedom by genealogy—to spread the capacity to choose one's ethical and political values oneself. As we'll see, his most polemical and outrageous assaults on morality function chiefly to "free" us from our sedimented values and to enable us to self select new values. And to an extent, we'll see, Nietzsche expects each other "free spirit" to choose somewhat *different* values from his own. All of this shifts the point of Nietzsche's revaluings, and to their credit.

Second, however, this is not to say that in freedom "anything goes," nor that the self selector will choose any ethical and political values whatsoever. Choosing freely sets some constraints on the content chosen. Here the second role of self selection comes in: Nietzsche thinks the self selector will choose as his/her basic value self selection itself. The latter is not just the method for choosing, but the first end chosen: to continue and indeed enhance one's freedom (partly by extending the genealogical insight on which that freedom depends). As such a basic end, freedom helps to constrain the ethical and political values that then get selected. So Nietzsche justifies *some* of his revaluings as necessary means to preserve and to improve one's freedom—means that will or should be chosen by any self selector.

This second role of self selection also puts Nietzsche's new values in a better light, I will try to show. It gives his new personal virtues, hardness and selfishness, a very different point than we had thought, and than they have for Social Darwinists. He selects them as virtues to serve that new ultimate personal project: he "exapts" the preexisting traits (which we read them as) to make them more functional for that project. So the hardness and selfishness we need for freedom are unlike the virtues Social Darwinists have praised. And this point changes as well the sense of his societal virtues, rank order and breeding.

Besides his basic value of self selection Nietzsche has many other differences from these Darwinists, and some of the others will play important roles here as well. So there are other main points from chapters 1 and 2 that I'll recall for their bearing on the ethics and politics. These points include: Nietzsche's characterization of natural selection as prevalently designing a will to power into us; social selection as herding and opposing this will to power; and the discontinuity between natural and social selection, with the consequent deep conflict built into us. We'll see that each of these plays a large role in Nietzsche's revaluings.

Our best route to clarifying all of this—and answering the problems raised in section 1—is to turn to the particular genealogies Nietzsche gives for pity and altruism. His genealogies generally proceed, we've seen, through two stages—natural and social selection. So in section 2 I'll look at whether/how those social virtues get selected naturally, and in section 3 at how they are then exapted by social selection. And I'll compare this Nietzschean story with the Social Darwinists' account of how morality evolves.

These Darwinists hold that the development of these social virtues represents "progress," and that it shows us the way to progress still further. Nietzsche vehemently rejects this claim about progress, and even seems to dispute whether the notion itself is coherent. This raises the question of whether he thinks it's possible to "improve" on these virtues, especially at the level of whole societies. If he rejects progress, how can he hope or intend to improve our society's values? In section 4 I'll examine his critique of progress and argue that it leaves untouched kinds of personal and social progress in which he still believes.

Finally, in sections 5–6 I discuss Nietzsche's ethical and political re-valuings, in turn. I try to show how these issue out of his genealogies of our prevailing values, and how they are guided by his ideal of self selection in the two ways distinguished above. Because of these differences, both revaluings work very differently than the similar-sounding positions of Social Darwinists. Pity and altruism, breeding and rank order have different aims than we suspect, hence also different characters.

1. Links with Social Darwinism

Many readers may feel that Nietzsche's relation to Social Darwinism is a stale and unpromising topic—that it was well laid to rest (and thank goodness!) in an earlier stage of discussion. Once upon a time people stressed this affinity, and read Nietzsche in its light.[3] And beginners are still often tempted into this view. But we (who know more) are aware of the arguments he makes *against* Social Darwinists, which should be proof against making that connection.

I'm guessing that many Nietzsche readers now feel, in the wake of that earlier debate, something like the following. First, admittedly, Nietz-sche makes various stray remarks—mostly in his notebooks—that may suggest affinities with Social Darwinism (I'll get to some of them in a moment). But second, he also says, more clearly and decidedly, that he *rejects* their views. So Spencer, and the Darwinists generally, are among his favorite targets; he expresses scorn for them personally, and announces fundamental disagreements with their positions, and especially with their values.[4] So how can it be right to associate him with them?

3. Russell (1945, 769) offers as a "fair analysis" of Nietzsche's ethics: "Victors in war, and their descendants, are usually biologically superior to the vanquished. It is therefore desireable that they should hold all the power, and should manage affairs exclusively in their own interests." (On the next page Russell finds an affinity to "'rugged individualists' against trade-unions.")

4. GS373: "[A] humanity with such Spencerian perspectives as its ultimate perspec-tives would seem to us worthy of contempt, of annihilation!" Nietzsche calls Spencer "mediocre" (BGE253), a "decadent" (TI.ix. 37, WP53 [1888]); he attributes to him a

We also have more visceral reasons for disliking the topic. We feel that (later) Social Darwinists have been among the worst *misusers* of Nietzsche—cousins, in this, to the fascists, whose abuse of him long inhibited Anglo-American attention to him.[5] Social Darwinists (whose positions partially overlap with the fascists') likewise build, out of Nietzsche's stray remarks, an outlook on social questions that is not just contradicted by him elsewhere, but that also depicts him in a highly unflattering way.[6]

We allow, of course, that the evidence here is strongly split, as it is for so many other topics in Nietzsche. We see that he says things that link him unappealingly with Social Darwinists. But we feel that it would be discharity to make very much of them. Even if he does, in some moments or some moods, say these things, we should, in fairness to him, recognize that he also, in other and better-judging moments, says things that quite renounce and cancel them. And shouldn't we mainly take him in his best-considered views, and not dwell on temptations he elsewhere rejects?[7]

If we are specialists in Nietzsche, we are in various ways invested in finding positions that show him in a favorable light. And with Social Darwinism in such discredit, sympathetic interpreters have motives against so reading him. These motives make us, I suspect, more satisfied with the textual evidence there is against this reading than is really warranted. For they make us ignore the precise character of Nietzsche's criticisms of Social Darwinists—as well as some *agreements* he has but doesn't flag.

I don't want to criticize the motive of reading him sympathetically. I share it myself. My interest in reviving this connection is not to paint Nietzsche in such unflattering terms that we can write him off, even on this topic. Nor is it that I have a taste for the Social Darwinist ethics and politics myself, and think that stressing Nietzsche's links with them shows him in a favorable light, after all. I'm convinced that these links go very

"shopkeeper-philosophy" (*Krämer-Philosophie*) showing "complete absence of an ideal, apart from that of the average human" (WP382 [1887]; cf. WP944 [1888]).

   5. Compare Schutte's diagnosis and critique of this "historical reaction" (1984, 162ff.).

   6. See Hawkins (1997, 272–91) on the connection between fascism and Social Darwinism.

   7. The great and contradictory *variety* of things Nietzsche says on any topic gives interpretation unusual latitude. The motive of a sympathetic reading has more room in which to operate with Nietzsche than it does with more univocal philosophers. Caution is required, of course.

deep—but that his differences do as well; my claim is that to grasp the latter we need to take adequate account of the former.[8]

What *is* "Social Darwinism"?[9] A historical movement, of course. But I'll take it to be characterized by certain claims, which fit together into an overall argument. My primary interest will be in this argument—and its relations to Nietzsche's—not in the views of individual Social Darwinists. Still, there is one of these individuals I think we should keep in view. Herbert Spencer stands out in the attention Nietzsche pays him. While Nietzsche's access to Darwin was mainly indirect, he read Spencer carefully, and key parts of his conception of English Darwinism come out of this study.[10] So I'll look at a little of the detail of Spencer's position.[11] (I'll shelve the interesting question of how far Darwin himself was a Social Darwinist.)[12]

8. Nietzsche's vehement attacks on Social Darwinists disguise his important affinity with them. This is an instance of a wider syndrome. We can, as a rule, read the list of Nietzsche's enemies as the list of positions he has incorporated (important parts of) into his own. It's only where he shares—and indeed borrows—that he's persistently engaged in rebutting. It's only positions that are always (not just with but) *in* him that he feels steadily challenged to rise above. So with Darwinism.

9. See Hawkins (1997, 3ff.) on the difficulties in defining Social Darwinism, and 30ff. for his own proposal (the crucial element is the use of selection to explain humans' "social existence . . . [including] reason, religion, and morality"). This definition is more encompassing than my own—also more (I think) than the common use of the expression "Social Darwinism": it's not just an effort to give Darwinian explanations of "social existence," but to draw value lessons, in ethics and politics, about the importance of selection and competition.

10. Brobjer (unpublished) says that Spencer is "the British philosopher Nietzsche refers to most frequently"; he describes Nietzsche's intensive reading of (a German translation of) *The Data of Ethics* in 1880–1881. Nietzsche also read (again in translation) Spencer's *Introduction to the Study of Sociology*. Among the others who might be classed as Social Darwinists and whom Nietzsche read are Walter Bagehot and Ernst Haeckel.

11. This position is all the more interesting because Spencer was so very popular and influential a philosopher (or intellectual authority) in the late nineteenth century. I'll look closest at Spencer's views in *The Data of Ethics* (1879), since this seems to be what Nietzsche read most closely. It occurs as part I in *The Principles of Ethics* (as volume I, pp. 31–335 in the edition I cite; I'll cite these pages as, e.g., *Data* 31).

12. It's now usual to say that he was not—often from that same preference for a sympathetic reading. But he shares in more of these positions than supposed; cf. Richards 1988/1998. Consider *Descent* I/168: "We civilised men . . . do our utmost to check the process of elimination; we build asylums for the imbecile, the maimed, and the sick; we institute poor-laws; and our medical men exert their utmost skill to save the life of every one to the last moment. . . . Thus the weak members of civilised societies propagate their

The positions that I'll identify with Social Darwinism will be, I hope, a familiar lot. Their overall aim is to draw certain valuative conclusions from an evolutionary story that purports to be mainly factual. That is, in our terms from the end of the last chapter, they pass from the study of values/s, to the valuing of values/v—and they think they can justify this step.

Their evolutionary story has a number of important elements. Some of these are (I put them quickly and loosely): that evolutionary development occurs via natural selection; that natural selection works by the "survival of the fittest"—i.e., by the more fit reproducing in greater numbers than the less fit; that if such selection is disrupted, and factors intervene such that the unfit reproduce as well as the fit, then the line will stagnate or even regress.

On the basis of such claims from their evolutionary theory, Social Darwinists draw their familiar *valuative* conclusions. Societies need to be organized to let natural selection work—which means that they must be careful not to still or flatten that competition, or the differential benefits that both fuel it and make success in it pay off reproductively. The need for such competition requires that we impose certain limits on our sympathetic and altruistic impulses. And it shows we should favor a social structure that rewards competitive success and penalizes failure. It's natural, legitimate, and desirable that societies be tiered into winners and losers, and that we struggle to be winners ourselves.

Now, it might be asked whether these Social Darwinists, instead of arguing so bluntly from facts to values, don't instead rely on an implicit or explicit value premise, such as "survival is good," or "evolution (by selection) is good." They would in this way avoid the "naturalistic fallacy," it could be urged. However, I think this just pushes back the site of their step from is to ought—it doesn't keep them from making it. For they think of this basic value of survival or evolution as singled out and justified by their general facts about how species evolve. They think that when we understand species evolution we'll have reason to accept that basic value.

What disturbs us about Nietzsche is that he seems to reach quite similar valuative conclusions, and from a similar argument about selection.

---

kind. No one who has attended to the breeding of domestic animals will doubt that this must be highly injurious to the race of man." Also *Descent* II/403. Hawkins 1997 surveys (14ff.) the cases for and against calling Darwin a Social Darwinist, and argues (36) that he was—but as I've noted Hawkins's notion of Social Darwinism is more expansive than mine.

He too insists on competition, and on a deep, hard floor (no safety net) for failure in it. Those four ethical and political campaigns mentioned before—against pity and altruism, equality and taming—seem part and parcel with Social Darwinism.

Indeed, Nietzsche's view looks even worse. For he himself mainly *attacks* Spencer and other Darwinists as *too favorable* toward, e.g., pity.[13] He attacks them, disconcertingly, for an excess in valuing what *we* think they value far too little. We must not mistake his scorn for those views with our own, and infer from shared dissent to shared grounds.[14] He attacks them on pretty much the *opposite* grounds to those we have: he thinks they're too "soft," whereas we're convinced they're much too hard.[15] And here Nietzsche is more true to the real emphasis of Spencer's own work: his main aim is to *validate* altruism, as the upshot of an overall evolutionary progress. It's this main point that Nietzsche remarks, whereas we remember more Spencer's *hedges* or limits on that value.[16]

Now let's survey some of the things Nietzsche says that suggest his affinity with Social Darwinists. We should have fresh before us some samples of his disturbing views. I'll organize these by the four "revaluings" introduced above: in ethics, the conversions of pity into hardness and altruism into selfishness; in politics, those of equality into rank order and civilizing into breeding.

I'll be mainly interested in pity and altruism considered *as personal virtues*, hence within what I'm calling Nietzsche's ethics. However, his

13. Besides passages given below, see WP53 [1888].

14. There's this strangeness in, for example, Dennett's treatment (1995) of the point: he begins one of his chapters on Nietzsche by referring to GM's attack on Social Darwinists, then in the next paragraph offers the kinds of criticisms of them that I think come first to all of us: "it is 'natural' for the strong to vanquish the weak, and for the rich to exploit the poor. This is simply bad thinking" (461); "efforts by do-gooders to provide nurture for the least fortunate members of society . . . permit those to replicate whom nature would wisely cull. These are abominable ideas, but they were not the primary target of Nietzsche's criticism" (462). Dennett then goes on to develop Nietzsche's critique as against their "historical naiveté," "their Panglossian optimism about the ready adaptability of human reason (or Prudence) to morality." But this obscures the fact that Nietzsche attacks them *from the opposite side*, for giving *too much* credit to altruism and pity, rather than too little.

15. Here we see Nietzsche's affinity with the cantankerous conservatism of Maistre, of whom Berlin says (1953/1993, 50): "Both the content and the tone of his writing are closer to Nietzsche, d'Annuncio and the heralds of modern Fascism than to the respectable royalists of his own time."

16. See Richards (1988/1998, e.g., 596) on this common misconception of Spencer.

attack on pity and altruism extends into his politics as well. That is, he attacks them *as social practices* and seems to advocate a society practicing hardness and selfishness instead. It's these attacks that link him most clearly with Social Darwinists, so let's start here.

Nietzsche gives the very argument I identified Social Darwinism by: that such practices (pity and altruism) *subvert selection*, by artificially aiding the weak and sick and preventing their being "selected out." See first how Nietzsche uses this general kind of argument (not directly about pity or altruism). BGE62: "[S]*overeign* religions are among the chief causes that have kept the type 'human' on a lower rung — they have preserved too much of *what should perish*." And WP246 [1888]: "Christianity is the counter-principle *against selection.* . . . The species requires that the ill-constituted, weak, degenerate perish: but it was precisely to them that Christianity turned as a *conserving* force."[17]

Nietzsche applies this kind of argument to *pity* in A7: "[P]ity crosses the law of evolution, which is the law of *selection*. It preserves what is ripe for destruction; it defends those who have been disinherited and condemned by life"; it "crosses those instincts which aim at the preservation of life and at the enhancement of its value." And WP54 [1888]: "That virtue of which Schopenhauer still taught that it is the highest, the only virtue, and the basis of all virtues: even that pity I recognized as more dangerous than any vice. To cross fundamentally selection in the species, its purification of waste — that has so far been called virtue *par excellence*."[18]

He argues similarly against *altruism* in EH.iv.8: "In the concept of the *good* human one sides with all that is weak, sick, failed, suffering of itself, with all *that ought to perish* —, that crosses the law of *selection*." 13.14[5] [1888]: "[T]hat promotes a practice, which is the antithesis of species-interest. The altruism of Christianity is a *life-endangering* conception; it sets everyone equal to one another."[19]

17. 13.14[5] [1888]: "The dangerous antinaturalness of Christianity: / — it crosses selection." See also BGE259; WP734 [1888]. Compare Spencer's statement of the argument: "Any arrangements which in a considerable degree prevent superiority from profiting by the rewards of superiority, or shield inferiority from the evils it entails . . . are arrangements diametrically opposed to the progress of organization and the reaching of a higher life" (*Data* 219; see also 227).

18. Also WP52 [1888].

19. Compare Spencer: "[T]o say that each individual shall reap the benefits brought to him by his own powers, inherited and acquired, is to enunciate egoism as an ultimate principle of conduct. It is to say that egoistic claims must take precedence of altruistic claims" (*Data* 219). Elsewhere: "There is a notion, always more or less prevalent and just now vociferously expressed that all social suffering is removable, and that it is the

These attacks on pity and altruism as social practices are joined by attacks on them at the level of individuals—i.e., on ethical rather than political grounds. Nietzsche argues against these personal traits for how they bear on the individual alone, not as a social member. He warns against the sentiment of pity and altruistic aims as *incompatible with* the selfish, aggressive impulses that are the sources of all individual achievement. Characteristically, he argues this incompatibility in both directions, which gives him two distinct angles of attack on the other-regarding virtues.

So he has two main strategies for discrediting pity in the individual, for dissuading us from it. First, he diagnoses it as *expressing* weakness or sickness; so GS13: "Pity is the most agreeable feeling among those who have little pride and no prospects of great conquests."[20] Here he discredits pity by what it's an effect and symptom of: he attributes it to motives we don't want to have. Second, he warns that pity *weakens or sickens*, as at WP368 [1886–1887]: "Pity [is] a squandering of feeling, a parasite harmful to moral health."[21] Here he discredits it by its *results*.[22] These two patterns of argument are pervasive in Nietzsche.

He argues in the same two-pronged way against altruism. First, altruism expresses weakness; so WP373 [1888]: "The preponderance of an altruistic mode of valuation is the consequence of an instinct for being ill-constituted. The value judgment at bottom says here: 'I am not worth

duty of somebody or other to remove it. Both these beliefs are false. To separate pain from ill-doing is to fight against the constitution of things, and will be followed by far more pain" (*Data* 32). He goes on to say (33) that science confirms the Christian view that "if any would not work neither should he eat," by "the law that a creature not energetic enough to maintain itself must die"; this is "a natural necessity." See Hofstadter 1944/ 1955 on Spencer's "ultra-conservative" political lessons—"Spencer deplored not only poor laws, but also state-supported education, sanitary supervision other than the suppression of nuisances, regulation of housing conditions, and even state protection of the ignorant from medical quacks" (41)—and the reception of his views in the United States.

20. GS338 treats pity as an easy way, reflecting a "religion of comfortableness," and flight from the rigors of keeping to one's "own way." EH.i.4: "[Neighbor love] counts for me as a weakness, a case of being incapable of resisting stimuli, — *pity* is called a virtue only among decadents." More elaborately, pity is presented as expressing "slave morality"; e.g., BGE260.

21. A7: "Pity stands opposed to the tonic affects, which heighten the energy of the feeling of life: it has a depressing effect. One loses strength, when one pities." GM.P.5: "I understood the ever spreading morality of pity that had seized even on philosophers and made them ill, as the most sinister symptom of a European culture that had itself become sinister." See again GS338; also D134, D137, A2.

22. He argues that it's harmful to the pitier, and also that it doesn't really help the pitied, in particular because it ignores "the personal necessity of distress" (GS338).

much': a merely physiological value judgment."[23] Second, altruism damages our interests. To make everyone altruistic "means to take from existence its *great* character, [it] means to castrate humanity" (EH.iv.4).[24]

We're troubled not only by these attacks on pity and altruism, but by what Nietzsche proposes to replace them with. In place of pity he preaches *hardness*, and in place of altruism *selfishness*. He appeals to us to control our sensitivity to suffering, our own or others', and to become "hard," "warlike," and so on.[25] And he commends to his readers a "healthy selfishness." So in Z.iii.10, Zarathustra "pronounced *selfishness* blessed, the wholesome, healthy selfishness that wells from a powerful soul." And in BGE265: "[E]goism belongs to the essence of a noble soul, I mean that unshakable faith that to a being such as 'we are' other beings must be subordinate by nature and have to sacrifice themselves."[26]

Turning from Nietzsche's ethics for individuals to his politics, consider his attacks on equality and civilizing (taming). He takes these to be our prevailing "societal virtues," i.e., ways we want society to be (or ways our society wants itself to be). "Equality" names a way for society to be structured (or its members to be related to one another). "Civilizing" names a way society shapes its members into proper parts of itself. Again, Nietzsche's attack on these prevailing virtues strikes nerves in us.

Against equality, he argues in that same dual fashion. He gives us two kinds of reasons not to count it a virtue in societies. First, equality (as a societal virtue or value) *expresses* the society's weakness or sickness. So TI.ix.37: "'Equality,' as a certain factual becoming-similar-to [*Anähnlichung*], that finds expression in the theory of 'equal rights,' belongs essentially to decline."[27] In particular, this value of equality expresses the herd

---

23. TI.ix.35: "An 'altruistic' morality, a morality in which selfishness *atrophies* —, remains a bad sign under all circumstances. This is so for individuals, it is especially so for peoples." Also WP785 [1887].

24. 9.6[74] [1880]: "The dominance of altruism seems to me to ruin [*zu Grunde zu richten*] humanity — a process of dying-off, euthanasia."

25. BGE260: "'A hard heart Wotan put into my breast,' says an old Scandinavian saga.... Such a type of man is actually proud of the fact that he is *not* made for pity. ... Noble and courageous human beings who think that way are furthest removed from that morality which finds the distinction of morality precisely in pity, or in acting for others, or in *désintéressement*." EH.i.4: "The overcoming of pity I count among the *noble* virtues."

26. See HH.iii.285 on selfishness as a precondition for the virtues. Also BGE2.

27. 9.6[163] [1880]: "[T]he common and *equal* human is only so desired, because the weak human fears the strong individual and wills rather the *general weakening*, instead of evolution to individuals."

instinct.[28] Second, equality (again, taken as a societal virtue) *makes* the society weak or sick. WP354 [1888]: "[I]t seems to be all over for a kind of human (people, race) when it becomes tolerant, allows equal rights and no longer thinks of willing to be master."[29] Nietzsche's many attacks on democracy and socialism also express this hostility to equality as a supposed virtue for societies.[30]

Against "civilizing"—which he often calls "taming" or "domesticating"[31]—he makes the same two arguments. First, civilizing (practiced as a societal virtue) *expresses* weakness. We want society to civilize our fellow members, because we're "threatened" by (i.e., fearful and envious of) their outbursts of drive energy.[32] Second, civilizing *renders* us weak. So A22: "Christianity wills to become master over *beasts of prey*; its method is to make them *sick*, — weakening is the Christian recipe for *taming*, for 'civilizing'." WP864 [1888]: "[I]ncreasing civilization . . . necessarily brings along with it the increase of morbid elements, the *neurotic-psychiatric* and the *criminal*."[33]

Again Nietzsche proposes new virtues to replace these—and again these positive views seem only to reinforce our distaste for his critique. In place of equality, he preaches rank order. BGE221: "One must force moralities to bow first of all before *rank-order*, . . . until they finally become clear with one another that it is *immoral* to say: 'what is right for one is fair for the other.'"[34] He prefers an "aristocracy" that seems to involve sharp inequalities of economic, political, and other kinds. Indeed, he speaks favorably of a "new slavery." BGE257: "Every elevation of the type 'human being' has so far been the work of an aristocratic society — and

28. WP925 [1888]: "[I]t is the *instinct of the herd* that finds its formula in it [the golden rule] — one is equal, one takes oneself for equal: as I to you, so you to me."
29. WP871 [1887–1888]: "Here the concept of the *'equal value* of humans *before God'* is extraordinarily harmful."
30. Against socialism: 8.25[1] [1877].
31. GM.i.11 speaks of "breeding out of the beast of prey 'human' a tame and civilized animal, a *house-animal* [*Hausthier*]." He also links "civilizing" and "taming" at GM.iii.13, A22; also 12.9[142] [1887], WP121 [1888].
32. See again GM.i.11.
33. GM.ii.15: "[P]unishment *tames* humans, but does not make them 'better' — one might with more justice assert the opposite." WP397 [1888]: "The taming of a beast is in most cases achieved through the harming of the beast: likewise the moralized [*vermoralisirte*] human is not a better human, but only a weaker one." 12.2[56] [1885–1886]: "*Corruption* of the forceful primitive human [*Naturmenschen*] [occurs] under constraint of the civilized state." See too GM.ii.16, GM.iii.21, TI.vii.2; also WP395 [1886–1887].
34. See also BGE62 and BGE228.

it will be so again and again: a society, which believes in a long ladder of the rank-order and difference in value between human and human, . . . needs slavery in some sense or other."[35]

And in place of civilizing he preaches breeding, which seems to mean *not* relying just on social selection (training) and the habits it superimposes on drives, but trying to control reproduction in ways to breed those drives themselves—so that people will stand in that rank order. We need to take charge of human evolution. A3: "The problem I thus pose is not what shall redeem humanity in the succession of beings [*Wesen*] (— the human is an end —): but what type of human one should *breed*, should *will*, as of higher value, worthier of life, surer of a future."[36] This breeding means *eugenics*, of which Nietzsche advocates both positive and negative methods: to help the really valuable to reproduce more, and to encourage the harmful or unworthy to reproduce less.[37]

It's because of passages like these that Nietzsche has appealed to later Social Darwinists, many of whom have cited his influence.[38] Together, these affinities put his ethical-political views in a very unappealing light. We fault both his arguments and his results: the former are flimsy, the latter horrific. However, I think that when we dig deeper into his positions we find conclusions less starkly disagreeable and arguments more instructive if not compelling. These details open up a clearer gap between Nietzsche and the Social Darwinists.

2. Roots of Pity and Altruism in Natural Selection?

To understand and assess Nietzsche's positions here, we need to look much more carefully at what he thinks pity and altruism are, and at his

35. GS377: "[W]e think about the necessity for new orders, also for a new slavery — for every strengthening and elevation of the type 'human being' also involves a new kind of enslavement."

36. See TI.vii.2–5 on the contrast between taming and breeding. But Nietzsche sometimes uses "taming" (*Zähmung*) to mean (I think) this breeding; WP398 [1888]: "[T]here is no worse confusion than when one confuses taming with weakening. . . . / Taming, as I understand it, is a means of storing up the tremendous forces of humanity, so that the generations can build upon the work of their ancestors — not only outwardly, but inwardly, organically growing out of them, into something *stronger*."

37. E.g., GS73 seems to favor killing a "wretched, misshapen" child. Also 8.23[59] [1876–1877]. See Moore (2002, 5f.) on the reception of Nietzsche's ideas by later eugenicists.

38. Cf. Strong (1996, 127).

genealogical story about how and why we have them. For it's precisely this genealogy that will orient self selection's choice about these values. (I'll defer until section 6 the parallel questions about the society-level virtues, equality and civilizing.) I'll try to show how Nietzsche's genealogical story gives him a new account of the self and its selfishness, against which pity and altruism then react.

So first, what *are* pity and altruism? Nietzsche is after, of course, not a definition to capture the ordinary meaning of these terms, but a naturalistic account of what's really there, in the vicinity where we apply them. By his usual ontology for organisms (analyzed in chapter 1), he thinks of pity and altruism as ultimately particular *drives*, in the general sense of dispositions or propensities. Generally, pity is the ingrained habit of *feeling* (about others) a certain way, and altruism is the habit of *acting* (toward others) a certain way. To determine these habits, we must specify these ways of feeling and acting.

What way of feeling is *pity* (*Mitleid*)? First, its broader genus is *sympathy* (*Mitgefühl* or *Sympathie*), which is "feeling as another feels"—though we must take this as the feeling's *intent*, not necessarily its achievement. Indeed, Nietzsche sometimes denies that people *ever do* feel the same as one another (whereas elsewhere he insists that they do, to their detriment). So sympathy is defined as a project: *trying and taking oneself* to feel as another feels.[39] And pity, which is Nietzsche's main concern, is just one kind of sympathy, because it tries to share in just one kind of feeling—the other's *suffering* (*Leiden*).[40] We'll see that Nietzsche objects to *Mitleid* on the ground of several of these essential elements: to the way it is *mit* (i.e., seeks to share), to the way it is *Leid* (i.e., shares suffering), and even to the way it is a feeling (passively experienced).

Whereas pity is (a drive or habit for) a feeling, *altruism* (*Altruismus*) is a policy or practice for behaving or acting—not merely undergone, but carried out. Like pity, we can treat it as falling under a genus, which I'll

39. WP279 [1886–1887] speaks of the inertia "in sympathy. It is a relief to make oneself the same, to try to feel the same, to *adopt* an existing feeling." D142, speaking of empathy (*Mitempfindung*), describes our great skill in imitating the feelings of others.

40. Again, Nietzsche sometimes denies that one ever feels the same (kind of) suffering. D133: "That pity . . . is the *same kind of thing* [*einartig*] as the suffering at the sight of which it arises, or that it possesses an especially subtle, penetrating understanding of suffering, are both contradicted by *experience*." Also HH.i.104, GS338. 9.2[52] [1880] extends this point against altruism. Note, by contrast, that Spencer's main term is "sympathy," which he uses in that broader way; we'll see it's important for his argument that it includes feeling not just pain but pleasure with another.

call "benevolence" (*Wohlwollen*); this is any policy directed at aiding or improving others. Altruism is then specifically the practice of benefiting others *instead of* oneself. Altruism, in other words, involves a perceived or intended *sacrifice* in one's own interests, in order to advance another's: one *limits* pursuit of one's interests (if only to the extent of paying no attention to them).[41] It's this attitude of self-sacrifice that Nietzsche will hold against altruism, whereas he will extol what he calls "the giving virtue."

We've noted that Nietzsche's main interest is not in the feeling of pity, nor in the altruistic act, but in what we might call the dispositions or tendencies to feel or act so. These drives or habits explain the events or episodes in which we so feel or act. Nietzsche then asks what explains these dispositions in turn. Why *do* we have these drives or habits or practices of pity and altruism? Genealogy uncovers what these dispositions were selected for; by it we find their hidden aim and point, for which many of their particular features turn out to be covertly functional.

Now as we saw in chapter 1, Nietzsche's genealogies of dispositions usually begin with a quasi-Darwinian natural selection: drives are initially designed as bodily propensities enhancing the fitness of the organism, i.e., its capacity for (what we now know to be) genetic copying. As we saw in chapter 2, these drives are then redesigned—or a second level of dispositions superimposed upon them—in the *social* phase of our species. Practices and habits are selected for their capacity at (what we call) memetic copying, which redesigns them for the group's cohesion. How has this two-stepped selection evolved our practices of pity and altruism in particular?

Put most simply, Nietzsche's claim is that pity and altruism evolve *only* by social selection—and *not* by natural selection, as he thinks Spencer believes. Of course natural selection makes various antecedents of these values—raw materials for them—but it's only the new memetic or social selection that generates these values themselves. Under natural selection, organisms are instead made to be "hard" and "selfish." So pity and altruism function originally for the special structural ends of social selection—for the sake of "herding" us, especially. One of Nietzsche's key complaints against Social Darwinists is that they've failed to recognize the special logic of this social process. (We should bear in mind a subtext in this disagreement about whether pity and altruism are selected naturally: Nietzsche implicitly concurs—though this may be only a rhetorical or

---

41. WP785 [1887]: "The disposition [*Gesinnung*] of altruism, thorough and without tartuffery, is an instinct for creating at least a *secondary value* for oneself, in service of *other* egoisms." (The note goes on to say that altruism is usually only apparent.)

polemical move—with Spencer's supposition that *natural selection legiti-mates*, i.e., that it counts in favor of a trait or behavior if it is rooted in such selection. So Spencer establishes the presence of altruism in all organisms, as a way to legitimate it, whereas Nietzsche denies or reduces its presence there, to delegitimate it. This is also the force of his argument that natural selection really breeds selfishness instead. I'll return to the question of how far he credits natural selection in section 4.)

Now Spencer finds altruistic conduct at the heart of life itself—in its very reproductivity. The parent sacrifices matter and effort to its off-spring: "[A]mong creatures of higher grades [than the protozoan], by fission or gemmation, parents bequeath parts of their bodies, more or less organized, to form offspring at the cost of their own individualities" (*Data* 232).[42] Altruism runs the gamut from these "lowest," unconscious, and automatic acts, up through birds and mammals where it becomes conscious (as we see from their display of emotions over offspring), and finally to human beings' conscious self-sacrifice. Altruism arises by selection and evolves up this scale because its higher levels render organisms more and more fit.

Nietzsche opposes Spencer's effort to build altruism into this crux of life (its reproductivity). 9.6[137] [1880]: "*Quite false* with *Spencer* to see in the care of the brood [*Brut*] and already in procreation an expression of the altruistic drive."[43] 9.1[110] [1880]: "The begetting [*Erzeugung*] of a posterity [*Nachkommenschaft*] is not altruistic. . . . The sacrifice for the brood is sacrifice for the own-closest [*Eigen-Nächste*]."[44] Instead of altruism, Nietz-sche claims, natural selection breeds selfishness.[45]

Put broadly this way, Nietzsche's view looks more like Spencer's than he admits. For Spencer stresses that *egoism* is even more basic and indispensable to life than altruism: "[E]thics has to recognize the truth,

42. Spencer gives this sense for altruism: "all action which, in the normal course of things, benefits others instead of benefiting self" (*Data* 231). In all cases he thinks it involves a sacrifice of "bodily substance," since every effort on another's behalf involves "waste of tissue" (*Data* 233).

43. In WP653 [1887] Nietzsche attacks the interpretation of propagation as altru-ism—but replaces it with another implausibility: that propagation is a "throwing off of ballast." See also WP680 [1886–1887].

44. Also 9.6[164] [1880], WP653 [1887].

45. He similarly argues that hardness (*Härte*) rather than pity is the "natural" virtue. WP52 [1888]: "Nature is not immoral when it is without pity for the degenerate: the growth of physiological and moral ills [*Übel*] in the human species is by contrast the *conse-quence of a sick and unnatural morality*." But he gives a fuller argument, and I think a more basic one, on behalf of selfishness in place of altruism, so I'll focus here.

recognized in unethical thought, that egoism comes before altruism" (*Data* 217).[46] Natural selection works, indeed, by the fitter organisms (selfishly) reaping the benefits of their fitness: "The uniform principle has been that better adaptation shall bring greater benefit; which greater benefit, while increasing the prosperity of the better adapted, shall increase also its ability to leave offspring inheriting more or less its better adaptation" (*Data* 218). And on this ground Spencer warns against "unduly subordinating" egoism to altruism: "Sentient beings have progressed from low to high types, under the law that the superior shall profit by their superiority and the inferior shall suffer from their inferiority" (*Data* 227). This association of natural selection with egoism—the notion that it tends to make organisms selfish, and that this justifies selfishness—is another part of Social Darwinism as we conceive it.

But of course Nietzsche knows that Spencer credits egoism in these ways,[47] and means to say that he doesn't go far enough—or even in the right direction. Spencer errs not just by dragging in altruism, but because he gets wrong the character of this basic selfishness. His view of it is distorted by his plan that it progress into altruism, as well as by such metaphysical errors as belief in the ego. Nietzsche thinks there are many more "selfish selves" at work in organisms—many different levels and kinds of selfishness built into them. Spencer conflates these many interested selves into a unified ego, because he's in thrall to a certain ideology (faith in the ego) selected both naturally and socially. The real challenge is to analyze this complex of competing self-interests.

A first self-interest is the one lodged, as it were, in natural selection itself. It is a thing's interest in "getting selected," i.e., in successfully replicating itself into the next generations; the thing has this "interest" by having

46. Spencer's main ground: "The acts which make continued life possible, must, on the average, be more peremptory than all those other acts which life makes possible; including the acts which benefit others" (*Data* 227). Note that *Data*, chapters 11–14, offers an extended account of the conflict between egoism and altruism, and their "conciliation"—a story it will be fruitful to compare with Nietzsche's.

47. WP784 [1887]: "[O]ne goes further, one seeks the *higher utility* in the preference of the egoistic viewpoint over the altruistic. . . . Thus: a preponderance of the rights of the ego, but under an extreme altruistic perspective ('total advantage of humanity') / one tries to reconcile the *altruistic* way of acting with *naturalness*, one seeks altruism in the ground of life; one seeks egoism like altruism as equally grounded in the essence of life and nature / one dreams of a disappearance of the antithesis in some future, when, through continual adaptation, egoism is at the same time altruism."

that end, i.e., by having been designed for that outcome. All of its adaptations are ultimately functional for such reproductive success. As we've seen, Nietzsche insists that this project is selfish (preserving itself in the other), rather than altruistic (giving to the other at its own expense). By this design organic parts and processes are all ultimately "for" a selfish outcome.

As we saw in chapter 1, Nietzsche treats selection as operating at several levels: it works on drives, on organisms, and on species or lineages. So each of these units of selection has this kind of selfish interest in its own replicative success—each has been designed for such success. A drive's features, including its goal, are designed to enable it to copy itself. Similarly the individual, as a complex of many such drives, is selected for the mutual fitness and effectiveness of these drives—for the system's ability to persist and copy itself. Finally, the whole lineage is selected for its capacity to persist and grow through generations of individuals. Natural selection designs "selves" at all three levels for and toward their own reproductive interest.

Nietzsche recognizes these selfishnesses involved in selection, but is more anxious to insist on a different kind of selfishness that issues out of it. Every drive is selected because it is reproductively fit, or serves the reproductive fitness of the organism or lineage. But each drive serves this fitness by being responsive and plastic toward some more concrete outcome: its particular function or goal. This outcome has aided reproduction *for the most part* in the population over time, though in some or many cases it is ineffective or even harmful. But the drive will pursue that outcome *even* in those cases: it is responsive toward the goal, but not toward the end (reproduction) for which the goal was selected. And Nietzsche often treats the drive's selfishness as aimed at this goal, rather than that end.[48]

I think it's this kind of selfishness he has in mind when he argues, as he often does, that some action is egoistic *because* it is caused by a drive: that source, just by itself, establishes selfishness. HH.i.57: "The *inclination for* [*Neigung zu*] *something* (wish, drive, desire) is present in all the mentioned cases [of love and seeming sacrifice]; to give in to it, with all the

---

48. This is connected with what we saw in chapter 2, section 2, that Nietzsche often takes drives' "values" to lie more in their goals than in the ultimate selective end; the latter, he prefers to put it, gives the "meaning" of those values, but is not itself valued because the drive is not "responsive" toward it.

consequences, is in any event not 'unegoistic'."[49] The selfishness lies not in the drive's design to replicate itself, but in its more immediate relation to its particular goal.

Why does the drive's effort at its goal count as selfish? Nietzsche counts it so because he thinks of the drive as pursuing its own "satisfaction" (*Befriedigung*) in that goal. This is, as it were, the character or structure of drives generally—how natural selection has designed them to work. They pursue the fitness-improving outcome most effectively by finding their satisfaction in it. Similarly the organism, as a system of these drives, selfishly pursues satisfaction of that system. So even a drive to help others is covertly egoistic, because one acts on it *in order* to satisfy it. And even though the behavior is also "in order" to help others, Nietzsche suggests that this other-interest is underlain and supported by that deeper self-interest in satisfying the drive.[50]

In his middle works (in the 1870s) Nietzsche treats this satisfaction as *pleasure*, so that the selfishness of drives and organisms is a kind of hedonism. The drive is plastic and responsive toward this pleasure, not the ultimate selective end. It's in this sense that Nietzsche says the sex drive aims at sexual pleasure, not at reproducing; 9.6[145] [1880]: "And there is no drive to will to preserve the species. . . . Generation is a matter of pleasure: its result is propagation." Similarly pity aims, according to HH.i.103, at "the pleasure of the emotion" and "the pleasure of gratification in the exercise of power," not at the other's pleasure.[51]

In his later (and more characteristic) view, the weight shifts from pleasure to *power*: drives have the structural aim not at mere pleasant release, but at the power their exercise involves. Drives satisfy themselves in power. GS13: "In benefiting and hurting one exercises his power on others — one wills no more than that!"[52] The pleasure in satisfying drives

49. HH.i.133: "[H]ow, indeed, should [a human] *be able* to do something, that had no reference [*Bezug*] to himself, hence without inner compulsion [*Nöthigung*] (which would have to have its ground in a personal need [*Bedürfniss*])?"

50. 9.6[141] [1880]: "Procreation is a commonly occurring incidental result of *one* kind of satisfaction of a sexual drive: *not* its intention, not its necessary working."

51. Similarly, D133 says that in pitying we "give way . . . to a *drive of pleasure* [*Antriebe der Lust*]," and goes on to list some forms this can take.

52. WP689 [1888]: "[S]triving is nothing other than striving after power." WP786 [1887]: "[F]inally, one grasps that altruistic actions are only a *species* of egoistic [actions], — and that the degree to which one loves, spends oneself, is proof of the degree of individual *power* and *personality*."

is (Nietzsche now thinks) just a side effect of the feeling of power. WP688 [1888]: "[P]leasure is only a symptom of the feeling of power attained, a consciousness of a difference — / — it does not strive after pleasure, but pleasure occurs, when it attains what it strives after: pleasure accompanies, pleasure does not motivate [*bewegt*]." So now the drive's selfishness lies in its designed plasticity toward its power in reaching its goal.

This analysis shows a much more complex selfishness than Spencer recognizes. Spencer's faith in the ego—that an organism and especially a person is a wholly single and united thing—lets him find a single selfishness that works by guiding deliberation and choice. This single and deliberative self can then be led to altruism. Nietzsche, by contrast, finds a welter of selves and interests—and finds them in drives that are not susceptible to being so led. Moreover, he will argue that this selfishness in the drives is indispensable for the organism's (person's) overall health. So his account of our natural selfishness embeds it far more deeply in us than Spencer's does.

3. Formation by Social Selection

The next question is how Nietzsche thinks the virtues of pity and altruism do arise, against the background of this natural selfishness. Like Spencer, he thinks that these values evolve within a *social* context; indeed, he takes over some main points in Spencer's account. But Spencer treats that "social evolution" as largely continuous with natural selection—merely operating at the level of groups, not individuals. Nietzsche finds a new logic at work in social selection—a logic that designs us for ends we don't at all suspect. He thinks Spencer misses this logic, and hence is subject to it: Spencer's own positions on pity and altruism are explained (not by an access to the truth, but) by the social processes that designed those virtues for us. And this different design reflects very differently on these virtues than Spencer can see.

a. Spencer: Selection Progresses to Sympathy and Altruism

Let me sketch here the Social Darwinist story which Nietzsche modifies. This story, as Spencer for example tells it, is largely familiar to us.

Spencer begins by extending to human behavior[53] and to the psychological traits it expresses the Darwinian strategy of explanation by natural selection. Selection designs behavior to serve our survival (and reproduction), and does so especially by shaping our "feelings"—which Spencer thinks supply the motives for action (*Data* 139). In particular, the feeling of pleasure is attached to behavior that serves survival, the feeling of pain to behavior that endangers it. So *Data* 115: "At the very outset, life is maintained by persistence in acts which conduce to it, and desistance from acts which impede it; and whenever sentiency makes its appearance as an accompaniment, its forms must be such that in the one case the produced feeling is of a kind that will be sought—pleasure, and in the other case is of a kind that will be shunned—pain."

Spencer then applies this explanatory strategy to our social or moral feelings, in particular. He gives an extended account of how pleasure has been attached in this way to the feeling of *sympathy* and to the practice of *altruism*—attached because of the ways they aid (Darwinian) survival. As noted before, this happens to an extent for all organisms: reproduction itself is a kind of altruism, a sacrifice of material resources by the parent. From this primitive case Spencer finds a continuum of cases rising up to our human altruism: "As there has been an advance by degrees from unconscious parental altruism to conscious parental altruism of the highest kind, so has there been an advance by degrees from the altruism of the family to social altruism" (*Data* 234). Evolution ascends in a straight line, even though the selective processes work a bit differently in the human case.

The higher, human levels of altruism are produced by what Spencer calls "social evolution"—by selection working in the social context that crucially characterizes humans. Although some other species form societies, "our own species is, on the whole, to be distinguished as having a formula for complete life which specially recognizes the relations of each individual to others, in presence of whom, and in cooperation with whom, he has to live" (*Data* 166). Sympathy and altruism have evolved in tandem with this social life, to facilitate it.

The chief difference Spencer recognizes in this social context is that evolution works by (what we now call) *group selection*. That is, selection works on a new "unit," not the individual organism but the group. Societies

53. Spencer's term is "conduct," defined as "either—acts adjusted to ends, or else— the adjustment of acts to ends; according as we contemplate the formed body of acts, or think of the form alone" (*Data* 39).

compete against societies and are "designed" for this. Members are likewise designed for the society's success, and not merely for their own.

Darwin had already introduced such group selection at just this point. He used it to solve a puzzle which he presciently recognized: how could altruism, understood as involving a sacrifice in fitness (reproductive prospects), ever have been selected? Darwin's answer was that we're altruists because *groups* with more altruists were more successful than groups with fewer—even if individual altruists did worse than egoists within the same group.[54]

Similarly, Spencer thinks that social altruism arose in a period when competing groups—groups in fact at war with one another—could only succeed and survive by subordinating the individual's welfare to the group's. So political, religious, and social factors that control the individual "have evolved with the evolution of society, as a means to social self-preservation" (*Data* 153).

Sympathy and altruism are products of this process. Social (as opposed to parental) altruism evolves to serve the group. And this behavior is assured or reinforced by selection attaching certain feelings and pleasures to it. Sympathy in particular evolves in this way (*Data* 273ff.); it gives us an egoistic interest in behaving altruistically. "From the laws of life it must be concluded that unceasing social discipline will so mold human nature, that eventually sympathetic pleasures will be spontaneously pursued to the fullest extent advantageous to each and all" (*Data* 278).

However, Spencer thinks this is only the *first* social setting. The evolution of sympathy and altruism eventually changes this selective context by bringing societies into a peaceful "industrial" age. The process that operated within societies increasingly also works between them: "[A]s fast as the dependence of societies on one another is increased by commercial intercourse, the internal welfare of each becomes a matter of concern to the others" (*Data* 246). The culmination will be a world of societies permanently at peace with one another (*Data* 53). In the absence of external opponents, that group selection will cease. The need for individual sacrifices to the welfare of the group will wither away, and individual welfare will become supreme.

Spencer sees this as a matter of an ultimate end achieving a priority it (in a sense) had long deserved. Even in those early conditions of social

54. *Descent* I/82: "In however complex a manner this feeling [sympathy] may have originated, as it is one of high importance to all those animals which aid and defend each other, it will have been increased, through natural selection; for those communities,

conflict, "social self-preservation" was merely a "proximate aim taking precedence of the ultimate aim, individual self-preservation" (*Data* 167). Spencer thinks individual welfare has always been ultimate, because he thinks of group selection as reducible to individual selection: group survival counts, because it's the survival of the most individuals.[55] But so long as societies fight one another, they must constrain their members to sacrifice their interests to the group's. In the future world at peace, the need for these constraints on individual self-interest will cease.[56] However, by that point individuals will have been designed to take pleasure in the well-being of others, so that they will continue to find their self-interest in altruism (*Data* 335). This will result in what Spencer calls the "conciliation" of egoism and altruism.

b. *Nietzsche's Critical Genealogy for Pity and Altruism*

Nietzsche accepts a surprising amount of this Darwinian story—but insists on retelling key parts of it in ways that give it a quite different effect. He shares, in particular, the (unsurprising) idea that it's humans' social context that has been decisive in evolving pity and altruism. He also shares the idea that selection now works at the level of societies as well as individuals and that in designing societies it designs individuals as functional members of them. But he has a different account of how this social design works—and of what kind of members it most favors. Moreover, he uses that social design to explain not only Spencer's explananda, but Spencer's explanations as well.

The kernel of this difference is, I claim, Nietzsche's analysis of the new kind of copying (replicating) that emerges in this social context—and that principally shapes this context. This copying is not genetic but mimetic

which included the greatest number of the most sympathetic members, would flourish best and rear the greatest number of offspring." See too *Descent* I/162.

55. *Data* 167: "As fast as the social state establishes itself, the preservation of the society becomes a means of preserving its units. Living together arose because, on the average, it proved more advantageous to each than living apart; and this implies that maintenance of combination is maintenance of the conditions to more satisfactory living than the combined persons would otherwise have."

56. *Data* 180: "In proportion as societies endanger one another less, the need for subordinating individual lives to the general life, decreases; and with approach to a peaceful state, the general life, having from the beginning had furtherance of individual lives as its ultimate purpose, comes to have this as its proximate purpose."

or "memetic": dispositions are transmitted not "in the blood" (as he puts it) but by imitation. Gradually a kind of animal is bred that can transmit and acquire habits or practices by such social copying. And as such practices become able to spread through a social medium, a new selection arises for them: selection as to *how well* they can copy themselves this way. So practices are selected to be "habit forming" and are progressively designed to be maximally so.

These practices are *partly* selected, of course, to serve the survival or expansion of their medium, the social group. Practices can succeed through the success of the group they inhabit; they depend on its surviving and can spread by its growing. So of course they will also, often, have been selected to help the society succeed. Here Nietzsche has common ground with the Darwinists and their explanation by group selection. Selection works not just between practices, but between societies. And individuals are designed, in part, to serve the group's success.[57]

Spencer, we've seen, is already concerned about how group selection subordinates individual self-interest to the interest of the group. He awaits a higher stage of society, a peaceful global society in which self-interest can be deconstrained. But Nietzsche's view of group selection is much grimmer. He diagnoses two further, disturbing features in it, which rule out the happy resolution Spencer expects.

First, he has a different theory about what traits, in particular, enable groups to survive and expand. The most important virtue is unity: how well the parts cohere into a whole. And this cohesion is achieved, above all, by a homogeneity in the members—a homogeneity that consists in their *sharing practices*. So the selection operating over groups will tend to design into members an instinct for this sharing.[58] Nietzsche thinks societies tighten or loosen these bonds in response to circumstances: they become more cohesive and homogeneous in the face of dangers and difficulties; they become less so in their "old age," or at peace.[59]

Second, Nietzsche rests this group selection in a memetic selection, which reinforces this insistence on sharing. Practices aren't selected just

57. We saw in chapter 2, section 3, how both the ethic of custom and morality evolve to serve the group's preservation and growth. See n. 38 there.

58. BGE268: "The more similar, the more common humans were and always are better off." (Note though that here it's selection over individuals that Nietzsche credits: an individual is fitter, by being more similar to his/her neighbors.) Cf. GS354.

59. See especially BGE262: "[T]he kind [*Art*] needs itself as a kind, as something that can prevail and make itself durable by virtue of its hardness, uniformity [*Gleichförmig-keit*], and simplicity of form, in a constant fight with its neighbors." (Compare 11.35[22]

to "serve" society (with its replicative ends of survival and growth). Practices are also designed to shape society into a more favorable medium for their own propagation. So practices are designed to habituate individuals to share their habits with one another. The most successful practices are those that help to bind us up into a "herd," through which they can more effectively disperse. Herd practices are an "evolutionarily stable strategy," in Maynard Smith's expression;[60] they resist "invasion" by new practices, which are discredited by their own rarity.

Social selection—Darwinian group selection modified in Nietzsche's two ways—breeds into us a *drive to copy*, i.e., to imitate others, to want to do the same as they do. It fixes in us the "metahabit" of learning habits by copying others. Nietzsche's name for this metahabit is, as we saw in chapter 2, "herd-instinct."[61] We should see it as the consequence of that social selective mechanism.

These new selective processes design dispositions that are "in the interest" not of the individual who adopts them, but of the society, and the society as *herd*. GS116: "These valuings and rank-orders [of a morality] are always the expression of needs of a community and herd: that which benefits *it* first — and second and third —, that is also the highest measure for the values of all individuals. With morality, the individual is trained to be a function of the herd, and to ascribe value to itself only as function."[62]

All four of the values or virtues we're considering—pity and altruism, equality and civilizing—are key elements in this new selective mechanism. So "equality" ultimately refers to this homogeneity among members, to their sharing practices (i.e., habits and values). And "civilizing" ("taming") refers to the methods by which individuals are trained and coerced into this sharing—are made to be, and to want to be, like one another. Both of these are virtues for societies, i.e., ways the whole is designed. Pity and

[1885].) BGE268: "The greater the danger, the greater is the need to come to agreement [*übereinzukommen*] quickly and easily about what must be done."

60. Maynard Smith 1974.

61. See chapter 2, section 3a. This herd instinct competes in its own right against other drives; so WP275 [1886–1887]: "My answer [to the question 'who speaks?' in our values], taken not from metaphysics but from animal physiology: *the herd instinct speaks.* It *wills* to be master: by its 'thou shalt!' it wills to let the single individual count only in the sense of the whole, for the best of the whole."

62. GS21: "Upbringing [*Erziehung*] always proceeds so: it tries to determine the individual through a series of attractions and advantages into a way of thinking and acting that, once it has become habit, drive, and passion, rules in him and over him *against his ultimate advantage*, but 'to the general good'."

altruism, then, are the virtues for persons, into which that civilizing trains people, so that they'll share practices. Nietzsche pays so much attention to pity and altruism because he thinks they're the principal traits by which persons are designed to be functional parts of the herd.[63]

So pity is a way of feeling that shapes us for group service. We have this feeling, in part, in order to make us behave as altruists. But besides this, pity—and more generally sympathy—plays a direct role in "herding" us. We're trained to feel as others feel, in order to be the more effective sharers in their practices. So WP766 [1886–1887] refers to sympathy as "what makes [us] herdlike."[64]

And altruism suits us for group service even more obviously. It is a habit of subordinating one's own interests to those of the whole. We get trained into it *because* it serves the interest of that social whole—by Nietzsche's modified group selection. So this habit in us really serves others, and not ourselves. GS21: "[W]hen virtues are praised, what's really praised is . . . the unreason in virtue thanks to which the individual lets himself be changed into a function of the whole."[65]

This way altruism really is other-interested is consistent with its *also* being self-interested, in precisely those ways that we saw (in section 2) belong to our drive nature. Natural selection has designed that deep selfishness into the altruist too, in the underlying effort to *satisfy* his/her drives or projects. The altruist just has a different project to satisfy: I find myself with this need to sacrifice myself, and when I "give in" to it, I do so for the sake of the pleasure or power in behaving so.

Social selection is parasitic on this deep selfishness: it hijacks the organism's desire-satisfaction mechanism. By giving the organism—the social member—altruistic projects, social selection manipulates its selfish aim at satisfaction, so that it sacrifices itself in other respects. And in these other respects the organism really does damage itself: it makes itself weaker and worse, even though it does so selfishly. So altruism has a very complex teleology. We think we sacrifice ourselves, but are deeply selfish. And yet,

63. 11.34[41] [1885] says that "'having-pity,' altruism, is the *hypocritical* expression" for herd morality.

64. Compare WP809 [1888].

65. WP286 [1886–1887]: "If one hears within oneself the moral imperative as altruism understands it, one belongs to the *herd.*" WP269 [1886–1887]: "[Altruism] has a meaning: namely, as the instinct of public spirit [*Instinkt des Gemeinsinns*] resting on the valuation that the single individual matters little, but all together matter very much, provided they form a *community* [*Gemeinschaft*] with a common feeling and a common conscience."

our selfishness has been manipulated by social selection, so that we really do sacrifice ourselves after all—and not just in the way we suppose. This gives us, as it were, the worst of both sides: we do indeed hurt our interests, but don't deserve the credit for it we claim.

This lets us reconcile two seemingly contradictory lines Nietzsche takes. Sometimes he insists that altruism doesn't really occur, that it's just disguised self-interest.[66] But other times he holds that it does occur, and really does sacrifice and damage our interests. This duality results from the complex selective processes that have designed these dispositions— there are two opposing teleologies that explain why we perform the altruistic act. We do it for the power in enacting that drive—but we have the drive by selection in the interests of the herd.

Besides hijacking this selfishness built into our drive mechanism, social selection also builds a new kind of selfishness in us. It builds a self-consciousness in which we regard ourselves as "egos" and form explicit conceptions of our interests. But this too is designed to herd us. We all take over the same conception of our own interest—what everyone thinks is best for anyone. And this common conception of "the human good" has evolved under selection for an ideal that unifies and homogenizes us. WP873 [1884]: "In ordinary 'egoism' it is precisely the 'not-ego,' the *deep average being* [*tiefe Durchschnittswesen*], the species-human, that wills its preservation'."

Now all of this "design" by social selection is superimposed on the much longer-standing work by natural selection. The latter has set into us drives and feelings that persist "in the blood" and are (as it were) continually trying to assert themselves against the social habits laid over them. The herd habits must be constantly bending us against our natural feelings and desires. Altruistic habits must override selfish drives, and social pleasures must counteract the natural pains that go with constraining our drives.[67]

It's the conflict between these two design programs that makes the human animal so distinctively sick and suffering. GM.ii.16: "But thus

66. D148: "If only those actions are moral which are performed for the sake of another and only for his sake, as one definition has it, then there are no moral actions!" 13.14[29] [1888]: "[T]he cult of altruism is a specific form of egoism, that occurs regularly under certain physiological presuppositions."

67. Spencer by contrast thinks of feelings as much more pliable, more able to be thoroughly redesigned. *Data* 214: "[T]he remolding of human nature into fitness for the requirements of social life, must eventually make all needful activities pleasurable, while it makes displeasurable all activities at variance with these requirements."

began the gravest and uncanniest illness, from which humanity has not yet recovered, man's suffering *of man, of himself* — the result of a forcible sundering from his animal past."[68] Suffering was uppermost in the long period in which those habits were being forcibly imposed, the period of the "ethic of custom" (*Sittlichkeit der Sitte*), when the human animal was being "domesticated" or socialized. Nietzsche dwells on the bloody and horrific aspects of this training. Sickness is uppermost now, as an effect of that suffering. To counteract those natural pains, social selection breeds into us "guilt," which is the habit of *blaming ourselves* for this suffering: the drives that resist social practice are evil, as is the body, and we ourselves.[69]

Nietzsche thinks Darwinists have either missed altogether these damaging features of social selection, or failed to appreciate how they *do* damage the individual.[70] They miss this because they're in the grip of these values, and on the hunt for justifications of them. So 9.8[35] [1880–1881]: "The value of altruism is *not* the conclusion of science; but the man of science lets himself be misled by the *currently predominant drive*, to believe that science confirms the wish of his drive! Cf. Spencer."[71] So they miss the real selective history of their morality.

4. Lessons from this Genealogy: Whether/How We Progress

These, then, are the facts about our ethical and political values—how they've evolved under selection, and what this selection has designed them for. Given these facts, what normative lesson does Nietzsche draw? How does this genealogy inform or orient his valuing's stance toward others? What lesson does he draw from his analysis of altruism's socializing role and how it is imposed on those underlying selfishnesses?

68. So the human is *"the* sick animal" (GM.iii.13). See also A14; 11.25[382] [1884], 13.15[120] [1888].
69. Nietzsche tells this story especially in GM.ii.
70. 9.10[D60] [1880–1881] suggests that Spencer fails to realize how he hopes to turn every individual into a useful tool, so rendering the individual ever weaker.
71. GS345: "These historians of morality (especially Englishmen) do not amount to much: usually they themselves stand unsuspectingly under the command of a particular morality, and serve, without knowing it, as its shield-bearers and followers." WP253 [1885–1886] cites Darwinism as one among many ways modern thought has been unable to break free from Christian values: "[E]ven the basic conditions of life are falsely interpreted for the benefit of morality: despite knowledge of the animal world and plant world."

We must take the start of our answer from the account of Nietzsche's metaethics in chapter 2, section 5. The fundamental lesson of genealogy is self selection: to use these facts to free oneself from how values *have* been made, so enabling one to make values for oneself. But what does this mean, concretely? How does it affect how one feels and acts toward others? How, in particular, does it affect our habits of pity and altruism? In the rest of this chapter I'll try to cash in the metaethics by showing how it issues in a Nietzschean ethics and politics.

First, in this section, I'll treat a metaethical issue crucial for orienting us to find those ethical and political lessons. This is the issue of **progress** (*Fortschritt*)—i.e., Nietzsche's views on what progress is (would be), and whether and when it occurs.[72] Nietzsche presents his position as sharply different from the Darwinists' here: they believe in progress and he denies it.[73] What does this denial involve? I will particularly consider whether it means that it's impossible for a person or society to "progress" in the simple, minimal sense of "getting better" or improving. If Nietzsche denies progress in this sense, it seems he couldn't have any practical or valuative lesson to suggest to us after all. If we can't improve, no lesson from him could help us. We must see what he thinks about progress before attributing any such lessons to him.

Nietzsche's comments on progress are often inflected by his association of the concept (and claim) with Spencer, whose position let's again note. As we partly saw above, Spencer presents progress as a pervasive cosmic tendency, the tendency of matter to pass from indefinite homogeneity to definite heterogeneity. He presents this tendency as manifesting or expressing itself at a series of higher levels. It is the crux to progress in organisms: each individual organism progresses by developing and organizing its parts. And species progress, in that evolution leads to higher species whose members are increasingly complex functionally. Finally the point applies to human societies, which progress by integrating ever-greater diversities of members.

Spencer thinks he observes this progress in human history, and he relies on it to predict a certain future development: this integration (a kind of harmonizing of differences) will rise to the global level, and societies will

72. On Nietzsche on progress see Moore (2002, 29–34).

73. Passages attacking Darwinists for their faith in progress include WP243 [1887], WP685 [1888], WP684 [1888]. I think Nietzsche hears an implication of progress even in the term "evolution" (*Entwicklung*); see 10.4[177] [1882–1883], which proposes instead "[t]he organic as degeneration [*Entartung*]."

come to be in concord with one another (while keeping their differences). At this point they will no longer need to constrain their members to defend them from other societies. Here progress reaches its limit and end, in the perfection of both individuals and societies.

Let's examine Nietzsche's disagreement with Spencer's story of progress. Does he reject every bit of it?

a. No Lesson?

Nietzsche's sharp attacks[74] on progress might well be taken to show that he can't derive *any* lesson from his genealogy of morality. He denies that evolution *does* progress. GM.ii.12: "The 'evolution' of a thing, a custom, an organ is thus by no means its *progressus* toward a goal."[75] He denies even that progress is *possible*. But then how could he think that his ideas could "improve" us, as individuals or society?

Since the primary application of the term "progress" is to cases of *evolutionary* change, i.e., change in a replicating line, let's focus here. This includes, we should remember, social practices, habits that replicate not genetically but by social diffusion; so societies also evolve and progress. But this excludes another application of the term, to the individual case— the way an organism itself might progress. I'll come back eventually to this nonevolutionary case.

It's obvious that "progress" contains the notion of an *advance* or *improvement* through time: evolution passes from a worse to a better state. What needs to be the general character of this process of improvement, in order that it count as progress?[76] Consider these increasingly strong definitions:

a. Progress = *any* evolutionary advance (passage from a worse to a better state).

Progress occurs when some replicating line improves from time 1 to time 2.

74. Here we focus on his mature views. In his "positivist" phase he is sympathetic to progress. See, e.g., HH.i.24, 26, 224, 236, HH.ii.4, HH.iii.183.
75. WP685 [1888]: "That *species* represent any progress is the most unreasonable assertion in the world; so far they represent one level." He maintains that humans are not a "progress" beyond animals: A14, WP90 [1888].
76. I here set aside cases in which Nietzsche attacks "progress" defined as change to a certain *content*, i.e., as implying a specific conception of how society will improve

b. Progress = an evolutionary advance that is *sustained*.

Progress requires that the replicating line improve over the long term, i.e., in such a way that episodes of advance are not nullified by those of retreat, but accumulate and build on one another.

c. Progress = a sustained advance that is not just accidental, but causally *necessary*.

Progress requires that this long-term improvement happen necessarily, i.e., by some causal mechanism that guarantees it (given some range of conditions, of course). There's a logic in the process that brings about such long-term advance.

d. Progress = an evolutionary advance that is sustained and necessary, because evolution *aims* at its end.

The mechanism that brings about this long-term advance is teleological—i.e., such that its outcome explains why it happens. Progress happens "for the sake of" the outcomes it reaches.

In which of these senses of progress does Nietzsche deny it? And are there any of them in which he affirms it (says it occurs, even values it)? Note that although each sense defines progress as a change, senses c and d refer this change to a particular kind of disposition or tendency inherent in evolution.

It's clearest that Nietzsche rejects evolutionary progress in sense d—though even here there's an abundance of passages in which he appears to affirm it.[77] He often and emphatically denies that evolution is teleological,

---

(what's better). He associates the term with an Enlightenment picture of the upward path to equality and democracy. So GS377: "[W]e do not work for 'progress,' we do not need to plug our ears in the market against the sirens of the future — what they sing about 'equal rights,' 'a free society,' 'no more masters and no servants' does not tempt us." Cf. BGE201, 242, 260, TI.ix.43; 12.2[13] [1885–1886].

77. Early, in *Untimely Meditations* (iii.6), he overtly posits a goal: "[T]here, where a kind reaches its limit and passes over into a higher kind, lies the goal of its evolution." See also HH.i.107. And even later he's often tempted this way; for example, he often uses organic similes to suggest that our species or society is "growing toward" the individual. See GS23 (individuals are the "fruit of fruits hang[ing] ripe and yellow on the tree of a people, — and this tree existed only for the sake of these fruits!"); GS149 ("the egg is becoming ripe and the eggshell is about to be broken"); GM.ii.2 ("the tree at last matures its fruit, [and] society and its ethic of custom at last bring to light *whereto* they were simply the means").

distinguishing himself from Darwinists, who (he supposes) think it is.[78] Yet he sometimes slips into the view himself, when he thinks about *will to power* in a particular way, when he treats it as a basic life force steering evolution. In chapter 1, I focused instead on his "recessive" view, which presents it as an adaptation produced by natural selection. But even when (in his "dominant" view) he sets will to power prior to selection, he prefers to think of it as playing the role we now give to random mutation: will to power generates the individual variations on which selection then works (see chapter 1, section 5a). An organism's will to power drives it to "grow" and distinguish itself; selection judges the resulting novelties, which are passed on (Lamarckianly) with varying success.[79] So will to power is an engine for diversity, but gives no overall direction to the evolutionary process.[80] It goes against Nietzsche's strong conviction to think "optimistically" that evolution is steered for the best by anything, will to power included.[81]

We've already seen that he rejects progress in sense c, as well. He denies that evolution *must* progress.[82] He thinks Darwinists believe in this inevitable progress.[83] One way he rebuts them is by denying that evolution

78. See GM.ii.12 (quoted above), and nn. 81 and 83 below. Many of the passages quoted or cited below against weaker notions of progress attack this stronger one too, either implicitly or explicitly.

79. And as we've seen, it's often not the "most powerful" that selection then favors.

80. The highly metaphysical vision of the world as will to power in WP1067 [1885] depicts it as "a sea of forces storming and flooding in themselves, eternally changing, eternally running back, with tremendous years of recurrence, with an ebb and flood of its forms." Moore (2002, 32): "For Nietzsche, evolution is a process of differentiation taking place within particular individuals. The species as a whole does not advance."

81. He attacks the Darwinian confidence in progress as a remnant of the Christian faith in divine providence; see WP243 [1887].

82. Even in *Human, All-Too-Human*, where he affirms progress, he doubts its necessity: HH.i.24: "[I]t is rash and almost nonsensical to believe that progress *necessarily* must follow; but how could one deny, that it is possible?"

83. 10.4[177] [1882–1883]: "History = *evolution of purposes in time*: so that always higher grow out of the lower. . . . *About* this the teleologists and the Darwinists are *united*, that it happens. . . . The opposite, that everything up to us is *decay*, is even provable. . . . The organic as degeneration." Note that Darwin also denies this necessity: "We must remember that progress is no invariable rule." He rejects "the tacit assumption . . . that there is some innate tendency towards continued development in mind and body. But development of all kinds depends on many concurrent favourable circumstances. Natural selection acts only in a tentative manner" (*Descent* I/178). On the other hand he also says: "And as natural selection works solely by and for the good of each being, all corporeal and mental endowments will tend to progress towards perfection" (*Origin* 489).

has progressed, in precisely the case they most have in mind—human societies and values. He denies that those on top today are better than those on the bottom, and that people today are better than those of the past. A4: "Humanity does *not* represent an evolution to the better or stronger or higher in the sense believed today. 'Progress' is merely a modern idea, that is, a false idea. The European of today is vastly inferior in value to the European of the Renaissance: further development is altogether *not* according to any necessity in the direction of elevation, enhancement, or strength."[84]

Nor does Nietzsche think this is just a "bump in the road"—or a dialectical step—on the way to an inevitable overall improvement. He thinks it's possible that humanity will degenerate into the "last men" famously described in *Zarathustra*'s prologue. He worries that a culture of *nihilism* or valuelessness will ensue, and that it may prove a lasting, terminal state—an evolutionarily stable strategy. Our culture will escape it only if certain special individuals, creators of new values, should happen to arise.[85]

Nietzsche also plainly rejects b, that evolutionary progress can be sustained indefinitely or over the very long term. Advances will only ever be temporary and local, eventually to be reversed and nullified.[86] His favorite reason is that growth is in power, but that *power is unstable*. At its highest levels, power is fragile and even self-dissolving.[87] The inevitability of decline is also one of the implications of the thought of eternal recurrence. Nietzsche stresses how this cyclicality makes all ascent transitory; this may be much of the doctrine's attraction for him. He especially notes the transitoriness of societies or "peoples": their health and strength are brief and ephemeral—a view ingrained in him from his model of the Greeks. Decline is inevitable, not just because external factors will break in, but by an internal logic of senescence or decay.

What of our minimal notion of progress, a? Does Nietzsche even deny that temporary advances or improvements in the course of evolution are

84. Also BGE52, TI.ix.37; WP90 [1888]. Nietzsche argues, as we saw in chapter 1, that social evolution favors a "lower" type—renders it fitter; e.g., 11.35[22] [1885].

85. GM.ii.24 says that this redeeming antichrist "must" come, but means it (I think) hopefully rather than assertorically.

86. WP684 [1888]: "The overall animal- and plant-world does not evolve from lower to higher.... But everything at the same time, and superimposed [*übereinander*] and confused [*durcheinander*] and opposed [*gegeneinander*]." See n. 80 above.

87. WP684 [1888]: "The richest and most complex forms ... perish more easily. ... Among humans too the higher types, the lucky cases of evolution, perish most easily under shifting fortune and misfortune." Also BGE276; WP987 [1884], WP996 [1885].

possible? If he denies that we can ever really improve at all, then clearly he can have no value lessons for us here—at the social level at least. And if he then prefers, e.g., hardness to pity, this won't be because we progress or advance by becoming so.

But on consideration I think we can see that Nietzsche actually accepts and affirms progress in sense a. Indeed, it's the fact that temporary improvements are possible—that we *can progress*—that motivates his vehemence against the current state of our society and values. He tries to show how these *can* be improved, though only *against* the grain of the selective process at work in societies. This is why the just-quoted A4 goes on to say that "in another sense" there *does* occur a "higher type," in the form of "fortunate accidents of great success."[88] And Nietzsche does indeed use the word "progress" in this sense.[89]

So the attack on progress doesn't rule out "higher" and "lower" types of persons altogether—nor the possibilities of evolutionary "ascent" and "decline" of these types. That these are possible is vital to Nietzsche, who talks continually about higher and lower, ascent and decline: "I have a subtler sense of smell for the signs of ascent and decline than any other human being before me; I am the teacher *par excellence* for this — I know both, I am both" (EH.i.1).

So even though progress isn't inevitable, and can't be indefinitely sustained—even though there's no logic or tendency in selection that ensures or favors it—we can still achieve a progress, and Nietzsche can try to show us how. He claims his title to show us from his genealogical insights into our evolution so far. But what in particular does he think these insights show? What do they tell us about how to progress?

b. Lesson: Restore Nature's Design?

I think there's one way of stating this lesson that immediately suggests itself from Nietzsche's writings. It appears that he wants to restore us,

88. See the quotation from TI.ix.48, in the text below. WP881 [1887] speaks of "the *whole human*, . . . the milestone-human, who shows, how far forward humanity has so far come. It goes forward *not* in a straight line; often an already-achieved type is lost again."
89. GM.ii.12: "The magnitude of a 'progress' is measured by the mass of all that had to be sacrificed to it; humanity as mass sacrificed to the growth of a single *stronger* species of human — that *would* be a progress." Also BGE216. WP1023 [1888]: "Progress: the strengthening of the type, the capacity for great willing: everything else is misunderstanding, danger."

from the unhealthy habits imposed by social selection, to the rule of our healthy, naturally selected drives. His lesson seems to be that the products of social selection are bad, those of natural selection good—and that we should favor the latter over the former within us. This seems an obvious inference from his genealogy, read as revealing how the healthy work of natural selection gets "sickened" by the herding tendencies of social (memetic) selection. Our goal would be to recapture the natural health in being ruled by drives.[90]

If this is Nietzsche's lesson, it would in effect attempt to *reverse* the development Spencer counts as progress. Spencer's moral progress is really a decline and degeneration, and we need to walk back along its false path.[91] The lesson is to restore the preeminence of the dispositions and goals we have through natural selection—by weeding out the moral values bred into us in order to herd us. So we would weed out, in particular, our habits of feeling pity and acting altruistically. Since these moral values are impressed particularly through language and consciousness—in our "spirit"—the lesson is to restore authority to our *body*.

Much evidence points this way. Nietzsche often contrasts our sick and "all too human" social instincts with a healthier animal nature which—it seems—he wants to revive or unrepress in us.[92] He calls morality "unnatural," to condemn it (WP52 [1888]). It's his common theme that "bodies know best"—that our intellect is a much less reliable guide to our interests than the drives built into us by our evolutionary past. He wants, familiarly, to restore a "good conscience" to our bodily drives and appetites, which often serve him as a touchstone for "health."[93] His stress on will to power and the value of our aggressive impulses sounds like an effort to revivify naturally selected drives.

All of this might suggest that pity and altruism are simply to be erased and eliminated. Nietzsche seems sometimes to offer strategies for precisely this, for example, in these passages from *The Gay Science*. GS.JCR.63 (see the context): "Pity should be sin for you." GS345: "'Selflessness' has no

90. This is related to the "intrinsic argument" described in chapter 2, section 5b.
91. 11.25[171] [1884]: "Basic *error*: we set *our* current moral feelings as standard, and measure progress and regress [*Rückschritt*] thereby. But each of these regresses would be a progress for an opposite ideal. /'Humanizing' — is a word full of judgment, and sounds to my ears nearly the opposite as to your ears."
92. For example Z.i.4 ("On the Despisers of the Body"), TI.v ("Morality as Anti-Nature").
93. WP124 [1887]: "That one gives back to man the *courage* to his natural drives. . . . /Progress towards 'naturalness' [*Natürlichkeit*]."

value either in heaven or on earth." GS289 (regarding the evil or unhappy or exceptional): "What is needful is not pity for them. We must learn to abandon this arrogant fancy, however long humanity has hitherto spent learning and practicing it."

But again I think this reading of Nietzsche can't be right in the end. It misses the main and best part of his position. Although he often does seem a *complete* opponent (rejecter) of all the products of social selection, this is rhetoric disguising a more nuanced stance.[94] Spencer's story of progress tried to show morality's height, by emphasizing the lowness of premoralized humans, i.e., "primitives." Nietzsche replies that he prefers the latter to tamed humans—but this isn't to say that these primitives are his ideal.

Although he sometimes seems to advise a kind of "return to nature," such a lesson is really too atavistic and primitivist to be his. He wants more than just a return to simple health—and the more is supplied by the "spirit" formed socially. TI.ix.48: "*Progress in my sense.* I too speak of a 'return to nature,' although it is really not a going back but a *coming up* [*Hinaufkommen*] — up into the high, free, even terrible nature and natural-ness, that plays with great tasks, that *may* play."[95]

c. Lesson: Redesign for Freedom

To put it plainly or crudely, I think Nietzsche's dominant aim is not to return us to "nature's values" from morality, but to *use* the first to redesign the second, and vice versa. Rather than denying (and trying to erase) the social virtues bred into us by herd or memetic selection, Nietzsche tries to "exapt" these inbred habits—to impose a new function on them, by a new selective pressure. And he tries to do the same with his drives and their values. Both habits and drives work by assigning certain *virtues* (ways to try to be), and Nietzsche's redesign works especially on and with these. HH.i.P.6: "You shall become master over yourself, master also over your virtues. Formerly *they* were your masters; but they must be only your

94. He takes this unmitigated stance in *The Antichrist*, whose tone is noticeably more extreme.

95. Compare WP120 [1887], which lists ways that nineteenth-century Europeans have become "more natural," but insists that this is not a "return to nature," since "there has never yet been a natural humanity"; instead these changes involve "a step further into civilization." Also TI.ix.43.

instruments beside other instruments." He tries to adapt them for an end or ideal not already present in nature, the end of *self selection*.[96]

In chapter 2, section 5b, we saw how Nietzsche *justifies* this new ideal in his empirical and psychological fashion.[97] He offers it as solving a problem our species faces, by its dual formation from natural and social selection. Our drives and social habits (especially our habits of thought) stand in a deep conflict that has made us "the sick animal." Nietzsche offers freedom as solving this conflict—and hence as advisable for any human capable of it (since we're all sick this way). This ideal is a kind of synthesis of the fundamental tendencies of both sides—of our drives and spirit. It takes up the core values of both: health and truth. And it turns both capacities—spirit's skeptical eye and body's healthy taste—to a new project of choosing values.

So Nietzsche's revaluation of values is best conceived as a quasi-Darwinian "exapting": he wants to take over structures that have evolved and been fixed in us for *one* end (social cohesion), and he wants to impose a new selective pressure, to redesign them for a different end. As we saw in chapter 1, section 4, he thinks one of his large differences from Darwin is his stress on such redesign; he likes especially to show how good things have ugly beginnings. And in making values himself, he makes them not from scratch, but from pieces of the very ones he attacks.

This shows us his fuller position on "progress." Although he denies there's any selective logic in evolution that "aims" at his ideal of self selection, or makes it inevitable, he does still think that a study of that logic—a genealogy—will suggest or point to this ideal as a suitable next step. It shows us a step we have an interest in taking, since we ourselves are made up of these conflicting tendencies and aims. By insight into these tendencies, we see how they oppose one another, in ways damaging to each. But this insight also reveals itself as a step in a new project with a new aim that takes up the best of both prior aims—and in this sense solves their conflict. We progress, by the standards of our existing values, into new values that then supersede them. We now value something more than

96. An early statement is HH.i.286: "I believe that everyone must have his own individual opinion concerning everything about which an opinion is possible, because he himself is an individual, unique thing which adopts a new posture.... Freedom of opinion is like health: both are individual, from neither can a universally valid concept be set up." An important later statement is GS335. I describe this ideal in chapter 2, section 4.

97. This was the "constructive argument," which accommodates—as the intrinsic argument couldn't—Nietzsche's insistence that he *creates* his values as *new*.

the sum of those old values: we value "taking control" over those values set into us, and selecting values ourselves.[98]

Since Nietzsche's progress lies not within natural or social selection, but in the step out of them, his way of grounding values in evolution is (in this sense) *opposite* the Social Darwinists'. The latter justify values as those projected within evolutionary history itself. But for Nietzsche ascent lies in overcoming this selective history, not revalidating it. He cites natural and social selection not in order to justify the values they issue in, but precisely in order to seize from them the power to make values himself.[99] (To be sure, he makes his values *out of* those values selected before.)

We must see how this redesign applies to pity and altruism: Nietzsche wants not to excise but to exapt them. I'll argue in the next section that his virtues of hardness and selfishness "take these up"—they involve descendant forms of pity and altruism.[100] They *must* do so, first because these virtues/habits are hard to erase, but also because those descendants are useful and indeed indispensable to the projects of freedom and power. And I'll argue in the final section of this chapter that Nietzsche's politics takes a similar tack with the society-level virtues, equality and taming. In all four cases I'll try to show that this way that Nietzsche's new virtues assimilate the old responds to our worries about his immoralism.

5. Self Selection's Ethics: Revaluing Pity and Altruism

Let's examine in more detail how self selection carries out a "redesign" of pity and altruism. This also lets us make more concrete our understand-

98. HH.i.24 is optimistic about the possibility of progress, now that we have a "conscious culture," by contrast with the old culture "which viewed as a whole has led an unconscious animal- and plant-life."

99. Darwinism, he says in WP243 [1887], involves "absurd trust in the course of things," in a kind of divine providence—this is the trust the Darwinists put in the upshot of natural (and social) selection. This trust expresses their failure to overcome values embedded in their drives. 9.8[35] [1880]: "The value of altruism is *not* the conclusion of science; but men of science let themselves be misled by the *now dominating drive*, to believe, that science confirms the wish of their drive! cf. Spencer." Note in UM.i.7 his complaint that Strauss, a self-claimed Darwinist, failed to "boldly deduce from the *bellum omnium contra omnes* and the privileged right of the stronger a moral code for life"; compare 7.27[2] [1873].

100. Compare Schacht's effort to show that Nietzsche's conclusions about selfless-ness and pity "are not as simply and completely negative as one might initially suppose" (1983, 455ff.).

ing of freedom as self selection—just how it chooses and creates. And it lets us assess, finally, Nietzsche's attacks on those social virtues.

If I achieve Nietzsche's special kind of freedom, and "see through" the reasons I have these particular drives/habits (the goals for which pity and altruism have been selected and set into me), how will this affect these dispositions in me? How will I try to change them? Nietzsche's general answer is that I change them into—or put them under the direction of— hardness and selfishness. The self selector will choose these "new virtues" as the personal traits he/she will try to instance. These virtues are, once again, not revivals of the natural or animal forms, but "exaptations" of these, toward new ends.

This is, in a sense, Nietzsche's "ethics": it's how he ultimately governs his stance toward others. But we should bear in mind from the start (what we'll see in section 6) that he does *not* mean it as an "ethics" in Aristotle's fuller sense, of constituting an (ideal or hoped-for) *ethos*, an overall social practice. Hardness and selfishness aren't virtues he wants the whole society to adopt and share—they aren't "universalizable." But in this section, I set aside what Nietzsche wants society to be like, to focus on why he thinks a *self selector* will choose them as personal virtues for him/herself. We're concerned with the virtues Nietzsche lives by himself, and commends to his favored readers.

Self selecting one's virtues is much harder than we suppose. It seems just a matter of becoming conscious of the question "how should I be?" and then deliberating and choosing some answer to it. But the problem is that this choice may only express the values that natural and social selection have set into me, quite unbeknown to me. So when I "choose" pity or altruism as a virtue for myself—a way to try to be, a feeling or behavior to cultivate—this choice expresses an allegiance bred and trained into me, for goals (functions) of which I've been unaware. Having failed to grasp *why* (for what goal) I favor pity and altruism, I can't genuinely choose them, after all.

As we saw in section 3, Nietzsche thinks the ethics of pity and altruism were principally designed to make us members of the herd. That is, it was selection for *this* result (function) that was most effective in fixing these practices into society, and that best explains their features. It explains what is otherwise so puzzling: why we have dispositions that run contrary to our selfish, bodily interests, in ways that both pain and sicken us. Once I identify this and related functions that my pity and altruism were designed to play, I become free to redesign them. The self selector will redesign them for a *selfish* end, though a different kind of such end than allowed for in Spencer's egoism.

To settle how Nietzsche wants to redesign pity and altruism, we obviously need to examine his *criticisms* of them—i.e., the grounds he expresses for his negative judgments about them. However, we must handle these criticisms carefully. For Nietzsche offers them, I will try to show, in two different ways, which give them different kinds of relevance to that redesign: they play different roles in his larger effort to help us to freedom.

That freedom depends, we've seen, on genealogical insight into the reasons for pity and altruism—an insight that gives me the distance from these virtues that is needed for a genuine choice about them. This insight must help me to step back from the value in showing me why I value it. So along with the insight must come a certain emotive effect on my visceral taste for things. It's in order to play this freeing and separating role that so many of Nietzsche's critiques are so shrill. His diagnoses are strongly slanted in order to show historical and psychological roots in the most unappealing aspect or light.[101]

Many of Nietzsche's critiques of pity and altruism are meant this way—to help free or distance us from them, in order to make us capable of self selection over them. Others, I think, are meant to guide the choice we exercise *while* we self select. I'll treat these in turn.

a. Freeing to Select Social Virtues

The first and hardest step in self selection is that step back or away from the values we've always valued. This removal is all the harder to the extent that the values in question are bred deeply into us and are hedged 'round with defensive mechanisms that inhibit questioning of them. This is the case with the virtues pity and altruism, because they're such important tools in the overall project of herding us.

It's this view of how deeply these values are entrenched in us that explains much of the rhetorical force—the hyperbole—in Nietzsche's at-

---

101. See A4 on how great spirits must be skeptics, because "[c]onvictions are prisons." GS347: "[O]ne could conceive of such a pleasure and power of self-determination, such a *freedom* of the will that the spirit would take leave of all faith and every wish for certainty, being practiced in maintaining himself on insubstantial ropes and possibilities."

tacks on them. He insists so emphatically and unqualifiedly against pity and altruism as a counterweight to the great but obscure forces that have thrust them into us. So his critique is (in this part) *tactical*—aimed to help us to step back and notice these impositions, the better to make our own choices about pity and altruism. He attacks them *as* ingrained in us—indeed as *most* deeply ingrained.

This rhetorical tactic is all the more needed because of the *kind* of grasp we need of our values' genealogy. For freedom it's not enough to grasp this diagnosis in a theory; we need to "incorporate" the lesson. So the critique of values' source must reach us "down in our drives," in our immediate feelings and reactions to cases. As we'll see in chapter 4, this involves a shift in our *aesthetic* responses. Nietzsche intensifies the emotive force of his diagnoses in order to produce this visceral effect.

A certain overstatement or one-sidedness is appropriate here. But this isn't to say that *lies* would do. It's crucial that the diagnoses that detach us from pity and altruism be true, since otherwise we simply fall under the power of the lie and the liar. (It can *only* be truth that "sets us free.") Still, this licenses Nietzsche, in these rhetorical moments, to tell only part of the truth—the part that strikes the greatest emotive resonance against pity and altruism, which is precisely the part that was most suppressed by the devices that defended these virtues.

This puts a different light on the strong distaste we feel for Nietzsche's attacks. It shows us how his point is precisely to offend us—and to make us inquire into that offense. He wants us to feel strongly that *we can't think that way* (that pity and altruism are bad, for example) and then to ask ourselves, what restrains us, exactly? By fingering this nerve, he hopes to make us pay attention to the workings of this social impulse—herd instinct—on us, and to test our independence from it. EH.P.3: "*Nitimur in vetitum* [we strive into *the forbidden*]: in this sign my philosophy will triumph one day, for what one forbade was fundamentally always only the truth."

I think we should read many of Nietzsche's critiques of pity and altruism in this light. They're addressed to us not as clinching arguments, but as data we need to take into account, in order to clinch our own arguments for ourselves. The critique operates, as it were, in a merely preliminary way—"en route" to our values, not as determining what those values should in the end be. He doesn't mean for us simply to accept those conclusions about pity and altruism, since that would forgo the work of self-choice that's precisely his point.

This intent in Nietzsche's critiques of pity and altruism is clearest in the places where he attacks their *sources* in unhealthy selection. It's plausible to read these as meant merely to show us our "bad motives" for holding these values—generally not motives at all, as we've thought them to be, but designs by selective mechanisms. This would leave open the possibility that we might come to hold those same values for "good motives." So they would allow us to respond to their critique not by changing our values, but by changing the reason we have them. They would allow us to adopt the same values again, after that freeing critique—to select them ourselves, rather than receiving them as naturally or socially selected.

This option of readopting the same values after the freeing critique, though from different motives, is clear in HH.iii.212: *"Free of morality. —* Now that minds are becoming freer and less narrow, it is certain that morality (inherited, handed down, instinctual acting *in accordance with moral feelings*) is on the decline: but the individual virtues, moderation, justice, repose of soul, are not — for when the conscious mind has attained its highest degree of freedom it is involuntarily led to them and comes to recognize how *useful* they are." Although Nietzsche hasn't yet his own special freedom in mind, I think he will make the same claim about it.[102]

b. Redesigning Social Virtues

But Nietzsche's criticisms of pity and altruism aren't *only* meant as freeing/ detaching—they don't all have just that rhetorical aim. His metavalue of self selecting his values has *consequences* for which further values he then selects: changing *how* he values limits or (somewhat) determines *what* he values. And he thinks it will work this way for self selectors generally. It guides, in particular, what the self selector chooses about the social virtues of pity and altruism. Nietzsche attacks these, after all, not just for their causes (the real reasons we value them), but for their *effects*, in inhibiting our pursuit of certain ends he presumes we share. So these attacks on pity and altruism are not just tactical or rhetorical (helping us to self selection) but *assertive* (of how we should then select).

We might compare this with the way Kant thinks that (his type of) freedom still dictates a particular choice: when you're free to choose, you

---

102. BGE293: "[W]hen such a man [who is by nature a master] has pity, well, *this* pity has value."

will, paradoxically, still choose a particular way. You are, as it were, constrained by the nature of freedom itself to decide as reason and the categorical imperative demand. Nietzsche argues in parallel that his quite different type of freedom also (partly) determines the value content the "free spirit" will choose. But in broad contrast with Kant, Nietzschean freedom leads through *empirical* discoveries, in genealogy.

When pity and altruism are weighed from the stance of this freedom—by one who has "incorporated" genealogical insight into his or her selected goals—they get revised ("exapted") to serve different functions than they had. They are reshaped to serve new ends, which Nietzsche expects the self selector will substitute for the ends—"herding" in particular—those virtues have so far been selected to serve. I'll argue that there are two such general ends, for (or toward) which Nietzsche thinks his self selector will redesign social virtues.

The first is the aim of self selection itself. I'll try to show how this aim exapts pity—into an empathy controlled by a hardness. I'll then argue that Nietzsche tries to ground in this aim a further one: the personal and also social project of "healing spirit." I'll try to show how this further aim exapts altruism—into a giving rooted in selfishness. In each case Nietzsche's virtue—hardness and selfishness—requires and uses a descendant of the original virtue. Hardness changes pity into empathy, as a tool for genealogy, and selfishness changes altruism into giving, for action.

i. HARDNESS VERSUS PITY

The chief end for which the self selector will exapt social virtues is *self selection itself*—the project of improving and extending one's insight into values' sources, and so one's ability to choose values. Some values that one might self select can interfere with this ongoing project of self selection. Even if one *does* choose them freely, they make it harder to *continue* to choose freely. This is so, for example, with the herd instinct itself, i.e., the value (roughly) of "feeling and doing as others do": if this value project of copying were freely chosen, it would inhibit and even bar one from freely choosing in the future. And this is also the case with pity, Nietzsche argues. So the self selector, if he/she retains this virtue at all, must exapt it to serve self selection.

Consider how pity is a kind of polar opposite to self selection. The pitier aims to mirror or copy an attitude taken by another. Moreover, the attitude it copies is itself a "suffering," i.e., consists in passively and negatively undergoing an experience—again opposite to actively shaping it. Pitying is a passive copying of a passive feeling. By habituating us to this copying, pity promotes the herd instinct in us, and discourages and inhibits the project of freedom. By its design, pity pulls us away from ourselves.[103]

Instead of such pity, Nietzsche promotes to us the virtue of *hardness*, as more helpful toward genealogy and freedom. This hardness serves, first of all, an *epistemic* end: the genealogist needs it to push through the inquiry into values. The self selector needs hardness against pity above all for the sake of the diagnostic *truth* that is a precondition for freedom. This different point to the virtue gives it a different character than it has for Spencer.

This hardness is turned, in the first instance, toward *oneself* and one's own suffering. The task of self selection depends on exposing and discrediting one's own ingrained values—which Nietzsche thinks inflict an especially damaging kind of suffering, one that undermines and demoralizes.[104] So hardness is first the courage to bear with this internal turmoil, and to press on with the very project of value critique that inflicts it.

But Nietzsche thinks genealogy also depends on a hardness toward suffering in *others* (and here the virtue lies in his "ethics"). BGE269: "The more a psychologist — a born and inexorable psychologist and unriddler of souls — turns toward the more choice cases and humans, the greater becomes his danger of suffocating from pity; he *needs* hardness and cheerfulness more than another human does."[105] Moreover, since the genealogist even *inflicts* suffering on those who find themselves exposed to his/her diagnoses—as Nietzsche on his honest readers, he thinks—the genealogist needs hardness at that too.[106] Indeed, Nietzsche aspires to turn some of

103. EH.i.4 says that pity "wills to attack [Zarathustra] like a final sin, to entice him away from *himself*."

104. His confidence that this suffering is "worse" than, e.g., poverty or physical pain looks like self-flattery, and may well be doubted. Note Nussbaum's doubts (1994, 159) about his insight into nonspiritual suffering: he only understands "bourgeois vulnerability," she argues.

105. Early, D134: "But whoever wills to serve humanity as physician *in any sense*, must become very cautious against that experience [pity], — it cripples him in every decisive moment."

106. GS.JCR.26: "I must away over a hundred steps, /I must upwards and hear you cry: /'You are hard! Are we then of stone?' /I must away over a hundred steps, /And nobody wants to be a step." And Z.iii.12.29: "And if your hardness does not will to flash and cut and cut through: how could you one day create with me? / For creators are hard. And it must seem blessedness to you to press your hand on millennia as on wax." This carries beyond the current epistemic point, however.

his readers into self selectors, and he often says he needs hardness toward the suffering this subjects them to.[107]

However, we need to notice about this hardness Nietzsche advocates: it's *not* a steady state of not-feeling for/about others, not a blank and persistent indifference (or hostility) toward them. Instead it's a capacity exercised at a certain point in a broader project, a project that involves "thinking or feeling one's way into" others' viewpoints and feelings—even or especially those of whom Nietzsche is most critical.[108] (One only understands a perspective, Nietzsche thinks, by *occupying* it. And the perspectives most at issue are not theoretical but *valuative*.) It's precisely because this broader project brings the suffering and the limitations of these others so sharply before the genealogist that he/she is so prone toward pity—and so in need of hardness.

So hardness is a virtue exercised at a certain dialectical moment. It responds to a problem that arises for a kind of inquiry—genealogy—that needs to use *empathy* as one of its best tools. The genealogist needs to be able to step into the perspectives he/she studies, and Nietzsche prides himself on this capacity.[109] Because this inquiry is focused on exposing the unattractive sources of our values, it is persistently exposing the weaknesses and sicknesses of the viewpoints it feels its way into. Pity is a danger, because it is a natural modification in this empathy that self selection depends on.

To be sure, this pity that Nietzsche needs hardness to hold in check is itself something different from Christian pity. It has a different object than pity has had—not suffering, but all the ways people fall short of freedom, of "becoming who they are." (So it's no longer "pity," by the definition I've been using, and which I think Nietzsche mostly presumes.) Nietzsche suffers from the sickness and pettiness of people, even where they don't suffer themselves. Conversely, he thinks that some kinds of suffering are helpful and even requisite for becoming free, so that he even welcomes them in others. So now, oddly, this (new) pity pities us for our (old) pity, as really damaging and weakening to us. BGE225: "*Our* pity is

107. I defer until subsection ii the question of why Nietzsche has an interest not only in becoming free himself, but in helping others become so.
108. EH.Z.6: "How gently [Zarathustra] handles even his adversaries, the priests, and suffers with them of them!"
109. EH.i.1: "Looking from the optics of the sick at *healthier* concepts and values, and conversely from the fullness and self-sureness of a *rich* life down into the secret work of the instinct of decadence — this was my longest training, my genuine experience, if in anything I became master in this."

a higher, more farsighted pity: — we see how *the human* makes himself smaller, how *you* make him smaller! — and there are moments when we observe *your* very pity with an indescribable anxiety, when we guard ourselves against this pity." Later: "Therefore pity *against* pity!"[110]

It's this new kind of pity that Nietzsche's hardness controls and limits. But the important point for us is that both pity and hardness occur within the scope of a prior commitment to a kind of empathy. Nietzsche (correctly) sees one of his greatest philosophical strengths as his ability to feel his way into the viewpoints of others, high and low, healthy and sick.[111] His sympathetic bent, his quick attunement to the stances of extremely diverse psychological types, sustain all his diagnoses. He sees himself, in fact, as building all these accessed viewpoints into himself, and enriching himself by them.[112] It's by this sympathetic access that he can make himself "synthetic" and "great-souled."

This empathy is prone to conversion into pity—that special version of pity Nietzsche feels. His main grounds for resisting this step are epistemic. Pity—even his refocused pity—is not as good for the understanding one needs for freedom. He often stresses pity's epistemic failings: the usual kind isn't even good at understanding suffering.[113] And even his own pity, focused not on suffering but on sickness and weakness, is a passive submission to those perspectives: it suffers over them, for the moment is paralyzed in and by them. By contrast, genealogy's empathy enters perspectives with an active purpose: to *diagnose* and *explain* each viewpoint, and so to "see through it."

Now we may well feel that this empathy is a poor substitute for pity. In the first place it seems directed mainly at "spiritual" suffering and not at physical suffering, which presumably holds less psychological interest.

---

110. In BGE269 pity is over "the corruption, the destruction of the higher humans." WP367 [1885]: "*My 'pity'.* — This is a feeling for which I find no name adequate: I sense it when I see a squandering of precious capabilities, for example at the sight of Luther"; he goes on to name two other circumstances, and concludes, "This is my kind of 'pity' [*Mitleid*]; though there is no suffering [*Leidenden*] *with* which I suffer." Also 11.25[19] [1884].

111. See especially EH.i.1–3 (and n. 109 above). EH.i.8: "[M]y humanity does *not* consist in sympathizing with [*mitzufühlen*] how humans are, but in *enduring* that I sympathize with them." Note HH.i.33.

112. Or, as he also likes to put it, these perspectives are rungs on a ladder up which he climbs. But again he carries these countless rungs along within him, as the great "depth" he claims. See n. 107 in chapter 2.

113. D133 says that experience contradicts the claim that pity "possesses an especially subtle, penetrating understanding of suffering." See n. 40 above.

Moreover its point seems to be simply to study this suffering, not to alleviate it. Indeed this aggressive curiosity into the limitations of other people may seem to express a hostility toward them that is really opposite rather than cousin to what we value in pity. Is it really "empathy," after all? We value pity, I think, because it wants the best for its objects, and because it leads to behavior to benefit those others—to correct the defects or limits it "feels" with them. But Nietzsche's empathy seems not to care for its objects in any way that will lead to benefiting actions.

So let's turn to the virtue by which Nietzsche governs not his feelings but his actions toward others—his "selfishness." At once this seems to confirm all our doubts against his empathy—that it is deployed quite coldly and leads to none of the helping behavior toward others that we attribute to pity. But here too I'll argue that Nietzsche's revaluing works differently than we first think.

ii. SELFISHNESS VERSUS ALTRUISM

I think that to see Nietzsche's argument about selfishness we need to add to the basic end he expects the self selector to choose. We've seen that he/she will choose freedom itself—to expand insight and control over the aims of values. But there are other ends Nietzsche expects "free spirits" to arrive at, based on some very general empirical facts that genealogy will expose. These facts concern the self selector's own character as a human animal; they reveal a problem in that character, to which Nietzsche thinks a certain kind of "selfishness" is the solution.

Genealogy's most general discovery—as we saw in chapter 2, section 5b—is of the *dual* selective processes that have made human values and practices. Genealogy shows how the values built into us by natural selection were later attacked and repressed by that socializing process, the better to herd us into like-minded communities. So our feelings and impulses reflect two value regimes, impelling us in incompatible directions. This conflict has rendered us a typically sick and suffering animal—perhaps the large-scale fact about us that Nietzsche most emphasizes.

He thinks this general genealogical insight can and should lead the self selector to adopt, besides the project of self selection itself, that of somehow reconciling those two value regimes—or rather of bringing them into a more fruitful tension/interaction. What standard judges "fruitful" here? As we also saw in chapter 2, section 5b, Nietzsche wants a "synthesis" of these two regimes that can realize values crucial to each. He thinks (his kind of) freedom brings them into an interaction in which each is "better" by (some of) its own criteria. On the side of natural selection, he takes up its key value of *health*. From social selection, he takes the value in which he thinks it culminates, *truth*. His new ideal will show how one can accomplish both, each better than was possible before.

How can our organic effort at health, and our spiritual effort at truth, be made to help rather than hinder one another? By marrying *genealogy* to the project of *healing* values. Genealogy reaches the most inaccessible and dangerous truths—about our values' aims—which human thinking had never been adequate to, and indeed had been designed *not* to see. So genealogical truth is the greatest achievement of "spirit." And now its truths can be used to recover what spirit had always had to sacrifice before: the health valued by the animal in us (the body). The ideal of self selection—Nietzschean freedom—achieves this higher synthesis when the genealogist proceeds to *heal* the social virtues he/she has as spirit.[114]

So Nietzsche thinks the self selector will "choose health" once his/ her diagnoses expose how our divided character has sickened and damaged us. And what specifically is this "health"? In its simple or "animal" form, it is simply fitness: the organism's capacity for the natural selective ends of survival and (especially) growth or power. More specifically, Nietzsche thinks of it as a matter of the organism's drives being directed toward goals that really serve growth—so that they carry it "in the right direction." The organism "wills" things that really are in its interest. So A6: "I call an animal, a species, an individual corrupt [*verdorben*] when it loses its instincts, when it chooses, when it *prefers*, what is disadvantageous for it."

This conception of "health" shows its very close connection with *selfishness*, for Nietzsche. The healthy organism is one well aimed at what is best for it—best by the values embedded in its natural design. Moreover (by Nietzsche's Heraclitean view) this depends on the organism's drives each single-mindedly and "selfishly" pursuing its own goals—rather than constraining itself to cooperate with other drives. So the healthy organism is a selfish synthesis of many selfish parts, its dispositions.

Social selection, the long history of custom and morality, has attacked and undermined this "healthy selfishness." It has done so for several connected reasons, including selection to constrain or suppress those drives to allow civil life, and selection to herd and homogenize individuals. In

114. Z.i.22.2: "Knowing, the body purifies itself; experimenting [*versuchend*] with knowledge, it elevates itself; in the knower all drives heal themselves; in the elevated the soul becomes gay."

social selection's most advanced stage, morality, it undermines selfishness by instilling an explicit ideology (a conscious value) against it: altruism.

As the project to sacrifice one's interests to others, altruism aims the organism to work against itself. The social practice of altruism, and the doctrine intermingled with it, have been designed to make us social "members," not to serve our own fitness and growth.[115] So it is not surprising that they are positively damaging to us. TI.ix.35: "The best is lacking when selfishness begins to be lacking. Instinctively to choose what is *self*-damaging, to be *enticed* by 'disinterested' motives, gives virtually the formula of decadence. . . . A human is finished when he becomes altruistic."

This social evolution not only advances altruism, it also corrupts or misdirects the selfishness that survives. It spreads the "sick selfishness" treated in section 3 above. We interpret even our own interest according to the common (herd) viewpoint.[116] We assume that the same life is best for all persons, and try to craft ourselves toward a common plan. Indeed, we want for ourselves whatever are the goods that others value; we measure our success by their standards and views of us. And so we lose our feeling and trust for the quite idiosyncratic set of drives that characterizes each of us.

Part of Nietzsche's response is to try to restore that healthy selfishness in the drives. We learn not to repress them, but to sublimate them—to find ways they can have "spiritual" expression, and be so satisfied and enjoyed. We give them back their voice in us.[117] This new graciousness toward the drives is also reflected in the role they play in the new truth project. The kind of truth that matters—insight into the aims and meanings of our values—depends on studying and indeed "inhabiting" those drives, as the first vehicles for those values.[118] The old truth project sought "objec-

115. GS21: "The praise of virtue is the praise of something privately harmful, — the praise of drives that deprive a human being of his noblest selfishness and the strength for the highest care [*Obhut*] for himself." GS328: "Surely, the faith preached so stubbornly and with so much conviction, that egoism is reprehensible, has on the whole harmed egoism (while *benefiting*, as I shall repeat a hundred times, *the herd instincts!*)."

116. 9.6[70] [1880] says that others' judgments "give us our *picture of ourselves*, according to which we measure ourselves, are well or poorly pleased with ourselves! Our own judgment is only an *offspring* of the combined foreign [judgments]."

117. WP918 [1888]: "For what is one penalized worst? For one's modesty; for having given no hearing to one's ownmost requirements; . . . for forfeiting a sharp ear for one's instincts."

118. In chapter 4, section 4, of Richardson 1996 I develop this "phenomenological" use of the drives.

tivity" through annulling the drives, but the genealogist learns by cultivating their subjectivity.

The rest of Nietzsche's response is to *use* this organic health to "heal spirit" and thereby achieve a "higher health" of the whole system of body (natural drives) and spirit (social habits). He founds a new selfishness by establishing a new interest or aim, which goes beyond those naturally in the drives. This is the aim of freedom or self selection.[119] The effort at this freedom has better claim to the title "selfish," inasmuch as it is the aim of really "becoming a self," more fully or adequately than ever before. Freedom strives to be selfish *in its own way* (to be "selfishly selfish").[120]

That altruism is defined as self-sacrifice means, I think, that it "can't be healed"—and that there's no room for it, even exapted, in Nietzsche's ideal.[121] And he is, I think, unrelentingly hostile toward it, never speaking of "our altruism" as he does of "our pity." Nevertheless, there's an element in altruism that *can* be taken up, and that does belong to his ideal. Nietzsche calls this "giving" (*Schenken*), and he builds it into his account of the ideally healthy individual.[122] (At issue will be whether we can accept this replacement.) This giving differs from altruism in two kinds of ways: it has a different conception of the other's good, but more important, it has a different kind of concern for that good.

119. In chapter 2, section 5b, above I distinguished two ways—"intrinsic" and "constructive"—in which Nietzsche defends this ur-value of freedom: as the highest achievement of power, and as solving our deep dividedness by synthesizing our natural and social value systems. Here I am elaborating the latter line.

120. Animals are selfish with this individuality, inasmuch as they aim only and precisely with the specific set of drives they comprise. They submit to no generalizing conceptions of what's good for members of their kind.

121. 9.11[40] [1881] says that altruism requires seeing others as similar to oneself, "But I think of the continuing *dissimilarity* and greatest possible *sovereignty* of the individual: therefore altruistic enjoyments must become rare, or *receive* the *form* of *joy in the other*, like our *current joy in nature*."

122. My position contrasts, on one side, with Appel (1999, 2): "[T]his book argues that his work is best understood as an uncompromising repudiation of both the ethic of benevolence and the notion of equality of persons." On the other side I disagree with Reginster (2000a, 2000b), who interprets Nietzsche as promoting altruism itself. I share Reginster's strategy of showing how Nietzsche values others, but disagree with calling this "altruism." Nietzsche is consistently negative about (what he calls) altruism; he prefers different terms for what he wants. I claim this is because he hears "altruism" to imply sacrifice of self-interest—whereas Reginster interprets it to mean just "for others." I agree with Reginster that Nietzsche has a value "in the vicinity," but think we need a different word for it.

So first, giving rests on a different notion of the other's good. Nietzsche means to benefit us under *his* conception of our good, not ours[123]—though his conception of our good is precisely that we should (truly) choose a good for ourselves. So he's interested in pushing and pulling us toward seeing through the ways values have been selected and imposed on us so far. He's not much interested, by contrast, in reducing our suffering—indeed quite the opposite, insofar as growth, to freedom in particular, is most achieved by and from suffering.[124] So he often wishes suffering upon us—and indeed wants his writings to *inflict* a kind of suffering on us. Of course we must bear in mind that he wants suffering not indiscriminately, but the *kinds* and *degrees* of suffering that help us in this way.[125]

Second, giving acts from avowed self-interest.[126] Zarathustra identifies the highest virtue as a "giving virtue" (*schenkende Tugend*) and celebrates its "whole and holy . . . selfishness" (Z.i.22).[127] In the first place, giving expresses—is a sign and confirmation of—the richness and strength of an individual; it displays one's excess.[128] More than this, giving positively

---

123. WP864 [1888]: "Misunderstanding of love. There is a *slavish* love that submits and gives away: that idealizes, and deceives itself — there is a *divine* love that despises and loves, and *reshapes, elevates* the beloved."

124. Z.ii.3: "[A]ll great love is even above all its pity: for it still wills to create the beloved."

125. Nussbaum (1994, 159) argues, in effect, that Nietzsche knows too little about some kinds of economic or physical suffering to do them justice; he thinks only of "bourgeois vulnerability" when he "holds that it is not so bad; it may even be good for the philosopher"; but "basic vulnerability" "he simply neglects."

126. EH.ii.9: "[N]eighbor love, living for others and other things *can* be a protective measure for preserving the hardest self-hood [*Selbstigkeit*]. This is the exception where, against my rule and conviction, I take the side of the 'selfless' drives: here they work in the service of *selfishness, self-discipline* [*Selbstsucht, Selbstzucht*]."

127. Further from Z.i.22: "Insatiably your soul strives for treasures and gems, because your virtue is insatiable in willing to give." In Z.ii.3, in the midst of his critique of pity, Zarathustra reaffirms, "But I am a giver: I give gladly, as friend to friend. Strangers and the poor however may pluck for themselves fruit from my tree: so they will be less ashamed." Zarathustra very often presents himself so, e.g., in Z.i.P.1, Z.iii.12.3, Z.iii.14.

128. BGE260: "[T]he noble human also helps the unfortunate, but not, or almost not, from pity, but more from an urge begotten by excess of power." WP932 [1887]: "The benevolent [*wohlwollenden*] helpful kind dispositions have absolutely *not* come to be honored for the sake of their usefulness: but because they are states of *richer souls,* which can bestow, and carry their value as feeling the fullness of life. Look at the eyes of benefactors! There is the opposite of self-denial, of the hatred for the *moi,* of 'Pascalism'." In D556, to be "magnanimous" (*grossmüthig*) (to the "defeated") is one of the "four cardinal virtues."

enhances strength, by extending one's reach into the other. That excess is not altogether ceded from oneself, but is a piece of oneself that takes root in the other and extends one's power into him/her.[129] And one's power is all the greater when this gift is something genuinely fine—when it truly benefits the other—as Nietzsche of course thinks about his own gifts of genealogy and freedom. He grows himself, by the growth he adds to us.[130]

This last case, Nietzsche's own, is his vision of the highest achievement of power, through giving the greatest gift. By diagnosing the sickness at work in morality and teaching us how to recognize and heal it, he plays a unique historical role. All philosophers, he thinks, have created values and found power in disseminating those values through society. Nietzsche aspires not just to join them, but to better them, by creating values that "see through" all of theirs, and genuinely heal our culture.[131]

More broadly, Nietzsche's self selector will "exapt" altruism into giving, by smelling out all the ways his benevolent impulses were designed to weaken him. He aims to give in the way that strengthens him, as an excess that extends his scope, and at the same time genuinely betters others. HH.i.95: "Even now we will to work, but only so far, as we find our own highest advantage in this work, no more, no less."

We need to ask, however, whether this giving does enough to redeem Nietzsche's ethics for us. Does it suffice to make the Nietzschean selfishness a policy we can admire or aspire to? Giving seems limited in ways altruism is not. First, it seems to be directed primarily toward potential self selectors, i.e., those capable of learning and profiting from Nietzsche's genealogies and values. These seem to be the only recipients of his gifts. And by his own account these are extremely few, both among his readers and among those around him with whom he interacts more directly (friends and

129. Z.iii.10 identifies the "giving virtue" with the "lust to rule" (*Herrschsucht*). WP964 [1884]: "The great man feels his *power* over a people, his temporary coincidence with a people or a millennium: this *enlargement* in his feeling himself as *causa* and *voluntas* is *misunderstood* as 'altruism'."

130. Compare D552's account of a (spiritual) pregnancy: "This is *ideal selfishness*: continually to watch over and care for and to keep our soul still, so that our fruitfulness shall *come to a happy fulfillment*! Thus, as intermediaries, we watch over and care for the *benefit of all*."

131. EH.iv.1: "*Revaluation of all values*: that is my formula for an act of supreme self-examination by humanity, become flesh and genius in me." EH.iv.2: "I am by far the most terrible human there has so far been; this does not exclude, that I shall be the most beneficial."

neighbors). Second, as aimed at making "free spirits," giving seems directed solely at a "spiritual" benefit. So it seems simply to ignore material needs and sufferings and the interests of all but a very few humans. It looks, on these grounds, to be a very inadequate substitute for our altruism.

Now I agree that Nietzsche's new virtue has its focus here—in giving spiritual help to free spirits. This is the application that he thinks and speaks of most often. However I think the arguments he uses to support this virtue allow it to apply much more broadly. If indeed we grow (take power) by helping others grow, this help can include anything that counts as real improvement, even if it lies at a much lower level on Nietzsche's scale of power than the rise to self selection. And it can even include whatever material benefits really are conditions for a genuine growth—despite how Nietzsche tends to ignore them. Indeed, even his ideal of freedom might be shared out more widely than he often implies: some of genealogy's insights can become widespread, freeing even "the many" from some of their subjection to values. The self selector can aspire to modest and incremental impacts on the great diversity of others with whom he/she interacts.

However, these extensions or generalizations of Nietzsche's views are not ones he usually makes. He resists this "democratization" of the others his free spirits care about. They care about those who can be like themselves, the "highest." Nor, usually, does Nietzsche think that growth by "freeing" can or should be widespread in society. To see why, we need to turn to his views about social structure, i.e., from his ethics to his politics.

6. Self Selection's Politics: Revaluing Equality and Civilizing

We've been considering, as Nietzsche's ethics, the virtues—hardness and selfishness—he commends to himself and to any readers he can attract to his basic project of self selection. We've set to the side the question of what role these virtues might play in his "politics," i.e., in his hopes or wishes for society in general. Now we must see whether he wants hardness and selfishness to become common practice. And we must also return to those "virtues for societies" introduced above: his critiques of equality and civilizing as ways for societies to try to be, and his effort to replace them with the virtues of rank order and breeding. More even than his ethics, it's his politics that seems to link Nietzsche with Social Darwinists, to his discredit.[132]

Let me start with some basic doubts that have been raised as to whether he really has a "political theory" at all. First is the charge, made strongly by Nussbaum, that Nietzsche's remarks on political topics are too unreflective, "puerile," and unargued to merit serious attention. She claims (1997, 2): "[O]n six of the seven issues [that are criteria for serious political thought], Nietzsche has nothing to offer that is not utterly childish"; on the seventh—moral psychology—"he makes a serious contribution, though one that could be argued to be quite pernicious."[133]

I will respond to some of Nussbaum's charges against Nietzsche in footnotes below. Some I will largely concede: there are important political questions about which he has nothing interesting to offer.[134] But I'll argue that this is because his attention is elsewhere—on what he thinks is *most crucial* about and for societies, the things we need to think about *first*. On this topic (in this region of political problems) he does have interesting things to say. The further challenge will be to see how this coheres with that "childishness" elsewhere.

A second way of denying a "political theory" to Nietzsche is more charitable to him: it says he has reasons for renouncing any such theory. This has been argued by several interpreters.[135] After all, Nietzsche proclaims that what matters is the single individual (or free spirit), standing apart from the social practice and seeing through it. Perhaps he doesn't care enough about that practice to offer a theory of how it should be. He might deliberately renounce the role of social architect. And in fact he sets himself so thoroughly against and away from "the state" that it's hard to see how he could have any plan to redesign it.

132. Schutte (1984, chapter 7) is useful for its presentation of the case against Nietzsche; she criticizes some previous scholars (Jaspers, Kaufmann) for avoiding his disturbing political views.

133. Nussbaum's seven criteria for serious political thought: "understanding of material need; procedural justification; liberty and its worth; racial, ethnic and religious difference; gender and family; justice between nations; and moral psychology" (1997, 1).

134. That is, nothing intrinsically interesting, i.e., that would be interesting apart from the fact that Nietzsche says it.

135. See Kaufmann (1950/1974, 412): "Nietzsche opposed both the idolatry of the State and political liberalism because he was basically '*antipolitical*' (EH.i.3) and, moreover, loathed the very idea of belonging to any 'party' whatever." See the critical discussion of this view by Detwiler (1990, 37ff.).

I will also try to do justice to this second doubt against a "Nietzschean politics." Indeed, in recognizing just how different his region of problems is, I partly concede that doubt. Nietzsche stretches our term "politics" to cover something new, something he sometimes calls "great politics." But I think this still does involve a kind of social architecture, operating at the same high level of generality as Plato's. Nietzsche doesn't limit himself to the question of how individuals should be, but judges and recommends for societies as well. Indeed, it's only in doing this that he counts himself a "philosopher" at all, by his own main sense for the term. A philosopher makes new values *for society*, and Nietzsche clearly aspires to this larger role.[136] Importantly, he wants different values to take hold in different *parts* of society, so that his values serve to articulate a certain social structure.

The key to Nietzsche's politics is once again his ideal of self selection; it is the way he conceives of freedom as decisively *from* society's values. His core idea here is the fundamental opposition—and also dependence— between ideal individuals and the social herd. Nietzsche aims to design a society to enable individuals to detach from society, and this dictates the distinctive features of his politics. It also gives a different point to his values of breeding and rank order than the latter have for Social Darwinists. Again the eventual question will be whether this special basis for his political claims—in a conception of freedom that may have some appeal for us—makes those claims more satisfactory than their Social Darwinist analogues.

So the kind of society Nietzsche wants is determined by that priority he puts on individuals, and by his identification of individuals as those who *overcome* their social constitution. They "see through" their social values—stepping back to remake them for themselves. This means that self selection could never become a social practice, and the best society can't be a society of self selectors.[137] And we can't get at Nietzsche's ideal society by taking an ideal individual and multiplying. The members he designs for society are disjoint from the individuals he aims to produce.[138]

136. BGE61 says that "we free spirits" understand the philosopher "as the human of the most comprehensive responsibility, who has the conscience for the overall evolution of the human."
137. Moore (2002, 136): "A 'species' of such superior beings would be a contradiction in terms."
138. Notice, however, that HH.iii.350 says that it's *our* age, the "age of the individual," in which only individuals can be free, not society in general; it implicitly anticipates a later time when society can be so too.

Hence the practices—habits and values—that pervade the society define not what the self selectors will do, but what they'll step away from. And his principal advice to free spirits is advice on how to escape these practices, not advice on how the practices should be. And so when he promotes the virtues of hardness and selfishness to self selectors, this doesn't show that he wants them to be general practice. Indeed, he insists on the great disparity between the virtues for the rule and those for the exceptions.

Yet it's a basic premise of Nietzsche's politics that there *must* be a practice which the bulk of society's members follow *because* it's the common practice: *the herd is necessary*. Society is only possible by shared practices, and practices will only in fact *be* so shared by being "planted" in members, not left to their individual initiatives. Members must take up practices by virtue of a common drive to share—a herd instinct. Nietzsche insists that this character of society is not something we should hope to overcome. Indeed it is also a necessary condition for those new individuals he advocates.[139]

But to say that the herd must persist is not to say that it should persist unchanged. Once again Nietzsche thinks of an exaptation or redesign. This herd, with its distinctive logic of memetic selection, needs to be subordinated and converted to a new selective end (criterion): the end of producing individuals who transcend it. Previously social selection designed the herd to be hostile and discouraging to individuals. Now self selectors—the "new philosophers"—will redesign it to encourage them. They do so by changes in the content of its "herd values."

One key point is that the herd's values must not "stick to" the candidates for freedom. So the herd must not insist on imposing its values on those potential individuals. The challenge is to "insulate" the latter from the former.[140] And this insulation also works in the other direction: to prevent the diagnosing insights of free spirits from undermining the herd's confidence in its values. One challenge in the following will be to characterize this "insulation."

---

139. WP132 [1885]: "[W]e support first of all [*zunächst*] the religions and moralities of the herd instinct, for these prepare a kind of human, that must one day fall into our hands, that must *desire* our hand. /Beyond good and evil, but we demand the unconditional holding-holy of the herd morality." WP660 [1885–1886]: "Inference about the evolution of humanity: perfecting consists in bringing forth the most powerful individuals, into whose tool the great mass will be made." See also WP954 [1885–1886]. The point is already in UM.iii.6.

140. WP287 [1886–1887]: "The sense of the herd should rule in the herd, — but not reach out above it."

It's partly to secure such insulation, I think, that Nietzsche insists there must be a second and elite class or caste in society, with values and practices distinct from the herd's. This class is intermediate, in certain respects, between herd and individuals. Free spirits emerge from this class, but the class's members are not themselves free: they belong to a type cleaving to a common practice, and are to this extent a second but less-inured herd. These are the "nobles," the aristocracy he promotes. Their values, discrete from the herd's, enable the self selectors.

I'll organize Nietzsche's plans for society under the two headings of breeding and rank order. As I've mentioned, I take these as basic projects of the society he wants, ways it tries to be, i.e., "societal virtues." The first is his substitute for our prevailing virtue of civilizing (taming): he wants to change society's general method of making its members. The second is his substitute for our virtue of equality: he wants to change the kind of members society makes. Putting his changes together: Nietzsche wants to "breed a rank order."

a. Breeding

Nietzsche's views on breeding (*Züchten*) are at the center of a group of opinions that are highly unsettling to most of us. These include his comments on *race*, his advocacy of *eugenics*, and his idea of gender relations. Most centrally, they include his insistence that we must try to "breed humanity higher." So EH.BT.4 speaks of "that new party of life, which takes in its hands the greatest of all tasks, the breeding higher of humanity." And A3: "The problem that I here pose is not what should succeed [*ablösen*] humanity in the succession of beings (— the human is an *end* —): but which type of human one should *breed*, should *will*, as higher in value, worthier of life, surer of a future."[141] All of these positions link Nietzsche with Social Darwinists. And all look highly unappealing to most of us today.[142]

---

141. He already thought so in *Untimely Meditations* (iii.6): "[H]umanity, because it can come to consciousness of its purpose, has to seek out and establish those favorable conditions, under which those great redeeming humans can arise."

142. E.g., Detwiler (1990, 193): "His racial and genetic theories, . . . and his views on women need no comment except to say they are probably the most thoroughly discredited aspects of his thought."

I will try to clarify these positions in my neo-Darwinian terms. What Nietzsche means by "breeding" is a particular way of relating the three selective mechanisms I've distinguished (natural, social, individual). It is a certain "functional" ordering of them, a way of making them mutually use and direct one another's projects. It's what Nietzsche would call a certain power relation among them. Most important, breeding is a way of making self selection—in the person of the "new philosophers" he anticipates—direct how genetic and social selection operate. But we'll see that the functional or power relations are more complex and mutual than this. Together, they give us the gist of the "great politics" (*grosse Politik*) he advocates.

Let's start with the contrast term. Nietzsche offers breeding to replace *civilizing* (*Civilisiren*), as the up-to-now way society has shaped its members. His negative assessment of this method is suggested in the other terms he interchanges with it, "taming" (*Zähmung*) and "domestication" (*Domestikation*).[143] He uses these terms to characterize a process or project of forming human beings, a process that he finds more or less widely at work. Most widely, he sees taming as the overall or dominant character of all the changes that have separated humans from other animals; all of human history (and prehistory) has worked this way. Somewhat more narrowly, he finds taming in the moralistic way of shaping humans that has characterized many societies, including European society since the Christianizing of Rome.

What does Nietzsche mean by this taming? What criteria does he use in applying it? We can distinguish two *kinds* of criteria.

Sometimes or in part, he understands these terms to refer to a certain *outcome* or *end* that the design (of members) aims at. Civilizing aims at a particular content or product—it tries to make a certain kind of human: morally good, peaceable, selfless, and so on. It aims, in fact, at the "herd animal."[144]

But elsewhere Nietzsche hears "civilizing" and its cohort as defined by a certain *method*, a *means* of instilling its content into humans. In particular, taming is distinguished by how it reviles and suppresses our bodily

143. See n. 31 above on this group of terms. Nietzsche sometimes speaks of civilizing as breeding; e.g., GM.i.11 says that it involves *"ein Hausthier herauszuzüchten."* Note that A62 also uses *herauszuzüchten* for this point.

144. WP121 [1888]: "Civilization wills something other than culture wills: perhaps something opposite"; the preceding sentence makes clear that civilizing wills to moralize people, at the expense of the most spiritual.

drives—by how it tries to turn us *against* these drives, for no matter what end.[145]

Of course these senses of taming are connected. Nietzsche is diagnosing a cultural phenomenon which has both aspects: it tries to make a particular kind of people, and it uses a characteristic method and means to do so—a method suited to that anticipated product. The kind of breeding he commends to us differs from civilizing in both respects—in its *means* and its *end*. I'll treat the difference in end in the following subsection, as the difference between rank order and equality. Here I'll focus on the difference in breeding's means or methods.

I think the current connotations of "breeding"—as of *Züchtung*—make us expect that the difference is this: whereas civilizing works memetically, i.e., by processes of training, disciplining, and teaching, breeding works genetically, i.e., by processes that change society "in the blood." Civilizing trains habits, whereas breeding alters (genetic) drives. So taming works by cultivating social habits and values, whereas breeding works by controlling procreation—who makes babies with whom.

This is an element in Nietzsche's view of the contrast, but by itself it's too simple. In fact, the strong eugenic connotations we now hear in "breeding/*Züchtung*" are misleading. Nietzsche doesn't consistently use the term in a genetic or biological sense, but in a broader sense in which it includes upbringing, training, teaching, and so on. Indeed, he seems *more* often to apply it in cases where the latter, and not manipulations of (genetic) inheritance, are clearly the point.[146] And the "breeding" he advocates often works in these nongenetic ways.[147]

Indeed, Nietzsche's Lamarckian tendencies—which we've noted before—erode the boundary between these two kinds of selection. Acquired

---

145. GM.ii.16 speaks of "this [human] animal that rubbed itself raw on the bars of its cage as one willed to 'tame' it." See too TI.vii.2.

146. Schank (2000, 336ff.) argues in detail that the nongenetic sense is dominant. Kaufmann (1950/1974, 304) stresses its "dual connotation"; in his translations he often renders it "cultivate," which unfortunately obscures the term's presence. An example of the broader use is EH.i.2: "He reacts slowly to every kind of stimulus, with that slowness which a long caution and a willed pride have bred into him"; presumably the caution and pride are the individual's own.

147. Notice the methods WP898 [1887] mentions for "the breeding of a *stronger race*": "The means would be those that history teaches: preservation-interests opposite the ones usual today; habituation [*Einübung*] in the opposite valuations; distance as pathos; free conscience in what's today most undervalued and forbidden."

traits can become heritable: habits can become drives. This means that genetic content can be altered not just by changing "who makes babies," but by changing the upbringing, education, and indeed all the social processes that work "memetically" on members.[148] It's clear that the new kind of breeding he advocates will work by both routes.

On the other hand, Nietzsche also believes that it is *difficult* to change drives this way—by changing habits.[149] Drives can be changed only in certain limited ways, even by the most rigorous inculcation of habits. And he thinks the changes that *can* be made this way are less firmly set into the heritable "blood" of descendants. WP684 [1888]: "[T]he domestication ('culture') of humans does not go deep. . . . Where it does go deep, it is at once degeneration (type: Christ)."

So although I deny that Nietzsche thinks breeding works only genetically, and civilizing only memetically, I do agree that he *stresses* (the need for) a more direct control on propagation—and calls his new method "breeding" to convey this stress. He thinks the reigning process of civilizing has paid too little attention to "marriage"—which stands for him as the means to a direct control of inheritance. He wants to take such control, while also working to change habits and values. He expresses this inclusive method in his frequent pairings of *Züchtung* and *Erziehung*.[150]

I've been discussing the special character of breeding's "how," but must also address a really prior question, as to "who" or "what" carries it out. Who or what is it that "breeds"—and how is this different from what "tames"? To answer, let's start with Nietzsche's most extended discussion of the contrast between taming and breeding. This is chapter 7 of *Twilight of the Idols*, on "The 'Improvers' of Humanity." This describes a method of breeding which is not Nietzsche's own, but with which he feels

148. BGE213: "For every high world one must be born; more clearly put, one must be *bred* for it: a right to philosophy — taking the word in the great sense — one has only thanks to his descent [*Abkunft*], the ancestors, the 'blood' decides here too. Many generations must have worked before the arising of the philosopher; his every virtue must have been individually acquired, nurtured, inherited, incorporated." Also WP942 [1885].

149. Both points are evident in BGE264: "One cannot wipe away from the soul of a human, what his ancestors have done most gladly and constantly"; "with the help of the best upbringing and education [*Erziehung und Bildung*] one will only succeed in *deceiving* about such a heredity."

150. Some examples from *Beyond Good and Evil*: BGE61 (*Züchtungs- und Erziehungswerke*), BGE62 (*Züchtungs- und Erziehungsmittel*), BGE201 (*gross-gezogen und gezüchtet*); also BGE199 (*geübt und gezüchtet*), BGE203 (*Zucht und Züchtung*).

an affinity: the Hindu caste system as laid out in the "law of Manu."[151] He contrasts it with the method of taming practiced by Christianity. He is critical of both systems, but clearly more favorable toward the Hindu "breeding." We can use this to point us toward the new method of breeding he advocates.

In this passage, Nietzsche presents both tamers and breeders as intended "improvers of humanity." He depicts them as deliberately, foresightedly identifying their (respective) ends, and calculating means accordingly. So he identifies the Christian tamer as "the priest," "the church" (2), and identifies improvers generally as "priests and philosophers" (5). He also suggests that the Hindu breeder "conceiv[es]" of this "plan [*Plan*] of breeding." And it is otherwise common for Nietzsche to "personalize" in this way the causes of such social processes.[152]

However, I think this personalization is misleading, because incomplete: it leaves out a further explanation he has of those individuals themselves. He treats them as tools of much vaster selective processes, from which they haven't managed to get free. Indeed I think the lack of awareness of both tamer and breeder is presupposed in TI.vii, since these improvers are discussed in order to illustrate how a moral judgment "reveals, for knowers at least, the most valuable realities of cultures and inwardnesses, which did not *know* enough to 'understand' themselves" (1). And the terms "taming" and "breeding" themselves express "zoological realities . . . of which the typical 'improver,' the priest, knows nothing — *wills* to know nothing" (2).

The priest or philosopher doesn't understand what he's doing.[153] And the most important thing he misses is the way he is being used by larger processes—in fact natural and social selection themselves. It's the latter that really set up end and means, and the individual "improver" is just one of those means. So the Christian priest, the tamer, seeks to con-

151. Elsewhere he attributes such breeding to an "aristocratic community" (BGE262).

152. A57 attributes foresight to a group: "At a certain point in the evolution of a people, the most circumspect level, that sees farthest back and ahead, declares the experience according to which one should live — i.e., *can* live —, to be concluded." WP142 [1888] is most emphatic: "One errs, when one supposes an *unconscious and naïve* evolution here [in the priest's holy lie], a kind of self-deception. . . . /The most cold-blooded reflection has worked here, the same kind of reflection, as a Plato had, when he thought out his 'Republic'."

153. See GM.iii.13 (quoted above in chapter 1, n. 86) and iii.28.

trol habits and practices—but in fact there is a logic in those habits them-selves that produces him, with his project. Similarly the Hindu priest, the breeder, really expresses the tendency of natural selection, to breed types stronger.

I think it's in this regard that Nietzsche's new breeding differs most dramatically from both taming and the breeding by Manu. The key differ-ence, he thinks, is not in the end or the means, but in *how* this teleology gets set up at all—the way it is directed or aimed. What's most important is that we take a new kind of control of human development, take it *away from* natural and social selection. Such control was never feasible before, because we lacked the (genealogical) self-knowledge it presupposes. Nietz-schean breeding is redesigning our drives and practices on the basis of insight into why we have them, i.e., what they *have* been for. Just as individuals can only be genuinely (Nietzscheanly) free now that such insight is feasible, so too for the society or lineage.

Nietzsche often stresses how, with this breeding, evolution can today for the first time be self-willed, self-guided. BGE203: "To teach man the future of man as his *will*, as dependent on a human will, and to prepare great ventures and over-all attempts of discipline [*Zucht*] and breeding [*Züchtung*] in order to make an end of that gruesome rule by nonsense [*Unsinns*] and chance [*Zufalls*], that has so far been called 'history'."[154] Yet this new opportunity has been ignored and wasted.[155]

Nietzsche calls for "new philosophers" to direct this new breeding. By their diagnostic insight they advance beyond all previous attempts by philosophers, priests, and rulers to improve society (or humanity).[156] The new philosophers choose methods on the basis of a better genealogy, psychology, and physiology. They understand our constitution of drives and habits as previous social architects never did. They see what's suscepti-ble to being changed and what's not, and whether change must come by

154. WP898 [1887]: "That which partly necessity [*Noth*], partly chance has achieved here and there, the conditions for the production of a *stronger kind*: we can now grasp and knowingly [*wissentlich*] *will*: we can create the conditions, under which such an elevation is possible."

155. See BGE203 on the anxiety of one who grasps just how much might be "bred from the human."

156. This is the gist of Nietzsche's "procedural justification" for his political vision—contra Nussbaum's claim (1997, 4) that he "[n]either asks [n]or answers the question, from what point of view or through what procedures are political institutions justified." Nietzsche defends his political values as those a self selector will choose.

memetic or genetic steps. So they will breed more "scientifically" than was ever possible before. Nietzsche puts great stress on this improvement in method.[157]

We can see this new breeding as the culmination of a long and difficult evolution in humans' epistemic powers. We saw in chapter 2, sections 3b–c, how these powers—memory, language, and consciousness— first arose under the long "ethic of custom," as devices for improving social cooperation, and how they were gradually designed into a morality, reinforcing social bonds with guilt, God, and other potent memes. But these epistemic powers also involve a "will to truth"—which likewise made them useful for those social purposes. Nietzsche thinks this will to truth progressively frees itself from that social service; it "sees through" those memes developed in its moral phase. And now, with the insights of genealogy, these epistemic powers make real freedom possible, first for individuals and then (in a sense) for society and indeed humanity as a whole.

The new breeding not only employs these epistemic powers, but also works to strengthen them. And it does so, I will argue below, at all levels of society. Even the herd will be "wiser" than it has been, inasmuch as its values will be purged of their moralistic force: they will no longer rest on lies about God or the soul, for example. A kind of herd will be bred that can cleave to its values even without such faith in their ultimacy or objectivity—and without resentment against those who reject them. This epistemic advance in the herd is important for the "insulation" of its values.

Outside (or "above") the herd Nietzsche anticipates a body of "potential individuals," in whom those epistemic powers will be bred still stronger. I'll return to this body in treating rank order, but for now what's important is that it will be selected for its capacity to live with the nihilistic truths that genealogy uncovers. To breed this strength, the device Nietzsche most stresses is the *thought of eternal return*: he often calls this a breeding agent. WP862 [1884]: "A doctrine is needed, strong enough to work for *breeding*: strengthening for the strong, crippling and shattering for the

---

157. Early, in HH.i.24: "But humans can resolve with *consciousness* to evolve themselves to a new culture, whereas formerly they evolved unconsciously and accidentally: they can now create better conditions for the arising of humans, their nutrition, upbringing, instruction." The note appended to GM.i describes the sorts of historical and physiological researches the new philosophers will rely on.

world-weary." And WP462 [1887]: "In place of metaphysics and religion: *the doctrine of eternal recurrence* (this as [a] means of breeding and selection)."[158]

I think Nietzsche uses his thought of eternal return as an emblem for the partiality of all values. It involves, in the first place, the overturning of all religious supports to values: no God, no future paradise (and hell) to confirm conclusively the value of certain values. The thought forces one to affirm values in the absence of such metaphysical validations. More generally, this thought of eternal return brings home the "partiality" of one's values, by stressing how temporary and small they stand in overall time. All that one's values *detest* will also recur, having likewise an eternal part in the whole. Indeed, the thought challenges one to *will* that these detested opposites recur. And this tests whether one's valuing can encompass these opposites as well—and hence reduce, to this degree, the partiality in this valuing. So the thought of eternal return is meant to effect the kind of distance from one's values that is needed for freedom.

As a breeding agent, the thought of eternal return works memetically, I think. It works on the values of the elite, selecting them to be as this thought demands. It alters the milieu of ideas of this elite, not their "blood." But we've already seen that Nietzsche's new philosophers will also use genetic means more aggressively. Insight into our physiology of drives shows the limits to engineering by habits or memes. Our prevailing sickness is due to the misguided effort to overpower drives with enforced habits. The new breeding sees the need to work on drives more directly, and so gives more weight to *eugenics* than the long regime of taming has done. Here the aim is of course not to breed drives weaker, but to keep them strong while making them more susceptible to sublimation into the spiritual project of freedom. For this Nietzsche advocates both *negative eugenics*—inducing the unworthy to reproduce less—and *positive eugenics*—inducing the valuable to reproduce more, and with valuable others.

One way to reduce propagation by the unworthy is by increasing their mortality. Nietzsche makes various concrete suggestions of this sort. In

---

158. WP1053 [1884]: "My philosophy brings the triumphant thought, by which every other mode of thought will ultimately perish. It is the great *breeding* thought: the races that cannot bear it, are condemned; those that experience it as greatest benefit are picked out to rule." That is, some people's practices are capable of dispensing with the illusions of progress and morality, whereas others will end as the illusions end.

TI.ix.36, for example, he calls on physicians to inculcate in some patients a responsibility to "choose death." Elsewhere he seems to favor infanticide and even restriction of social resources.[159]

But the main means of genetic change is by controlling marriage and reproduction. This includes preventing some from procreating altogether. WP734 [1888]:

> [H]ere society has a *duty* to fulfill: there are few such pressing and basic demands on it. Society, as great trustee of life, is responsible *before* life itself for every failed life, — it also has to pay for it: hence it should prevent [*verhindern*] it. Society *should* prevent [*vorbeugen*] procreation in many cases: for this it may hold in readiness, without regard to descent, rank and spirit, the hardest measures of constraint, withdrawals of freedom, in some cases castration.[160]

On the positive side, he anticipates exceptional men and women being permitted to marry with multiple partners (9.11[179] [1881]).

Nietzsche also advocates a broad revision in the motives for marriage: he wants to reverse the modern tendency toward marriage "for love," i.e., on the basis of erotic attraction. TI.ix.39: "[The rationality of marriage] lay also in the family's responsibility for the choice of spouse. With the growing indulgence in favor of *love* matches, one has eliminated the foundation of marriage, that which first *makes* an institution of it."[161] Our sex drive responds to physical features quite different from the spiritual and epistemic strengths needed in breeding for freedom. So society needs to prevent this drive from determining marriage partners. Nietzsche sometimes implies

159. See n. 37 above. TI.vi.3 seems favorable toward the sick-making restrictions the laws of Manu impose on the chandala, such as no clean water. A2: "The weak and failures [*Missrathnen*] should perish [*zu Grunde gehn*]: first principle of *our* love of humans. And one should even help them thereto." WP964 [1884] speaks of the "annihilation [*Vernichtung*] of millions of failures." There are also many vaguer remarks, such as EH.BT.4: "the relentless destruction of everything degenerating and parasitical."

160. On castration see also 9.10[100] [1881]. On the more general preventative point, 9.14[16] [1881].

161. 9.5[38] [1880]: "One should not make the satisfaction of the [sex] drive into a practice by which the race suffers, i.e., where no selection at all takes place any more, but everyone mates and makes children. The *dying-out* of many kinds of humans is just as *desirable* as any propagation." Also D151; WP732 [1886]. Moore (2002, 136–37) notes that Nietzsche favors prostitution to divert sexual energies and prevent them from determining marriages (see again 9.5[38] [1880], also 9.11[82] [1881]).

that society must exert some kind of bureaucratic control over this choice, to counter that drive.[162]

However, I think these suggestions of an authoritarian legal control of the sex drive mask the change Nietzsche is really interested in—a change in *values*. Here what's at stake are the values in this sex drive itself, what stirs and what depresses it. Rather than distracting or suppressing this drive, I think Nietzsche most wants to modify or exapt it, to alter its "taste." This better accords with his general aim to "sublimate" drives rather than suppress them. Society should breed sexual taste to favor the epistemic powers germane to freedom. In chapter 4 I'll lay out Nietzsche's theory of the sex drive, and the "beauty" it judges. I'll show how he thinks this taste has been revised by social selection, and how he means to revise it again, to advance self selection. And I hope this account will show a part or aspect of his viewpoint on sex that merits an attention those cruder authoritarian statements do not.[163]

Nietzsche thinks that in their control of marriage his new social architects will take "race" into account. They will work strategically upon the various races brought together in society, mixing or isolating different ones. Here (I think) Nietzsche means by "race" simply a large human clade, i.e., a group of shared descent, which also shares a set of practices that enable *this* blood to live in this environment at this time. The differences among races makes them so many different instruments for social design, put to work in different ways.[164]

Sometimes the social architect will try to "breed pure" a race. But Nietzsche thinks that today the main challenge is to find the right way to "mix races"—all the races making up Europe, for a start. WP862 [1884] recommends "[t]o strive for fullness of nature through pairing of opposites: race-mixture thereto. "[165] Nietzsche is especially eager to mix into European

162. WP733 [1888]: "[E]very marriage [should be] warranted and sanctioned by a certain number of trusted men [*Männer*] of the community, as a community concern."

163. Nussbaum (1997, 5–6) criticizes Nietzsche's many "silly" remarks on sex, as no more interesting than those of a twelve-year-old boy. Nietzsche himself sometimes seems to recognize the limits of his vision here. But the ideas I'll develop in the next chapter show a more serious and appealing aspect to his reflections here.

164. It must be admitted, however, that Nietzsche sometimes thinks some races will be no longer useful for this design: WP862 [1884]: "The annihilation [*Vernichtung*] of the decaying races." 8.19[79] [1876]: "Economy of the earth, letting-die-off of bad races, breeding of better."

165. WP960 [1885–1886]: "[T]he possibility has been created for the formation of international racial unions [*Geschlechts-Verbänden*], which set themselves the task of breeding up a master-race, the future 'masters of the earth'."

blood "the strongest, toughest, and purest race now living in Europe," the Jews (BGE251).

Again I think Nietzsche here states in crudely political fashion ideas that are more interesting when read as a reform of values, and for the sake of freedom. For we can think of this "race management," too, as effected not via direct intervention by authorities, but in a general shift in the values or tastes of members—in their aesthetic and sexual judgment. Again this shifts the taste to improve *epistemic* powers. Individuals from one clade need to judge more accurately the limitations it saddles them with—and to find their advantage in mixing (their memes and/or their genes) with other clades.[166] Again the main point is to enable that kind of distance from one's own values, which is required for freedom. Racial mixtures can be a means to such distance—building multiple viewpoints into individuals, enabling them to judge each perspective from others.

b. Rank Order

All of this discussion of Nietzschean breeding has shelved what is really a prior question: what does this breeding aim at? Let's turn now from the method, breeding, to the end, i.e., the kind of members society breeds for itself—as well as the kind of *relations among* these members.

In the case of taming, our current method for making social members, the aim is indeed *more* at a kind of relation: it tries to render us more alike. Taming designs members *so that* they can stand in this relation, which is the main thing—the thing most selected for (by the logic of social selection analyzed back in chapter 2, section 3a). It's for the sake of this similarity that taming makes members in the further ways discussed above, e.g., as moral and God-fearing.

Similarly, although Nietzsche's breeding aims chiefly at a kind of "member," it understands this kind as defined by its *difference* from other members. It is hard to say, I think, whether Nietzsche values this kind for its intrinsic character, or because of that difference and distinction from others.[167] In any case his breeding crucially pursues a "rank order" (*Rangord-*

166. On the topic of race, Nussbaum criticizes (1997, 6–7) Nietzsche's "unsorted and incoherent group of remarks that don't really add up to anything." Again, my modest aim is to isolate a subset of his views that cohere with the large-scale, neo-Darwinian argument this book develops and that look better in this context.

167. I discuss the comparative or relational character of power in Richardson 1996, chapter 1, section 1.2.

nung) or *hierarchy*, which he thinks is indispensable to making the strong and free individuals he advocates.

This account of breeding's end is more disturbing than even the method was. And again there are several associated claims that are still less appealing, including Nietzsche's attack on *democracy*, his praise for *aristocracy*, and his favorable comments on *slavery*. And on all these points his positions remind us once more of Social Darwinism.

My strategy for responding to these doubts will be to stress how this rank order is crucially a necessary range of degrees of *freedom*. Making oneself, by making one's values, is the best a human can be. But human life also depends on society—on a background of shared values and practices, to which there must be very general allegiance. This allegiance in turn depends on a shared metavalue on agreeing and sharing, a value that must be a strong instinct in order to support effective social practice, an *ethos*. In his thought about rank order, what matters most for Nietzsche is the necessary grades of *escape* from this dominant social instinct. So he thinks of a radically different kind of hierarchy than the Social Darwinists do.

The principal difference in rank—the one Nietzsche really cares about—is in this new kind of freedom. And the economic and (more narrowly) political differences he sometimes speculates on are secondary. He can afford to be wrong about them, because his main allegiance is to that other point. And that other point—the core idea of a necessary hierarchy in freedom—is an idea worth taking seriously and separating off from the crude applications he often gives it. Often, indeed, we find that the crudity is in our hearing—that we have missed the kind of social difference or hierarchy he's talking about. Elsewhere, when there is no mistaking his intent, we should ask why he thinks his core idea has these particular economic and political implications, and whether in truth it does.[168]

i. KINDS OF SOCIAL DIFFERENCE

Again let's start with the contrast term (to rank order). The value *equality* (*Gleichheit*) is a way for a society to be structured, *taken as* a goal or virtue by that society. That is, Nietzsche naturalizes it—as he does all ends and values—as the object of a valuing, in this case not by an individual but

---

168. At this point my strategy resembles that of Warren (1988, 209): "Nietzsche's philosophy *underdetermines* his politics, and in crucial respects is also at odds with it."

by a social group. And it's an "end" for that group in his etiological sense: equality is the outcome that explains the group's shared practices—explains them by being the social structure those practices have been designed to bring about. The group "aims" at equality not by intending it, but by having been designed for it.

Nietzsche thinks that not just some but all societies have this value of equality, by the logic of selection over social habits. There's a steady selective pressure in all social groups in favor of *likening* their members, making them herd. This is so even in social groups in which equality is never "posited" as a goal linguistically or consciously. As we saw in chapter 2, section 3b, language and consciousness are themselves, by Nietzsche's diagnosis, designed to help "herd" us. So when they appear they are directly employed to *voice* that value of equality and to bring it into conscious *view*. And so societies come eventually to "value" equality in our more usual sense of naming and thinking it valuable.

But equality is especially the tendency of our modern age, Nietzsche thinks. BGE242: "One calls that in which the distinction of the European is sought 'civilization' or 'humanization' or 'progress'; one calls it simply . . . Europe's *democratic* movement." Even in this case the thought and spoken (conscious and linguistic) ideal of equality rests on a deeper process; he continues: "[B]ehind all the moral and political foregrounds, to which such formulas point, a tremendous *physiological* process is taking place, which comes ever more on, — the process of a becoming-similar [*Anähnlichung*] of Europeans." This process is served and strengthened by the *moral* form it has been given, first by Christianity and later by the enlightened arguments of philosophers such as Kant and Mill. The physiological and philosophical projects of equality are both parts of this large cultural dynamic.

Now what, more precisely, is this outcome of equality, toward which this large dynamic tends? As a "social structure," it's a relation among society's members, but what relation? I think we can distinguish three main points Nietzsche has in mind. Members are equal by virtue of (a) sharing practices and values, (b) having similar abilities and attainments, and (c) standing level in their power relations.

Nietzsche depicts himself as countering this broad and now especially intense social tendency toward equality with his ideal of rank order or difference.[169] He proposes it as a new end—though reviving and revising

169. WP854 [1884]: "I am compelled, in an age of *suffrage universel*, i.e., where everyone may sit in judgment over everyone and everything, to establish again *rank order*."

an old one—for which society should be engineered. Rank order differs from equality in those same three aspects; it makes members different by (a) individualizing their habits and values, (b) separating their degrees of ability and attainment, and (c) cultivating relations of command and obedience among them.

Taming tends, by the logic of social selection, to gather us into the same practices and values. But since each of us is a quite specific system of drives, with distinctive physiological needs, those blanket values fail to address those needs—their one size can't fit all. Nietzsche often attacks morality's insistence that the same values are right and best for all. Instead, different persons need different values, fine-tuned to their drive systems— they need the values that bring those drives into their most effective synthesis and working. Each needs to make values for his/her own case. This self-differentiation is the first main kind of "difference" he advocates.[170]

It's only the self selector who really or most accomplishes this—who really "sees through" the common values, and creates values of his/her own. By this, the free spirit steps out of the group, and is no longer truly a member. Nietzsche thinks this achievement will always be rare. However, I think he also promotes an analogue to this "difference" even among members—i.e., even within the shared practices. In the new herd he antici-pates, these practices will be (as it were) more adjustable to the psycho-physiological differences among members. They will reflect new scientific insights into our constitution by naturally selected drives—and into how varied this constitution can be. There will be more "variants" in the practice, suitable for individuals made differently in their drives. Members will learn to study themselves and to pick the variants that serve best in their cases.[171]

Such differences among members don't themselves raise one above another, however; they merely adjust the shared values to their peculiar cases. What really sets them into a hierarchy is their different capacities to "see through" those shared values, and to make themselves indepen-

---

170. A11: "A virtue must be *our* invention, *our* most personal defence and need [*Nothwehr und Nothdurft*]: in every other sense it is simply a danger. . . . The opposite [to Kant's universal duty] is commanded by the deepest laws of preservation and growth: that everyone invent *his* virtue, *his* categorical imperative." See also BGE221, TI.v.6.

171. I think Nietzsche advocates this individualized attention to one's life conditions in EH.ii, with its emphasis on finding the nutrition, climate, and so on in which one best thrives. So in ii.1 he poses the question: "'[H]ow do *you* in particular [*gerade*] have to eat, in order to arrive at your maximum of strength, of *virtù* in the Renaissance style, of moraline-free virtue?'"

dently of them. This core distinction supports Nietzsche's two further claims about rank order.

Taming has worked to shrink the natural variation among individuals in their abilities and achievements. Reinforced by the herd's resentment of exceptions, civilizing has set up mechanisms that inhibit exceptional abilities and suppress exceptional achievements. Against this, Nietzsche wants society to magnify these disparities. Z.ii.7: "For justice speaks to *me* thus: 'humans are not equal.' / And they should not become so! What would my love of the overman be if I spoke otherwise?"[172] The most exceptional achievement, the overman's, is of course to make new values in freedom. If there can be both such superhuman individuals, and at the same time others who are merely herd, this difference will stretch out as far as possible.

Nietzsche wants to redesign society, so that it functions not for average or overall well-being, but for high individual achievements—especially the high achievement of individuality. One of the ways society should favor such achievements is by dispersing widely the recognition or acceptance that there *are* higher and lower human levels—that individual types lie not on a plain of equal validity or worth, but vertically on a "ladder" of steps or levels.[173]

Again this changes even the common practices and values of the herd. It's not that the herd members take up for themselves the ideal or goal of freedom: they don't try for it themselves, and esteem others who have more of it. Nietzsche often complains how high achievements get spoiled when the herd tries to share in them.[174] They might not admire or even approve of those "free spirits." But Nietzsche thinks the herd must at least not *resent* the exceptions, and must not try to moralize them back into the herd. This is another part of the "insulation" needed between the values of the many and the few.

Taming has set members level with one another a further way: it has flattened the relations of "command and obedience" between them. Or, indeed, in the wake of Christianity's slave revolt it has even reversed these relations, so that the weaker command. Nietzsche wants breeding to restore this kind of difference as well: it's not enough that there be higher and

172. Also Z.ii.16.
173. Z.ii.7: "Life itself wills to build itself up into the heights with pillars and steps: it wills to look into wide distances and out towards blessed beauties, — *therefore* it requires height! / And because it requires height, it requires steps and contradiction among the steps and climbers!"
174. E.g., Z.ii.6 ("On the Rabble").

lower, but the higher should "rule." WP861 [1884]: "A declaration of war by *higher humans* on the masses is needed! Everywhere the mediocre are coming together in order to make themselves master!"[175]

It is this third point, of course, that most disturbs us. What kind of "command" or "rule" does Nietzsche have in mind? We can imagine a range of answers to this key question, running perhaps between these extremes: (i) the elites command only by formulating values the herd then accepts, or (ii) they command in the full political and economic sense we find in, e.g., the Greek state. These extremes give us very different ways of hearing the kind of "slavery" Nietzsche often advocates. This could be as relatively innocuous as (i) the herd's uncritical embrace of prevailing values, or as disturbing as (ii) a political and economic suppression of this group. I'll return to this key issue below.

Now I've been treating these three kinds of "difference" Nietzsche means to breed as differences among individual members. In this aspect, rank order grades individuals along a long and complex continuum of human types, the "ladder" of possibilities. But Nietzsche also thinks these differences need to be instantiated in clearer divisions between social *classes* or *castes*. There must be a higher class that rules and a lower one that obeys. Such an "aristocracy" is necessary for that overall project of breeding exceptions. WP752 [1884]: "Aristocracy represents the belief in an elite-humanity and higher caste. Democracy represents the disbelief in great humans and an elite-society: 'Everyone is equal to everyone.' 'At bottom we are all together self-serving cattle and mob.'" The difference between the castes is a conspicuous emblem of the society's overall commitment to making humans stronger and better.

In treating Nietzsche's views about class or caste I will exaggerate a simplification he often makes, and speak only of *two* classes, his "nobles" (elite) and his herd. These correspond, roughly, to Plato's spirited and appetitive classes—and types of soul. The analogues to Plato's philosopher-kings are of course Nietzsche's new philosophers and overmen, but he insists they don't form a class, and can't directly be bred.[176] His philoso-

---

175. To be sure, Nietzsche thinks there have been selective advantages behind this rule of the weak and sick. And he sometimes speculates, as in WP401 [1888], that it's better that they rule (since the masters would suppress the spirituality evolved through the sick). But I think his usual view is that although the reign by slave values has developed new human strengths, we will only best use them by effecting his "revaluation."

176. Here again I focus on *one* line Nietzsche takes. I acknowledge that he often speaks as if his ideal individuals, the overmen, *do* form a class or kind, and do constitute the "new aristocracy." Detwiler (1990, 100) reads him so.

phers, nobles, and herd also correspond to the three castes set up by the law of Manu: the spiritual, the strong, and the mediocre.[177] Nietzsche defends these castes as merely acknowledging natural differences among us; so A57: "The order of castes, the *rank order*, merely formulates the highest law of life itself, the separation of the three types is necessary for the preservation of society, for making possible higher and highest types."

Nietzsche's redesign of society establishes a functional relation among these three groups: the herd is mainly designed for the sake of the elite, who are mainly designed for the sake of the exceptions. To be sure, we'll see that the elite and even the herd are *also* designed for their own sakes—to be "as good as they can be." But because their best is less valuable than the exceptions, design proceeds mainly from the latter. So the new philosopher mainly conceives of these exceptions, and asks what elite practices will best induce some members to step free—and then, what herd practices will sustain that elite. I'll treat these designs of elite and herd in turn.

In each case the redesign will principally work, Nietzsche thinks, by instilling *values*. Each caste has different values, and also "has" its values in a different way. Here again he contradicts morality's assumption that values should be uniform throughout society. Elite and herd need different values in order to play their different functional roles. To preserve this difference there needs to be, we've seen he insists, a certain insulation between these values. Each must be prevented from spoiling or infecting the other. It's the failure in such insulation that brought about our great cultural tragedy: the slaves' resentment and then subversion of the masters. Much of Nietzsche's redesign of hierarchy is aimed at preventing this.

ii. THE NEW ELITE

Since exceptions can't be bred directly, the new breeding tries to make this top caste, from which they will emerge.[178] It tries to breed an elite that shares the virtues requisite for self selection—a "new nobility" based not in economic but in spiritual power.[179] It equips members of this elite with

177. Nietzsche becomes very interested in these Hindu laws in 1888. See especially TI.vii and A55–57. He traces Plato's caste morality to Manu in 13.14[191] [1888].

178. See WP907 [1884] on the difficulty in foreseeing the most favorable conditions for the highest individuals, but on the virtues ("courage, insight, hardness, independence") we can inculcate in order to improve the odds.

179. Z.iii.12.12: "O my brothers, I dedicate and direct you towards a new nobility: you should become procreators and breeders for me and sowers of the future, — / —

the abilities and values necessary for that leap to free creation, though these traits are not sufficient: few even in the elite will accomplish it, he thinks. Still, the virtues of this elite are mainly designed for that freedom.

I must acknowledge from the start, however, that Nietzsche sometimes gives this elite a more primary role: he speaks as if these "nobles" were themselves the ultimate point. His ideal sometimes seems less rigorously exceptional, more the members of a class or caste, which he often calls a higher kind or species or race (e.g., WP898 [1887]).[180]

But more often, I think, he puts his strongest emphasis on a new kind of creative individual who steps outside of every caste or social group—even from that new elite—and makes something new and his/her "own." And he favors his new elite over all elites before, precisely because it prepares for these exceptions. It's this peculiar ideal that gives Nietzsche's thoughts about social class their most distinctive character—and that renders them serious and interesting.

Nietzsche most often characterizes his new masters in vague terms as "strong" and so on. We commonly read these terms to state a Social Darwinist vision that is unattractive to most of us. But I think they should instead be read in the light of his core ideal of freedom as self selection. The new elite are bred toward this ideal, and the privilege they have is shaped to this purpose. WP978 [1885]: "The new philosopher can only arise in connection with a ruling caste, as its highest spiritualization." Why does Nietzsche think that his ideal requires such an elite?

Self selection depends on certain *virtues*—ways one ably tries to be—that can only be bred in a minority group, not in the general herd. Freedom is far harder than we suspect; Nietzsche gives it a heroic and questing character. It requires various intellectual and emotional strengths that are hard to inculcate, because they go so much against our natural design—and also against the instinct to share and agree, which the bulk of society must share. Moreover, these strengths entail weaknesses for other tasks: they're ineffective and even disabling with respect to the many other things a person might do, besides making his/her own values. Since society will need most of its members to do these other things, it can't breed *just* this elite.

truly, not towards a nobility that you could buy like shopkeepers and with shopkeepers' gold: for everything that has its price is of little value."
   180. BGE251: "[T]he 'European problem,' as I understand it, [is] the breeding of a new caste ruling over Europe." WP957 [1885]: "[F]irst of all *a new kind* must be bred up, in which the needed will, the needed instinct will be guaranteed duration through many generations [*Geschlechter*]: a new master-kind and -caste."

Nietzsche stresses what we might call the "martial" virtues needed for his freedom—but they really have an *epistemic* point. It requires new kinds of *strength* and *courage* to carry out a skeptical genealogy of the prevailing values—the values one had taken for granted. One needs courage before the existential pains in upsetting and spoiling these values.[181] Indeed, one even needs a kind of *cruelty*, directed at oneself and one's culture—a malicious will to find and touch the most sensitive nerves. Self selection presupposes a training in these and other traits, which can't extend to society at large—because most of society will always have functions this training and these traits would undermine. These skeptical traits destroy, most broadly, the straightforward confidence in the value of one's practical goals, needed for effective action.

These martial virtues are developed by unrepressing certain deep bodily drives. WP957 [1885]: "To prepare a *reversal of values* for a certain strong kind of human of the highest spirituality and strength of will and to this purpose slowly and with caution to unfetter a host of instincts now kept in check and slandered: whoever reflects on this belongs to us, the free spirits." The task is to design a society that *can* unfetter these drives, without splintering its social cohesion altogether. And Nietzsche's solution is to breed these virtues in a discrete "caste," so that they are somewhat insulated from the herd, and the herd from them.

Now of course in self selection these virtues are exercised in a *spiritual* way. The philosopher's courage and strength are exerted upon *ideas*; his/her command lies in *persuading* others into these ideas. But how should we understand the broader elite? Does Nietzsche think it will have these virtues primarily in *non*spiritual forms? This has surely been the character of the "aristocracies" we know from the past. But I think Nietzsche means a new kind of elite, for the sake of his new ideal. What makes the members elite is that they share not just the spiritual turn, but the self-awareness achieved by genealogy.

I think Nietzsche means the new elite to value and pursue "strength of spirit." The members compete with one another in this. They understand this strength to lie in skepticism and suspicion.[182] And they understand the ultimate test of this strength to be being able to will "eternal return." Unlike the *Genealogy*'s old "masters," who inhabited their values unreflec-

181. I treat Nietzsche's chief epistemic virtues, courage and honesty, in Richardson 1996, chapter 4, section 4.
182. A54: "[G]reat spirits are skeptics. . . . Strength, *freedom* through the strength and overstrength of spirit, *proves* itself by skepticism."

tively and had their strength in this, Nietzsche's new elite incorporates the insights of genealogy. Its members live with naturalized values, not (strictly speaking) a morality.

This shows us that the task of "breeding" this new elite is mainly a matter of inculcating an intellectual tradition, centered on the work of cultural diagnosis and self-scrutiny. Z.i.22.2: "You solitaries of today, you who have separated yourselves, you shall some day be a people: from you, who have selected out [*auswähltet*] yourselves, a chosen [*auserwähltes*] people shall grow: — and out of it the overman."

I've been treating the primary function of this new elite, which is to cultivate the strengths that give a chance for freedom. But Nietzsche also assigns a second function to this class, one that stands in some tension with the first. For this elite also plays the secondary role of assimilating and implementing the revolutionary advances of the exceptions.

An overman accomplishes a fresh diagnosis of social values, exposing some large aspect of their real design and enabling individuals really to choose, in this light, about them. Further, the overman points the general way for this choice, by using the diagnosis to *revalue* those social values. The broader elite, although not able to create this freeing step itself, appreciates its advance, and reconstructs its practice in its light. The elite's members implement the overman's diagnoses and revaluations, working out their implications for concrete practices.

So the new elite secondly functions to "incorporate" the overman's revaluings at the social level—analogously to the incorporation we saw was necessary for individual freedom (chapter 2, section 4b). They incorporate it into their own attitudes and actions. So, for example, Nietzsche's own diagnosis of the *ressentiment* in moral values would be incorporated by fully exposing its effect on those attitudes and actions—and revising them to overcome its influence. He wants a new elite that will live in the light of his diagnosis, remaking values free from that resentful aim. And by embodying the new insight themselves, the elite members diffuse it even into the general practice of the herd (to which I'll return shortly).

This second function of the new elite stands in some tension with the first. The members must be on the one hand the embodiment of new values won by old diagnoses and revaluings. But they must also be the reservoir of critical and skeptical impulses that will eventually expose and undermine those new values in turn. Indeed, this tension of living on sand, of striving and caring in ways one is simultaneously working to "see through," is the distress and strain that shows their strength, above that of those who can only live with the whole-hearted values of the herd.

When we see these two basic functions of the new elite, we see how the economic and (narrowly) political status of this elite is something secondary—which can be settled only by difficult judgments on how best to effect those functions. For example, the question of how this elite can best "incorporate" new values into the general social practice—whether by example and instruction, or by the exercise of some kind of political authority—is open and unresolved. To consider how Nietzsche addresses it we must widen our view, and look at the new herd this elite somehow "rules."

ii. THE NEW HERD

Before the new elite is fully possible, Nietzsche thinks there must be in place a particular lower caste, an appropriate herd.[183] He thinks this new herd is now being shaped, unknowingly, by a very large-scale social and genetic process at work in Europe and beyond. He expresses alarm and contempt for the "small" and homogeneous kind of persons he thinks are the multiplying products of this process. But his second thought is that these can be profitably taken up by the new breeder's further design.

We've seen that it's the overall tendency of social selection to reduce us to a common level as herd. In the modern age this reduction serves a highly developed and specialized economic machinery. WP866 [1887]: "Once we have that inevitable impending overall economic management of the earth, then humanity *can* find its best meaning as machinery in its service: as a tremendous gear-work of ever smaller, ever more finely 'adapted' gears; . . . as a whole of tremendous force, whose individual factors represent *minimal forces, minimal values*."

This process will be *merely* a diminution if this machinery isn't put to better use, to support the elite and exceptions—i.e., to enable there to be *individuals*, as well as this herd. Again WP866 [1887]: "Otherwise it would in fact only be the overall diminishment, *value* diminishment of the *type* human, — a *regress-phenomenon* in the greatest style." By the redesign of these economic gears to enable the elite, they get more meaning than they would otherwise have.

---

183. WP903 [1887]: "Temporary preponderance of the social value-feelings comprehensible and useful: it is a question of creating a foundation"; WP890 [1887]: "a broad foundation has to be created"; WP894 [1887]: "the continued existence of the rule is a precondition for the value of the exception".

So the new herd now evolving is exapted for a new purpose, different from the reason it has emerged. WP898 [1887]: "The *homogenizing* [*Ausgleichung*] of European humans is the great process that is not to be obstructed: one should even accelerate it. . . . / This *homogenized* species requires a *justification*, as soon as it is achieved: it lies in service of a higher, sovereign kind, which stands upon it and can lift itself to its task only upon it."[184]

This returns us to the key issue raised before: what kind of "service" (of herd to elite) does Nietzsche mean? In what ways does he think the elite depends on or requires or uses this herd caste, and in what way does the elite "rule" them? We need to specify the economic and (narrowly) political character of this service.[185] And we especially want to know whether this service *damages the interests* of the herd or majority: in serving the elite are they worse off than they would otherwise be?

It's clearest, I think, that this service has an *economic* side. The elite members must be freed from the work of meeting material needs; they give this labor over to the herd. They'll depend on that economic gear work but not be part of it. WP864 [1888]: "Handicraft, trade, agriculture, science, a great part of art—all that can only stand on a broad base, on a strong and healthy consolidated mediocrity."[186] As this sentence makes clear, this labor upon which the elite depends will include certain kinds of intellectual labor which Nietzsche thinks is best performed by the mediocre—for example, most science. Where this labor does not depend on the critical and skeptical powers germane to freedom, it is best carried out within the herd. So the "economic" privilege of the elite is its exemption from routine labor of both physical and mental kinds; this labor is taken over by others.

Regarding this economic support, we should ask whether it extends past providing the elite with material necessities, to greater luxuries. Apart from their leisure, will the new elite members "have more" than the herd—

184. WP955 [1885]: "The sight of today's Europeans gives me much hope: a daring ruling race is developing, upon the breadth of an extremely intelligent herd-mass." See n. 139 above.

185. In the broad sense of "political" I've been using so far, it takes in everything to do with society and its structure. In a narrower sense it concerns the control or influence of the society's laws.

186. This note is revised into A57. BGE61 speaks of "ordinary humans . . . , the most-of-all, who are there for service and general advantage, and only thus far *may* be there." Earlier, in HH.i.439: "A higher culture can only arise where there are two different castes in society: that of the laborers and that of the idle, those capable of true idleness; or expressed more strongly: the caste of enforced-labor and the caste of free-labor."

more of the physical goods the herd's labor generates? Here I don't think Nietzsche has a settled view. Sometimes he seems to expect such "luxury."[187] And we expect, on other grounds, that his new elite will not deny or suppress the body, in the way he blames Christian morality for doing. But elsewhere his model seems to be Plato's ascetic guardians.[188] And his free spirits might be ascetics after all, for the same reason he says philosophers are in GM.iii.7: asceticism offers "the optimum conditions for a highest and bravest spirituality." Nietzsche himself lived in great simplicity, and I think it most likely this is also his picture of his elite.

It's harder, I think, to determine the kind of *political* power he wants his new elite to exercise. He often implies a traditional kind of "rule" or "mastery"—even a military authority that puts to different use the "martial" virtues treated above. He predicts that "wars" will need to be fought in order to demoralize our culture, and we suspect his "new masters" will be the ones to fight and win them. Mostly, however, his allusions to "rule" are ambiguous—they can as easily mean the kind of spiritual control involved in disseminating new values. And since we've seen the latter is the crucial function he needs his elite to play, his further speculations about this rule are dispensable.

What Nietzsche's new elite members certainly need, in order to perform their two functions stated above, is the economic independence to pursue their diagnostic inquiries and the capacity to direct the values of the herd accordingly. We can ask whether the herd is damaged by *these* inequalities, which are the really indispensable ones in Nietzsche's political ideal.

Nietzsche often suggests that a healthy elite does knowingly damage the many. BGE258: "[A good and healthy aristocracy] accepts with a good conscience the sacrifice of untold humans, who *for its sake* must be pressed

187. WP898 [1887]: "[A]n *affirming* race . . . may grant itself every great luxury [*Luxus*] . . . , [may be] strong enough to have no need of the tyranny of the virtue-imperative, rich enough to have no need of thrift and pedantry, beyond good and evil; a hothouse for strange and choice plants." But this and other passages are ambiguous, and may be read to mean intellectual or spiritual luxuries.

188. WP764 [1883]: "The workers shall some day live as the bourgeois do now: but above them the *higher caste*, distinguished by [their] frugality [*Bedürfnislosigkeit*]! Therefore poorer [*ärmer*] and simpler, but in possession of power." See HH.iii.285, which on the one hand rejects Plato's abolition of property (since it would undermine a needed egoism), but on the other argues to prevent the accumulation of "great wealth," and to "regard those who possess too much as being as great a danger to society as those who possess nothing." And see WP915 [1887] on "naturalizing" asceticism.

down and diminished to incomplete humans, to slaves, to instruments."[189] And it's clear that he thinks "it's worth it" to sacrifice the many to the few; the latter have a surpassing value that outweighs the interests of any numbers of the weak and mediocre. Still, there are reasons to doubt whether he thinks his new hierarchy does impose such sacrifice on the herd. It is even important to him, I will try to show, that in his new society the herd will be better off, both in their own terms and in his.

First is a point we've seen: this diminution of humans is *already happening*, is even inevitable, by the logic of large social and economic processes that long predate Nietzsche and his new elite. The elite doesn't "push down" the herd, but finds it already at hand; it simply "exapts" the gear work (and "slaves") otherwise made.[190] So if the herd is worse off, it was made so by that long moralizing process, not by Nietzsche's new masters.

Second and more important, Nietzsche thinks that the special character of these elite members—their genealogical insight—will enable them to redesign the herd *to the latter's own advantage*. The new philosophers create in a new and better way: they make a healthy herd, so reversing the long-term sickening by our socialization. This reversal is the epochal achievement by these new philosophers: they heal our society, culture, and even our species. They heal for several reasons.[191]

They heal the herd because they can: only with Nietzschean genealogy can anyone recognize and understand those subtle and extremely large-scale processes that have made our values. The devices of previous "improvers" were harsh partly by their own ignorance and mistakes, for example, about the effects of suppression on ingrained drives. The new planners will judge better how to render these drives consistent with the demands of close civil life, without suppressing and demonizing them or

189. In the early essay "The Greek State": "So that there is a broad, deep, and productive foundation for the evolution of art, the enormous majority must be slavishly subject to life's troubles [*Lebensnoth*] in service of a minority, *beyond* the measure of their individual need. At their expense, through their extra labor, that privileged class shall be removed from the struggle for existence, in order to create and satisfy a new world of need."

190. BGE242: "[T]he democratization of Europe leads to the production [*Erzeugung*] of a type prepared for *slavery* in the subtlest sense." Also BGE203; WP128 [1884], WP898 [1887]. To be sure, Nietzsche often advocates advancing or hastening this process; e.g., WP889 [1887].

191. Besides those I go on to treat, Nietzsche once, anomalously, calls it a matter of duty, due to the way culture depends on the herd: "When the exceptional human handles the mediocre with gentler fingers than [he does] himself and his equals, this is not mere politeness of heart, — it is simply his *duty* [*Pflicht*]" (A57).

inducing guilt for them—the "unhealthy means" which have made us sick over them.

This will change how the virtues of pity and altruism are practiced, for example. The herd can learn to pity not only suffering, but the failure to grow to potential. It can learn that some kinds of suffering are spurs to that growth, and not to be pitied or removed—either in oneself or others. Similarly, the herd practice of altruism shifts: it learns to give gifts that help others to grow their abilities (rather than stepping in for them, so that they're preempted from using their abilities). And it learns to see this benevolence as a way of extending one's own scope or power, and not as a sacrifice.

Next, the new elite heals the herd, because this healing is a great achievement—it magnifies the elite members over all previous "improvers." Their achievement lies in *genuinely* improving, on the basis of their real insight into social selection. This improvement is their "selfish gift," by which they not only extend their influence into the herd, but do so by making it finer and better. WP964 [1884]: "They will to en-form themselves [*sich hineingestalten*] in great communities, they will to give one form to the multifarious, disordered." In section 5b.ii of this chapter, I showed how Nietzsche thinks an "enlightened" selfishness will have this motive to give. In chapter 4 I will describe how this remaking of the herd is an *aesthetic* act—a great feat of cultural shaping and beautifying that, again, expresses the preeminent power of the new elite.

Finally, they heal the herd because this makes the herd less dangerous. It was the herd's unhealthy resentment of the masters which energized its subversion of them. This resentment broke down the insulation between classes and accomplished the revolt and reversal of values. To make a hierarchy that will *last*, as even the Roman Empire could not do, the herd must be bred into a health not feasible before. In place of the priest's unhealthy drugs, which distracted the herd from the sufferings of socialization by giving its members someone to *blame* for them, the new elite will help the herd to find that "green-pasture happiness" it wants.

This new health will be partly achieved simply by the demoralizing of the herd's values. Unlike the previous caste systems of Manu and Plato, Nietzsche's hierarchy won't be enforced or justified by a morality—nor will the herd feel a moral attachment to its herd values.[192] A member will

---

192. WP143 [1888] says that in Manu the "*spirit of the priest* is worse than anywhere else" (though see too WP145 [1888]).

cleave to these values because they're "what one does," but will dispense with the moralistic insistence that these values are absolute and universally binding in a way that makes nonadherence "evil." The herd will be *less* "subject" to the elite in a way that is most vital for its members' spiritual health: they will not be obsessed with the elite in the combined envy and bitterness that Nietzsche calls *ressentiment*.

This demoralization of the herd brings the members epistemic benefits that are enormously important to Nietzsche.[193] Their values will no longer be artificially supported by a superstructure of lies, beginning with God, free will, and the afterlife.[194] Instead of shaping herd values with the kind of "holy lie" needed by previous "improvers," the new elite will expose the lies of those predecessors. The new herd will be more honest in its values: it will share in a part of the metaethical insight into the perspectival character of all values, will share in the amount of that insight it can bear, given its need for a solid good.

To be sure, this need for settled and stable values, which is the crucial limitation in the herd, means that it can't be exposed to the full dose of skepticism faced by the elite. In this direction too there must be "insulation": the herd must be protected from the undermining effects of a thorough scrutiny of its practices. The members "just do it"; they don't think about it. But they also don't have to tell themselves lies about why they do it.

For these several reasons I think Nietzsche aspires to make even the herd better off in his new society. It is better off in its own terms, by having more of the kind of happiness it wants. As he puts it bluntly in A57: "For the mediocre it is a happiness to be mediocre."[195] And the members are better off in Nietzsche's terms, by their better health and their better understanding of themselves and their values.

193. 13.14[203] [1888] (a note headed "*Kritik Manus:*") blames the constraint of the three castes to a moral-religious law for "making stupid" these castes, so that only the outcast chandala develop an empirical intelligence. On the other hand, see how TI.ix.40 complains that the education of workers spoils them for their best social role.

194. Although the new herd values won't be moral, they may still be religious. But this will be a demoralized and "poetizing" religion, explicitly inventive, and one that reveres higher humans rather than an infinite God. I'll look more closely at it in chapter 4.

195. A57 also says that a higher life is harder; it stresses the "privilege" of the mediocre. WP901 [1887] says that the conditions needed by the strong would destroy the weak.

c. Assessing the Politics

My account of Nietzsche's politics has been partial and compressed. But it has brought out a variety of points that count for or against his stance. I want to pull together some of these points into a very quick assessment of his politics, as it looks in my quasi-Darwinian light. Does this light improve the look of his values of breeding and rank order, or are they as or more unsavory than when we started?

I think Nietzsche's political views have their best chance to be interesting to us to the extent that they express his distinctive ideal of freedom as self selection. Insofar as he *justifies* "breeding rank order" as the best way to make (some of) us free, we may at least be curious why he thinks so. And to the extent that he *modifies* his hierarchy to reflect this ideal, his picture will be quite different from the Social Darwinists' and may have more appeal.

In the first place this hierarchy runs in a different dimension than we expect: it is not—primarily at least—a hierarchy of levels of wealth or political clout. It is a hierarchy of levels of freedom, i.e., of the capacity to "see through" the sources of one's values and to remake these values for oneself. The essential way in which the many are "slaves"—as Nietzsche provokingly puts it—is by being herd, i.e., by being content to have their values because they are "what one does," the very same thing that others do.[196] And the essential way in which the elite stands over the herd is by having the critical and skeptical strength for this self-diagnosis. The economic and political inequalities Nietzsche sometimes suggests are secondary and contingent—he's not at all sure they're what's needed to establish the hierarchy he really cares about.

Second, although Nietzsche often implies that the herd is "sacrificed" in supporting the elite, he also aspires to make a new herd that is better off in both its own terms and in his. His new elite will reconfigure herd practices and values to demoralize and heal the members. The elite will use the new biological and genealogical insights into our constitution to find less damaging ways of constraining natural drives to the needs of social life. And to the extent possible the elite will disperse this insight into the herd itself, improving its grasp of the status of the elite's goals and values.

196. See A54 on the "higher sense" of slavery, in which it refers to a kind of compulsion the weak-willed need.

To be sure, not all of Nietzsche's political assertions express his core ideal of freedom. Some are "free wheels," not meshed with the system revolving on that ideal. Moreover he sometimes draws from this ideal political lessons that we abhor. But I suggest that we have some latitude here: we can conclude that he has drawn the *wrong* lessons from his own central thoughts, that he has missed the concrete economic and political conditions that will best secure the hierarchy in freedom he above all wants. We may conclude, for example, that rather more self selectors are feasible than he thinks, or that a rather different social design will best effect them. So we might cleave to this crux of Nietzsche's politics—its redesign for freedom—while jettisoning some of his least palatable thoughts.

I've emphasized that self selection, and the epistemic strength he associates with it, are not narrowly restricted to those exceptions, but reach down, in diminished form, into the elite and even the herd. Although Nietzsche stresses that society's functional parts—its classes or castes— should each have *its own* values and that these different values should be "insulated" from one another, still he thinks these values will all reflect, to different degrees, the peculiar kind of "enlightenment" his naturalization of values achieves.

Nietzsche seems an avowed enemy of the Enlightenment, with its vision of an ongoing *progress* due to improving *reason*. Yet his conception of the benefits of his genealogy shows that he really aims at a novel kind of enlightenment. Genealogy's *understanding* of herd and slave morality—its truth about why we have our values—gives us the ability to heal and free ourselves and to become a higher and stronger kind of person than there ever has been. To be sure, the fullest levels of freedom and strength will only be achieved by rare exceptions—new philosophers and value creators. But the latter will partly diffuse both these truths and the benefits of these truths through the rest of society, by the new values they make for it. So the benefits of this new truth, and even the truth itself, reach down into the herd, despite Nietzsche's fatalism and contempt about it.

Summary

For the Darwinists, natural selection, working in the human social medium, tends "up" to altruism and morality—which serves to justify them as the *fittest* social practices. At the same time, the lesson of evolution also shows that society must sustain competition and struggle, and hence moderate pity for less successful competitors. The upshot is a *limited* pity and altruism, commended as the overall practice that renders the society fittest and best able to evolve (improve).

We've seen that Nietzsche has a different way of rooting his values in his evolutionary facts. His critique of social selection shows him the possibility of a self selection that surpasses it. So he offers this ideal not as already contained in natural or social selection—as what succeeds best in their projects—but as a step beyond them, by seeing through them. Whereas Darwinists offer their values as set by natural/social selection itself, Nietzsche offers his precisely as overcoming this determination.

My ultimate strategy for ameliorating Nietzsche's attacks on pity and altruism, equality and civilizing, has been to develop this positive value of self selection and to show the precise sense this gives to those attacks. If that value—and the way Nietzsche roots it in his evolutionary story—is persuasive, then along with explaining those attacks it will also somewhat persuade us to them. And it will force upon us the work of trying to reconcile these attacks with our attachments to those social virtues—to take seriously Nietzsche's suggestions for *reform*.

4

Aesthetics

In treating Nietzsche's values in chapters 2 and 3, I have managed to ignore a distinctive and striking feature of them, their "aesthetic" character. Nietzsche suggests that he means his values aesthetically, rather than morally or ethically.[1] Indeed, he suggests that he means his philosophy as a whole somehow aesthetically—as an artwork, the product of his creative imagination.[2] He thinks that both points set him apart from philosophers before him, and are crucial for understanding both his values and his ideas generally. How seriously should we take these remarks?

This self-description raises yet another large problem for his view. Nietzsche's "aestheticism" threatens to render his values frivolous: it sug-

1. E.g., the well-known remark in BT5: "[O]nly as *aesthetic phenomenon* is reality and the world eternally *justified*"; repeated in BT24 and then in BT.ASC.5. Compare 8.30[51] [1878]. GS107 says that "as an aesthetic phenomenon existence is always still *bearable* for us," and that we need the aesthetic in order to be "able to stand *above* morality." WP353 [1887–1888]: "[T]his is basically a question of taste and of *aesthetics*: would it be desirable, that the 'most respectable,' i.e., the most boring species of human should be left?" Also 9.11[79] [1881], 11.26[64] [1884]. Sometimes the suggestion is that (not just Nietzsche's but) all values are really aesthetic; Z.ii.13 says that "all life is conflict over taste [*Geschmack*] and tasting [*Schmecken*]."

2. WP1048 [1885–1886]: "[This is] an anti-metaphysical world-view — yes, but an artistic one." GS301 suggests that "we contemplatives" embrace a creative role—not as spectators but as poets of life. See also nn. 7 and 8 below.

gests that they express the preferences of an aesthetic taste that we simply don't trust for this role—a taste that judges by superficial and even sensory properties, which cannot be the right criteria to decide basic values. Moreover, reliance on aesthetic powers seems even less legitimate in the other parts of his philosophy, e.g., where he seems to make ontological or social or psychological claims. Why should we be persuaded by these, if we learn that they're driven by aesthetic motives—a liking for the "look" of a theory, perhaps—rather than by *epistemic* ones such as attention to evidence and argument?

Indeed, the problem is worse than this, by Nietzsche's own account. For he often presents the aesthetic as a kind of *opposite* to the epistemic. He insists that art and beauty "lie," so that our aesthetic appreciation for them involves being taken in by a lie.[3] (By a "lie" he means, let's say for now, a falsehood that is not a mere mistake but somehow *aimed* at.)[4] In this case, it seems that judging values by their aesthetic qualities even involves approving of lies. And making one's philosophy aesthetically would involve making a lie.

These worries about Nietzsche's self-descriptions are reinforced by the character of his work. His writing has obvious aesthetic features, which often in various ways seem to interfere with our assessing it as presenting philosophical claims and arguments. This is most obvious for his poetry and for *Thus Spoke Zarathustra*, whose claims are embedded in a dramatic story that greatly complicates their force. But much of his other writing has a marked literary character as well, and many of his best-known ideas (eternal return, master and slave, the overman) seem as much images or stories as concepts. Sober readers often distrust him in just the ways his self-accounts alert us to.

Can Nietzsche justify using his aesthetic faculty for so serious a purpose as judging or deciding basic values? We need to hear reasons that this faculty merits such trust. And can he justify offering his philosophy in general as an aesthetic product? We need to know why this shouldn't confirm our suspicion that his writings' extraordinary artistry is irrelevant and out of place, insofar as his and our interest is in *truth*.

Once again, I'll argue that we only really locate his position—and find its real strength—by setting it down on its crucial *Darwinian* ground.

---

3. WP602 [1884]: "Only by a certain dullness of vision, a will to simplicity, does the 'beautiful,' the 'valuable' occur; in itself it is, *I know not what*." See also n. 5 below.

4. A55: "By lie I mean willing *not* to see something that one sees; willing not to see something *as* one sees it."

Nietzsche explains our aesthetic taste as first arising by natural selection: to understand it we need to see how it was designed to serve reproductive interests. However, this is only the *start* of his account; here too he grafts his own further diagnoses—especially about the *social* development of this taste—onto this Darwinian stem. It's by this biological and cultural story that he justifies his own aesthetic values, and the use he puts them to. He thinks that when we see how his aesthetic values respond to this history—to how aesthetic experience has worked so far—we'll see that they *merit* the unusual role he gives them in his philosophy.

In section 1 I'll lay out the key problem here, which is the "opposition" between beauty and truth, and the way Nietzsche seems to divide his loyalty between them.[5] The following sections try to show how we can answer this problem, by looking at Nietzsche's genealogy of our aesthetic aims and at the lesson he draws from it. This genealogy treats in turn (section 2) the design of aesthetic drives by natural selection, and (section 3) the redesign of these drives by social selection, into aesthetic habits or practices. In the last section (4) I try to state the lesson I think Nietzsche proposes, on the basis of this genealogy—how he wants us to redesign our aesthetic aims once again, by "self selecting" them.

This fourth locus of Darwinism in Nietzsche is probably the most surprising of all. His aesthetics may well be the last place we'd expect to find this a factor in his thinking. We associate Nietzsche's aesthetic bent with his attacks on science and don't expect to find his science guiding his aestheticism. When we do find it there in that role, we see how pervasive his Darwinian element really is.

1. Art versus Truth

"Art lies," Nietzsche often says.[6] But, in his peculiar view, this may not be a criticism of art—or at least may not prevent him from embracing it

---

5. Heidegger stresses the "discordance" (*Zwiespalt*) between truth and art in his treatment of Nietzsche's aesthetics (1961/1979–1982, 142ff.). One of the titles Nietzsche considers for a book he plans in 1872–1873 is "The Philosopher: Reflections on the Struggle [*Kampf*] between Art and Knowledge"; some notes for this are collected in P&T.

6. GM.iii.25: "[A]rt, [is that] in which precisely the *lie* is sanctified." WP804 [1887]: "*Judgments of beauty* and *ugliness* are *short-sighted* — they always have the understanding *against* them —: but [they are] *persuasive in the highest degree*," and "[t]o experience a thing as beautiful means: to experience it necessarily falsely." See Z.ii.2 and 17, and Z.iv.14 on how poets lie. Also HH.i.234, HH.ii.188; WP853 [1887–1888].

to a degree philosophers before him had not. He says: "In the main, I give the artists more credit than all philosophers hitherto: they have not lost the great clue [*Spur*] concerning life" (WP820 [1885]). And, it's quite clear, he means to bring artistry into philosophy itself—to become himself something new, an "*artist*-philosopher" (WP795 [1885–1886]),[7] a "Socrates who practices music" (BT14).[8]

It's clear that both projects—*aesthetic* and *epistemic*, as I'll call them—are important to Nietzsche. Yet he stresses that these projects are at odds, and pull directly against one another. Each has a value or goal that negates the other's value: beauty depends on lies, and truth is ugly.[9] This inconsistency makes an issue of *how* he combines these projects in himself. How—we might put it—does he "insulate" the projects from each other, so that each can proceed without interference from the other (so that the effort at truth is not inhibited by aesthetic distaste for truth, or the effort at beauty hurt by repugnance for lies)? And how can his writings possess the opposite virtues of (ugly) truth and (lying) beauty?[10]

Now I think we expect that these aesthetic and epistemic projects are not ultimately equal for Nietzsche, but that one has preponderance, or runs deeper (or longer) in him. He resolves the conflict, we expect, in the main favor of one side. But which is it? Our interest, as throughout, is in determining Nietzsche's "mature" position, i.e., from about 1881 (when he was writing *The Gay Science*). This position is more complex and ambiguous than his earlier views. He takes a strongly pro-aesthetic stance in *The Birth of Tragedy*, but is hostile to it by the time of *Human, All-Too-Human*. He throws his lot first with art, then with science. If he oscillates in this way, where does he end?[11]

---

7. In GS.P.3–4 Nietzsche speaks "as" both a philosopher and an artist. Also 7.19[39] [1872–1873] (P&T15) on the "philosopher-artist."

8. EH.Z.1: "Perhaps the whole of *Zarathustra* may be reckoned as music"; see how he goes on to cite his music for "Hymn to Life." Seven of *Zarathustra*'s chapters are labeled as songs, and the rest has an obvious poetic character. He wrote sets of poems, some of which he appended to his works ("Joke, Cunning, and Revenge" and "Songs of Prince Vogelfrei," added as Prelude and Appendix to *The Gay Science*; "From High Mountains," an Aftersong to *Beyond Good and Evil*), others of which stand on their own (*Idylls from Messina, Dionysus-Dithyrambs*).

9. WP822 [1888]: "For a philosopher to say, 'the good and the beautiful are one,' is infamy; if he goes on to add, 'also the true,' one ought to thrash him. Truth is ugly." Also WP598 [1887–1888].

10. EH.ii.9 describes how in his task of revaluing values he needed "oppositions of capacities, without these disturbing, destroying one another."

11. Young 1992 gives a detailed review of Nietzsche's shifting views about art.

A case can be made for either an aesthetic or an epistemic upshot—that is, that the mature Nietzsche puts either beauty or truth foremost. Both cases *have* been made. The choice between them tends to coincide with whether the reader comes to Nietzsche from literary studies or from philosophy. Each side naturally finds uppermost its own project—with some exceptions.[12] So this issue is a natural battleground between these approaches.

It might be, on the one hand, that the epistemic project is primary.[13] When Nietzsche introduces poetry and other "literary" features into his works, this would serve his primary effort at (finding and conveying) insight and truth. In this case, we would take his images and turns of phrase—his pervasive stylistic effects—as intended to contain and convey real insights, or at least to assist us toward them. His literary devices would be just a strategy for communicating his truth.

Or, on the other hand, his main allegiance may be to the aesthetic.[14] Even his argumentative prose might be deeply literary in intent, aimed to appeal aesthetically and not (mainly) by its explicit reasons. The charm of Nietzsche's writing would be all (or most) of its point, and we would leave off trying to dig under it to truths. His point might be merely to convey this aesthetic attitude, and to dissuade us from our will to truth. So we would apply to himself his words in a note from 1872–1873: "That an *unprovable* [*unbeweisbares*] philosophizing still has a value, usually more than a scientific proposition, has its ground in the aesthetic *value* of such a philosophizing, i.e., through its beauty and sublimity."[15]

12. Such as Heidegger and Habermas, among philosophers; see n. 94 below.

13. In his "positivist" period (the late 1870s) Nietzsche's preference for truth over beauty is clear; see HH.i.145–223, e.g., 222: "The scientific human is the further evolution of the artistic." Also HH.ii.206. (Though see too HH.i.276, quoted in n. 22 below.) For expression of a similar priority in his mature period, see, e.g., A13: "In the end one might well ask whether it was not really an *aesthetic* taste that kept mankind in blindness for so long: a picturesque effect was demanded of the truth." Also WP572 [1886–1887]: "The artist endures no reality, he looks away."

14. WP853 [1888] describes *The Birth of Tragedy* as teaching "that art is *worth more* than truth." WP1011 [1886–1887] suggests that "the lie — and *not* the truth — is divine." The preference seems common in the early notebooks, e.g., 7.19[121] [1872–1873] (P&T32): "Absolute skepticism: necessity of art and illusion"; on the next page: "Not in *knowing*, [but] in *creating* lies our good [*Heil*]!" From the mature period, see, e.g., WP585 [1887]: "'Will to *truth*' — as impotence of the will to create." Megill (1985, 50) says that Nietzsche "gives primacy to the aesthetic . . . [because] it is explicitly a realm of illusion, and as such it stands in opposition to the unacknowledged illusion of logic and dialectic."

15. 7.19[76] [1872–1873] (P&T23). Later in this note: "[T]he little proved [*wenig erwiesene*] philosophy of Heraclitus has a greater artistic value than all the propositions of Aristotle."

Now there's a way that Nietzsche could resolve this conflict without sacrificing either project (aesthetic or epistemic): he could *re-aim* one or the other. If beauty and truth conflict, he could decide either that his aesthetic impulse doesn't need beauty, or that his epistemic impulse doesn't need truth. Nietzsche clearly considers both options.

So, with "beauty," he questions whether this is the proper or most important goal of the aesthetic drive. Beauty is indeed illusion, but there's another aesthetic aim that is more reconcilable with an allegiance to truth. This is a key part of his conception of the Dionysian art drive in *The Birth of Tragedy*. Famously, he identifies the Apollonian with "beautiful illusion" (*schöne Schein*), but attributes to the Dionysian a deep grasp of truth.[16] So a Dionysian aesthetic—aiming at the sublime instead of beauty—could be reconciled with the truth project, and might even be indispensable for it.

But I don't think Nietzsche sticks with this resolution. He is reconvinced of the conflict between art (in general) and truth. Indeed even in *The Birth of Tragedy* he insists that the Dionysian also transforms reality, doesn't give it as it is in itself.[17] And although in his later writings he sometimes revives the distinction between Apollonian and Dionysian art, he gives up the Schopenhauerian attribution of insight or truth to the latter.[18] Moreover, he speaks quite generally, as we've seen, of art and the aesthetic as involving lies. So we can't solve the conflict by denying that his aesthetic interest is in beauty.

So might it be that Nietzsche redefines "truth" instead—redefines it as a kind of lie, after all? In that case the epistemic project would not conflict with the aesthetic; at most they'd be after different kinds of lies. This is the line Heidegger offers (1961/1979–1982): he reads Nietzsche to mean by "truth" "the constant" (I, 215), i.e., perspectives that have become fixed or petrified in a person or (especially) a society. Art, by contrast, is the activity of shaping new perspectives. On this reading Nietzsche can easily renounce truth, because he's only giving up those fixed viewpoints.[19]

16. BT4: "The muses of the arts of 'illusion' paled before an art, that in its *Rausch* spoke the truth."

17. Schacht (1983, 486) argues that the Dionysian also involves a "transfiguration" of reality.

18. See these later accounts of the Dionysian: TI.ix.10; WP1050 [1888], WP799 [1888].

19. So Heidegger thinks Nietzsche concludes: "*Art, as transfiguration, is more enhancing to life than truth, as fixation of an apparition*" (1961/1979–1982, I, 216–17). Note, however, that allegiance to truth isn't really given up, because the argument works by its suggestion that art, as not petrifying, is really "truer." In a later lecture on Nietzsche, Heidegger

But I think this takes too easy a way out of the conflict between art and truth. It leaves Nietzsche no motive for allegiance to the truth side of that conflict, whereas in fact he has, I think, great allegiance to it—he sustains a very strong "will to truth." So EH.iv.1: "[T]he truth speaks out of me. — But my truth is *terrible*; for so far one has called *lies* truth. . . . I was the first to *discover* the truth by being the first to experience — to *smell* — lies as lies." Although he sometimes does call our fixed and accepted viewpoints truths, this is often in scare quotes—"truths" are just things commonly so called.[20] It's in a quite different sense, I think, that he mainly treats truth as antithetical to art. Truth opposes art in the way it's true, not in the way it's false. And art "lies" in more than just the sense of breaking from fixed perspectives.

We can reinforce this by noticing how much of Nietzsche's truth consists in *finding false*. His will to truth is strongly *skeptical* (or critical or negative), so that many (but not all) of the truths he finds are the insights that we *can't have* truths of some sorts we had sought. Since the truth project is so importantly the project of exposing lies, its discordance with art—as making and promoting lies—is all the stronger. The truth that clashes with art is not the "truths"—the settled myths—that Heidegger fingers, but the skeptical effort to lay bare all our pleasing illusions. Truth is ugly, because it cuts into the illusions that have always sustained us in life.[21] And it's art that makes these sustaining illusions.

Truth opposes art, and it also opposes values. Not only does art involve a kind of value—aesthetic as opposed to moral or ethical—but *all* values are "created lies" just as art is. Nietzsche's worries about truth are worries over the way it undermines values. And he so prizes art because of its special role in establishing values—as well as because of the special *way* it establishes them. Nevertheless, truth's hostility to values—i.e., the way that the truth project tends to undermine them—is still consistent with its playing crucial roles in Nietzsche's own values, as I'll try to show.

So Nietzsche doesn't resolve the conflict between truth and beauty by abandoning either. The epistemic and aesthetic projects continue to

makes this explicit: "In the unequivocal essential definition of truth as error, truth is necessarily thought twice, and each time differently, hence ambiguously: once as fixation of the constant, and then as harmony with the actual. Only on the basis of this essence of truth as harmony can truth as constancy be an error" (III, 126). He goes on to say that art involves that "harmony" with becoming.

20. E.g., BGE211; WP540 [1885], WP853 [1887–1888].

21. Foucault (1971/2001, 351) puts Nietzsche's point succinctly: "[K]nowledge is not made for understanding; it is made for cutting."

conflict—neither is revised to match the other.[22] As always, Nietzsche wants a certain "balance of opposition" between these tendencies: he wants to preserve this conflict, but to "heal" it in the general way we've seen in previous chapters. Or, he wants to "synthesize" these contraries into a further project that gives a better expression to *both* of their aims. And indeed, it's the synthesis of *these* contraries that is probably most crucial of all. Nietzsche thinks of it as a "marriage" of his male and female sides, and depicts it so in the climactic scene of *Thus Spoke Zarathustra*.[23]

In this synthesis and solution of the conflict between truth and beauty it's very hard to say whether either side rules or dominates. Still, I want to show that Nietzsche's "will to truth" plays a very much larger role in this interaction than we suspect. He insists, to begin with, on finding out *the truth about art*. The truth he finds is a highly scientific and naturalistic one.[24] It's the truth (no surprise) of how our aesthetic drives and practices have arisen by selection. It's this truth (together with a similar genealogy for our epistemic drives) that then suggests the new synthesis—just as we saw for Nietzsche's other values, above.

Nietzsche's naturalistic approach to art sets him apart not just from Heidegger, but from Kant and Schopenhauer, his main philosophical predecessors on the topic. He approaches art *from science*, in a way none of those other three attempts. And in this respect we can say that he not only "agrees more with artists" than these others, but also that he "agrees more with scientists." Indeed, he agrees with artists *because* of what he thinks he learns through science.[25]

In his naturalistic story, Nietzsche understands both the aesthetic and epistemic as ultimately "drives," in the broad sense that includes habits or practices. They are behavioral dispositions that are "plastic toward" bringing about certain outcomes—*and* they are explained by those out-

22. Nietzsche already thinks part of the point in HH.i.276: "Supposing someone lives just as much in the love for the plastic arts or for music as he is swept away by the spirit of science, and he sees it as impossible to resolve [*aufzuheben*] this contradiction through the destruction of one and complete unchaining of the other: so it only remains for him to shape out of himself so large a building of culture, that both those powers can dwell in it, if only at different ends."

23. See especially the account of this drama in Lampert 1986.

24. In GM.iii.8 Nietzsche anticipates a future work treating the "physiology of aesthetics."

25. So too, when Nietzsche avows the project "to see science under the optics of the artist, but art under those of life" (BT.ASC.2), we should understand this to be compatible with his *also* looking at both art and life "under the optics" of the scientist.

comes, which are therefore their "ends" and "values." **Beauty** (*Schönheit*) is of course the distinctive value of these aesthetic dispositions; as was true for other values, so beauty too exists only *as* the "value for a valuing," i.e., as the goal for such a disposition.[26] These dispositions "aim" at beauty, in the sense that the latter is the outcome that explains them—the outcome they were selected to reach. And by analyzing *why* drives were selected to pursue beauty, Nietzsche discovers the deeper ends and meanings designed into that value: he discovers what we have it for.

I'll lay out this naturalistic account of art in sections 2–3. Nietzsche begins with a Darwinian explanation of aesthetic impulses, but then tries to build *past* the Darwinists—to a better understanding of art and beauty than they had. In particular, he thinks he better understands the new way selection works in human societies—and how it redesigns those aesthetic drives for different ends. And he thinks his better science points the way to his different lessons about what art and (our experience of) beauty *should* be. I'll proceed to these lessons in section 4.

2. Aesthetic Drives

Nietzsche's naturalistic account of art begins with natural selection. This sets into us aesthetic "drives" in a narrow sense—dispositions that evolved in our ancestral, even animal past and that we inherit "in the blood." Originally our art, and our aesthetic value of beauty, were selected for how they served the organism's (or the lineage's) survival and growth. These aesthetic drives were selected to make us more fit, and they do so especially by virtue of a way they "lie"; in this they belong among many human traits selected for their fruitful, fit-making lies. The original home of these drives, finally, is in our *sexual* attitudes: aesthetic experience begins as a sexual response. All of this, I'll argue, is the seldom-noticed start of Nietzsche's aesthetic theory.[27]

Once again we focus on Nietzsche's *mature* theory. To be sure, in aesthetics—as not in this book's earlier topics—Nietzsche's most famous views are his earliest ones: the accounts of the Apollonian and Dionysian "art-drives" (*Kunsttrieben*) in *The Birth of Tragedy*. Already there, let's note,

26. CW.Epilogue: "[A] 'beauty in itself [*Schönes an sich*]' is a figment of the imagination."

27. The best account of Nietzsche's "physiology of art" is by Moore (2002, chapter 3).

Nietzsche is explaining aesthetic experience by "drives."[28] But in that first book these drives are mainly thought of in *Schopenhauer's* way, as manifestations of a metaphysical, noumenal will. This early aesthetics is premised as responding to this noumenal reality: both Apollonian and Dionysian art drives are ways of coping with that reality of Schopenhauerian will.

But Nietzsche soon insists on thinking of drives scientifically—not only of *what* they are (the body's abilities), but of *why* we have them (evolution by selection).[29] I presented this Darwinian view of drives in chapter 1. It's in aesthetics that this step into naturalism moves Nietzsche furthest from Schopenhauer. For Schopenhauer had depicted our aesthetic experience as (unlike intellect) genuinely a *disengagement* from willing: it really achieves the objectivity we only thought we could have in our science. But Nietzsche insists that it too expresses a (naturalized) will and drive—and "serves life" by making us more fit. As such, the aesthetic attitude is not "disinterested" or "disengaged" at all, as not just Schopenhauer but Kant had found it. Nietzsche now scorns their notion of it.[30] The aesthetic attitude in fact involves a heightening of our engagement and feeling.

These drives, in which art and aesthetic experience are ultimately rooted, are something ancient and fixed in us. Indeed, artistic drives have been designed into all organisms.[31] They were set into our bodies and our "blood" in our presocietal deep history, and persist there today beneath the layers of customs and habits that societies have superimposed on them (to exploit them, or counteract them, or both). By acting on these drives, beauty works on the "animal" in us—directly on the body, on the "muscles and senses" (WP809 [1888]), and the drives embedded in them. Our bodies

28. I'll flag in notes below some other ways the mature view is already present in BT. The prevalence of *Trieb* in BT is concealed in Kaufmann's translation, which renders it variously, especially as "impulse" and "tendency."

29. Clark (1998, 57f.) suggests that Nietzsche got his empiricism and naturalism from Schopenhauer, by subtracting his metaphysic of noumenal will. But, though Schopenhauer may well be a main source for the instrumental view of intellect, surely there are other sources for the empiricism and naturalism—ones not requiring the major surgery needed on Schopenhauer.

30. Against the notion in Kant: GM.iii.6; 10.7[18] [1883], 10.7[154] [1883]. Against the notion in Schopenhauer: WP821 [1888], WP812 [1888], WP851 [1888]. See Z.ii.15, e.g.: "Where is beauty? Where I must will with all my will."

31. 7.19[50] [1871–1872] (P&T18): "[Higher physiology] will say, that with the *organic* the *artistic* also *begins*."

themselves have a taste for certain kinds of beauty—above all the beauty of human bodies.[32]

Just how do these aesthetic drives work? We'll see they have a complex analysis, but I think there's one central point that gives us the key. These drives work in one most distinctive way: they induce or permit the experience of *Rausch*—rush. They "quicken" the organism, and bring its other drives too into their most potent condition. Both early and late, Nietzsche thinks of aesthetic experience as characterized by this "visceral" excitement or heightening.

It's important that this *Rausch* isn't merely the characteristic *effect* of those aesthetic drives; it's also their (etiological) *function*—i.e., what they were selected for, and why we have them. It's by inducing this experience that those drives have "served life," i.e., enhanced fitness, back through our deep species past: it's this effect that brought them on board the organism. Let's look first at what this *Rausch* is, before examining (Nietzsche's story about) how it arises by selection.[33]

a. *Forms of* Rausch

So aesthetic drives involve, especially, a capacity for undergoing or inducing *Rausch*.[34] TI.ix.8: "For there to be art, for there to be any aesthetic doing and seeing, one physiological precondition is indispensable: *Rausch*. *Rausch* must first have enhanced the excitability [*Erregbarkeit*] of the whole ma-

---

32. TI.ix.19: "In the beautiful, man posits himself as the measure of perfection. ... A species can*not* do otherwise than thus say yes to itself alone. Its *lowest* instinct, that of self-preservation and self-expansion, still radiates in such sublimities." This is also why "aesthetics is nothing but an applied physiology" (NCW2).

33. This stress on *Rausch* contradicts the Kantian-Schopenhauerian claim of "disinterestedness" in two ways. First, this experience (was selected because it) "serves our interest"—i.e., our reproductive interest, a point that has nothing to do with our "intending" it so. But second, this experience is also in its own right an intentionality of an especially "interested" kind—it is a hyperbolic and intemperate way of *feeling* about a thing or oneself or the world.

34. *Rausch* makes a very early appearance in Nietzsche's books, in BT1, where it is used to identify the Dionysian. In his "positivistic" phase after *The Birth of Tragedy*, Nietzsche is often suspicious or critical of *Rausch*; see HH.i.114, 149, HH.iii.170, D50, 52. But it regains a more positive role in his mature works, now often as something common to both Apollonian and Dionysian: TI.ix.10; 13.17[9] [1888]. It grows especially important to Nietzsche in his last year.

chine: else there is no art." *Rausch*—which I'll leave untranslated—is Nietzsche's favorite among a cluster of terms for this key aesthetic condition;
other common ones are "excitement" (*Erregung*) and "rapture" (*Verzück-
ung*).[35] Ultimately "beauty" must be understood in relation to this *Rausch*;
roughly, something is beautiful if and only if it can (or does) produce
Rausch.

It often seems that *Rausch* is simply the "feeling of power" itself. TI.ix.8:
"What is essential in such *Rausch* is the feeling of increased strength and
fullness."[36] This connects *Rausch* to Nietzsche's most important explanatory
and evaluative notion, power. In *Rausch* the organism feels its capacities
at a peak, and takes pleasure in this heightened potency. These capacities
are drives to work on the world, and in *Rausch* one feels oneself "overfull"
with them, bursting to change things to fit oneself.[37] It's by inducing such
Rausch that art is "the great stimulus to life" (TI.ix.24).

Here Nietzsche treats *Rausch* as a "feeling of" this power or potency.[38]
And elsewhere he allows that this feeling can be deceptive: it can be caused
"pathologically," such that one has only the *illusion* of power enhanced.[39]
Still, for the most part he treats *Rausch* as reflecting a genuine strengthening,
so that terms like "excitement" mean that *both* capacity and feeling are
heightened.[40] And it is, as he says above, a "physiological" condition, a
state of the organism, and in particular a state of its telic apparatus, the
wills or drives by which it aims at goals. *Rausch*—in the usual cases—is

35. Other allied terms are *Reiz* and *Stimulans*, both of which I'll translate as "stimulus"; they are applied to the thing that induces this excitation.

36. WP800 [1888]: "The state of pleasure that one calls *Rausch* is precisely a high
feeling of *power*."

37. TI.ix.8: "Out of this feeling one lends to things, one *forces* them to take from
us, one *violates* them, — this process is called *idealizing*." GS368 describes what his body
expects from music: "[A]ll animal functions should be quickened [*beschleunigt*] by easy,
bold, exuberant, self-assured rhythms."

38. *Rausch* is a "feeling of power" *not* in the sense that it's the feeling typically
caused by the physiological state of heightened potency (though that is true), but in the
sense that it's a feeling "directed upon" this potency—or "about" it intentionally, in
Nietzsche's very minimal sense. It's a feeling of *pleasure at* this power.

39. WP48 [1888]: "Here the experience of *Rausch* was misleading. . . . /this *increases*
in the highest degree the feeling of power /therefore, naively judged, *power*. . . . /there
are two starting-points of *Rausch*: the over-great fullness of life and a state of pathological
nourishment of the brain." See WP826 [1887]. Compare HH.i.127.

40. WP800 [1888]: "The feeling of *Rausch* [*Rauschgefühl*], in fact correspond[s] to
an *increase of strength*."

a state of excitement or elevation in these drives, which in some minimal way is "felt," and felt as pleasure.[41]

As a capacity for *Rausch*, the aesthetic drive is therefore a capacity for a change in the *other* drives. This capacity can take either of two forms, and this is the principal way aesthetic drives differ from one another: the capacity for *Rausch* can be *active* or *passive*. Some aesthetic drives are capacities for *self*-quickening, whereas others are capacities to be quickened by something else (the beautiful thing). Sometimes Nietzsche views this even as a difference in kind.[42] Other times he treats it as reflecting a difference in strength of a single such drive: it's the stronger cases or conditions of the aesthetic drive that take the active form.[43]

These active and passive capacities for *Rausch* are correlated with two aesthetic attitudes that Nietzsche often and familiarly distinguishes: (1) the *creative* (making beauty) and (2) the *receptive* (enjoying beauty). I will argue that there is also a third attitude he associates with *Rausch*, though less conspicuously: (3) the *discriminative* (judging beauty). By going through these types in turn, we can map how aesthetic drives function.

The first aesthetic attitude or condition is to "create" (*schaffen*) beauty. (Bear in mind that this creating is never ex nihilo, but always changes something preexisting—so it is also a remaking.) Nietzsche thinks creation of many kinds is fundamental to life—and pervasive in the activities of all living things. In the most general sense, the drive to create is simply will to power itself, the aim to extend one's capacities over oneself and other life.[44] But there's also a specifically aesthetic form of creating, which brings in that distinctively aesthetic feeling of *Rausch*.

This aesthetic creating is a "beautifying" (*Verschönern*), an "idealizing" (*Idealisieren*), a "perfecting" (*Vollkommen*) of something. It changes, in the

41. WP801 [1887]: "[A] blending of these very delicate nuances of animal feeling-well and desires is the *aesthetic state*. The latter appears only in natures capable of that bestowing and overflowing fullness of bodily *vigor*."

42. WP811 [1888]: "This distinguishes the artist from the layman (the artistically-susceptible): the latter has his high point of sensitivity in receiving, the former in giving — so that an antagonism between these two gifts is not only natural but desirable. The optics of these two states are opposite."

43. WP821 [1888]: "[T]he effect of the artwork is the *exciting of the art-creating state*, of *Rausch*."

44. We saw above how closely WP800 [1888] links *Rausch* and power; also WP801 [1887]. In the early 1870s especially Nietzsche thinks of human artistry as expressing an art drive at the heart of life or nature; see Moore (2002, 91ff.), who cites 7.7[117] [1870–

main case, the "look" of that thing—thus it's literally "aisthetic." It can make this change either physically, by working on the thing itself, or mentally, by changing viewpoints on the thing (e.g., telling a story about it). Creating art—in our narrow sense of a fine art's "artwork"—is only one form of this attitude.[45] There are everyday forms of it, and there are also forms much *grander* than fine art, in Nietzsche's view: he thinks of creating values, creating practices, creating societies.[46]

How (toward what) does this aesthetic creating change the look of the thing? This is where *Rausch* comes in: it serves as the criterion or objective for that change. Beautifying changes the thing so that it (a) resembles and (b) becomes able to evoke—Nietzsche runs back and forth between these—the *Rausch* the creator feels. In the main case, Nietzsche thinks of the artist as using his/her own experience of *Rausch* as a kind of touchstone or clue—shaping the work so that it pushes this *Rausch* higher and higher.[47] The artist's creative choices are guided by his/her intuitive sense of what changes in the work will most enhance this state. By following this clue the artist makes a thing that is able to induce *Rausch* even in those less susceptible to it. So in TI.ix.9: "A man in this state [of *Rausch*] transforms things until they mirror his power — until they are reflections of his perfection. This *having* to transform into perfection is — art."[48] The creator not only feels *Rausch*, but uses it as a sign and goal.

Now given this analysis of aesthetic creating, it's surprising that Nietzsche should insist that it inevitably and essentially involves a "lie"—that it always makes the world "look" a way it is not.[49] Why should it be, after

1871]: "The *artwork* and the *individual* is a *repetition of the ur-process*, from which the world has arisen."

45. HH.ii.174 insists that artworks are secondary products of an excess of "beautifying, concealing, and reinterpreting forces," which are "art" in the primary sense.

46. E.g., WP796 [1885–1886]. It's the "artist-philosopher" who creates at this cultural level: WP795 [1885–1886]. See n. 133 below.

47. We'll see the further reason he connects *Rausch* and beauty below, in the originally sexual character of this *Rausch*.

48. WP811 [1888] identifies *Rausch* as "the enhanced power-feeling; the inner need to make of things a reflection of one's own fullness and perfection." WP801 [1887] includes *Rausch* among "the states in which we lay a *transfiguration and fullness* into things and poetize about them until they mirror back our fullness and joy in life." 13.16[40] [1888]: "[H]e counts everything beautiful, that reminds him of the feeling of perfection."

49. WP800 [1888]: "[A]rtists should see nothing as it is, but fuller, simpler, stronger." WP853 [1887–1888]: "[A] human must be a liar by nature, he must more than anything else be an *artist*." (We saw many other such passages in section 1.)

all, that it's only lies that can induce that special excitement, *Rausch*? For now I'll defer a closer look at this epistemic assessment, but we'll need to ask: *how* is it a lie, to make things resemble or induce *Rausch*? And does the artist tell this lie *knowingly*, or is he himself taken in by it?

The secondary aesthetic attitude is to "receive" (*empfangen*) beauty, i.e., to enjoy or admire some prior creation. Nietzsche thinks that earlier aesthetic theories have been fixated here, hence aside from the main point.[50] He treats this attitude, in comparison to the creative attitude, more or less harshly. Sometimes he degrades it as so thoroughly passive, so devoid of creative spark, as to be really a separate thing.[51] But more often (I think) he points out ways even "mere" enjoyment of art involves its own creative act—though a lesser or weaker one than the artist's. Just to *see* the artwork as perfect or beautiful, the audience has to *make* it seem so—to create this seeming of it.[52] An artwork is designed to facilitate the audience's own making (of its appearance into beauty) but never takes all the work from the audience.

What makes it hard for the audience to make the artwork beautiful—and to enjoy it genuinely—is that this too requires *Rausch*, albeit in a less intense and absorbing form. The aesthetic enjoyer has a fainter version of the artist's own experience, Nietzsche thinks. WP801 [1887]: "Conversely: when we are confronted with things that show this transfiguration [*Verklä-rung*] and fullness, the animal being [*Dasein*] answers with an *excitation of those spheres*, where all those pleasure-states have their seat: — and a mixing of these very delicate nuances of animal well-being and desires is the *aesthetic state*."[53]

Like the artist, the audience needs *Rausch* as the standard for remaking the object. The enjoyer makes the object look to him/her as it must, to

50. WP811 [1888]: "Our aesthetics has up to now been a woman's aesthetics insofar as only the receivers of art have formulated their experience of 'what is beautiful?' In all philosophy up to now the artist is lacking."

51. See n. 42 above. And he derides those who think of art from this viewpoint. GM.iii.6: "Kant, like all philosophers, instead of sighting the aesthetic problem from the experiences of the artist (the creator), considered art and the beautiful solely from that of the 'spectator [*Zuschauer*]'."

52. WP341 [1887–1888] speaks of "the 'aesthetic' states . . . in which the world is *seen* fuller, rounder, *more perfect*."

53. WP802 [1887] presents art as transmission from the creative to the receptive stance: "Art reminds us of states of animal vigor; it is on the one hand an excess and overflow of blooming physicality into the world of images and desires; on the other, an excitation of the animal function through the images and desires of intensified life; — an enhancement of the feeling of life, a stimulant to it." Also EH.iii.4.

most fit and prompt the enjoyer's own *Rausch*. The enjoyer perfects it in how he/she imagines it, and the standard for this perfection is that it should inspire *Rausch*. So the enjoyer shapes the object's look—noticing and synthesizing particular aspects—so that it extends and strengthens a condition the enjoyer is already "on the scent of."

It's because even mere enjoyment of art depends on an ability to deploy this standard, and hence to recognize *Rausch* and know how to close in on it, that (genuine) enjoyment of art is rare. Again WP801 [1887]: "The sober, the weary, the exhausted, the dried-up (e.g., scholars) can receive absolutely nothing from art, because they do not have the artistic ur-force, the pressure of riches: whoever cannot give, also receives nothing." Indeed, it might even be that only artists can really enjoy art, because this enjoying requires *reviving* or *remembering Rausch* first felt in the creative form.[54]

A last and important feature that this aesthetic enjoying shares with creating is that it *falsifies*. WP804 [1887]: "To experience a thing as beautiful means: to experience it necessarily falsely." Again let's defer the key questions: why does enjoyment's *Rausch*—the audience seeing art's beauty— also involve a lie? And is the audience taken in by this lie (which presumably it tells to itself)?

Even though we don't yet see how, it's unsurprising that both creating and enjoying involve lies on Nietzsche's account, since we've seen that he stresses this falseness about the aesthetic generally. Still, I'll now try to show, there's also a way he thinks the aesthetic attitude *knows*, which is crucial to his full view but is shaded and obscured by his stress on those lies. We need to mark this third aesthetic attitude right from the start, in its earliest and underlying form, because it will evolve into the aesthetic "taste" with which Nietzsche will replace our moral judgment. This positive epistemic within Nietzsche's aesthetics emerges from the way both creating and enjoying are related to *Rausch*.

Both creating and enjoying, as able efforts to make or see the thing as beautiful, i.e., as fit to cause *Rausch*, depend upon a certain power to *judge* (*urtheilen*)—to judge whether the thing *is* fit in this way.[55] The artist

54. WP809 [1888]: "All art works *tonically*, increases strength, kindles pleasure (i.e., the feeling of strength), excites all the more subtle recollections of *Rausch*, — there is a special memory that penetrates such states." WP821 [1888]: "[A]ll distinct things, all nuances, to the extent that they recall the extreme enhancements of strength that *Rausch* produces, awaken back this feeling of *Rausch*."

55. HH.i.155 says that artists depend not on inspiration but on an *Urtheilskraft* working to cull the good, bad, and mediocre products of imagination. WP662 [1883–1884]: "Creating — as *selecting* and *finishing* the selected."

must be able to judge that the "look" his/her work is moving toward *will* induce *Rausch*. And so too for the art enjoyer, shaping the look in his/her own eyes. Nietzsche thinks that people differ dramatically in their ability to make these judgments. Many may lack it altogether: with no experience of *Rausch*, they also lack any sense of when a thing's look is "on the way" to inducing *Rausch*. It's only someone who can "get it right," and make or see the thing so that it *is* fit for *Rausch*, who really belongs to the aesthetic at all, as artist or audience. In judging well, both creating and enjoying *know*.

So the aesthetic attitudes possess, Nietzsche thinks, a certain epistemic power or competency, owing to their relation to *Rausch*. Moreover, he thinks the condition of *Rausch* has epistemic benefits of its own: raising our powers generally, it improves our perceptive ones too, in several ways. So WP800 [1888] lists several effects of *Rausch*:

> The condition of pleasure called *Rausch* is precisely a high feeling of *power*[.] — /the sensations of space and time are altered: tremendous distances are surveyed and as it were first *apprehended*. . . . / the *refinement of the organ* for the apprehension of much that is very small and fleeting /*divination*, the power of understanding with only the slightest aids, from any suggestion, "intelligent" *sensuality* — /*strength* as a feeling of mastery in the muscles, as suppleness and pleasure in movement, as dance, as levity and *presto*.

So *Rausch* heightens sensory acuity generally. But its main epistemic benefit lies in its acuity regarding the thing that one creates or enjoys. *Rausch* improves one's ability to judge the thing aesthetically. One is judging it, after all, in its fitness for inducing *Rausch*—and where better to judge this from, than that state itself? Both creating and enjoying beauty involve series of such judgments about the thing. They are "on the track" of that *Rausch*, and remake and resee the thing, progressively, such that it more and more strengthens and confirms that state.

We can think of this judging or discriminating attitude as a third main stance at work in the aesthetic, along with creating and enjoying. We've seen that these stances are not mutually exclusive, but indeed are involved and contained in one another. So, judging occurs not just in the critic, but in the artist and audience, as they steer their views of the thing toward *Rausch*. And judging is itself penetrated by creating and enjoying.

This account of *Rausch* suggests that it helps one see better, not worse. But how are we to square this new verdict with the old one we saw Nietzsche mostly makes—that "art lies"? We need some way to fit and reconcile these opposite assessments of art's epistemic value. I think the answer comes in seeing Nietzsche's Darwinian basis for this story.

b. Roots in Sexuality

With all of this we haven't reached the bottom of Nietzsche's theory of aesthetic drives. For we haven't seen *why we have these drives*, by his account. *Why*, in particular, this *Rausch*? It's only this explanation that makes Nietzsche's claims about *Rausch*, and his schema of aesthetic attitudes, very interesting. Without it, they seem free-floating and personal expressions about what aesthetic experience "should" be—or what it happens to be in *his* case. Nietzsche's quasi-Darwinian account of how we all have come to have this experience greatly enhances his analysis, by tying it down to facts.

Importantly, it's the third, judging or discriminating, stance that has priority in Nietzsche's causal story; creating and enjoying are subordinate to it. The main aesthetic ability that natural selection bred into us was a capacity to *judge* things as beautiful or not. There were selective benefits to picking out—by that response of *Rausch*—certain classes of things as beautiful, and to rejecting others as ugly. Humans (and even animals) were selected for their capacity to *recognize* things in these classes and to judge them accordingly. Our aesthetic taste was originally bred as an *epistemic* ability.

So, in the beginning, aesthetic experience was designed to find beautiful certain things that served our fitness. So WP804 [1887]: "On the origin of the *beautiful* and the *ugly*. What instinctively *repels* us, aesthetically, is proved by humanity's longest experience to be harmful, dangerous, worthy of distrust: the suddenly voiced aesthetic instinct (in disgust, e.g.) contains a *judgment* [*Urtheil*]."[56] Aesthetic responses were designed, initially, to recognize harmful or dangerous things—to dissuade us from them.

But the main locus of our beauty judgments is narrower than this. There's one thing in particular that we're mainly bred to find beautiful. The beauty of congenial landscapes, or of food (where the mainstay aesthetic term "taste" originates) is peripheral or secondary. It's the human

---

56. 13.16[75] [1888]: "[T]he general proposition . . . that supplies for me the foundation of all aesthetics [is]: that the aesthetic values rest upon biological values, that the aesthetic feeling-well [*Wohlgefühle*] is a biological feeling-well."

that we find preeminently beautiful, and in particular the "ascending" human. TI.ix.19: "Nothing is more conditioned, let us say *narrower*, than our feeling of beauty. Whoever would think of it apart from the pleasure of humans in humans, would immediately lose ground and footing." And this gives us, I think, a crucial further clue to Nietzsche's conception of these aesthetic drives. For it brings us to the roots of these drives in our *sexuality*: our aesthetic taste for "ascending" humans, and our feeling of *Rausch* toward their beauty, were originally sexual responses. Aesthetic drives are ultimately modifications of sexual ones, Nietzsche thinks—and it's here that the Darwinian character of his view emerges most clearly. For of course it's just here that Darwin himself found the origin of the sense of beauty, both in humans and in animals.[57]

This tie to our sexuality is one of Nietzsche's commonest points about the aesthetic.[58] In TI.ix.22, for example, he mocks Schopenhauer's notion that beauty negates the drive to procreate: "Someone is contradicting you, I'm afraid, it is nature. *For what* is there any beauty in tone, color, fragrance, or rhythmic movement in nature?"[59] He then approves a view he attributes to Plato: "[A]ll beauty incites procreation [*Zeugung*], — . . . just this is the *proprium* of its working, from the most sensual up to the most spiritual."

Beauty incites procreation by inciting *Rausch*, which is likewise ultimately sexual. WP805 [1887] describes the association between aesthetic beauty and sexual love: "[E]verything *perfect* and *beautiful* works as unconscious reminder[s] of that enamored state and its way of seeing — every *perfection*, all *beauty* of things reawakens through *continguity* [Nietzsche uses Hume's English] the aphrodisiac bliss."[60]

Now the precedent Nietzsche himself remarks, for his rooting of aesthetic experience in sexuality, is not Darwin but Plato. And of course his notion of *Rausch* is also akin to Plato's account of *eros*. But the connection with Darwin is more helpful to him, because it lets him set his aesthetic theory down into the science of his day—a grounding that can still be plausible for us in our own day. It gives him a *good reason* for connecting

57. See Darwin in *Descent*, e.g., I/63ff., II/108ff., /338ff.
58. See, e.g., GM.i.6, GM.iii.8, TI.x.4; WP801 [1887], WP799 [1888], WP800 [1888], WP808 [1888], WP815 [1888]. He makes the connection early, in 7.19[152] [1872–1873]: "The sense of *beauty* hang[s] together with procreation." On this connection see especially Moore (2002, 102–11). Compare Young (1992, 126ff.).
59. See also GM.iii.8 for this criticism of Schopenhauer.
60. See TI.x.4 on "the orgiastic." Moore (2002, 106): "[The aesthetic state] resembles—or rather, it *is actually a species of*—sexual arousal."

art and sexuality.[61] Moreover, it's this evolutionary way of connecting them that explains how the aesthetic ultimately involves both truth and lie.

We can mark how far this agreement with Darwin extends by seeing how both of them explain all three aesthetic attitudes by that sexual/ evolutionary story. So for Darwin, the effort to beautify, the response to beauty, and the ability to judge it were all originally formed in a sexual context.[62] All three stances or projects first evolved by selection for their role in our sexual dealings—for how they enhanced fitness there. And Nietzsche also treats each of these attitudes as rooted in our sexuality; I'll go through them in reverse order.

In this "sexual selection" where the aesthetic emerges, it's the third, judging or discriminative, attitude that has priority. What's bred into us, originally, is not a mere susceptibility to beauty, but an eye for qualities that are signs of fitness. We are bred to recognize in potential mates such qualities as strength and health—"ascending life"—that would improve the prospects of our offspring. Nietzsche stresses this primary sense for "beautiful" and "ugly." TI.ix.20: "Nothing is beautiful, only the human is beautiful: all aesthetics rests on this naïveté, which is its *first* truth. Let us immediately add the second: nothing is ugly except the *degenerating* [*entartende*] human, — and with this the realm of aesthetic judgment is circumscribed." In the ugly, one hates "the *decline of his type*. Here he hates out of the deepest instinct of the species; . . . it is the deepest hatred there is. It is by virtue of this that art is *deep*."[63]

To be sure, Nietzsche sometimes voices doubts as to whether such judgment is actually deployed in choosing mates. So in WP684 [1888]

61. Contra Young (1992, 129), who denies Nietzsche has a reason here.
62. Darwin on beautifying: "[A]n English philosopher goes so far as to maintain that clothes were first made for ornament and not for warmth" (*Descent* II/338). On admiring: "[I]t is impossible to doubt that the female[bird]s admire the beauty of their male partners" (with their "plumes and splendid colors") (I/63). On judging: "[T]he more vigorous female[bird]s, which are the first to breed, will have the choice of many males; and though they may not always select the strongest or best armed, they will select those which are vigorous and well armed, and in other respects the most attractive" (I/262).
63. WP800 [1888]: "Ugliness signifies the decadence of a type, contradiction and lack of co-ordination between the inner [parts] — signifies a decline in organizing strength, in 'will,' to speak psychologically." Perhaps this is why Nietzsche thinks that aesthetic judgments are the ultimate bases for our values: "The *aesthetic* judgments (taste, displeasure, disgust, etc.) are what make up the ground of the *table of goods*. This in turn is the ground of *moral* judgments" (9.11[78] [1881]).

(which itemizes many criticisms of Darwinism): "One has exaggerated the *selection of the most beautiful* [*Auslese der Schönsten*] in a way that goes far beyond the beauty-drive [*Schönheitstrieb*] of our own race! In fact the most beautiful pair with quite disinherited creatures, the greatest with the smallest. We almost always see male and female take advantage of any chance encounter and show themselves completely unselective [*nicht wählerisch*]." However, as we'll see in section 3, his main view is that humans have *lost* a selective capacity possessed by other species—lost it precisely by that corrupting overlay of socializing habits. These have spoiled a natural taste, which needs to be reinstituted, for the benefit of our kind.

It's important that there is a standard for *truth* in our aesthetic judgments, supplied by this sexual and evolutionary context. These judgments were only of selective advantage, because they tended to pick out mates that were in fact (on average) fitter. So these judgments rely on epistemic abilities designed to "get right" these assessments of others. WP801 [1887] says that in the aesthetic state we value "what the deepest instinct recognizes [*anerkennt*] as higher, more desirable, more valuable in general, the upward movement of the type." We have a discerning eye—or Nietzsche often prefers to say "nose"—for signs of ascent and decline. So in this original sexual context the aesthetic already involves a truth project, though one with limited scope: it aims at only a single truth about others—their fitness (and suitability as mates).[64] In this ur-aesthetic there *is* a truth about what's beautiful: healthy and ascending life.

This judgment is expressed, we need to remember, not in any thought or proposition that "this is beautiful," but immediately in the feeling of *Rausch*. It's the body that judges, and it judges beauty precisely in order to act sexually toward it. Since *Rausch* is requisite for so acting, the judgment (if positive) issues directly in this feeling—or rather the judgment simply *is* this feeling. My body concludes that X is beautiful in and by the *Rausch* that prepares it to pursue X.

However, this means of effecting the judgment is damaging to the epistemic progress of the judgment. This is an instance of a more general point: the need for quick and decisive action requires simplifications and generalizations. Action requires that epistemic effort be constrained and cut short, and to this extent the decisions the epistemic powers transmit

---

64. WP804 [1887]: "Thus the beautiful and ugly are recognized as *conditioned*; namely with regard to our undermost *preservation-values*. To want to posit a beautiful and an ugly apart from that, is senseless."

are inevitably "lies."[65] But the lie is greater in the sexual case than else-where, because here effective action depends on a condition of fascination and frenzy (traits not as effective or requisite in other contexts). The lover must feel the beloved to be the very heart of the world, the best beauty there is.

This brings us from aesthetic judging to aesthetic *enjoying*, i.e., the reception or appreciation of beauty, which spurs action toward the other (organism, person). Whereas aesthetic judging was selected to discriminate fitness, aesthetic enjoying is selected to spur sexual pursuit. To this end selection evolves the same means as for other activities that are indispens-able "existence conditions" for an organism: it attaches a great *pleasure* to this activity.[66] It motivates sexual pursuit of the other, for the sake of that pleasure. It submerges judgment's aim at the truth (about the other's fitness) in a new aim at sexual pleasure in the other.

We've seen that in Nietzsche's view this admiring of beauty is intrinsi-cally active and "beautifying." Although it doesn't physically work on the object as the artist does, it shapes the object in its view of it—shapes it the better to enjoy it in *Rausch*. It looks for aspects of the other that please it this way. And it's this beautifying that contradicts aesthetic judgment's epistemic aim. Once the body's judgment is made, and issues in *Rausch* toward the thing, the capacity for judgment is drastically eclipsed by that feeling. The organism re-aims itself toward "perfecting" the object within its own view: it tries to see the object as perfectly beautiful, and to shape its look to build higher and higher its own *Rausch* toward it.[67]

This is responsible, I suggest Nietzsche thinks, for a first main "lie" in our aesthetic responses: *Rausch* goes on to beautify the thing far beyond that original judgment. It sets aside those epistemic powers (to judge fitness) and tries to see only aspects of the object that enhance its own *Rausch*, and the pleasures this gives. So it positions itself to lie to itself, by

65. See chapter 1, section 4, for Nietzsche's general account of selection in favor of error.

66. Chapter 1, section 4, also gives Nietzsche's account of how selection attaches pleasure as a "reward" to drives, to spur their performance; also chapter 3, section 2.

67. WP804 [1887]: "[O]nce the aesthetic drive is at work, a whole host of other perfections, originating elsewhere, crystallize around 'the beautiful one.' It is not possible to remain *objective*, or to suspend the interpretive, additive, completing, poetizing force. . . . The sight of a 'beautiful woman'." WP806 [1887]: "[A]s man sees woman and, as it were, makes her a present of everything preferred, so the sensuality of the artist lays into one object anything else that he honors and esteems — in this way he *perfects* [*vollendet*] an object."

inflating the beauty on which it fixes—as one does in love, Nietzsche thinks.[68] Again, we can see this as a claim about the "fittest strategy": the sexual attitude that succeeds best is an initial discriminating judgment, followed by a passionate fixation in which judgment is swamped.

This sexual desire is a more complete or intense form of a "partiality" Nietzsche thinks is involved in all willing and valuing. The defect lies not in seeing a beauty that isn't really there, but in exaggerating this beauty and ignoring all others. It lies in the "perspectivity" of the assessment, and in particular in the *limits* or *horizons* to this perspective.[69] This defect is of course pandemic among perspectives, but they suffer it to differing degrees. Nietzsche thinks of two ways this defect is reduced: by widening the perspective to include others, or by somehow recognizing the perspective's limits.[70] But *Rausch* intensifies the defect in both respects: it exaggerates this one beauty to the exclusion and detriment of any others. It is "partial" to an extreme degree.

What about the third aesthetic stance Nietzsche treats, and indeed puts greatest weight on—aesthetic creating? Where does this third stance occur in the original sexual context of the aesthetic? Here creating means making things beautiful by changing them (not just by changing one's view of them, as already happens in aesthetic enjoying). What "makes" sexual beauty in this stronger sense? We can distinguish two ways this happens.

First, sexual beauty gets made by individuals working on others or (especially) themselves, to improve their beauty by the criteria of the prevailing judgment. In self-beautifying, one gives oneself the marks of ascending life, of procreative desirability. The means include grooming, clothes, and ornament. Once again Nietzsche treats this as a matter of making "lies": one creates artificial aids to one's appearance, so that one

68. WP808 [1888]: "Does one want astonishing proof of how far the transfiguring power of *Rausch* goes? 'Love' is this proof. . . . *Rausch* will be finished with reality in such a way that the cause [of love] is extinguished in the consciousness of the lover, and something else seems to find itself in its place — a vibrating and glittering of all the magic mirrors of Circe."

69. In chapter 2, section 5c, I treated this partiality as the ultimate and ineliminable lie in all valuing.

70. See, e.g., how TI.ix.19 alludes to this fuller perspective on beauty: "[I]s the world really beautified by the fact that man takes it for beautiful? He has *humanized* it: that is all. But nothing, quite nothing, guarantees us that man should furnish the model of beauty. Who knows what he may look like in the eyes of a higher judge of taste [*Geschmacksrichters*]?"

looks fitter and more reproductively suitable than one is. Nietzsche, as we know, attributes this sexual stratagem to women in particular. WP806 [1887]: "Woman, conscious of man's feelings concerning women, assists his efforts at idealization by adorning herself, walking beautifully."[71] And she does so, he thinks, because men have a more intense aesthetic responsiveness to sexual beauty—hence are more susceptible to being fooled by such sexual lies.[72]

The second way beauty gets made is more basic: selection favors beauty, so the lineage evolves toward more and more beautiful members.[73] This selection presupposes that initial aesthetic judgment in the members: they choose mates by the criteria by which they've evolved to judge fitness. This judgment is a selective pressure that favors those meeting these criteria. So the lineage evolves so that members have more and more the "look" of health and fitness, by those criteria. The artificial aids of grooming and so on are superimposed on a sexual beauty already made genetically.

Nietzsche thinks this second way of making beauty likewise involves a lie. The lineage tries, as it were, to trick its own members. It evolves by selection toward members with the signs of health that appeal to the current aesthetic judgment. Of course selection already favors organisms that *are* healthy, but now there is an additional selective pressure in favor of organisms that *appear* healthy to potential mates. And there may be ways for organisms to improve their success by giving signs of a greater health or vigor than they possess. Nietzsche anticipates our current biology's picture of the sexes as competing with one another to use this sexual selection to their advantage. Each tries to manipulate the aesthetic judgment of the other.

So in sum about aesthetic drives: what's bred into us first is the disposition to respond by *Rausch* to physical and behavioral features that have been, on average, reliable predictors of health and fitness. And it's this judging aesthetic attitude that is then the presupposition for the other

71. BGE232: "I do think self-adorning belongs to the eternal-feminine? . . . her great art is the lie, her highest concern is appearance and beauty."

72. See especially 8.18[43] [1876]: "If women had been as devoted to the beauty of men, it would in the end be the rule among men to be beautiful and vain — as it is now the rule among women. . . . It shows the greater understanding and soberness of women (perhaps also their deficiency in aesthetic sense), that women also accept ugly men; they look more at what matters here: protection, maintenance; men more at the beautiful appearance."

73. Very early, 7.7[121] [1870–1871]: "Nature strains to arrive at beauty: if this is achieved somewhere, it concerns itself with propagating it."

two—for creating and enjoying (sexual) beauty. These latter arise by a secondary selection, which presupposes the presence of that judging. The lies they tell presuppose the truth project involved in aesthetic judging— they are lies to that judgment. They presuppose that something counts as "getting it right." In this original locus of the aesthetic, there is indeed a "standard of beauty"; it's embedded in the selective process that "de-signed" our responses to beauty. What *is* beautiful is the "ascending" human. More basic than those aesthetic lies is this aesthetic knowledge or truth.[74] On the other hand, this is only a *first* such truth about beauty.

3. Aesthetic Practices

Nietzsche doesn't think that this Darwinian process is the *only* one that has shaped our aesthetic attitudes. These naturally selected drives are the deep basis for those attitudes, but superimposed on them is a second level of formation, which Nietzsche thinks happens not "in the blood," but in habits or social practices. Humans are distinctively able to acquire such nongenetic dispositions—to "learn" them from one another by imitation. And, as we saw in chapter 2, section 3, this new way for behavioral dispositions to "replicate" themselves sets up a new selective regime with a somewhat different logic than the old. And this "social selection" rede-signs our aesthetic behaviors and values toward a rather different overall end.

Let's quickly recall some general features of this new selective regime. It has the same overall and probabilistic character as natural selection. It makes behaviors "for" or "toward" certain outcomes *independently* of whether individuals "choose" these outcomes or "aim" at them, either consciously or not. Social practices, like inbred drives, get their meanings and ends from this selective history—and when I join in such a practice, what I do has ends determined not by my own motives or intentions, but by that history. So here again Nietzsche rejects our usual motives model for explaining ourselves, and denies the transparency this model attributes to our actions. We don't, in fact, know why we do what we do, and we need genealogy to find out.

---

74. To be sure, even this truth involves another kind of lie—one that will be important to Nietzsche. Our beauty judgments still lie, insofar as we're ignorant of how they have arisen by selection. (We may even suppose that beauty is "just there" in people, independent of that "biological" interest in fitness.) In this ignorance, we are

This suspicion—that our practices have different meanings than we think—is reinforced by Nietzsche's analysis of the principal tendency of this new selective regime. The chief way it diverges from natural selection is by favoring habits or practices that bind us more tightly and efficiently together into a collective unit. The (memetic) "fitness" of habits lies chiefly in how they *herd* us, i.e., render us more similar to one another, and more anxious to be similar. This herding requires, above all, a constraining of our bodily instincts, which drive us apart toward their selfish pleasures; it favors an "ascetic ideal." Because they've been selected for this chief end of herding and taming us, our habits have very different functions and goals than we suppose. Our standard motives model for understanding ourselves was designed, in fact, precisely to conceal these real meanings.

These general points apply in Nietzsche's diagnosis of our aesthetic practices. Natural selection bred into us aesthetic drives to function in the ways we've seen, in service to the ultimate selective criterion of biological fitness. Now these aesthetic drives are "exapted" by social selection and turned to new functions, especially to functions serving the chief end of socializing or herding us, and especially by constraining our selfish instincts. Aesthetic practices are superimposed on those aesthetic drives, to push and pull them toward those new functions. These divert that key experience of *Rausch*, in particular. And they revise the criteria for the "beauty" to which *Rausch* and aesthetic judgments respond.

Now to be sure, this adaptation for herding is only *part* of Nietzsche's story of how aesthetic practices evolve. There are many other factors that affect this history—which is therefore not a simple linear development by the more and more thorough exapting of aesthetic drives for herd purposes. Nietzsche distinguishes healthier and sicker phases in our cultural history, and healthier and sicker forms of art.[75] Nevertheless I think he believes that a broad tendency is indeed steadily at work in the background behind all these more conspicuous ups and downs: the tendency to herd and moralize us, and to use art for this task. The healthier societies and art worlds have the character of exceptions or resistances to this structural momentum. This tendency has the broad effect of subjecting aesthetic

(as it were) "used" by selection in these judgments, we don't see what they mean as we make them.

75. CW.Epilogue: "Aesthetics is tied indissolubly to these biological presuppositions [of ascending or declining life]: there is a *décadence*-aesthetic, there is a *classical* aesthetic." On decadent art see Moore (2002, 168ff.).

impulses to what Nietzsche calls the "ascetic ideal"; we'll see that this is the aspect of morality that bears most directly upon art and the aesthetic.

Nietzsche thinks of aesthetic drives and values as inherently *resistant* to that broad tendency. They are less susceptible to that redesign (under the ascetic ideal) than many of our other bodily drives and values, and constitute a reservoir of health. Nietzsche thinks the aesthetic has often helped societies and individuals to regain a healthier stance, against that herding, taming tendency. WP853 [1888] speaks of "[a]rt as the only superior counterforce against all will to denial of life, as the antichristian, antibuddhist, antinihilistic *par excellence*." So when the artist *is* coopted into service of that taming, this goes against the pronounced grain of the aesthetic. GM.iii.25: "An artist-servitude in service of the ascetic ideal is therefore the most genuine artist-*corruption* there can be, sadly also one of the most common."[76]

What determines whether art has been coopted this way is its relation to custom and morality. Aesthetic experience gets exapted for herding by being subordinated to ethical or moral purposes.[77] (Recall from chapter 2, section 3, that the ethic of custom and morality are the two main phases into which Nietzsche divides our social evolution.) The criteria for beauty shift: the most beautiful is no longer the "flourishing physicality" loved by aesthetic drives; now it's ethical or moral virtue.[78] Nietzsche is of course hostile to this subordination of aesthetic to moral values.

Take first art's function within the *ethic of custom*. Indeed, it's here that art really begins—that aesthetic drives are exercised upon art in our usual sense. Earlier there was "art" only in individuals' self-beautifyings—their ways of giving themselves the look of health and sexual fitness. But as a social practice, art arises to play a socializing and herding function—to bind members into a social unit. Art serves custom by providing orienting images that help align members to shared practices. The artwork is set up in public view, to announce and propagate a common life and outlook. It gives infectious images of the kinds of persons the social members need

76. WP821 [1888]: "What is essential in art remains . . . its production of perfection and plenitude; art is essentially *affirmation, blessing, deification of existence*[.]— What does a *pessimistic* art signify? Is it not a *contradictio*?" WP851 [1888] says that if Schopenhauer were right and tragedy taught resignation, then this would be an art "in which art denies itself."

77. This is exemplified in Socrates' conception of the Aesopian fable as the proper poetry; see BT14.

78. WP804 [1887]: "[T]he *herd-human* will have the *value feeling of the beautiful* through different things than will the *exceptional*- or over-human."

to aspire to be. It sets forth the virtues and ideals that are to be common or standard—sets them forth in pleasing form, the better to spread this standard. It works in particular by making beautiful images of gods.[79]

This socializing function of art takes up a power already present in our "animal" (or naturally selected) aesthetic drives. WP809 [1888]: "The aesthetic state has an overrichness of *means of communication*, together with an extreme *receptivity* for stimuli and signs. It is the high point of communicativeness and transmissiveness between living beings, — it is the source of language."[80] This communicative power originated in the sexual context, to align partners' aims and feelings to the sexual end. Now, in the social context of custom and convention, this power gets used for a special kind of "communication" (*Mittheilung*), of the *ethos*, the common views and actions to which members need to align themselves. Art makes certain aims and feelings "public," i.e., widely shared.[81] Nietzsche found this herding role of art most overtly and repellently enacted in Wagner's Bayreuth festivals.[82] Here the herd ideal is not just the message, but the medium.

The ethic of custom is already hostile to the drives, which pull individuals apart into private and selfish projects. So it begins the work of opposing to those drives an **ascetic ideal** (*asketische Ideal*), which rejects their goals and pleasures. By setting up images of lives that limit or renounce bodily pleasures, art already serves this ascetic ideal.

But this ideal is developed much further in the phase of *morality*. Now social members get trained to feel a "bad conscience" for their selfish impulses—for everything that would carry them apart from the common practice. The frustration and vilification of the drives is pushed further, and with it the suffering and sickness of members. Now art and aesthetic experience are adapted more drastically—both to control the drives and to ease the suffering this inflicts. Art becomes a vehicle for religions to

79. Z.ii.17: "[A]ll gods are poets' parable, poets' smuggling [*Dichter-Gleichniss, Dichter-Erschleichniss*]." Z.ii.2 attacks the "conjecture" of God, because it "reaches beyond your creative will"; we could not *make* a God (though we could the overman); here too Zarathustra associates this unfeasible ideal with the poets, who "lie too much."
80. 13.17[9] [1888]: "art . . . as means of communication."
81. GS39: "How does the general taste change? Because individuals who are powerful and influential announce without shame . . . the judgment of their taste and disgust, and tyrannically accomplish it."
82. CW.Postscript makes the point about Bayreuth part of a criticism of "theatre" generally: "The theatre is a form of demolatry in matters of taste; the theatre is a revolt of the masses." See too NCW2 (a revision of GS368).

teach that bodily appetites are evil and that the sufferers are themselves to blame for them.

So rather than invigorating the drives, a moralizing art is used either to deaden them or to divert them from their natural objects. And now the aesthetic works almost in reverse of its natural tendency, which was to activate and energize the other drives, and our sexuality in particular. Instead art is used to effect a "false strengthening" of the will and feeling, which Nietzsche associates especially with romanticism.[83] And here we find the new role that *Rausch* is exapted to play. A moralized art still evokes *Rausch*—it still excites the drives—but it uses this heightening for an opposite effect. *Rausch* now gets used as a narcotic, to "wear out" the drives and leave them weaker than before.[84]

This subversion of art by the ascetic ideal is best represented, Nietzsche thinks, by Schopenhauer. (Plato is a less complete case.)[85] Schopenhauer insists that the special function of art is to quiet the will, and that aesthetic pleasure is a pleasure in the resulting disinterestedness. By this reinterpretation of art's point, Schopenhauer carries Christianity further: he can affirm art (as the latter doesn't), "though in a christian, which means nihilistic sense" (TI.ix.21). So Schopenhauer shows the upshot toward which this moralization of art tends. He brings it to the point at which the ascetic ideal undermines itself, in nihilism; it's this that then makes possible self selection.

We can sum up these changes wrought by the social redesign of our aesthetic drives by returning to the three basic aesthetic stances (toward beauty) distinguished above—judging, enjoying, and making—and seeing how each gets transformed when art gets moralized and is subjected to the ascetic ideal. This brings out the *aesthetic deficiencies* of our moralized values, and of the life they give us. It shows that his well-known aesthetic criticism of morality has more facets than are usually seen: it's not merely that "morality makes ugly people," but that it makes people whose lives

83. WP826 [1887], which is entitled "False 'Strengthening'": "[I]n *romanticism*: the constant *espressivo* is no sign of strength, but of a deficiency of feeling."

84. *Rausch* is described so in WP29 [1883–1884]. CW5: "Wagner increases exhaustion: *therefore* he attracts the weak and exhausted." His art does this precisely by "exciting" their "weak nerves." Compare HH.iii.170. See GM.iii.19 on how the ascetic priest promotes an *"orgy [Ausschweifung] of feeling* . . . as the most effective means of deadening dull, crippling, protracted painfulness."

85. Plato's more positive relation to the drives—and sexuality in particular—is expressed in TI.ix.22–23. On the other hand GM.iii.25 calls him "the greatest enemy of art that Europe has so far produced."

are stunted by flaws in their own aesthetic stance. These aesthetic flaws will need to be corrected in the new values we self select.

Within a moralized aesthetic, how does *judging* work? Since the beautiful is the morally good, we must use our moral reasoning to judge beauty; our standard must be this same moral reasoning in whomever we judge.[86] It's not beauty of body but beauty of soul or character that we should admire—the beauty that lies in subduing one's instincts to a rational assessment of what's morally right. When we judge this kind of beauty, our natural power to discern and respond to health or sexual fitness becomes quite irrelevant.[87] We need to develop entirely different epistemic skills— above all to learn to reason morally ourselves. Since this moral reason is independent of all instincts and interests, beauty is a kind of disinterestedness—and it needs to be judged from that same stance. This results in what BGE33 calls "the aesthetics of 'disinterested contemplation,' under which the emasculation of art seeks seductively to create a good conscience for itself."[88] Aesthetic judgment is assimilated into moral judgment. And Nietzsche thinks this spoils this taste or judgment.[89]

How, second, does this moralization affect aesthetic *enjoying*? It's for the sake of this enjoying that morality cares to assimilate aesthetic experience: morality improves allegiance to itself by attaching aesthetic pleasures to itself. It diverts our aesthetic drives from their natural objects and "sublimates" or "spiritualizes" them.[90] It trains them to find their satisfaction not in physical beauties, but in moral ones. However this training inevitably drains much of the intensity from these pleasures; the spiritualized forms are faint and "bloodless" echoes of the originals. Not only are these pleasures fainter, they are also "unhealthy pleasures." They fail to play the invigorating role for which aesthetic pleasures were naturally

---

86. BT14 says that in the wake of Euripides and Socrates "the virtuous hero must be a dialectician; now there must be a necessary, visible connection between virtue and knowledge, faith and morality."

87. It's not irrelevant to Plato, of course—which is a way his aesthetic position is healthier and less fully moralized than Schopenhauer's.

88. WP30 [1887–1888]: "[C]ontempt for 'naturalness,' for desire, the ego: [an] attempt to understand even the highest spirituality and art as consequence of a depersonalization and as *désintéressement*."

89. GM.iii.22: "The ascetic priest . . . has also spoiled *taste in artibus et litteris*, — he is still spoiling it."

90. GM.iii.8 suggests that "sensuality is not annulled [*aufgehoben*] by the entry of the aesthetic state, as Schopenhauer thought, but only transfigured [*transfigurirt*] and no longer enters consciousness as sexual excitement."

selected. Even the *Rausch* that we've seen is still stirred in this enjoyment is merely an artificial heightening that dampens the drives in the end.

Third, in a moralized aesthetic, beauty gets *created* differently too. Since artists are now selected to appeal to this moral and unhealthy taste, they are themselves unhealthy. D269: "Do you not realize that if you demand art when you are sick you make sick the artists?" Such artists create, for the most part, out of a lack or deficiency, not from the excess and abundance of healthy artists.[91] They attempt to supply the deficiency in their drives with their conscious intelligence, which is not really an aesthetic power at all.[92] Nietzsche's arch-example is of course Wagner, whom he treats as *the* artist of decadence—of morality in a very ripe stage.[93] Wagner shows how far the processes of social selection have transformed and deformed the original aesthetic.

4. The New Aesthetics

We come now to the main issue. Given this account of what art and aesthetic experience *have been* (and indeed still are), what does Nietzsche *want* them to be? What does he attempt to make of them, in his life and writings? And, in particular, in what relation does he want art and the aesthetic now to stand, toward truth? With this, we come back to (try to) settle our opening problem: his characterization of *art as lie*, and how this affects his allegiance to truth.

A first important point is that Nietzsche clearly uses the above *truths about* how art and aesthetic experience have been so far to justify his aesthetic prescriptions to us. Although his aesthetic values aren't derived *solely* from those facts, he clearly uses those facts as an indispensable *part* of his defense of his values to us. These facts help give us part of a reason to adopt his new aesthetic values ourselves. So Nietzsche's truth project is at least "primary" in this limited sense, that its findings give an initial impulse and orientation to his aesthetic project: truths guide his choice of

91. Nietzsche lays great weight on this distinction in GS370; also WP845 [1885–1886].
92. See BT12 on Euripides: "as a poet, above all the echo of his conscious knowledge," "the poet of aesthetic Socratism."
93. CW5: "Precisely because nothing is more modern than this total sickness, this lateness and overexcitement of the nervous machinery, Wagner is the *modern artist par excellence*."

it. The further question is whether he designs this aesthetic project *for* truth.

Now it might seem he *can't* want to use art for truth. Nietzsche is mostly "on the attack" against truth and truth claims, questioning whether we can have truth, and whether we should want it. He seems to use his evolutionary story to undermine or discredit that will to truth, and to elevate art above it. So evolutionary truth teaches us to care about art more than truth: *this* truth sets us free from caring about truth (so much). This is the reading of Nietzsche by Heidegger and Habermas.[94] It has in its favor some explicit and emphatic statements by Nietzsche, and in these very terms: "art is *worth more* than truth."[95]

It also has in its favor, it seems, the large-scale argument of the third essay in *On the Genealogy of Morals*. This essay, which I think is especially synoptic, addresses the question of what ascetic ideals mean (*bedeuten*). It gives a genealogy for these values, as the priest's remedy for the pervasive suffering from frustrated drives. It depicts this ascetic ideal as the large-scale point of our values now—as the *only* meaning we have found to make that suffering bearable (GM.iii.28). This ideal is most clearly at work in Christianity (and religions generally), which moralizes against the drives and discounts this life for a life to come. But we must not suppose that we escape this ideal when we become enlightened scientists. The essay culminates in an argument that the will to truth is itself part of the ascetic ideal, its very "kernel" (*Kern*) (iii.27). Nietzsche hints that only art can save us: "[A]rt, in which precisely the *lie* is sanctified, and the *will to deception* has a good conscience at its side, is much more fundamentally opposed to the ascetic ideal than is science" (iii.25). And to play this saving role it seems that art must free itself from any allegiance to truth, as ascetic.

I'll argue, against this reading, for a close and complementary relation between art and truth, at this ultimate point in Nietzsche's position. The ideal of freedom as self selection gives us the solution to this relation: art and truth—our aesthetic and epistemic stances—complement one another by being indispensable parts of this self selection, and of the life this

94. Heidegger (I, 218): "Art as will to semblance is the supreme configuration of will to power." Also see Habermas (1985/1990, 96).

95. In WP853 [1888] he says that the author of *The Birth of Tragedy* believed this; see n. 14 above. WP1011 [1886–1887] suggests that "the lie — and *not* the truth — is divine." This view is prominent in Nietzsche's 1872–1873 notebooks, where he favors constraining the knowledge drive, for the benefit of an "artistic culture" (7.19[34] [1872–1873] [P&T11]).

chooses.[96] They get held together in a synthesis we need to analyze. This means also to analyze the complementary roles of beauty and truth as virtues or values of the self selector.

We will need to consider two ways that Nietzsche's new ideal bears on the aesthetic. First is the question of what aesthetic values the self selector will choose. Once I genealogize my aesthetic drives and practices, and so am able to self select these values, *what* such values will I choose? Second, but more crucial, is the question of what aesthetic values might be involved in self selection itself, i.e., in *how* this freedom chooses. For we'll see that when I self select my values this puts me into a kind of aesthetic relation to them—unlike the relation to values I had in morality.

As to the aesthetic values the self selector will choose, a first point is obvious: he/she will choose a "healthy" art and aesthetics, by contrast with the decadent aesthetics characteristic of our modern age and epitomized by Schopenhauer and Wagner. Nietzsche's account of the long social process by which art is moralized and made to serve the ascetic ideal sets up his own task of healing art. This is a necessary stage in an overall cultural therapy, which will lead us "through" nihilism and out the other side. He wants to cure first our art, in order to use especially it to cure the rest of us. He sees art in this role both early—this is a main point of *The Birth of Tragedy*—and late, e.g., WP794 [1888]: "Our religion, morality, and philosophy are decadence forms of man. / The *countermovement: art.*"

But what exactly is the character of this cure? One tempting answer to "what Nietzsche wants" is to *return* us from social, decadent art to those natural, animal art drives and art functions—to return us to art as it was naturally selected and to a simple, sensual health in our aesthetic attitudes. Perhaps this will involve resexualizing (or resensualizing) aesthetic experience—and somehow lodging it back in our bodies. And perhaps it will involve restoring art to the role it played in pre-Christian and premoralized "master" societies. In any case Nietzsche would aim to restore society in general to that simpler health, and would hope to do so by an art that regained the ability to express the natural drives, cured from their inversion by herd forces. Art would play the role of restoring our natural taste, our ability to judge health and fitness—the epistemic role of the aesthetic that we saw in section 2.

This is close to Nietzsche's point; it *is* his point, much of the time. But

---

96. WP495 [1884] puts it succinctly: "Both senses [for truth and for beauty] stand beside one another — the sense for the real is the means, to get in hand the power to shape things after our liking."

I think that by itself it suggests an "atavism" or "primitivism" that is not his dominant view.[97] He's not advocating a return to that simple and unreflective past of healthy masters, nor to our animal nature—he's not advocating it even within the realm of art, or in our aesthetic practice. (In chapter 3, section 4's discussion of "progress" we saw that it's also not his aim regarding our "values toward others.") Nietzsche sets his sights not on merely restoring an original health, but on ascending to a "higher health" with a rather different logic, never feasible before.[98] To help us to that higher health, art takes a new form, which involves especially a new relation to truth. So the self selector will redesign art for this higher health.

There's another way to state the goal of this redesign. This higher health is typified, above all, by the stance of self selection itself. So what the self selector will choose is to continue to self select, since it's in this very stance that his/her higher health lies. (This shows how our two questions above overlap.) So another way to see the new function of art and aesthetic experience is to see what role they play within self selection itself. And indeed, we discover that this stance of self selecting one's values puts one into the new aesthetic stance toward those values. Self selection itself carries us out of a moral way of having values, and drops us into an aesthetic one.

In redesigning aesthetic experience to serve freedom as self selection, Nietzsche assigns it new functions. I think we can pick out *three* ways he wants art to serve freedom. I'll take these from least to most direct: art serves freedom, either as (a) an external means, or as (b) a less or (c) a more integral *part* of freedom. I'll interpret these three new functions as versions of the three aesthetic attitudes we've had in view all along: the functions are exercised, respectively, in the attitudes of aesthetically (a) enjoying, (b) judging, and (c) making beauty. Nietzsche "exapts" each of these attitudes, as they have evolved under natural and social selection, so that they can serve as means or parts of the new ideal of self selection.

a. Aesthesis as Recuperative Play

Let's begin with the use Nietzsche speaks of most often: art, and the aesthetic attitudes it expresses and promotes, are employed as "recreation

97. See Nehamas's criticism (1996, 234) of Habermas's reading of Nietzsche as advocating a "return to the archaic."

98. Here I repeat points developed more fully in Richardson 1996, e.g., 137–38.

for the truth-seeker": the latter *turns aside* from the truth project, to rest and recuperate in beautiful illusions. Here aesthetic experience serves truth indirectly—as an external means to the truth project, a separate interlude that then enables one to resume that project more effectively.

This point has very early roots in Nietzsche, though it takes a different form there. One of the chief positions in his notebooks in 1872–1874[99] is that philosophy must act as cultural physician, by using art to "restrain" (*bändigen*) the knowledge drive. 7.19[51] [1872–1873] (P&T157) speaks of "[t]he restraining of knowledge as the drive of art. / We *live* only through these illusions of art." This is likewise the role that *The Birth of Tragedy* gives to Apollonian art: we suspend our epistemic powers to enjoy its beautiful illusions. So here already art and aesthetics are a realm apart from theory, a supplement just as necessary for life as dreaming sleep.

But in this early book and notes, the weight of Nietzsche's allegiance is on the side of art.[100] The "knowledge-drive" expressed in our science has a deep flaw, he thinks: it inevitably reaches out to its own limits, and by discovering them undermines itself. Finding that the knowledge it wants is unobtainable, it drives itself to a paralyzing skepticism. Moreover it has the same undermining effect on the cultural values that are requisite for societal health: it destroys commitment to any values it examines. The philosopher's role is to see these harmful effects of the unrestrained knowledge drive. The philosopher must teach society to defend its illusions, conveyed in its art and religion, by refusing to bring that skeptical, undermining viewpoint to bear on them. Here—in this early view—the aesthetic lies are, as it were, the best part of society, and not just a necessary exception to a truth project ranked higher. Here Nietzsche is decidedly hostile to the theoretical or scientific drive, which he calls "Socratic" in distinction from the Apollonian and Dionysian art drives.

99. Many of these notes are collected in Breazeale 1979 (which I am citing as P&T); see too Breazeale's introduction on this topic.

100. In BT4 Nietzsche reverses the priority we accord to waking over dreaming (the analogue of Apollonian art); he continues: "For the more I become aware of those omnipotent art-drives in nature, and in them an ardent longing for illusion, for redemption through illusion, the more I feel myself impelled to the metaphysical assumption that the truly existent and primal unity, as the eternally suffering and contradictory, also needs the rapturous vision, the pleasurable illusion, for its continuous redemption." And in WP853 [1888] he recalls this viewpoint: "But truth does not count as the supreme value-measure. . . . The will to appearance, to illusion, to deception . . . here counts as deeper, more primal, more metaphysical than the will to truth." See also n. 14 above.

But as we noted briefly before, Nietzsche soon casts off the Wagner-permeated viewpoint of *The Birth of Tragedy*, and passes into a "positivist" phase—in *Human, All-Too-Human* especially—in which he is strongly critical of art and the aesthetic and sets his allegiance clearly with truth.[101] Art is a refuge for metaphysical sentiments that we will gradually outgrow the need for. HH.i.220: "[A]rtists of all periods . . . are the glorifiers of the religious and philosophical errors of humanity." Art has given us sustaining pleasures, but we will learn to find them elsewhere. HH.i.222: "[A]fter a disappearance of art the intensity and multifariousness of the joy in life it has implanted would still demand satisfaction. The scientific human is a further evolution of the artistic." Eventually the scientist will no longer need to recuperate in aesthetic enjoyments, but will find them in knowledge itself.

However Nietzsche's views shift once again. He learns, as it were, to disassociate art from Wagner, and sways back to a more favorable view of it in his maturity. In particular, he revives the idea that art is needed as an antidote to truth. But now, I think, the weight is on the side of truth. The greatest power and the highest health belong to freedom as self selection, and this freedom depends crucially (as we've seen) on a diagnostic insight into the sources and aims of one's values. But freedom has that high status precisely because the truth it requires is so very daunting and discouraging. And art is needed as a recuperative interlude for someone struggling for such truths.

To choose our own values we need to "see through" our values so far. We need genealogical truths about the real meanings of our values: how they have been designed by social processes for very different purposes than we suppose. We need such truths precisely to loosen the grip of those values on us—and hence must "incorporate" these truths as dispositional counters to the drives and habits that carry those values. Grasping and incorporating these truths is the hardest thing we can do, and freedom's power and health are supreme because it has to be won this way. This is why the will to truth, even and especially in Nietzsche's version of it, is *ascetic*. Devaluing our own values is painful and depressing, and pushes us toward *nihilism*, as a loss of ability to care or strive.

So the first way Nietzsche redesigns aesthetic experience is to help us to cope with this specific pain. He uses it medicinally, to make his new

101. See n. 13 above. Young (1992, 73ff.) shows that already in *Assorted Opinions and Maxims* and *The Wanderer and His Shadow*, the immediately following works now

epistemic project more livable. Even the strongest and bravest inquirers will need interludes in which they restore their pleasure in life by enjoying artistic illusions. They need to refresh themselves by suspending their diagnostic and skeptical efforts—the better to resume them later on. Here art serves as rest and recuperation. We can take this use of art to be exemplified in Nietzsche's own passion for *Carmen*.

GS107 is important here. Art is a "counterforce" to our honesty, which lets us bear our skeptical insight into "delusion and error as a condition of knowing and perceiving." "As an aesthetic phenomenon existence is still *bearable* for us. . . . [W]e must now and then be glad about our folly, or we cannot remain glad about our wisdom."[102]

In this role as diversion and distraction from the truth project, the passive pleasure in art or beauty is sufficient—and indeed what serves best.[103] So when Nietzsche prescribes aesthetic experience for this role, he stresses its attitude of *enjoying* beauty; he'll put the other attitudes (judging and making) to work in different ways. Here what's important is to restore or make good the quantum of pleasure in the drives that Nietzsche thinks our organism requires, to keep itself healthily functional. Aesthetic enjoyment, which evolved under natural and social selection for the functions we've seen, is revised for this new function of refreshing the self selector.

This enjoyment comes in spectating art.[104] Nietzsche here appropriates his own earlier idea that a culture needs art's Apollonian illusions in order to sustain itself. He transfers this benefit from the whole culture to the individual life he advocates. Art revives the free spirit's pleasure or joy in living, which is constantly being sapped by the undermining work of the will to truth. Art is an antidote to the asceticism of that will: it prevents

incorporated as volume 2 of *Human, All-Too-Human* (and which I cite as HH.ii and HH.iii), Nietzsche finds more use for art.

102. Note the order of ends in 9.11[162] [1881]: "For the sake of knowledge, to love and further life, for the sake of life to will and further erring, illusions. To give existence an aesthetic meaning, *to increase our taste in it*, is [the] basic condition of all passion of knowledge." WP853 [1888] speaks of "[a]rt as the *redemption of the knower*, — of the one who sees the terrifying and questionable character of existence, who wills to see it, the tragic-knower [*Tragisch-Erkennenden*]." See also GS.P.4.

103. Here I disagree with Soll, who argues (1998, 107ff.) that Nietzsche gives too little attention or weight to the aesthetic experience of the spectator.

104. Perhaps it also comes in enjoying natural beauty. Nietzsche little mentions this in theoretical contexts, but this kind of aesthetic experience was clearly important to him as well: it (and not the chance to see art or hear music) was a main factor in his choice of homes, and in Sils Maria especially he had the habit of very long walks.

this asceticism from dragging the inquirer down into nihilism. Any individual who presses a diagnostic critique of his/her values will need to balance this effort at truth with aesthetic pleasures whose enjoyment depends on stilling that effort. Where the balance is struck will depend on the strength of the individual—on how able his/her body is to flourish even under the weight of that effort. In periods of "convalescence," for example, such saving pleasures (in illusions) are more necessary.

We've seen that aesthetic enjoyment occurs in the condition of *Rausch*, which excites the drives generally. In its natural or animal form this excitement functions to energize the drives for sexual effort, but under society and morality this excitement is redeployed to exhaust and numb the drives, which are painful because unactable. Now Nietzsche wants to adapt *Rausch* again, to energize drives not for sexual pursuit, but for the "spiritual" project of freedom. Thus he claims in his own case that his enjoyment of *Carmen* makes him "fertile" and "a better philosopher" (CW1).

Because beauty here serves truth "from without," i.e., not as a part of inquiry but as a state to which one "steps away," it can serve truth even though it is itself false, a lie. Still, precisely in experiencing art as rest and diversion, one doesn't inhabit these lies wholeheartedly. In taking them *as* recuperative play, one enters them knowingly, and temporarily, and within the scope of a dominant project of freedom and self-discovery. Recognizing that "untruth is a condition for life," one deploys these untruths deliberately, as side pleasures to sustain the main pursuit. Hence this first new use of aesthetic experience preserves a feature Nietzsche values in it from early on: "So art treats *appearance as appearance*, hence does *not* will to deceive, *is true*" (7.29[17] [1873] [P&T96]).

b. Aesthesis as Diagnostic "Scent"

But the new aesthetic does more than just serve the knower's diversion. It's clear that it *must* do more, both because diversion is too minor a role for art to play, and because it plays this role with only a lesser part of itself. As diversion, art engages the self selector only "as spectator," which we've seen Nietzsche treats as the least important aesthetic stance. He wants to take up aesthetic judging and creating as well—and he wants to make them more integral to his new ideal. He means to put aesthetic powers to direct work within his project of truth and freedom.

Let's look next at the use he makes of aesthetic judging. He exapts this power—already designed and redesigned by natural and social selection—to serve a new function, within his new project of self selection. The latter requires diagnosing the aims (values) of the dispositions that make our behavior—and then "incorporating" these diagnoses in dispositions of their own. Nietzsche thinks this special truth project requires a different epistemic power than science has relied on: *not* a neutral and objective detachment, but a certain aesthetic taste or judgment. Here the aesthetic is not just an external aid to Nietzschean truth, but an element in it.[105] Taste is needed for genealogy, hence for freedom.

This is why Nietzsche so often presents his critical eye on values as making an aesthetic judgment on them—a judgment expressed in an intense and visceral distaste or (in his favorite term here) *disgust* (*Ekel*, often translated as "nausea" by Kaufmann). Z.i.P.3: "What is the greatest experience you can have? It is the hour of the great contempt [*Verachtung*]. The hour in which even your happiness arouses your disgust, as well as your reason and your virtue."

Nietzsche defends this weight he puts on taste in Z.ii.13: "And you tell me, friends, that there should be no disputing [*streiten*] about taste and tasting? But all life is dispute about taste and tasting! / Taste: that is equally weight and scales and weigher; and woe to any living thing that wills to live without dispute about weight and scales and weighing!" Nietzsche thinks he can have the strongest case in such disputes—that he has a most discerning taste.

This second role in a sense runs contrary to the first. Rather than serving us with illusions in which we recuperate from our skeptical inquiries, the aesthetic here plays a skeptical role itself—it is used to lay bare and detach us from errors we'd been subjected by. Nietzsche's main use for aesthetic taste is *critical*: to "smell" the sickness or weakness in our values—both in order to discover it, and to detach from it. Aesthetic judgment discriminates the unsavory elements in our values and practices, and does so in just the distancing and alienating manner we need in order to be free. As principally critical in this way, aesthetic taste joins in the asceticism of the will to truth.[106]

105. Here contrast Habermas, who notes the possibility of an "aesthetic reason," but denies that Nietzsche allows it: "Nietzsche enthrones taste, 'the Yes and the No of the palate,' as the organ of a knowledge beyond true and false, beyond good and evil. But he cannot legitimate the criteria of aesthetic judgment that he holds on to because he . . . does not recognize as a moment of reason the critical capacity for assessing value that was sharpened through dealing with modern art" (1985/1990, 96).

106. For an ascetic, this taste is also dangerous: if exercised too far, it can lead to a nihilistic despair at the "smallness" of all humans. So Nietzsche says his greatest

The free spirit needs this taste to work not just (and not primarily) in explicit inquiries or deliberations, but "down" in his/her bodily drives—in the many little instinctive responses to the circumstances of life.[107] Values—as the designed goals of drives and habits—work subtly and unconsciously to shape our everyday behavior. It's not enough to diagnose these values in reflective thought—we need to incorporate these insights by bringing them into effect in the concrete everyday contexts where those values already work. Only so do we counteract those values and put them "out of play." Aesthetic taste is crucial for such incorporation, because it—unlike deliberate or reasoning judgment—can work effectively down at this level.

It's to reflect this implicit and bodily way the taste works that Nietzsche prefers to call it a sense of smell, rather than of sight or hearing. EH.i.1: "I have a subtler [*feiner*] sense of smell [*Witterung*] for the signs of ascent and decline than any human has had, I am the teacher *par excellence* for this, — I know both, I am both."[108] And EH.i.8: "I possess a perfectly uncanny sensitivity of the cleanliness-instinct, so that I physiologically perceive — *smell* [*rieche*] — . . . the 'entrails' of every soul."[109]

Aesthetic taste can work in this subliminal way because it is already lodged in our bodily drives. The first challenge, Nietzsche thinks, is to unrepress and activate this inbred taste, which has been "given a bad conscience" by morality.[110] And the second challenge is to re-aim this taste a certain way: to train it for the work of diagnosis, to "sniff out" precisely those things that interfere with self selection.

danger is "disgust at humans, at 'rabble'" (EH.i.8). The recuperative use of aesthetic enjoyment, just described, is an antidote for this.

107. So it's not enough simply to give us a new aesthetic concept, as he puts it in an early note; 7.19[51] [1872–1873] (P&T157): "The aesthetic concept of the great and sublime: the task is to educate to this."

108. Compare GM.iii.7: "[E]very animal abhors, just as instinctively and with a subtlety of smell [*Feinheit der Witterung*] that is 'higher than all reason,' every kind of disturbance or hindrance that lies or could lie in its path towards the optimum." CW.Postscript praises the "*Instinkt-Witterung* for the harmful and dangerous," which reacts against Wagner's music despite the prevailing decadence.

109. EH.BT.2 says that one who conceives himself as Dionysian "needs no refutation of Plato or Christianity or Schopenhauer — he *smells the decay*." BGE190 says that a Socratic argument "smells of the *rabble*." See also Z.iv.14.1, BGE271, GM.i.12, GM.iii.14, A59.

110. Z.i.3: "Listen instead, my brothers, to the voice of the healthy body: this is a more honest and purer voice."

The taste bred into our bodies by natural selection is a taste for a "flourishing physicality"; it involves a quasi-sexual attraction to the bodily fit and healthy, and repugnance for the weak and sick. Here as elsewhere, Nietzsche doesn't take this biological value of (reproductive) fitness as an ultimate standard. It's precisely by using that taste this way that he has "power over" that bodily taste as well. He wants to train this taste to judge a certain kind of "spiritual" health and—especially—sickness instead.[111] He wants to train it to recognize the distinctive ways that social selection has misshaped and weakened us, above all by making us "herd" and "common." So EH.i.4: "[P]ity . . . smells [*riecht*] of the rabble." The self selector develops his/her "nose" for the herd instinct at work in usual thoughts and practices.

Nietzsche wants his own books to help in this training. One of their most pronounced aims and effects is to induce us to judge "ugly" our constant inclination to do and think the same as others. His diagnoses convey not just facts about the working of this herd instinct, but this aesthetic revulsion against it. Since "whatever reminds us in the least of degeneration causes in us the judgment of 'ugly'" (TI.ix.20), Nietzsche constantly insists on the sickness of that herd tendency.[112] He tries to inculcate a new habit of judging ourselves, by coopting those inbred aesthetic responses.

Although the primary use of this new aesthetic taste is critical, Nietzsche also makes a role for positive judgments. A well-formed person has "a taste only for what is good for him" (EH.i.2). This taste begins in an instinctive preference for the physical conditions for bodily health—which Nietzsche thinks we socialized, moralized, intellectualized humans suppress or ignore. We need to learn to listen to the judgments of our bodies about food, climate, and amusement. But again we need to train this taste to admire a new "spiritual" health—the higher health of his new ideal.

Finally, this new aesthetic taste plays a crucial role in the "breeding" Nietzsche wants to institute. As we saw in chapter 3, section 6a, this breeding crucially works by affecting "marriage," i.e., choice of reproductive partners. Nietzsche often complains that marriage "for love" joins

111. Natural selection hasn't bred us to recognize the sickness of Christianity, for example. But insofar as it bred us to detest (aesthetically) "declining life," it prepares us to respond to Nietzsche's arguments that Christianity is such.
112. CW.Epilogue: "Aesthetics is indissolubly tied to these biological presuppositions" of ascending or declining life.

partners poorly, because they choose one another by a sexual taste that either fixes on crude signs of a "flourishing physicality," or has been diverted from this to the tamed "moral" virtues valued in the herd. Nietzsche argues for familial, communal, or legal controls on marriage to override this sexual taste. But I noted that he has another and more interesting strategy in mind as well: to "exapt" that sexual taste so that it picks out precisely the qualities that conduce to freedom.[113]

This is, I suggest, one aim in Nietzsche's romanticizing portraits of his free spirits and overmen—and of himself. He gives them a dash and charisma suited to evoke an erotic response. This is also an aim in the hyper-"masculine" traits he so gratingly gives them—his characterizations of these intellectual heroes as "warriors," for example. Though speaking very little of their sexuality, he still renders his new philosophers "sexy" in a way that taps erotic impulses. He trains those impulses to respond—in *Rausch*—to new traits. To be sure, this re-aiming of sexuality is quite one-sided: he insists that women forfeit their sexual attractiveness when they take on these same spiritual traits. His own attractions, however, were to independent and intellectual women—Lou Salomé most famously—and we may perhaps take this as a better indicator of the type of women he imagines his "best" will marry.

c. Aesthesis as Making New Beauty

But there's a further and even more intimate role for aesthetic experience to play in freedom. We find it by asking how, once we've diagnosed the animal and the herd in our values (our drives and practices), Nietzsche thinks we then go on to live and value. Having detached ourselves by "seeing through" our values, he wants us neither to reembrace those same values, nor to remain valueless.[114] Instead, he familiarly insists, we need to "create new values." This creating, which completes Nietzsche's freedom (self selection), is the third and most crucial new function he proposes for art and aesthetic experience.

113. This fits with Nietzsche's general strategy of re-aiming rather than suppressing our appetites. In 9.6[155] [1880] he praises the sex drive as "anti-social, and den[ying] the general equality and the equal value of human to human. . . . the *decline* of a people happens to the extent that the individual passion slackens, and the social grounds for marriage *preponderate*."

114. On the insufficiency of escaping morality's yoke, Z.i.17: "There are many who threw away their last value, when they threw away their servitude."

This third function of Nietzsche's new aesthetic works in the opposite direction from the second: it reverses the skeptical and destructive momentum of diagnosis, and builds new values. One passes from *judging* values and practices, to *making* new ones—which is also, we should bear in mind, a *remaking* of the old ones, since the new ones aren't made from scratch. Freedom requires not just "seeing through" current values, but revaluing them, an act that gets carried out by aesthetic powers (attitudes) in us. The selection of new values is performed *as a creating of beauty* in these values.

This brings us back to a point left underdeveloped back in chapter 2's presentation of freedom as self selection: the positive side to the "revaluation" of values. I have stressed the negative side of freedom—the critical genealogy of our values—and not yet done full justice to the affirmative, to just how the new values are made. This is what that freedom is "for," Nietzsche often says: it's the consequence that explains why that critical freedom is pursued.[115] Z.i.1: "To create new values — that even the lion cannot do: but to create freedom for oneself for new creating — that the power of the lion can do." And Z.iii.12.16: "And you shall learn *only* for creating."

I hope to complete my account of Nietzsche's transition from his genealogical facts to his new values by now showing how he "aesthetically creates" them, in his new way. I will particularly respond to the opening questions about Nietzsche's "aestheticism": what's the epistemic standing of this creating? Doesn't it lie? For doesn't it, in this last step, "make things up," rather than follow the facts?

The creating in which Nietzsche is principally interested is of *values*.[116] He claims for himself the role he thinks philosophers have always played—a role that scientists never come to, and that artists perform only under the direction of philosophers (as Socrates directed Euripides, and Schopenhauer directed Wagner).[117] But to see what it means to "create values," we must also bring in several other things that get created along with values, as Nietzsche also thinks. I'll focus on three: in creating his new values, he at the same time creates (a) himself, (b) his audience (us and our society), and (c) his works.

115. Indeed Nietzsche connects these more closely: he makes the annulment of the old depend on instituting the new; the old is never fully swept away until something new has been put in its place. GS58: "Only as creators can we destroy!" See Nehamas (1985, 61).
116. BGE211: "[The philosopher's task] demands that he *create values.*"
117. On Socrates/Euripides see BT11–13; on Schopenhauer/Wagner see GM.iii.4–5.

Values, we've seen, are the "ends" that explain life processes. (So they're *not* what we might have thought, the things a person *thinks* or *says* his/her values are. We've seen Nietzsche's argument that these stated values are both superficial and deceptive [chapter 2, sections 3–4].) A person's values are the ends that explain his/her drives and habits—the goals of the dispositions ("wills") that effect his/her thought and behavior. In the usual case, the person has these drives and habits either genetically or by social copying, and in either case the explaining end is set by the natural or social selective process *from* which the person received the drive or habit. By contrast a person "creates new values" by giving him/herself dispositions with new aims—or by re-aiming existing drives or practices.[118]

So the first sense in which Nietzsche "creates new values" is by re-aiming his own drives and habits—the dispositions by which his concrete thoughts/feelings/behaviors are guided. By this he "creates himself." And he describes this self-creating as an aesthetic task. GS299: "[A]ll this we should learn from the artists while being otherwise wiser than they. For with them this subtle strength [making beautiful] usually ends where art ends and life begins; but *we* will to be poets of our lives, and in the smallest and most everyday things first."[119] We make new values to beautify ourselves or our lives.

But Nietzsche is not so modest as to intend to create new values only for himself.[120] Genuine philosophers have always also created values *for society*, and it's clear that Nietzsche intends this too. The "new philosopher" will be a "legislator" of new values.[121] Nietzsche treats others—the audience, the society, the species—as raw material upon which he (as a philosopher) works. And again he presents this remaking in aesthetic terms: the task is to beautify others, or society, by so changing their values.[122] By

118. Z.i.17: "Can you give yourself your evil and your good and hang your own will over yourself as a law? Can you be your own judge and avenger of your law?"

119. GS290: "*One thing is needed.* To 'give style' to one's character — a great and rare art! It is practiced by one who surveys everything that his nature offers of strengths and weaknesses, and then fits them into an artistic plan, until every one appears as art and reason, and even the weaknesses delight the eye." Nehamas (1985, chapter 6) gives an important account of this.

120. See Z.ii.15 on the "will to create *über sich hinaus*," in a way that involves risking and sacrificing oneself.

121. BGE203: "Towards *new philosophers*, there is no choice; towards spirits strong and original enough to give the impulse for opposite valuations and to revalue and invert 'eternal values'." Also BGE211; WP979 [1885], WP978 [1885].

122. One of Nietzsche's recurring images is of himself/Zarathustra as *sculpting*, in stone and with a hammer, the *Mensch* into *Übermensch*. Z.ii.2: "Oh, you humans, there

working artistically on his whole society or culture, he thinks his will takes the greatest power.

The third thing Nietzsche creates, his work or philosophy, serves obviously to mediate between the first two creations. His works communicate the values by which he has remade himself. They induce or invite his readers to similarly remake themselves—and thereby spread those values. His works are created as vehicles for his values, above all the value of freedom as self selection. Here too this creating has an obvious aesthetic character: Nietzsche gives his works various kinds of "literary" qualities not usual in philosophy.

So Nietzsche thinks that other philosophers have created values in these same three places, though not in his own aesthetic fashion. They have failed to be "artist-philosophers."[123] Just what does this difference amount to, in these three cases?

The best-known account of Nietzsche's "aestheticism" is by Nehamas (1985), and I'll present my own in contrast with it. Nehamas likewise attributes to Nietzsche an ideal of self-creating that is strongly "aesthetic," and reflected in the aesthetic character of his works. But Nehamas develops this aesthetic aspect at the expense (I think) of Nietzsche's allegiance to truth, in several ways that tend to align Nietzsche with postmodernists (who of course often cite him as forebear). I will argue against this that Nietzsche carries out those three creatings in ways that reflect his persisting allegiance to truth—as postmodernism usually denies.

Let me start with Nehamas's account of self-creating.[124] Famously, he argues that the goal of this self-creating is to give oneself the kind of coherence possessed by literary characters: "Every detail concerning a character has, at least in principle, a point; it is to that extent essential to that character" (165). To create a self is to unify and connect all of one's "effects," i.e., one's thoughts, desires, and deeds; one makes these cohere with one another both by revising them, and by telling an organizing story about them. By doing so one "gives style to one's character" (Nehamas quotes GS290). By "blending . . . into a perfectly coherent whole" (188–89) all of my thoughts and deeds, I make them all essential to me, and become "willing to acknowledge all my doings as my own" (190). Nehamas ex-

sleeps for me in the stone an image [*Bild*], the image of my images! Oh, that it must sleep in the hardest, ugliest stone! . . . / The beauty of the overman came to me as a shadow." (He also quotes this in EH.Z.8.)

123. See n. 7 above; also nn. 2 and 8.

124. Nehamas (1985, 187, 195) notes that Nietzsche also calls this ideal "freedom."

264   *Nietzsche's New Darwinism*

plains the thought of eternal return as Nietzsche's test for whether one can affirm all of one's effects in this way.

Second, Nehamas likewise thinks that Nietzsche's main writerly goal is to communicate this ideal. But this task is complicated by the special logic of self-creating. Because this involves individualizing oneself, it is impossible to give any general description of what the goal is, or any rules for achieving it: "A true individual is precisely one who is different from the rest of the world, and there is no formula, no set of rules, no code of conduct that can possibly capture in informative terms what it is to be like that" (225). So not only does Nietzsche not offer this ideal with the universality of moral demands, it's not even a "code of conduct" directed to a few.

Finally, Nehamas argues that Nietzsche creates his philosophical works so that they can convey this unusual ideal. Because no general description of self-creating is feasible, it can only be communicated by displaying an example or instance. And this is just what those works do: they show their readers Nietzsche's own process of creating himself, in the writing of those works: "Nietzsche's texts therefore do not describe but, in exquisitely elaborate detail, exemplify the perfect instance of his ideal character. And this character is none other than the character these very texts constitute: Nietzsche himself" (232–33). By this special strategy he makes conspicuous the particularity of every self-creation.[125] This indeed is true of great art generally: "[T]he ability to exemplify greatness without demonstrating the means of achieving it, and without even caring to require that anyone else achieve it, is one of the most essential features of great artworks" (137).

What reasons does Nietzsche have for adopting and promoting this ideal of self-creation, according to Nehamas? The ideal is connected to Nietzsche's attacks on certain metaphysical notions—against the thing-in-itself, the substance, the subject: "A thing is . . . for Nietzsche not a subject that has effects but simply a collection of interrelated effects, selected from some particular point of view from within a much larger similar set" (92). The only unity we can have, therefore, is what we can achieve by making these effects "cohere" in the way we've seen. Nehamas insists however that Nietzsche's attacks on the subject do not themselves express an ontological

---

125. Self-creating involves this recognition of the particularity of one's case: "The main feature of this character type is that each of the specific characters in which it is manifested is aware of the fact that it too is only one among many possible characters" (38). This shows a further sense in which each self-creating is "aesthetic."

position (a truth) of his own: it is "not an alternative to the metaphysics of substance and accident"; "he wants to show that the world has no ontological structure," that it is "radically indeterminate" (96–97). In this regard the world in general (and not just the person) is like a literary text, which "can be interpreted equally well in vastly different and deeply incompatible ways" (3). So Nehamas at least much reduces the extent to which the aim of aesthetic creating is based in truths about the world.

My main disagreements with Nehamas concern this relation between Nietzsche's aesthetic and epistemic moves. They especially concern the *telic* relation between these projects, the ways he pursues one "for the sake of" the other—or in Nietzsche's own terms the way one "rules" or "directs" the other. Nehamas understates, I think, the extent to which the truth value still guides those aesthetic creations, even though they create falsehoods.[126] He also understates how far it is truths that justify and motivate Nietzsche's aesthetic turn. To be sure, Nehamas does mention, in scattered places, many of the epistemic/aesthetic connections I'll cite—but to do them justice we must pull them together.

One place Nehamas recognizes the role of truth within self-creating is (in the point) that we can't achieve unity by simply deceiving ourselves and "refusing to acknowledge an existing multiplicity"; this would give us "only the feeling of unity, and not unity itself" (186). So there are limits on the kind of story I can tell about myself, in unifying my effects. Similarly, my ability to will eternal return counts for nothing, if I accomplish it by deceiving myself about the contents of the past life I affirm (cf. 159). I can give my past deeds new meaning by relating them to a different future, but I must not simply lie those deeds away. So these aesthetic deeds only have merit or value if they satisfy these epistemic demands—if they grasp certain truths.

These epistemic constraints on self-creating, the ways it is beholden to truth,[127] are important in themselves, and fit uneasily into the context of Nehamas's reading, I think. Although he stresses that Nietzsche's perspectivism is not a relativism "that holds that any view is as good as any other" (72), Nehamas seems unwilling to say that some perspectives are better by being truer. The radical indeterminacy of the world seems to

---

126. I likewise disagree with Megill (1985, 88): "Nietzsche saw himself as an artist and mythmaker (which is not to deny that he was also, in some respects, a critic; but the critical, demythologizing part of his enterprise was entirely subordinate to his remythologizing)."

127. See nn. 96 and 102 above.

preclude there being any facts about our deeds for self-creating to be constrained to recognize.

But more than this, I think these truths function for Nietzsche not just as preconditions for self-creating, but as key criteria for its success. It's not simply a minimal condition on an adequate self-creating that it be true to these deeds.[128] It's rather a matter of the *degree to which* it is true to them: this is Nietzsche's main criterion for how "high" a self-creating is.[129] Besides the unity and richness Nehamas stresses, what counts for self-creating is *how much* of this diagnostic truth it reflects. Moreover the truth it needs to reflect is not simply a matter of what my thoughts, desires, and deeds concretely are, but of what they *mean*, i.e., why I do them, what they're for. It depends, in other words, on the kind of genealogical insight we've seen.[130]

Here again Nehamas recognizes a part of this point. He sees that the project of self-creating is picked out in the first place on the basis of certain skeptical insights: that there is no substantial subject distinct from those "effects," that there are no moral universals to constrain my self-change. So art is valued because (it's true that) there is no truth (cf. 73). In effect, art expresses a metatruth, and it's as such, I think, that Nehamas makes the project of self-creating appealing to his readers. But I don't think he recognizes the extent to which Nietzsche counts quite specific insights to be key in the self-creating he prizes: I need to "see through" the specific values that possess me, so that I can revalue and thereby possess them. (Nehamas seems closest to this point on page 61.)

Nor is it merely that skeptical, genealogical insights need to *precede* my revaluing, because they need to "clear the ground" on which I then build my new values. In this case it would be quite open how I go on to rebuild; the skeptical truth would play a merely destructive role, and would not be involved in the new creation. I think this reading is widespread but wrong. A Nietzschean self-creating needs to carry along those skeptical insights, and embed them in the new beauty it creates. So the new creations

128. Nietzsche won't treat it as a minimal condition, easily satisfied, precisely because truth, as perspectival, is a matter of *degree*. Perspectives can be higher or wider than others; they can encompass others.

129. E.g., A54: "Strength, *freedom* through the force and superforce of the spirit, *proves* itself through skepticism." See also chapter 2, n. 117.

130. See GS335 on the way that self-creating depends on a self-discovery, e.g.: "[Y]ou have still not discovered yourself, still not created for yourself an own, ownmost ideal."

carry lessons both particular and general, and have legitimate claim to be called "true."[131]

First, the new creating draws specific lessons from those diagnoses: it shapes the new values to avoid particular weaknesses or sicknesses it detects in them. The new philosophers Nietzsche anticipates will create not just any new values, but ones that render persons stronger and healthier than existing ones do—and stronger in part by *knowing not* to value out of the old weakness or sickness. In chapter 3, section 5b, I described how the existing virtues of pity and altruism are redesigned in the light of new insight into how they *were* designed, by social selection, to herd and control us. That redesign creates new virtues that salvage some of the old and turn them to better account.

Second, the new creating draws certain *general* lessons from the failure of the existing values, lessons that affect the *way* it then values the new. The new philosophers learn from genealogy not just the specific flaws of prevailing values, but the true perspectivity of all values. They infer from their own skeptical insights that all values are subject to such critique, from a perspective high or full enough. So they abandon the moralistic faith in the absolute or objective status of their values that philosophers used to have. They create values in the expectation that they will be seen through in turn. Let me return to the three ways (or places) Nietzsche "creates values," to see how these points affect the aesthetic character of these creatings.

Nietzschean *self*-creation builds on self-diagnosis. I revise my dispositions—my habits of thinking, feeling, acting—in the light of a diagnostic critique of them, which of course I need to carry out myself. I re-aim them by mixing into them a "distaste" for the features by which these dispositions tended to herd or weaken me. So my new empathy, for example, has a nose to steer clear of the forms of pity that subject and ensnare me. This is the epistemic aspect of self-creating; the artistry comes in being able to invent *positive* values that contain these critical lessons.

It's not a matter simply of taking the old values and adding the critical insight—which would leave me with *less* to value. I need to "sculpt" my

---

131. Perhaps he has some of this in mind in WP552 [1887]: "Truth is therefore not something that is there, to be found or discovered — but something *to be created* and that gives the name for a *process*, or rather for a will for overcoming, that has in itself no end." And WP616 [1885–1886]: "[E]very *elevation of the human* brings with it the overcoming of narrow interpretations."

valuing drives and habits into a form and unity that I can regard as beautiful. Exposing that diagnosed ugliness, and even holding it in view, I need to invent a way for myself, my life, and the world around me to be beautiful again.[132] I need to "recathect" my values, after incorporating that skeptical insight into them. My aims or goods must engage me bodily, above all by stimulating my *Rausch*. And I can only identify such lucky values by "listening to my body," and its nose for *Rausch*.

There is a similar synthesis of epistemic and aesthetic in the new philosophers' creation of new societies. Again the redesign is informed by critical diagnoses. And again the critical insights are incorporated into the new value perspective (not for the whole society perhaps, since the herd should still enjoy its herd pleasures, but at least for the individuals it flowers in). But again the creators cannot calculate or reason to the new values, since what's needed is a system that engages and invigorates individuals. They must rely on their aesthetic and bodily tastes to make and select values that engage in this way.

At the broadest and most ambitious level, this creating proceeds by "breeding" a new kind of human being. So breeding too is aesthetic work.[133] As we saw above, it tries to reconfigure sexual tastes and practices, in order to make more likely that "best will breed with best," and so continue their characters. One important strategy will be to change what's sexually attractive: the new values make new kinds of individuals beautiful—those who are suited for freedom. Along with this is a new idea of the beauty to be "brought forth upon" that loved beauty. Z.i.20: "Thirst of the creator, an arrow and longing towards the overman: speak, my brother, is this your will to marriage?" These sexual attitudes will also affect memetic copying. So Nietzsche builds in his readers a quasi-sexual attraction toward Dionysus and the overman. This shows the significance of the sexual dramas in *Thus Spoke Zarathustra*, between Dionysus and Ariadne, and Zarathustra and life.

We find the same fusion of epistemic and aesthetic in Nietzsche's creation of his works. These works—philosophical, poetic, philosophi-

132. Z.ii.13 says that the "sublime" one (*Erhabene*) returning with "ugly truths" hunted in the "forest of knowledge" needs to "become beautiful."
133. See WP960 [1885–1886] on the need for "philosophical strongmen and artist-tyrants" to "breed-up a master-race [*Herren-Rasse*]" through "international race-unions [*Geschlechts-Verbänden*]." GS113: "[E]ven now the time seems remote when artistic energies and the practical wisdom of life will join with scientific thinking to form a higher organic system in relation to which scholars, physicians, artists, and legislators — as we know them at present—would have to look like paltry relics of ancient times."

poetic—communicate not just his newly created values, but certain skepti-cal/diagnostic insights that are indeed inseparable from those values. They communicate a skill in self-diagnosis, and also specific diagnoses the audi-ence is invited to apply to itself.

So when Nietzsche plays the poet's role he does so in a different way than poets did before. They—most strikingly Wagner—played their role unknowingly, at the behest of some philosopher, and more deeply at the behest of very large-scale social selective forces. Nietzsche thinks himself a novelty both in being a poet who is also a philosopher (and so poetizes his own ideas), and in being a philosopher who is also a scientist (and so makes his ideas in the light of selection's truth).

Kofman (1972/1993, 102) says that Nietzsche replaces concepts with metaphors: "Metaphor foregrounds the 'personality' which is effaced by and in the concept." I agree that Nietzsche makes metaphors too, but think they are tangled up with his concepts and truth claims. His metaphors house his new ideal in beautiful images or scenarios. But the ideal can also, I think, be described, as Nehamas denies. Nietzsche wishes indeed to "exemplify" his ideal of self selection, and to give us pictures of people carrying it out. But he also wants to describe it[134]—and needs to describe it because he needs to convey the crucial diagnoses the new ideal must incorporate. These include the diagnosis of Christian, ascetic, and herd values.

Let me sum up my account of Nietzschean creating. I have argued that we need to understand it as a move within self selection. As such, this aesthetic creating is complexly intertwined with epistemic aims and insights. This creating makes new values that incorporate truths about the old—and this is what lets that creating *advance*. For this new purpose, Nietzsche "exapts" an existing aesthetic attitude, made by natural and social selection to serve, ultimately, a pair of functions: our reproductive success, and success of the herd in us. He tries to superimpose upon these ultimate aims of the attitude his new aim, and to redesign creating for it.

So aesthetic creating, like enjoying and judging, gets converted in Nietzsche's revaluing into an activity that follows and values truths— insights into the social and psychological sources of values and practices.

---

134. To be sure, there is great flexibility in this ideal—as the ideal of creating and "individualizing" oneself. But there is also a lot that can be said to describe or analyze the common features of such creating—as I've tried to show in my account of self selection above. See also Leiter (1992, 287–88) against Nehamas's claim that Nietzsche exemplifies instead of describes his ideal.

These insights, I've tried to show, have their root in the Darwinian view of life as bearing a deep noncognitive design. From this root Nietzsche generates a distinctive naturalistic account of humans, as compounds of natural drives and social habits, pressing us toward conflicting sets of ends. Nietzschean creation—what he practices himself and what he commends to his audience—does not cast loose from these biological/genealogical truths, but makes values that let us live, more freely, in the light of them.

Vocabulary

Translations are my own, often revising the well-known ones by Walter Kaufmann and R. J. Hollingdale. I have aimed for literalness and consistency in rendering the vocabulary that bears most on my topics. I have also tried to preserve Nietzsche's punctuation as far as feasible—as well as the telegraphic and ungrammatical character of some of his notes. I mark paragraph breaks with a slash (/).

The following are some of the stand-ins I'll use for Nietzsche's German. My aim is to enable readers to infer the German within my quotations. Where I depart from these equivalents, I'll mark it by giving the German in brackets.

1. Evolution

adaptation = *Anpassung*
akin = *verwandt*
ancestors = *Vorfahren*
descent = *Abkunft*
evolution = *Entwicklung*
existence = *Dasein* or *Existenz*
fit = *lebensfähig*

fitness = *Lebensfähigkeit*
generation = *Generation*
heredity = *Vererbung*
inborn = *angeboren*
kind = *Art*
life = *Leben*
lineage = *Linie*
nourishment = *Ernährung*
posterity = *Nachkommenschaft*
preservation = *Erhaltung*
procreation = *Zeugung*
propagation = *Fortpflanzung*
race = *Rasse*
selection = *Selektion* or *Selection* or *Auswahl* or *Auslese*
self-preservation drive = *Selbsterhaltungstrieb*
sexual = *geschlechtlich*
species = *Gattung*
struggle = *Kampf*
struggle for existence = *Kampf um Dasein/Existenz*
survival = *Fortleben* or *Bestehen*
survival of the fittest = *Bestehen des Lebensfähigste*

2. Teleology

advantage = *Vortheil*
agreeable = *Angenehm*
degenerate = *degenerirt*
drive = *Trieb*
employment = *Verwendung*
favorable = *begünstigend*
function = *Funktion*
goal = *Ziel*
healthy = *gesund*
instinct = *Instinkt*
intention = *Absicht*
intentional = *beabsichtig*
intentionality = *Absichtlichkeit*
means = *Mittel*
motive = *Motiv*
pleasure = *Lust*

progress = *Fortschritt*
purpose = *Zweck*
purposiveness = *Zweckmässigkeit*
satisfaction = *Befriedigung*
sick = *krank*
(to) strive = *streben*
useful = *nützlich*
utility = *Nützlichkeit*

3. Society and Values

altruism = *Altruismus*
benevolence = *Wohlwollen*
(to) breed = *züchten*
breeding = *Züchtung*
caste = *Kaste*
civilization = *Civilisation*
class = *Stand*
domestication = *Domestikation*
habit = *Gewohnheit*
habituation = *Gewöhnung*
hardness = *Härte*
level = *Schicht*
nobility = *Adel*
pity = *Mitleid*
practice = *Brauch*
rank-order = *Rangordnung*
society = *Gesellschaft*
taming = *Zähmung*
upbringing = *Erziehung*
valuation = *Schätzung* or *Werthschätzung*
value = *Werthe*

Bibliography

Primary Sources

For Nietzsche's German text I have relied on:

Colli, G., and Montinari, M. 1980. *Sämtliche Werke: Kritische Studienausgabe in 15 Bänden*. Berlin: de Gruyter.

Where I provide the German, it reproduces this edition.

Nietzsche's Published Works

Here is a table that gives Nietzsche's published works and any prefaces, separately numbered chapters, and so on that I refer to. I give these works' approximate years of composition—which permits coordination with Nietzsche's *Nachlass* notes (whose dates I supply when citing them). This table also gives my abbreviations for these prefaces, and notes if they were written and added later.

BT   *The Birth of Tragedy* (1869–1871)
          .ASC "Attempt at a Self-Criticism," a preface written in 1886
UM   *Untimely Meditations* (1873–1876)

.i "David Strauss: The Confessor and the Writer"
.ii "On the Uses and Disadvantages of History for Life"
.iii "Schopenhauer as Educator"
.iv "Richard Wagner in Bayreuth"

HH *Human, All-Too-Human* (1876–1879)
.i Volume I
.ii Volume II, part I: "Mixed Opinions and Maxims"
.iii Volume II, part II: "The Wanderer and His Shadow"
.i.P, .ii.P Prefaces to both volumes, written in 1886

D *Daybreak* (1880–1881)
.P Preface written in 1886

GS *The Gay Science* (1881–1882)
.JCR "'Joke, Cunning, and Revenge': Prelude in German Rhymes"
.P Preface written in 1886
Book V (sections 343–83) written in 1886

Z *Thus Spoke Zarathustra* (1882–1885)
.i–.iv Four parts
.i.P "Zarathustra's Preface" to part I
Nietzsche doesn't number the sections in his parts—we must add them. Some of the sections have numbered sub-sections, which I cite as, e.g., Z.iii.12.20.

BGE *Beyond Good and Evil* (1885–1886)
.P Preface

GM *On the Genealogy of Morals* (1887)
.P Preface
.i–.iii Three essays

CW *The Case of Wagner* (1888)
.F Foreword
.E Epilogue

TI *Twilight of the Idols* (1888)
.F Foreword
.i–.xi Eleven chapters (not numbered by Nietzsche)

A *The Antichrist* (1888)

EH *Ecce Homo* (1888)
.F Foreword
.i–.iv Four parts (not numbered by Nietzsche)
.BT, .UM, etc. Subparts of .iii on Nietzsche's earlier works

NCW *Nietzsche contra Wagner* (1888)
.E Epilogue

Nietzsche's Nachlass

As described in the note on citations, I cite Nietzsche's unpublished essays—all dated 1870–1873—simply by their titles (e.g., "The Greek State"). I cite his notes by their appearance in the *Kritische Studienausgabe* (volume number, then notebook number, then note number in brackets), unless the note was collected into *The Will to Power*, in which case I cite it by **WP** and the note number there. In both cases I append the note's year of composition, to allow it to be placed against the published works. There is also the following useful collection of some of Nietzsche's early notes:

Breazeale, D. (ed. and trans.) 1979. *Philosophy and Truth: Selections from Nietzsche's Notebooks of the Early 1870s*. Atlantic Highlands, N.J.: Humanities Press.

For notes included in this volume I append to the *Kritische Studienausgabe* citation a reference to **P&T**, followed by page number.

I refer to a few of Nietzsche's letters, identifying them by their addressee, and month and year. These appear in

Colli, G., and Montinari, M. 1986. *Sämtliche Briefe: Kritische Studienausgabe in 8 Bänden*. Berlin: de Gruyter.

Secondary Sources

I cite the following in the scientific format, except for the two books by Darwin and one by Spencer, which I abbreviate as ***Origin, Descent,*** and ***Data***, respectively. Where I give two years separated by a slash (/), the second is the date of the edition cited; the first is the work's original appearance.

Allen, C., M. Bekoff, and G. Lauder. (eds.) 1998. *Nature's Purposes: Analyses of Function and Design in Biology*. Cambridge, Mass.: MIT Press.

Anderson, R. L. 1994. "Nietzsche's Will to Power as a Doctrine of the Unity of Science," *Studies in the History and Philosophy of Science* 25(5):729–50.

Ansell Pearson, K. 1997. *Viroid Life: Reflections on Nietzsche and the Transhuman Condition*. London and New York: Routledge.

Appel, F. 1999. *Nietzsche contra Democracy*. Ithaca, N.Y.: Cornell University Press.

Ayala, F. J. 1970. "Teleological Explanations in Evolutionary Biology," *Philosophy of Science* 37:1–15.

Bedau, M. 1991. "Can Biological Teleology be Naturalized?" *Journal of Philosophy* 88:647–55.

————. 1992. "Where's the Good in Teleology?" *Philosophy and Phenomenological Research* 52:781–805.

Bennett, J. 1976/1990. *Linguistic Behavior.* London: Cambridge University Press. Reprint. Indianapolis, Ind.: Hackett.

Berlin, I. 1953/1993. *The Hedgehog and the Fox.* London: Weidenfeld and Nicolson. Rev. ed. Chicago: Dee.

Bigelow, J., and Pargetter, R. 1987. "Functions," *Journal of Philosophy* 84(4): 181–96.

Bowler, P. J. 1992. "Lamarckism," in Keller and Lloyd (eds.) 1992.

Braithwaite, R. B. 1953. *Scientific Explanation.* Cambridge: Cambridge University Press.

Brandon, R. N. 1978/1996. "Adaptation and Evolutionary Theory," *Studies in the History and Philosophy of Science* 9(3):181–206. Reprinted in Brandon 1996.

————. 1981/1996. "Biological Teleology: Questions and Explanations," *Studies in the History and Philosophy of Science* 12(2):91–105. Reprinted in Brandon 1996.

————. 1996. *Concepts and Methods in Evolutionary Biology.* Cambridge: Cambridge University Press.

Breazeale, D. 1979. Introduction to *Philosophy and Truth: Selections from Nietzsche's Notebooks of the Early 1870's.* Atlantic Highlands, N.J.: Humanities Press.

Brobjer, T. (unpublished). "Nietzsche's Knowledge of Philosophy."

Canfield, J. 1964. "Teleological Explanation in Biology," *British Journal for the Philosophy of Science* 14:285–95.

Clark, M. 1990. *Nietzsche on Truth and Philosophy.* Cambridge: Cambridge University Press.

————. 1998. "On Knowledge, Truth, and Value: Nietzsche's Debt to Schopenhauer and the Development of his Empiricism," in Janaway (ed.) 1998.

Conway, D. W. 2002. "*Ecce Caesar*: Nietzsche's Imperial Aspirations," in Golomb and Wistrich (eds.) 2002.

Cummins, R. 1975. "Functional Analysis," *Journal of Philosophy* 72:741–64.

Danto, A. C. 1965. *Nietzsche as Philosopher.* New York: Macmillan.

Darwall, S., A. Gibbard, and P. Railton. 1992. "Toward *Fin de siècle* Ethics: Some Trends," *Philosophical Review* 101(1):115–89.

Darwin, C. 1859/1961. *On the Origin of Species.* London: Murray. Facsimile ed. Cambridge, Mass.: Harvard University Press. (I cite this as *Origin*, followed by page number.)

————. 1871/1981. *The Descent of Man, and Selection in Relation to Sex.* London: Murray. Facsimile ed. Princeton, N.J.: Princeton University Press. (I cite this as *Descent*, followed by volume and page number.)

————. 1877. "A Biographical Sketch of an Infant," *Mind* 2:285–94.

Dawkins, R. 1976/1989. *The Selfish Gene.* Oxford: Oxford University Press.

————. 1982. *The Extended Phenotype: The Long Reach of the Gene.* Oxford: Oxford University Press.

Dennett, D. C. 1995. *Darwin's Dangerous Idea: Evolution and the Meanings of Life.* New York: Simon and Schuster.

Detwiler, B. 1990. *Nietzsche and the Politics of Aristocratic Radicalism.* Chicago: University of Chicago Press.

Foucault, M. 1971/2001. "Nietzsche, Genealogy, History." Orig. pub. in *Hommage à Jean Hyppolite,* Paris: Presses Universitaires de France. Trans. D. F. Bouchard and S. Simon in D. F. Bouchard (ed.) *Language, Counter-Memory, Practice: Selected Essays and Interviews by Michel Foucault.* Ithaca, N.Y.: Cornell University Press, 1977. Reprinted in Richardson and Leiter (eds.) 2001.

Gibbard, A. 1990. *Wise Choices, Apt Feelings: A Theory of Normative Judgment.* Cambridge, Mass.: Harvard University Press.

Godfrey-Smith, P. 1994a. "A Modern History Theory of Functions," *Nous* 28(3): 344–62.

———. 1994b/1996. "Spencer and Dewey on Life and Mind," in R. A. Brooks and P. Maes (eds.) *Artificial Life IV* (Proceedings of the Fourth International Workshop on the Synthesis of Living Systems), Cambridge, Mass.: MIT Press. Reprinted in M. Boden (ed.) *The Philosophy of Artificial Life,* New York: Oxford University Press.

Golomb, J., and R. S. Wistrich. (eds.) 2002. *Nietzsche, Godfather of Fascism? On the Uses and Abuses of a Philosophy.* Princeton, N.J.: Princeton University Press.

Gould, S. J., and E. Vrba. 1982/1998. "Exaptation: A Missing Term in the Science of Form," *Paleobiology* 8:4–15. Reprinted in Hull and Ruse (eds.) 1998.

Habermas, J. 1985/1990. *The Philosophical Discourse of Modernity: Twelve Lectures.* Orig. pub. as *Der philosophische Diskurs der Moderne: Zwölf Vorlesungen,* Frankfurt: Suhrkamp Verlag. Trans. F. Lawrence, Cambridge, Mass.: MIT Press.

Hawkins, M. 1997. *Social Darwinism in European and American Thought, 1860–1945.* Cambridge: Cambridge University Press.

Heidegger, M. 1961/1979–1982. *Nietzsche.* Orig. pub. in 2 vols., Pfullingen: Verlag Günther Neske. Trans. F. A. Capuzzi, D. F. Krell, and J. Stambaugh in 4 vols., San Francisco, Calif.: Harper and Row.

Hofstadter, R. 1944/1955. *Social Darwinism in American Thought.* Philadelphia: University of Pennsylvania Press. Rev. ed. Boston: Beacon.

Hull, D. L. 1978. "A Matter of Individuality," *Philosophy of Science* 45:335–60.

———. 1980. "Individuality and Selection," *Annual Review of Ecology and Systematics* 11:311–32.

Hull, D. L., and M. Ruse. (eds.) 1998. *The Philosophy of Biology.* Oxford: Oxford University Press.

Hussain, N. (unpublished). "Honest Illusion: Valuing for Nietzsche's Free Spirits."

James, W. 1878/1992. "Remarks on Spencer's Definition of Mind as Correspondence," *Journal of Speculative Philosophy* 12 (Jan.):1–18. Reprinted in *William James: Writings 1878–1899,* New York: Library of America.

Janaway, C. (ed.) 1998. *Willing and Nothingness: Schopenhauer as Nietzsche's Educator.* Oxford: Oxford University Press.

Kaufmann, W. 1950/1974. *Nietzsche: Philosopher, Psychologist, Antichrist.* 4th ed. Princeton, N.J.: Princeton University Press.

Keller, E. F. 1992. "Competition: Current Usages," in Keller and Lloyd (eds.) 1992.

Keller, E. F., and E. A. Lloyd. (eds.) 1992. *Keywords in Evolutionary Biology.* Cambridge, Mass.: Harvard University Press.

Kitcher, P. 1993/1998. "Function and Design," in P. A. French, T. E. Uehling, and H. K. Weltstein (eds.) *Midwest Studies in Philosophy* xviii, Notre Dame, Ind.: University of Notre Dame Press. Reprinted in Hull and Ruse (eds.) 1998.

Kofman, S. 1972/1993. *Nietzsche and Metaphor.* Orig. pub. as *Nietzsche et la métaphore,* Paris: Payot. Trans. D. Large. Stanford: Stanford University Press.

Lampert, L. 1986. *Nietzsche's Teaching: An Interpretation of "Thus Spoke Zarathustra."* New Haven, Conn.: Yale University Press.

Lange, F. A. 1866/1950. *The History of Materialism and Criticism of Its Present Importance.* Orig. pub. as *Geschichte des Materialismus und Kritik seiner Bedeutung in der Gegenwart,* Leipzig: Baedeker. Trans. E. C. Thomas, 3d ed. New York: Humanities Press.

Leiter, B. 1992. "Nietzsche and Aestheticism," in *Journal of the History of Philosophy* 30(2):275–90.

———. 1995. "Morality in the Pejorative Sense: On the Logic of Nietzsche's Critique of Morality," *British Journal for the History of Philosophy* 3:113–45.

———. 1998a. "The Paradox of Fatalism and Self-Creation in Nietzsche," in Janaway (ed.) 1998.

———. 1998b. "Nietzsche's Respect for Natural Science," *Times Literary Supplement* 4983(2 Oct.):30–31.

———. 2002. *Nietzsche on Morality.* London: Routledge.

Lennox, J. G. 1992. "Teleology," in Keller and Lloyd (eds.) 1992.

Lenoir, T. 1982/1989. *The Strategy of Life: Teleology and Mechanics in Nineteenth-Century German Biology.* Dordrecht: Reidel. Reprint. Chicago: University of Chicago Press.

Lewontin, R. C. 1996. "Evolution as Engineering," in J. Collado-Vides, B. Magasanik, and T. F. Smith (eds.) *Integrative Approaches to Molecular Biology,* Cambridge, Mass.: MIT Press.

Magnus, B., and K. M. Higgins. (eds.) 1996. *The Cambridge Companion to Nietzsche.* Cambridge: Cambridge University Press.

Maynard Smith, J. 1974. "The Theory of Games and the Evolution of Animal Conflicts," *Journal of Theoretical Biology* 47:209–21.

Megill, A. 1985. *Prophets of Extremity: Nietzsche, Heidegger, Foucault, Derrida.* Berkeley: University of California Press.

Millikan, R. 1989. "In Defense of Proper Functions," *Philosophy of Science* 56:288–302.

Mills, S. K., and J. H. Beatty. 1979. "The Propensity Interpretation of Fitness," *Philosophy of Science* 46:263–86.

Moore, G. 2002. *Nietzsche, Biology and Metaphor.* Cambridge: Cambridge University Press.

Morrison, R. G. 1997. *Nietzsche and Buddhism: A Study in Nihilism and Ironic Affinities.* Oxford: Oxford University Press.

Müller-Lauter, W. 1971/1999. *Nietzsche: His Philosophy of Contradictions and the Contradictions of His Philosophy.* Orig. pub. as *Nietzsche: Seine Philosophie der Gegensätze und die Gegensätze Seiner Philosophie*, Berlin: de Gruyter. Trans. D. J. Parent. Urbana: University of Illinois Press.

Nagel, E. 1977. "Teleology Revisited," *Journal of Philosophy* 74(5):261–301.

Nehamas, A. 1985. *Nietzsche: Life as Literature.* Cambridge, Mass.: Harvard University Press.

———. 1996. "Nietzsche, Modernity, Aestheticism," in Magnus and Higgins (eds.) 1996.

Nietzsches Bibliothek. 1942. *Vierzehnte Jahresgabe der Gesellschaft der Freunde des Nietzsche-Archivs.* Weimar: Wagner Sohn.

Nussbaum, M. C. 1994. "Pity and Mercy: Nietzsche's Stoicism," in Schacht (ed.) 1994.

———. 1997. "Is Nietzsche a Political Thinker?" *International Journal of Philosophical Studies* 5(1):1–13.

Poellner, P. 1995. *Nietzsche and Metaphysics.* Oxford: Oxford University Press.

Quine, W. V. O. 1969. "Natural Kinds," in *Ontological Relativity and Other Essays.* New York: Columbia University Press.

Reginster, B. 2000a. "Nietzsche on Selflessness and the Value of Altruism," *History of Philosophy Quarterly* 17(2):177–200.

———. 2000b. "Nietzsche's 'Revaluation' of Altruism," *Nietzsche-Studien* 29: 199–219.

Richards, R. J. 1988/1998. "The Moral Foundations of the Idea of Evolutionary Progress: Darwin, Spencer, and the Neo-Darwinians," in M. H. Nitecki (ed.) *Evolutionary Progress*, Chicago: University of Chicago Press. Reprinted in Hull and Ruse (eds.) 1998.

Richardson, J. 1996. *Nietzsche's System.* New York: Oxford University Press.

Richardson, J., and B. Leiter. (eds.) 2001. *Nietzsche.* Oxford: Oxford University Press.

Russell, B. 1945. *A History of Western Philosophy.* New York: Simon and Schuster.

Schacht, R. 1983. *Nietzsche.* London: Routledge and Kegan Paul.

Schacht, R. (ed.) 1994. *Nietzsche, Genealogy, Morality: Essays on Nietzsche's Genealogy of Morals.* Berkeley: University of California Press.

Schank, G. 2000. *"Rasse" und "Züchtung" bei Nietzsche.* Berlin: de Gruyter.

Schutte, O. 1984. *Beyond Nihilism: Nietzsche without Masks.* Chicago: University of Chicago Press.

Simmel, G. 1907/1991. *Schopenhauer and Nietzsche.* Orig. pub. as *Schopenhauer und Nietzsche: Ein Vortragszyklus*, Leipzig: Duncker und Humblot. Trans. H. Loiskandl, D. Weinstein, and M. Weinstein. Urbana: University of Illinois Press.

Sober, E. 1980. "Evolution, Population Thinking, and Essentialism," *Philosophy of Science* 47:350–83.

Soll, I. 1998. "Schopenhauer, Nietzsche, and the Redemption of Life through Art," in Janaway (ed.) 1998.

Spencer, H. 1879/1978. *The Data of Ethics.* Reprinted as part I of *The Principles of Ethics*, 1893. The latter was reprinted in 2 vols., Indianapolis, Ind.: Liberty

Fund. (*The Data of Ethics* appears on pp. 31–335 in volume 1. I cite this as *Data* followed by page number.)

Stack, G. J. 1983. *Lange and Nietzsche*. New York and Berlin: de Gruyter.

Stegmaier, W. 1987. "Darwin, Darwinismus, Nietzsche. Zum Problem der Evolution," *Nietzsche-Studien* 16:264–87.

Strong, T. B. 1996. "Nietzsche's Political Misappropriation," in Magnus and Higgins (eds.) 1996.

Warren, M. 1988. *Nietzsche and Political Thought*. Cambridge, Mass.: MIT Press.

West-Eberhard, M. J. 1992. "Adaptation: Current Usages," in Keller and Lloyd (eds.) 1992.

Williams, G. C. 1966/1996. *Adaptation and Natural Selection*. Princeton, N.J.: Princeton University Press. Reprinted with new preface.

Woodfield, A. 1976. *Teleology*. Cambridge: Cambridge University Press.

Wright, L. 1973. "Functions," *Philosophical Review* 82:139–68.

Young, J. 1992. *Nietzsche's Philosophy of Art*. Cambridge: Cambridge University Press.

Name Index

I include the names of (real) persons—as well as the names' adjectival forms. I exclude Nietzsche and Darwin, as too numerous.

Subject Index

References are topical and selective: not to all occurrences of the word, but to main developments of the topic.